FRONTIERS IN CREATIVE AND INNOVATIVE MANAGEMENT

SERIES ON ECONOMETRICS AND MANAGEMENT SCIENCES

This is one of a series of books on econometrics and the management sciences sponsored by the IC² Institute of the University of Texas at Austin, under the general editorship of W. W. Cooper and Henri Theil. In this series, econometrics and management sciences are to be interpreted broadly, providing an opportunity to introduce new topics that can influence future activities in these fields as well as allow for new contributions to established lines of research in both disciplines. The books will be priced to make them available to a wide and diverse audience.

Volumes in the Series:

Volume 1: EXPLOITING CONTINUITY: Maximum Entropy Estimation of Continuous Distributions, by Henri Theil and Denzil G. Fiebig

Volume 2: CREATIVE AND INNOVATIVE MANAGEMENT: Essays in Honor of George Kozmetsky, edited by A. Charnes and W. W. Cooper

Volume 3: TRANSFORMATIONAL MANAGEMENT, by George Kozmetsky

Volume 4: FRONTIERS IN CREATIVE AND INNOVATIVE MANAGEMENT, edited by Robert Lawrence Kuhn

FRONTIERS IN CREATIVE AND INNOVATIVE MANAGEMENT

Volume 4 of Series on
Econometrics and Management Sciences

Edited by
ROBERT LAWRENCE KUHN

1985

BALLINGER PUBLISHING COMPANY
Cambridge, Massachusetts
A Subsidiary of Harper & Row, Publishers, Inc.

International Standard Book Number: 0-88730-057-X

Library of Congress Catalog Card Number: 85-15125

Printed in the United States of America

Library of Congress Cataloging in Publication Data

Main entry under title:

Frontiers in creative and innovative management.

(Series on econometrics and management sciences ; v. 4)
"Papers presented at the Second International Conference on Creative and Innovative Management, held in Miami on 7-9 November 1984 ... sponsored by the RGK Foundation and the IC² Institute of the University of Texas at Austin"—P.
Includes index.
1. Creative ability in business—Congresses.
2. Management—Congresses. 3. Organizational change—Congresses. I. Kuhn, Robert Lawrence. II. International Conference on Creative and Innovative Management (2nd : 1984 : Miami, Fla.) III. RGK Foundation.
IV. IC² Institute. V. Series.
HD53.F76   1985   658.4   85-15125
ISBN 0-88730-057-X

CONTENTS

LIST OF FIGURES

LIST OF TABLES

OVERVIEW

Robert Lawrence Kuhn

Creative and innovative management is the cutting edge of contemporary organizations, the new formulation of strategy, the new implementation of structure.
This volume, the second in a series on creative and innovative management,
brings together leaders and scholars of intellectual institutions, organizations
whose output is knowledge and information. The rich mixture of participants —
from diverse disciplines, sectors, and cultures — exemplifies the broad impact of
the field. We mingle practitioners with researchers, presidents with scientists,
those who run creative and innovative institutions with those who study how
they do it. We explore the frontiers of managerial novelty. We seek relevance
and responsiveness to real-world turbulence and organizational discontinuity.
We seek a new discipline of business management.

   This volume is derived from papers presented at The Second International
Conference on Creative and Innovative Management, held in Miami on 7–9
November 1984 and entitled "Frontiers in Creative and Innovative Manage-
ment: A Research Agenda." The conference was hosted by the University of
Miami and sponsored by the RGK Foundation and the IC² Institute at the Uni-
versity of Texas at Austin.

   The preceding volume in this series — *Creative and Innovative Management:
Essays in Honor of George Kozmetsky,* edited by A. Charnes and W. W. Cooper
(Cambridge: Ballinger, 1984) — was concerned with identifying problems and
opportunities for creative and innovative management in private enterprise, government, not-for-profit institutions, and other societal activities. The current

volume focuses on managing creativity and innovation in centers of intellectual output: universities, scientific laboratories, high technology companies, advanced research institutes, policy research institutes, and similar organizations whose central purpose is the generation, development, or dissemination of original knowledge, irrespective of sector. Emphasis is placed on evaluating fresh ideas and approaches to the management of these institutions and to making them more responsive to the needs and wants of society.

The object of this volume is to stimulate further interest in creative and innovative management and to begin to identify critical issues that will help guide research and encourage development. Articulating areas of research is preparatory to providing a needed underpinning for a new academic field. It is believed that the topics of creative and innovative management, so vital for business, are not being adequately addressed in schools of management, even at advanced levels of research and teaching. A primary objective is to provide a continuing basis for systematic attention to this developing field of study—in teaching, research, symposia, publishing, and related academic activities.

Our distinguished contributors represent five countries: Canada, France, Israel, West Germany, and the United States. They come together to share their expertise, insight, and experiences for defining the frontiers of creative and innovative management. The result is a cross-cultural identification of issues, problems, disciplines, concepts, themes, methodologies, and techniques directed toward developing the required research agenda. These contributions and interactions are dedicated to our core purpose: advancing the study and facilitating the practice of creative and innovative management.

Dr. George Kozmetsky introduces the subject by describing the boundaries of creative and innovative management, characterizing its outposts, and providing a framework for future discussion. Creative and innovative management is seen as the only successful response to society's demands and needs within a hypercompetitive environment. The development of a self-sustaining academic field—Dr. Kozmetsky's clarion call in Part VIII—is catalyzed by formulating a rigorous research agenda implemented by a bold "act of management."

To handle creative organizations, we must first touch the fundamental essence of creativity. Professor Herbert Simon explores creativity's deep cognitive structure in terms of required knowledge (50,000 "chunks") and problem-solving process, and with elegance and wit he both decreases the mystery and increases the wonder.

Dr. James Botkin considers how creativity is transformed into innovation, focusing on management style and approach. Professor Abraham Zaleznick discusses the psychodynamics of creativity and innovation, differentiating the two by "habit"—disrupted for creativity, utilized for innovation. He posits, provocatively, that real creativity is an act of the individual not the group.

Dr. Arthur Porter cautions us not to overly manage the creative process. Professor Gerhard Mensch sees innovation being "harder and riskier than necessary," and he seeks to exploit the "structural readiness for basic innovation" emerging in various industries.

"Big Bang" innovations are characterized by Frederick Gluck as being both unfortunately rare and exceedingly vital. Radical change, he states, must be viewed as an opportunity not a problem. Captains of industry cannot be satisfied with spoon-fed summaries; they must immerse themselves in the raw, primary data of competition and customers.

Gerard Roche's "Route to the Top" forces academic theorists to face the real world of corporate business. How do companies develop creativity and innovation when their prime criterion for executive leadership is consistency and stability in bottom-line management?

Dr. George Geis and I probe the relationship between individual personality and organizational creativity. Commitment—which we define as "the link between personal meaning and company mission"—is considered a critical force in corporate creativity. Risk attitudes and personality traits are also addressed.

Creativity in the public sector is viewed from two perspectives by Professor Yair Aharoni of Israel and Senator Michael J. L. Kirby of Canada. Professor Aharoni highlights the opportunities and pecularities of state-owned enterprises, calling for competition among government agencies as a public sector surrogate for private sector markets. Senator Kirby presents ten innovative alternatives (not mutually exclusive) for delivering and financing essential social services.

The creative management of "intellectual institutions" is explored by two chief executives of such organizations: Professor Meinolf Dierkes (Wissenschaftszentrum Berlin) and Dr. Donald Kerr (Los Alamos National Laboratory). They radiate the increasing importance of advancing knowledge, in the social and natural sciences respectively. Leadership of the modern world is dynamically dependent on the creation and control of information, a critical factor for building comprehensive national security (see the papers in Part X on "strategic thinking" by Dr. Robert Kupperman and on "the creative power of American science" by me).

Professors Timothy Ruefli and George Huber attack a prime objective of the volume; they develop a clear topography for creative and innovative management as an academic field by enumerating issues and establishing guidelines. Professor Ruefli presents a schedule of strategic milestones while Professor Huber offers strategies to facilitate implementation.

The creative management of universities is discussed brilliantly in two contrasting papers. President Richard Cyert (Carnegie–Mellon University) stresses "attention focus, reward systems, and upward communication" in describing how administration and faculty must interact. Chancellor Joseph Murphy (City University of New York) goes for the jugular, explaining how university CEOs *really* get innovative things done, whether academic theorists like it or not.

The Discussion sections, generated at the precursor conference in animated give-and-take, posed an editorial dilemma. On the one hand, the erupting ideas were unusual, insightful, and, in some cases, unexpected. On the other hand, they were random, fragmented, and often unrelated to previous papers. What to do? The easy answer was to edit out. The conversion from spoken to written word is, to begin with, no mean task, however elegant the original aural sounds. What finally tipped the scales was the nature of our quest: creativity and innovation *require* "random, fragmented and often unrelated" material. To exclude the spontaneous, we concluded, would be criminal, leaving too much good stuff a permanent prisoner of floppy disks. To include all—the other extreme—would be both laborious and excessive. Thus we chose snippets and driblets from the Discussions, tasty morsels for hungry readers—whom we again advise not to expect order, coherence, and relevance but rather to seek idea, insight, and inspiration.

What we have, in short, is creative and innovative management emerging as a new field of academic business, with broad implications for theoretical analysis and practical application. This book, perhaps, can be a milestone.

—Robert Lawrence Kuhn

Austin, Texas
New York, New York
June 1985

ACKNOWLEDGMENTS

Frontiers in Creative and Innovative Management is, in a real sense, the personification of George Kozmetsky. It is the reflection of his intellectual ideals as much as it is the expression of his visionary quests. Dr. Kozmetsky is a true pioneer of creative and innovative management; he is an original industrialist, a technology entrepreneur, a creative university administrator, an innovative scholar, and an imaginative thinker. It was his vision that catalyzed the concept of creative and innovative management, and it is his intensity and conviction that carries it forward. Those of us privileged to share the opportunity to develop this new field are grateful for his leadership. On a personal note, I would like to express my profound appreciation to George for portraying the emergence, for showing me a new way of looking at the world of business, and, most important, for energizing me with the fire of creative and innovative management.

One cannot express appreciation to George without doing the same for his wife, Ronya. In truth they are a partnership. As president of the RGK Foundation, she is responsible for the coordination and logistics of all conferences and activities. A remarkable job she does.

The intellectual foundation of this volume is the product of numerous people. My special appreciation to my friends, colleagues, and co-chairmen: Professor William W. Cooper, whose tough rigor and brilliant insight made preparations stimulating and rewarding; Dr. Bertram Brown, whose creative vigor constantly bursts traditional boundaries; and Professor Abraham Charnes,

Professor Maurice Saias, and Dean Jack Borsting whose support was central and solid. A special thanks to Dr. Borsting and the University of Miami for hosting the Conference, and to Dr. Raymond Smilor, associate director of the IC² Institute, for his creative coordination.

—Robert Lawrence Kuhn

Introduction

FRONTIERS IN CREATIVE AND INNOVATIVE MANAGEMENT
The Development of a Research Agenda

George Kozmetsky

Frontiers generally begin where charted lands end. The field of creative and innovative management is yet to be mapped. In some respects, as we learn from the papers that follow, it is a field filled with academic and professional risks, doubts, and reservations, but these are intrinsic to the nature of discovery and exploration. On the other hand, it is a field of increasing interest to leaders in private and public sector institutions. Many executives are becoming concerned about how to manage complex, unstructured, and volatile problems that beset each of their institutions. Their interests focus on prospects, processes, and problems associated with the innovative development of newer technologies, including managerial concepts from idea generation to commercialization, with more efficient and effective utilization of resources—human as well as financial—and with the creation of strategies that provide for flexibility and adaptability to changing socioeconomic conditions. Those charged with the development, diffusion, and transfer of state-of-the-art science, for example, are recognizing that effective integration and application of technical, managerial, and marketing skills are needed to make things happen successfully in a hypercompetitive global environment.

Managers in both public and private sectors are looking for ways to improve the domestic economy, meet international competition, and advance their particular firm's, community's, or state's competitive positions—positions that generate new jobs, stimulate economic growth, encourage emerging industries, and renew basic industries.

It has been difficult for Americans to accept the fact that some of our industries are losing their strategic edge in domestic and worldwide markets. Competition in creativity and innovation on a global basis has become more than an individual firm's concern; it is a national need. The transformation requires the establishment of creative and innovative environments in each of our institutions, individual and institutional managerial risk taking and risk sharing, and the utilization of newer motivational methods. Today's theories, methodologies, techniques, and practices are the knowledge building blocks from which we can begin the discovery and exploration of the hypermodern dimensions of creative and innovative management. That the knowledge building blocks have limitations and problems is not sufficient cause to delay establishing creative and innovative management as a field. We must proceed with vigor to extend our current body of knowledge for both understanding and use.

Abraham Charnes and W. W. Cooper, co-editors of the first volume in this series, established the basic framework for the exploration of creative and innovative management.

> For purposes of creative and innovative management, we need to begin to drop old distinctions, and the distinctions between entrepreneur, manager, and administrator is surely a candidate for elimination. Thus, by creative management, we refer to new conceptions and new ideas, new entities and new methods that can also be used to provide new directions or new modes of operation for already existing organizations and activities. By innovative management, we refer to the ability to implement new ideas and/or to move successfully in such new direction. Making things work successfully is an old and abiding task of management. It is the coupling of this task with new ideas, directions, and the like that makes it innovative and creative. Finally, it is the ability to induce these kinds of activities in others in an organized way that makes it an act of management rather than only the act of an individual.[1]

Let us examine the key words and build from them three constructs: creative management, innovative management, and creative and innovative management.

The construct *creative management* would consist of new concepts, new ideas, new methods, new directions, and new modes of operation. The operative word is "new."

The construct *innovative management* would consist of the ability to implement creative ideas and/or to move successfully in such new directions. The operative words are "to implement" and "to move successfully."

The construct *creative and innovative management* focuses on coupling; that is, linking creative and innovative management constructs. The operative notion here is an "act of management" rather than an act of an individual.

These constructs make it evident that this book's explorations for a research agenda does not deal solely with "sparks or strokes of genius." The papers deal with identifying the "knowledge blocks" for creative processes and their transformation in a management context. They do, of course, deal with creative and innovative managers in research institutes, academia, business, and government and what they do or need to do. Here we differentiate between managers and management. This differentiation recognizes all levels of managers as well as all functions from scientific creation through commercialization to ultimate use. The orchestration of these managers' activities and functions with the concomitant body of knowledge, experience, and judgment (or "chunks" of knowledge to quote Herbert A. Simon) is an act of management. This is what Robert Kuhn, editor of this volume, referred to when he wrote:

> The coordination of myriad quanta of information is beyond any person's capacity, but decisions can be made with confidence and commitment when appropriate data reduction is combined with directed insights. Creative management, almost by definition, defies upfront quantification and early verification. Creative solutions are often suboptimal when measured by conventional yardsticks. Yet such suboptimal initiatives can often overwhelm reason and blow out logic. These startling mental processes, performed constantly without awareness by corporate executives, must be subjected to study and analysis. This, then, is the new academic frontier.[2]

My own experiences from idea generation through commercialization suggest that when managerial knowledge is still in its infancy, it is essential to integrate and assimilate scientific knowledge and methods with practical applications and use. Practical applications provide valuable data for scientific analysis, which in turn directly affects acts of managers. In addition, they build the required expertise and experience for understanding the act of management. The reverse process—from scientific study to application—is also true for the above objectives. There is, at this time, a real need to converge the applied, experiential research streams in order to advance the field of creative and innovative management and facilitate its timely implementation.

The needs for creative and innovative management can best be introduced from a societal point of view rather than as the needs of specific disciplines or managerial professions. A viable research agenda for such an unstructured field must do more than bring changes in attitude. It must remove barriers to risk taking and risk sharing across institutions including centers of intellectual output. What seems to be evident today is that there are societal needs or stimulants for creative and innovative management that should be converted into effective demands.

There are a series of "drivers" that are catalysts for a fundamental reassessment of the *act* of management. These drivers, classified as demands and needs, can forge the field of creative and innovative management.

Demands

The following drivers are currently receiving funds and other resources in response to longer term social demands.

1. Federal government large-scale programs or projects for defense, space, health, and the public infrastructure for the next generation.
2. Leading-edge state government growth initiatives for economic development and high technology diversification.
3. Imaginative collaborative relationships between universities and corporations.
4. Pioneering programs and couplings among government, universities and corporations.
5. Innovative private consortia for cooperative research and development.
6. A blossoming venture capital industry.
7. Creative institutional arrangements among public, private, and nonprofit sectors.
8. Imaginative local community initiatives for economic growth and social developments.

Needs

The following social needs can reshape the theory and practice of management.

1. Worldwide technology race and scientific competition for preeminence.
2. Expanding needs for large-scale programs (those that constitute more than $100 million each) on a global basis.
3. Shortages of highly trained scientists and engineers.
4. Difficulty in keeping up to date with scientific and technological and managerial developments.
5. Gaps in new technology transfer especially when it requires pulling together basic research from different disciplines.
6. A determination to diffuse research and development (R & D) activities across wider geographic areas.

Creative and innovative management is a way to respond to the societal demands and needs within a hypercompetitive environment. We live in a hypercompetitive world. The competition is national between states, cities, universities and colleges, industries, sizes of business, as well as international between highly industrialized foreign nations. The competition is taking the form of a worldwide scientific, technological, and economic race for preeminence. This volume deals directly with hypercompetition and the role of creative and innovative management in meeting it.

NOTES

1. A. Charnes and W. W. Cooper, *Creative and Innovative Management* (Cambridge, Mass.: Ballinger Publishing Company, 1984), p. xvii.
2. *Ibid.*, p. 28.

Part I

THE NATURE
OF CREATIVITY

Chapter 1

WHAT WE KNOW ABOUT THE CREATIVE PROCESS

Herbert A. Simon

Research on creativity has been carried out most often in the natural sciences, to a lesser extent in the arts and humanities, and to a very slight extent in professional domains like management or the law. Under these circumstances, unless we are willing to assume that creativity, in whatever domain it appears, relies upon essentially the same processes, there is little we can say about the processes of creative management. However, I think there is much reason to believe that there is, indeed, a great commonality among the creative processes, wherever they appear. If that is so, a review of the processes as they evidence themselves in scientific discovery will be of interest and value to all concerned with managerial creativity.

In this paper, I should like to review some recent research on scientific discovery and to describe the creative process as that research reveals it. Then, in the final sections, I would like to draw some lessons for creativity in management.

CREATIVITY

At one point in history, about forty years ago, the federal courts put themselves in the position of requiring that for an invention to be patentable there must be proof that a "spark of genius" had occurred. The language was Mr. Justice Hand's, and it plagued the courts for at least a decade until it was mercifully more or less forgotten.

3

The trouble with sparks of genius, and similar evidences of creativity, is that they are not photographable, hence are difficult to introduce into evidence in a federal courtroom. As long as we refer to acts of creativity with awe and emphasize their unfathomability, we are unlikely to achieve an understanding of their processes. And without such an understanding, we are unlikely to be able to provide usable advice as to how to encourage and enhance them.

Fortunately, it is not necessary to surround creativity with mystery and obfuscation. No sparks of genius need be postulated to account for human invention, discovery, creation. These acts are acts of the human brain, the same brain that helps us dress in the morning, arrive at our office, and go through our daily chores, however uncreative most of these chores may be. Today we have a substantial body of empirical evidence about the processes that people use to think and to solve problems, and evidence, as well, that these same processes can account for the thinking and problem solving that is adjudged creative.

Symbol Systems

The evidence to which I have just referred, and which I will presently develop in more detail, supports two central hypotheses:

1. Thinking is information processing that involves reading symbols, writing symbols, assembling symbols in relational symbol structures, storing symbols, comparing symbols for identity or difference, and branching on the outcome of the comparison. Intelligence calls for these, and only these, processes.
2. The processes required for creative acts are the same as those required for all intelligent acts.

The first hypothesis, sometimes referred to as the Physical Symbol System Hypothesis, has as corollaries, first, the assertion that computers (since they are symbol systems with the requisite processes) can be programmed to behave intelligently, and second, that human beings use these same symbolic processes (embodied in distinctly different "hardware" from computers) to accomplish thinking and other intelligent acts. None of these assertions need be taken on faith: they are all empirical hypotheses that can be (and have been, extensively) tested in the laboratory. The first corollary can be tested by programming computers to behave intelligently, the second by analyzing the processes that people use in handling difficult intellectual tasks.

Definition of Creativity

But let me start at the beginning. My basic claim is that creativity is "thinking writ large." Before we can test this claim, we must have a definition of creativity. The simplest way to find such a definition is to observe when people apply the term "creative" to some human act. What is the basis for such an attribution?

Acts are judged to be creative when they produce something that is novel and that is thought to be interesting or to have social value. Interesting or valuable novelty is the touchstone of the creative. Acquaintance with a creative act, one's own or another's, is often accompanied by surprise: "How did he (or she) manage to do *that?*" This quality of unobviousness partly accounts for the sense of mystery and awe that creativity often evokes.

Novelty can have either of two meanings: it can mean wholly new in the world or it can mean new to the discoverer. Usually, the medal of creativity goes only to the *first* discoverer. Second discovery, however independent, wins no awards from the U.S. Patent Office. There are exceptions, however. We celebrate the birthday of Columbus, although his discovery was rather thoroughly anticipated by the American Indians. Histories of science are also sometimes kind to independent discoverers. They remember Leibnitz as an inventor of the calculus, although the historical record shows that Newton had ten years' clear headstart. Newton failed to publish promptly, however, and it was Leibnitz's version of the calculus that was diffused and developed.

Independent discovery may also be used as evidence of the discoverer's abilities, for the processes must be the same as those employed in first discovery. When the young Gauss immediately found the formula for the sum of the first N integers, his teacher correctly predicted that he would be a creative mathematician, even though the formula was old hat to trained mathematicians. Thus, we have creativity in the weaker, or individual, sense, and creativity in the stronger, or social, sense, and rightly regard the former as a harbinger of the latter.

Of other uses of the term "creativity"—"creative advertising" or "creative writing"—I have little to say. One has the impression that such language is loose, or at least generous to the products to which it is applied. But in the last analysis, each field must make its own judgments of creativity; each must decide what is novel and what products are interesting or valuable. There are no reasons to suppose that the basic processes underlying the humbler forms of creativity are different in kind from those that account for the great leaps (which are not really leaps but successions of tiny steps) of a Newton or a Leibnitz. I think that even applies to singing commercials. What we wish to understand, then, are the sequences of processes that enable a man or a woman or a child to bring into being something that is novel and interesting or valuable.

The Discovery of Planck's Law

People make little discoveries daily or hourly in their everyday lives. Great discoveries are, by definition, rare events. Our hypothesis is that the processes that underlie both little and great discoveries are basically the same. Since we cannot ordinarily produce great discoveries in the laboratory, most of our evidence for the processes of significant invention must be historical. Let me recount to you one piece of evidence that is a little more direct.

The so-called problem of black-body radiation was posed by the great physicist, Kirchoff, in about 1860. The problem was to find the formula describing the intensities of radiation of different wavelengths that would be given off by a perfectly absorbing cavity ("black body") at a given temperature. Many distinguished physicists struggled with the problem over the next forty years, among them the young Max Planck. The problem was both experimental (to devise apparatus permitting the radiation to be measured over wider and wider ranges of wavelengths) and theoretical (to find both a formula that would fit the empirical observations and a physical explanation for the formula).

By about 1896, it was thought that an answer had been found. A formula called Wien's Law provided an excellent fit to the data then available. Moreover, in 1899, Planck believed that he had proved, from basic classical physical principles, that Wien's Law was the only acceptable formula. Alas, in science, new experimental data can always be counted on to cause trouble. By the middle of the year 1900, experimentalists, penetrating a new range of wavelengths, had made observations that could in no way be fitted by Wien's Law. Where Wien's Law called for an exponential function, in the new range the observed function was linear.

On Sunday afternoon, 7 October 1900, Heinrich Rubens, one of the experimentalists in Berlin working on black-body radiation, called with his wife upon the Plancks and described the new findings that clearly violated Wien's Law. Before he went to bed that night, Planck had conjectured a new formula to replace the defective one and had mailed a postcard to Rubens describing it. The new formula is what we have known ever since as Planck's quantum-theoretic law of black-body radiation. Its public announcement on 19 October 1900 marked the beginning of twentieth century physics.

How did Planck do it? In the spirit of casual empiricism, I have carried out the following experiment. On eight occasions I have sat down at lunch with colleagues who are good applied mathematicians and said to them: "I have a problem that you can perhaps help me with. I have some very nice data that can be fitted very accurately for large values of the independent variable by an exponential function, but for small values they fit a linear function accurately. Can you suggest a smooth function that will give me a good fit through the whole range?"

None of my colleagues recognized the problem as Planck's—and there was no reason why they should have. Five of the eight proposed Planck's Law as the answer, each within the space of two minutes or less. When asked how they arrived at it, all five described rather standard methods of interpolation. (The most common was to expand the exponential into a Taylor's series and to observe that for small values of the independent variable the resulting function, less unity, was linear through the origin.)

The moral of the story, I suppose, is that Planck was the right person at the right place at the right time. The role of time and place are obvious. None of my colleagues will receive the Nobel Prize for solving Planck's problem. As to the person, Planck clearly possessed both an ardent interest in the problem and the mathematical skills to solve it.

But the story has a sequel. Finding Planck's Law did not provide a physical explanation of why it should hold. Planck discovered such an explanation in the two months following his discovery of the law and published it before the year was out. He later described the activity of these two months as the hardest work of his life.

He began with the rationalization he had earlier derived of the faulty Wien's Law, seeking the loophole in his derivation. He also had the "correct" new formula to guide him—he could work backward from this answer and could reject any purported explanation that did not lead to it. In the event, he succeeded by introducing a probability assumption that was quite unusual and that had no particular justification except that it produced the desired result. Moreover, it required the introduction of a particular constant (which we now call "Planck's constant" or the quantum constant, h), which first appeared to him as merely a computational-trick. In fact, it took five years, and the work of other physicists including Einstein and Ehrenfurst, before the truly revolutionary import of these assumptions began to become apparent. One could say that physics backed into quantum theory through the constraints imposed by an empirical law upon the possible physical explanations for a phenomenon.

It does not in any way demean Planck's achievement to trace its history in this detailed way, to observe how little of the final result was anticipated, and to note that the sequence of events seems to have proceeded along a quite normal course of problem solving. In science, we do not wonder at natural phenomena because they are mysterious. We wonder at them because we find that the beauties and complexities of nature can be understood in terms of relatively simple and orderly underlying mechanisms. The magic is that there is no magic. The natural phenomena are truly "natural."

Moreover, it was no accident that it was Planck who provided a physical rationalization for the new black-body radiation formula. By 1900 he had already devoted a decade of his life to intense work on the problem. There were probably not more than two or three other theoretical physicists who came even close to him in the amount of effort spent in probing the problem and conjecturing sets of possible physical mechanisms that could contribute to its solution. As Thomas Kuhn's detailed study of the background of the discovery has shown, Planck had studied thoroughly all of the branches of physics—electromagnetism, thermodynamics, statistical mechanics—that played a role in the mechanism he finally postulated. Chance, in the words of Pasteur, had favored the prepared mind.

THE (RE)DISCOVERIES OF BACON

There are not many opportunities to test the processes of scientific discovery in the way in which I was able to recreate Planck's discovery of his formula. An alternative way is to see how far we can go toward constructing a computer program capable of making significant discoveries. A computer is patently a physical symbol system—nothing more. We know exactly what operations it can perform, and we can examine its programs to determine exactly what operations those programs employ to accomplish their work. If a program can make discoveries that, if made by a human, would be regarded as creative, then the processes it used (unless they amounted to nothing more than blind trial and error) will tell us something about the creative process.

The program I should like to tell you about is named BACON, in honor of Sir Francis Bacon, whose theory of discovery by induction provides much of the groundwork for BACON's procedures. In its earliest form, BACON (the program, not the man) was created by Pat Langley as his doctoral thesis, and it has since undergone extensive development at the hands of a research team including Langley, Gary Bradshaw, Jan Zytkow, and me.[1]

At least in its simplest forms, BACON, following the principles proposed by its namesake, is a data-drive inductive system. Its inputs are raw observational or experimental data, and its outputs, when it is successful, are scientific laws that describe the data parsimoniously. Now I do not wish to suggest that data-driven induction is the only mode of scientific discovery, although a study of the history of science shows that it is an exceedingly common one. In many cases, discovery is guided not only by data but also by relevant theory, and in domains of science where strong theories are already in place, logical deduction can often lead to the prediction of new data or empirical phenomena, which are subsequently observed.

Nor do I wish to claim that the extraction of laws from data and/or theory is the sole important aspect of scientific research. The process of defining problems for study and selecting relevant data is also important (although it is worth observing in passing that the problem Planck solved was one that had been defined for him by others, and that there was no ambiguity as to what data were relevant). Also important are the design of experiments and the devising of new instruments of observation. All of these activities, and others, call for creativity. Nevertheless, the induction of laws will provide us with a useful domain within which we can examine creative processes.

BACON at Work

When BACON is given data on the distances of the planets from the sun and their periods of revolution about the sun, it produces (in less than a minute on a computer of moderate size) Kepler's Third Law: the period, P, varies as the $3/2$ power of the distance, D. Kepler's Third Law was a scientific discovery of the first magnitude; hence BACON's independent rediscovery must be accounted to be creative. How was it accomplished?

BACON generates and considers possible laws very selectively, being guided in its search by selective heuristics, or rules of thumb. In the search for Kepler's Law, two heuristics allow BACON to arrive at the result very quickly. A scientific law expresses some invariant of the data. BACON's first heuristic leads it, when it finds that two variables are positively correlated, to compute their ratio and test it to see if it is invariant. (If the variables are negatively correlated, BACON computes and tests their product.) Its second heuristic leads it, when the result of the first step is unsuccessful, to add the newly computed variable to its set of data and try the same process over again.

Thus, BACON notices that period and distance are positively correlated, and computes the ratio, P/D, which is not a constant. It now notices that D and P/D are positively correlated and computes the ratio, P/D^2, which again is not constant. Next, BACON notices that P/D and P/D^2 are negatively correlated, hence computes their product, obtaining P^2/D^3, which is an invariant. Hence, P varies as the $3/2$ power of D.

An even more interesting case is BACON's rediscovery of the law of conservation of momentum. In this case, the only data given BACON are the relative accelerations of pairs of bodies connected by a stretched spring that is released. BACON first discovers, using the same heuristics as before, that for any given pair of bodies, the ratio of accelerations is always constant — but with different constants for different pairs. When BACON discovers an invariant relation between pairs of objects, it conjectures that this relation can be stated more simply by attributing a new property to each of the objects, and expressing the relation in terms of that property. In this case, BACON invents, and assigns to each body, a property (which we call *inertial mass*) and finds that the product of these masses by the corresponding accelerations, summed over the pair of bodies, is zero. This, of course, is the law of conservation of momentum.

In the same way, when BACON is given data on the temperatures of liquids and their mixtures, it introduces the concept of specific heat and discovers Black's Law of temperature equilibrium. When given data on the refraction of light passing from one medium to another, it introduces the concept that we know as the index of refraction. BACON is not limited, then, to discovering numerical laws; it can also invent new concepts.

Various extensions of BACON, which we have named GLAUBER and STAHL in honor of distinguished chemists who made important discoveries in the early history of modern chemistry, are capable of using qualitative information about the inputs and outputs of chemical reactions to discover qualitative laws. GLAUBER, for example, by searching for common components in different reactions, is able to define such classes as *acid, base,* and *salt.* STAHL, given information about reactions involving combustion, arrives at either the (erroneous) phlogiston theory of combustion or the (correct) oxygen theory, depending upon the way in which the reactions are described.

More recent experiments with BACON are aimed at discovering laws that do not merely describe phenomena but explain them as well. For example, if it is known or conjectured that the quantity of heat is conserved when liquids are mixed and that the mass of the mixture is equal to the sum of the masses of the components, then simple inferences can be used to *deduce* Black's Law of temperature equilibrium, instead of inducing the law from the experimental data. Thus, conservation laws, laws of symmetry, and other a priori assumptions can be introduced to guide the search for scientific laws, making the search (when successful) far more efficient than when it depends solely on examining the empirical data and providing explanations of the regularities in terms of conservation or symmetry.

Another offspring of BACON, which we call DALTON, uses a simple atomic hypothesis to guide its search. It starts with the assumption (as nineteenth century chemists did) that chemical substances are made up of atoms "packaged" in molecules. It assumes further that the total numbers of each kind of atom are conserved in chemical reactions, and (Gay–Lussac) that equal volumes of gases under standard conditions of pressure and temperature represent equal numbers of molecules. With these assumptions, it is able to infer the chemical makeup of many molecules and to demonstrate, for example, that gases like oxygen and hydrogen are diatomic, a fact that eluded chemists for many years in the nineteenth century. With small modifications in its structure, DALTON can induce from Mendel's original data on sweet peas the laws of Mendelian inheritance.

All of these experiments were aimed at showing that scientific discovery is an understandable phenomenon that can be explained in terms of the same kinds of basic information processes that account for other kinds of human problem solving and thinking. It involves search through large spaces of possibilities, the search being guided and made efficient by the use of heuristic principles and previously developed theory.

The Prepared Mind

Earlier, I quoted the saying of Pasteur that "chance favors the prepared mind." "Accidental" discoveries are exceedingly common in the history of science. All of us are familiar with the story of Becquerel's discovery of radioactivity, or Fleming's of penicillin. Those discoveries could have been made by other scientists than Becquerel or Fleming, but they could not have been made by just anyone. Assigning the "accidents" to randomly chosen members of the population would not have done the trick.

To exploit an accident — the image that appeared on Becquerel's photographic plate or the destruction of bacteria in proximity to the penicillium molds — one must observe the phenomenon and understand that something surprising has happened. No one who did not know what a dish of bacteria was supposed to look like could have noticed the pathology of the dish that was infected by the mold nor would have been surprised if it had been called to his or her attention. It is the surprise, the departure from the expected, that creates the fruitful accident; and there are no surprises without expectations, nor expectations without knowledge.

A study by my colleague John R. Hayes of world-class experts in a number of different domains, including chessplaying, painting, and musical composition, shows that no one reaches a world-class level before he or she has devoted a decade or more of intensive effort to acquiring knowledge and skill about the domain of expertise. (Bobby Fisher, who became a grandmaster only nine years and some months after learning the game of chess, is a near-exception, but the only one.) Child prodigies are not exempt from this rule. Mozart was composing music (but not especially creative music) by age four, but his first world-class compositions were written no earlier than his late teens or early twenties (depending on one's standard). Picasso, whose father was a professional painter, painted from early childhood, but his productions were not world class until after his move to Paris in early adulthood.

Expertness, in turn, is the prerequisite to creativity. One need only visit a regional art exhibit and then an international one to realize that amateurs are not a major source of the world's important innovations. In making his claim, we must be careful: the vital point is the possession of *relevant* skill and knowledge, and at certain key periods in the history of science and of other domains, the relevant knowledge comes from a field other than the one to which it is applied. That is why many of the major discoveries of modern molecular biology were made by biochemists or even physicists, rather than by traditionally trained biologists. The ten years of dues that the world-class expert must pay must be paid in the right field, and choosing that field may itself involve accident and gambler's luck.

We even have some knowledge about how *much* knowledge the world-class expert needs and how it is organized in his mind and brain. A college graduate is likely to have a vocabulary of 50,000 words (or even twice or four times that) in his or her native language vocabulary. Each word is immediately recognizable when it is heard or seen in print and, upon recognition, evokes from long-term memory a more or less rich set of meanings and associations. A psychologist would say that each person has 50,000 familiar chunks of knowledge, each accessing information in long-term memory through an act of perceptual recognition. A computer specialist might call each of these chunks a production, a pair consisting of a set of conditions to be tested and an action to be taken whenever these conditions are tested. The conditions are, of course, the recognition cues; the action is the evoking of the associated information from memory.

Several estimates have been made of the number of chunks (in this case, patterns of pieces that recur frequently on the chessboard during games) held by a chess grandmaster. These estimates again range around 50,000. Fifty thousand is not a surprising number, given the ten years of effort during which the grandmaster is acquiring these chunks. Now that we are beginning, in artificial intelligence, to build expert systems in a number of domains, these projects are also providing us with estimates of the amounts of knowledge required. None of the systems built thus far, with the possible exception of the CADUSEUS medical diagnosis program, comes close to 50,000 chunks; but of course, most of the extant systems are relatively primitive and quite restricted in the range of their expertness.

Until we have better numbers, ten years and 50,000 chunks will serve as informative parameters for indicating the effort and knowledge that is prerequisite to expertness and, hence, to creativity. If these are necessary conditions, it would be unreasonable to claim they are sufficient conditions. Yet they suggest that hard work and persistence represent a very large part of the ingredients that go into creative performance. We should not be surprised if we find that many (most?) highly creative people behave like workaholics.

Taking Risks

Science is an occupation for gamblers. Of course, journeyman science can be done without much risk taking, but highly creative science almost always requires a calculated gamble. By its very nature, scientific discovery derives from exploring previously unexplored lands. If it were already known which path to take, there would be no major discovery—and the path would most likely have previously been explored by others.

In this respect, successful scientific research has much in common with successful stock market investment. Information is only valuable if others do not have it or do not believe it strongly enough to act on it. The investor is pitting his knowledge, beliefs, and guesses against the knowledge, beliefs, and guesses of other investors.

In neither domain—science or the stock market—is the professional looking for a "fair bet." On the contrary, he or she is looking for a situation where superior knowledge—knowledge not yet available to others—can be made, with some reasonable assurance, to pay off. Sometimes that superior knowledge comes from persistence in acquiring more "chunks" than most others have. Sometimes it comes from the accidents that have already been mentioned. But whatever its source, it seldom completely eliminates the element of risk. Investors and scientists require a "contrarian" streak that gives them the self-confidence to pit their own knowledge and judgment against the common wisdom and belief of their colleagues.

CREATIVITY IN MANAGEMENT

If we wish to talk about creativity in management, we must use the same definition of creativity that we use when we talk about scientific discovery. We attribute creativity to behavior when it produces interesting or useful novelty. What are the evidences we can use to detect or identify managerial creativity?

The peculiar characteristic of managerial creativity is that we must assess it, not by the personal accomplishments of managers, but by the achievements of the organizations for which they are responsible. Because of this characteristic we may expect that the motivation for managerial creativity may be rather different than the motivation for individual creativity of other sorts. We may also wonder whether there are fundamental differences in the creative processes — that is, the cognitive aspects — as well.

Motivations

There is no reason to believe that the basic motivations of managers are different from those of other people, although the admixture may not be exactly the same. People receive satisfaction from accomplishment (solving the problem), from material rewards, from the esteem of others, and from power. Undoubtedly there are other motives, but these are generally acknowledged to be prominent and powerful ones, and they will suffice for our purposes. In our kind of society, management probably offers more than average opportunities for material rewards and for power, but it differs in these respects from other occupations only in degree. Preeminence in the arts and in science can also lead to wealth and to power.

What would seem to distinguish management most sharply from other kinds of work is the nature of the sense of accomplishment it provides. In most other endeavors, accomplishment is a highly personal matter — the direct product of the working of one's own head and hands. An author writes books, a scientist carries out research and publishes papers, a painter produces canvases. The sense of accomplishment of managers, on the other hand, arises out of what they see others doing. For this to provide satisfaction, managers must see or imagine a causal nexus connecting the works of their organizations with their own efforts in organizing, directing, and staffing them.

In all human affairs, the assignment of credit and blame is a difficult matter. I have already alluded to the role of accident, hence of luck, in scientific discovery. Management inserts another step of indirectness in the causal chain connecting personal behavior with outcomes, thus making assessment correspondingly more difficult. Moreover, "hands on" accomplishment generates, for many people, a qualitatively different affect from accomplishment by indirection. Even the intervention of a power tool may alter radically the feelings associated with handicraft activities. True, there has been more romantic speculation about these matters than hard empirical evidence, but we have only to consult our own feelings to know that there are differences, and often important ones.

Inability to delegate effectively is a very common managerial failing. It is usually attributed to feelings of responsibility for the results and unwillingness to depend on others for the discharge of that responsibility. It may also be due to the diminished satisfactions some managers feel when delegation deprives them of the opportunity to participate directly in the problem-solving process. They may get greater satisfactions from the exercise of their problem-solving skills than from the exercise of their skills of influencing other people.

Creative managers, then, are people who, by their own propensities or through learning, can receive great satisfaction from creative outcomes even when their role in producing those outcomes has been an indirect one—specifically, a managerial one.

We should not suppose that this peculiarity of motivation, though characteristic of management, is wholly limited to business occupations. It has often been noticed in recent years that, with the growth of Big Science, scientific activity itself becomes more and more managerial, carried out through organized research teams. This has been a cause of no little malaise to scientists attached to the traditional values and modes of operation; but probably also a source of satisfaction to scientists who have good managerial skills and who can now participate in the scientific enterprise with a success they could not otherwise have had.

Even before the advent of Big Science, the scientist was often also a teacher. In teaching, and especially in guiding the activities of graduate students, there is a major shift in satisfactions from problem solving to facilitating the work of others, and one can see the proclivities of scientists reflected in their attitudes toward the direction of graduate work and their styles of supervision and guidance.

When all is said and done, however, management is the discipline *par excellence* that depends for its achievement satisfactions on influencing the accomplishments of others. No one is likely to succeed in management, or to be creative in it, for whom this particular kind of achievement is not congenial.

The Cognitive Aspects of Managerial Creativity

Since my thesis is that creativity consists of good problem solving, in considering the creative process in management I need mainly to point out that the principal kinds of problems that confront managers where creativity is called for. First, however, I should like to make some comments on the nature of managerial expertness. In what are managers expert, and how does that expertness reveal itself in their behavior?

We have seen that a major component of expertise is the ability to recognize a very large number of specific relevant cues when they are present in any situation and then to retrieve from memory information about what to do when those particular cues are noticed. Because of this knowledge and recognition capability, experts can respond to new situations very rapidly — and usually with considerable accuracy. Of course, on further thought, the initial reaction may not be the correct one, but it is correct in a substantial number of cases and is rarely irrelevant. Chess grandmasters, looking at a chessboard, will generally form a hypothesis about the best move within less than five seconds, and in four out of five cases, this initial hypothesis will be the move they ultimately prefer. Moreover, it can be shown that this ability accounts for a very large proportion of their chess skill. For, if required to play very rapidly, the grandmaster may not maintain a grandmaster level of play but will almost always maintain a master level. But in rapid play, there is time for almost nothing but to react to the first cues that are noticed on the board.

We usually use the word "intuition" — sometimes also "judgment" or even "creativity" — to refer to this ability of experts to respond to situations in their domains of expertise almost instantaneously and relatively accurately. The streetwise slum resident has good intuitions about how to react to the situations that are often encountered in a slum environment. The manager has good intuitions about how to react to the situations that are often encountered in organizations. Both skills have the same basis in knowledge and recognition capability.

Present a capable and experienced business manager with the summary accounts of a business firm and he or she, within a matter of minutes, will make some shrewd conjectures about the firm's strengths and weaknesses. Present the same manager with a case describing a personnel problem, and a diagnosis of the difficulty and comments on possible courses of action will be forthcoming almost at once.

The point is not that managers either do or should act on impulse. Rather, it is that the expert ones have learned their 50,000 chunks and, with them, the ability to respond "intuitively" to business situations as they present themselves. It follows from this that schools of business, even the best, do not produce expert managers. They do not charge the ten years' dues that expertness would call for, nor can they provide the full environment of organizational situations in which the perceptual cues can be learned and practiced. But I think that this conclusion will surprise none of us.

As a surrogate for some of this experience and as an alternative means for developing the perceptual recognition skills that underlie expertness, business schools often use the case method as one of their instructional techniques, as well as the business game. These techniques could probably be used more effectively if they were recognized for what they are: methods for giving students opportunities to practice searching for relevant and important cues in business situations and for associating potentially useful responses to these cues. By these methods, the business school can at least start its students on the way toward accumulating the 50,000 chunks they will need as managers.

A more difficult question has to do with the content of the chunks. What does a streetwise—or, more accurately, organization-wise—manger know? The requisite inventory has never been taken, but we can conjecture that managerial knowledge falls into two main categories: on the one hand, knowledge about human behavior in organization and about how organizations operate, and, on the other, knowledge about the content of the organization's work—knowledge that may be largely specific to an industry or even to a particular company or plant.

It has sometimes been argued that managerial expertise is a general skill that can be transferred from any organizational environment to any other. I don't think the evidence bears out this claim. The Peter Principle is a refutation as it applies to vertical transfer, and we can see as many instances of failure as of success in horizontal transfer between organizations. The hypothesis of transferability probably appoaches most closely the truth toward the top levels of very large corporations or governmental organizations. In the former, the responsibilities at the top levels, in addition to the selection of key personnel, are most likely to resemble those of an investment banker. In the latter, responsibilities for mediation between political and administrative levels are likely to bulk large.

In any case, it would seem that knowledge of technical content of an organization's work can be harmful to managers only if it tempts them to resist delegation of responsibility. Nevertheless, it is characteristic of managerial jobs that managers are continually in the position of directing operations whose technical content they cannot fully master. To cope with this difficulty, they develop a number of strategies. One strategy is to encourage multiple channels of communication from below, so that they will not be the captives of any one set of experts. Another strategy is to develop skills of cross-examination—specifically, skills in inducing experts to reveal the hidden assumptions on which their conclusions and recommendations are based. A third strategy is to strengthen the identifications of their associates and subordinates with the top-level goals of the organization, weakening their attachments to subgoals.

One way to probe the content of the knowledge (whether possessed by executives or by members of their organization) that underlies organizational success is to enumerate the various ways in which an organization can enjoy an advantage over its competitors and then to assess the historical role these different forms of competitive advantage have played in the growth of especially successful organizations. I don't know that a systematic study of this kind has ever been undertaken and can therefore only guess what it would reveal.

Even in the absence of systematic data of this kind, we can point to a very large number of different dimensions in which organizations have behaved creatively and prospered as a consequence. We can think of instances of innovation in manufacturing methods (interchangeable parts and the assembly line) and even a few instances of innovation in organizational form (divisionalization by product groups).

Technical innovation, the creation of new products, undoubtedly is the major factor accounting for the rise of whole new industries. But within individual industries, the forms of creativity that provide particular firms with competitive advantage are more difficult to specify. The identification of these factors of advantage would provide an excellent focus of research on the species of creativity that are specifically managerial.

Managerial Risk Taking

Is every expert manager creative? What are the additional ingredients, beyond the intuitive skills based upon the 50,000 chunks of knowledge, that are required for creativity? Perhaps we can return to our understanding of scientific creativity for part of the answer. There are, in science as in business, competent journeymen and especially creative masters.

From our review of scientific discovery, we have seen that at least three stigmata seem to characterize scientists who are unusually creative: first, sensitivity to "accidents" and readiness to respond to them, even abandoning an ongoing program (as the Curies did in their search for radium); second, care and thoughtfulness in defining and selecting research goals and research problems; third, a propensity for risk taking. (Of course, we must interpret this last characteristic with care, for the creative scientists we know of are the ones whose bets paid off.)

Translated into terms of business and management, these traits sound rather familiar. The first is sensitivity to opportunity and the ability to marshal fluid resources to initiate new programs of activity. The second is attention to strategic planning, to understanding relevant future trends and developments, and to the setting of long-term goals. The third is a willingness to adventure, even with risks of failure. You will understand that I am not recommending any particular level of risk preference but simply claiming that the opportunity to be creative can seldom be fully separated from the opportunity to fail.

The common romantic scenario for the creative hero postulates an underdog who is willing to risk all to achieve his or her visionary goals and who finally reaches those goals after surviving many perils and overcoming many obstacles. We have seen that a more realistic scenario pictures the creative person as a professional gambler who prefers odds that are stacked in his or her favor and who secures those odds by acquiring superior knowledge about the domain in which the gamble is taking place. I put the matter this way not to discount the genuine element of risk associated with most creative accomplishment but rather to emphasize the skill and knowledge (the 50,000 chunks) that form the foundation to most successful risk taking.

CONCLUSION

William Larimer Mellon, the benefactor of the Graduate School of Industrial Administration at Carnegie–Mellon University, said: "Industrial opportunity means the opportunity to create." That motto is engraved in stone in the lobby of the school's building, where I hope it is still read and pondered by the students who pass by it. The motto does not spell out, of course, how the opportunity is to be seized.

What I have tried to do in this paper is to review what is known about the creative process. Most of my evidence was derived from research on scientific creativity, but I am confident that the foundations of creativity are the same in management as they are in science.

My review of the evidence emphasizes the conclusion that the creative processes are problem-solving processes—that we do not have to postulate any special kind of "genius" to explain the creative act. The evidence shows, further, that effective problem solving rests on knowledge, including the kind of knowledge that permits the expert to grasp situations intuitively and rapidly. But intuition is no mysterious talent. It is the direct byproduct of training and experience that has been stored as knowledge.

Creative performance results from taking calculated risks, where the accuracy of the calculations rests, again, on the foundation of superior knowledge. What appears to be the reckless gamble of the successful creator may be just that; more likely it was much less a gamble than it appears, just because the risk taker understood the situation better than competitors did.

Earlier, I maintained that science does not demean phenomena by explaining them. Creativity is not less challenging or exciting when the mystery is stripped from the creative process. The most beautiful flowers grow under careful cultivation from common soil. The most admirable products of human effort grow from the cultivation of ordinary knowledge by the solid processes of problem solving. Understandable, but no less admirable for that.

NOTE

1. This section of my paper is based upon our joint work. An introduction to it, and references to other publications, will be found in Gary F. Bradshaw, Patrick W. Langley, and Herbert A. Simon, "Studying Scientific Discovery by Computer Simulation," *Science* 222 (2 December 1983): 971–75.

DISCUSSION

W. W. Cooper

W. W. Cooper: How do you design an organization to induce creativity?

Herbert Simon: We do not yet have a full or satisfactory theory of how we design organizations to be creative. In order to build such a theory, we must examine examples of organizations that have been unusually creative (at least during their *periods* of creativity, which are not always long lasting). We should determine if what they do or do not do fits the model of the creative process that I have presented. If we could find actual instances of executives seeing unusual patterns in situations, we could understand such organizational creativity in terms of the model. But there has still not been a thorough study of innovative organizations.

W. W. Cooper: Is there any difference between creativity and innovation?

Herbert Simon: No. I do not understand the distinction that others make between creativity and innovation, and my definition indicated that.

W. W. Cooper: What can we do to instill in our students a spark of creativity other than contribute to the 50,000 bits of information and the ten years of experience?

Herbert Simon: Chunks! They are much richer than bits. Chunk building is certainly one of the things we can do. The second thing is to give students some understanding of the creative process and of the nature of real risk taking. I would particularly stress the point that chunk building and risk taking are not isolated components of creativity but that effective risk taking must be based on knowledge and understanding.

W. W. Cooper: Can educators devise mechanisms to get students to absorb chunks more rapidly?

Herbert Simon: Yes, indeed, but first some caution. When we talk about "absorbing chunks," we better be careful. We are not talking about memorizing information. I hope I made that clear in the nature of the capability that has to be exhibited as evidence of the mastery of chunks. One must be capable of triggering these complex symbols at the appropriate times. It is a perceptual skill. There is research going on about the kind of learning that would underlie such skill. One way is through a process that is best described as learning from examples. We know a good deal now about how people learn from examples, and this theory has even been carried to the point of using such techniques (based on the theory) to teach high school algebra to young kids, to teach them how to solve linear equations, how to factor quadratics, and so on. There have been a number of experiments run—interestingly enough, most of them in China. So there are beginning to be some developments in pedagogy arising out of information processing psychology that may, within a space of five or ten years, yield dramatic advance.

W. W. Cooper: Would you comment on the case method of teaching in business school?

Herbert Simon: The case, of course, is simply a rock you bring into a geology lab or a fish into a biology lab. There are all sorts of ways of looking at rocks and fish. There is nothing special about "the case method." I've taught cases. I've watched some of the Harvard people, in the early and most orthodox days of the case method, teaching cases. And I've seen lots of different things going on in the classroom under that heading.

Learning to deal with other people in complex situations is a very important managerial skill. We should strive to find ways within the business school setting to help students acquire chunks that involve, not merely the situations in cases, but the behavior of fellow students. When I taught a course on organization theory—especially during a period when most students were fresh from undergraduate college—the big problem was to construct situations where they could learn to recognize the kind of phenomena that occur between people in organizations. Creating that experience in the classroom would be a very valuable part of managerial education.

Part II

GENERATING CREATIVITY; TRANSFORMING CREATIVITY INTO INNOVATION

Chapter 2

TRANSFORMING CREATIVITY INTO INNOVATION
Processes, Prospects, and Problems

James W. Botkin

Private and public interest in the process of innovation is skyrocketing. Senior executives want to know how to accelerate innovation in their companies. Public officials in state government want to promote innovation in their regions. In the Congress, there is a committee to "target the process of innovation" as a national priority. President Reagan has formed a task force under the chairmanship of Hewlett–Packard president John Young to investigate productivity, national competitiveness, and innovation. Educators, too, are rightly concerned with innovation in terms of new teaching methods as well as new products of research.

Everyone is talking about innovation. What is it, and where does it come from? Assuming it can and should be increased, accelerated, or enhanced, who should do what to make it happen?

For the past several years, my colleagues and I at the Technology and Strategy Group have investigated the processes, prospects, and problems of the kinds of innovation associated with new technologies, new commercial products, and new manufacturing processes. What we found surprised us. Among the findings were several prominent myths, such as the following:

- Most industrial innovation is in high technology. (Not so; this is only half the story.)
- America is innovative while Japan and other Asian countries are imitative. (Careful, it could change.)

- Innovation is synonymous with creativity. (It is not.)
- Innovation is not a "group thing"; it comes from talented individuals. (A nonhelpful oversimplification.)

By examining each of these myths in turn, we can build a more accurate picture of the process of innovation. We see the enormous number of cooperative tasks and activities that have to be undertaken by an incredible diversity of actors in order to make innovation work. We also see the rising importance of education and new management philosophies as key ingredients to successful innovation. Finally, I stress the concept of "centers of excellence" as the most promising source today of new implementable ideas consistent with the needs of the rest of this century.

INNOVATION AND ADVANCED TECHNOLOGY

Philip Caldwell, chairman of the Ford Motor Company, said recently: "The smokestack reference should be banished from our vocabulary as being bad for the health of thinking people and confusing to the public. The industrial revolution which is transforming the U.S. automobile is essentially a high-tech, space-age revolution."[2]

Caldwell's statement captures the essence of what is happening in high technology today. When we speak of 64K RAMs, it is useful to note that one of the largest makers of chips is Indiana-based Delco, which supplies ICs to the auto industry. When we speak of CAD/CAM, you have to realize that 70 percent of such computer aided design systems are in so-called "mature" businesses. So it is not high tech versus smokestack but a complementarity between the two. Said in another way, innovation is coming not only from Silicon Valley but also from linking Silicon and Lehigh Valleys.

New technologies are reinventing the manufacturing business. A recent report by Morgan Stanley shows that one third of all capital investment last year went into the new technologies. The effect completely reverses Henry Ford's concept of a mass production assembly line. Indeed, Henry Ford, Sr. would no longer recognize his own Dearborn Engine Plant, which is now one of the most advanced and massive computer users anywhere. Others, like the Harris Corporation's automated plant in Kennedale, Texas (computerized machining line) or FANUC in Japan (machine tools and robots) are targeted to have an optimal lot size of one. Lot sizes of one have a special appeal because they induce producers and buyers to think innovatively.

In the service sector, we find a similar story. Office automation is having an even greater impact than the flexible factory, and 72 percent of the U.S. work force is in services. This puts a terrific premium on education. John Filer, chairman of the board of the Aetna Life and Casualty Company, said: "The resource that will most clearly distinguish us from others over time is our people — their education, training, motivation, and resourcefulness. This will determine our success as a nation, as a corporation, and as individuals."[3] At Aetna, one of IBM's biggest customers where 100,000 claims are paid every night, there will be one terminal for every two people by next year. At American Express, computers process 250,000 transactions daily throughout the world with an average response time of five seconds.

The quest for productivity increase at Aetna has taken on a new dimension. The strategic edge becomes how quickly new products and services can be introduced, which translates into how fast their 20,000 person sales force can understand and absorb the new information. Aetna has founded a Corporate Institute for Education. It intends to operate one of the most advanced educational systems yet devised — a laser-driven interactive videodisc that can hook into their SBS satellite. The company's ability to train a sales force efficiently and effectively is becoming a great strategic advantage.

While it is true that computers, electronics, and telecommunications are "drivers" of significant change, they by themselves are only half the story. The real payoff of these innovations are not as products per se but as tools that radically or incrementally change other older production processes or service delivery systems. The dramatic performance of the price / performance ratios of computers is an indicator of the fast pace of innovation in the electronics field. For example, a projection by Xerox shows how the computing power that had to be cost justified by 4,800 people in 1970 will be justified by only two employees in 1990. The computers that used to cost $48 million can now be bought for $100,000. Another study details how computing costs will increase by a factor of seven over the next decade.[4] Equally important will be those yet to be developed indicators that show the relentless pace of innovation as these tools are incorporated into agriculture, manufacturing, and services.

It is also critical to recognize that this "first line" innovation is not restricted to computers and electronics. Even while the Japanese and Americans race for the fifth generation computer, the next race is already shaping up between Japan's ceramic engine and an American reinforced plastic prototype. All the designs for the car of the future replace much of their steel, aluminum, and rubber with composites, epoxy and carbon fibers and high-strength reinforced plastics. The rate of innovation in advanced materials is breathtaking, as it is in other advanced technologies like biotechnology, aerospace, and deep-sea mining. Again, the real payoff is in the application of these areas to more basic businesses.

INNOVATION AND INTERNATIONAL COMPETITION

Since we are still in an era of *national* industrial strategies, the question of which culture or countries are most innovative is intriguing and politically important. Researchers have tracked the geographic origins of inventions and their implementation. A recent study showed that "in the late 1950s, over 80 percent of the world's major innovations were introduced first in the United States. By 1965, this figure had declined to 55 percent."[5] Another indicator often cited is patent applications. Here the figures show that Japan has had more patents in recent years than any other country.[6]

These concerns have led to something of an international race in innovativeness. In Europe, for example, the ESPRIT project has been formed by the European Community to stimulate new projects and cooperation in the electronics field. This program was launched in response to Japan's announcement of their fifth generation computer project, which in turn has led the United States to form not one but at least three programs — the DoD's Strategic Computing Project, the IBM-led Semiconductor Research Cooperative, and the CDC-inspired Microelectronics and Computer Technology Corporation (MCC). All are focused on producing the components for an innovative computer with speech and vision capabilities that have vast implications for nearly every form of business, government, and educational activity.

Japan has been the most explicit in formulating a national innovation strategy, which is called "creating creativity" but in fact focuses more on innovation — that is, the implementation of new ideas as well as their inception. In MITI's words, "Creativity should be brought into full play in developing software and systems technologies and in commercializing new technologies by utilizing Japanese characteristics. At the same time, it is necessary to attach importance to basic research, to take risks, and *to pioneer in unexplored fields and thus become the world's [leading] innovator.*"[7]

If we focus on *implementation* of new ideas, the tiny island country of Singapore has to be a world leader. In the short span of the past five years, the country has transformed itself from an old labor-intensive economy to one of the most modern knowledge-intensive societies. Under the slogan "computerize the island," the latest in CAD/CAM, telecommunications, computer information systems, and the facilities to train knowledgeable workers, managers, and researchers have all been installed. What we used to call "Yankee ingenuity" and what Max Weber called the "Protestant work ethic" has been surpassed by Singapore's (predominantly Chinese) inventiveness and Confucian purity.

Our own prognosis is that the Asian Pacific region is well on its way from imitation to innovation. Already in 1982, the trade patterns reflected this fact when the volume of international trade in the Asian Pacific exceeded that across the North Atlantic. This international movement of innovation is following an older historical pattern. The United States began its industrialization by bringing ideas primarily from England and implementing them in New England (an example is Francis Cabot Lowell's importing and adapting British textile technology to Massachusetts in 1821). The post–World War Two years are often cited as especially innovative ones in America—except that many of the innovators were Europeans displaced by the war.

The international dynamic today is, in fact, changing to a global one. While governments talk of national strategies for innovation, business people in multinational corporations know that no one culture has a monopoly on new ideas and the ability to implement them. New ideas are flowing with increasing speed across national boundaries—ask the MIT researchers who conceived the concepts behind a fifth generation machine first launched in Tokyo. In genetic engineering, for example, we have interesting international developments. National innovation in biotechnology today is likely to be determined less by some innate cultural propensity to innovate than by government regulations. Biogen or Advanced Genetics can and will locate in many places in Asia or Europe if American courts challenge their research programs with excessive vigor. Recent decisions against the deployment of genetically-engineered frost-resistant substances in the United States are another interesting twist on innovation, where the judicial system seeks to curtail possible hazards even while the executive seeks to enhance potential economic benefits.

INNOVATION DISTINGUISHED FROM CREATIVITY: A MODEL OF THE INNOVATION PROCESS

"Innovation" is a link in the chain that follows "creativity." James Utterback, professor of industrial history at MIT, puts the emphasis on translating original ideas into marketable products and processes to increase productivity.

Our innovation model starts by assuming a level of creativity and then focuses on four issues: education, management style, research and development, and capital costs (Figure 2–1). The model is useful in the context of present policymaking; it singles out something obvious yet forgotten, and something else

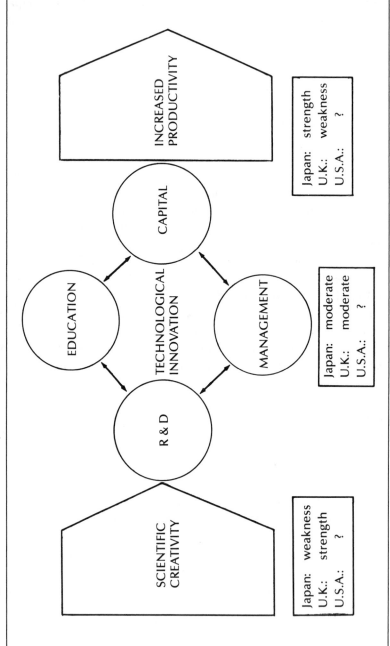

Figure 2–1. The Four Components of Innovation.

Source: THE INNOVATORS, Rediscovering America's Creative Energy.

nonobvious and also forgotten. The obvious is that for industrial innovation, management's ability to create an environment to enhance innovation is probably the single most important feature. One can enact any law, seed any program, broadcast government exhortations, but if the managers and employees don't want to innovate, they won't.

The less obvious factor is the role education is coming to play in innovation. Unlike the time of Thomas Edison or Benjamin Franklin, invention today is an organized process that requires the cooperation of many people. Because technology is so fast-paced and organization so complex, a larger base of understanding is required to be effective. Education, or trained human resources, is the single greatest factor in shifting to a knowledge society or so-called "information age."

Education

Consider education for electrical engineering and computer sciences (EE/CS). It is undergoing significant changes—part of a larger movement or revolution imminent in all education. The immediate problem in engineering education is both obsolescence—the half life of computer science knowledge is five years; the time to produce a graduate averages 4.5—and shortages.

Our college and university system produces only a 1.7 percent net increase of electrical engineers and computer scientists each year, after factoring out retirement and promotion. Our studies estimate that America's 287 accredited engineering departments are increasing the 206,000 EE/CS pool by 7.7 percent, but retirement, death, and promotion reduces this to 1.7 percent. But even conservative estimates of demand run at least 2.6 percent per year. Actually the demand may be higher, since the Bureau of Labor Statistics has been consistently understating demand recently after it feared it overestimated it back in the 1960s and 1970s. This translates into a nearly 30 percent shortfall.

The problem is not a lack of students. Universities are obliged to limit access to their programs. For example, the University of Texas had to reduce undergraduate engineering enrollment. Don Kennedy, president of Stanford, has capped his university's enrollments in electrical engineering. So did two-thirds of the country's engineering schools. In new materials the situation is also serious. Rustum Roy, chairman of Pennsylvania's Materials Advisory Panel, says that "in the area of materials, the technological posture of the United States is deteriorating very fast."[8]

The main problem is financial. Offers for graduates to work in industry and defense are draining the sources of future faculty. An MIT bachelor of science

Figure 2–2.   Human Resources: Japan vs. the United States.

Number of Professionals per 10,000 Population	U.S.A.	Japan
Accountants	40	3
Lawyers	20	1
Engineers	25	35
BA Graduates (Engineering)	16	29
MS & PhD Graduates	3	1.5
Software Engineers	9	1.5
Programmers	13	2

Sources: Various—NEC Corporation, McKinsey & Co., *Global Stakes,* adapted by J. Botkin.

in electrical engineering earns $2,000 per month in industry versus $750 per month as a teaching assistant. Industrial starting salaries for EE/CS graduate students are often more than their tenured professors' take-home pay.

Many people think Japan does a better job at educating its engineers than America does. The famous statistic is that on a per capita basis, Japan turns out twice the number of engineers as the United States (Figure 2–2). This is true at the B.A. level. The Japanese have twenty-nine engineers to every sixteen American ones on a per capita basis. A lesser-known fact is that at the masters and doctoral level, the figure is reversed. There are only 1.5 Japanese engineers with advanced training for every three in the United States. In software and programming, the situation even more favors the United States. So why is Japan so successful? Michio Nagai, the former Minister of Education in Japan, puts it this way: "An irony of history is that because Japanese universities have failed, the rest of society has been forced to compensate."⁹ Singapore, incidentally, by 1990 will have the greatest per capita concentration of EE/CS talent in the world. Fortunately for us, the country is only 1/100th the size of the United States.

When we put this discussion into a global context, the imbalance becomes severe (Figure 2–3). The number of R & D scientists and engineers in America, Europe, and Japan form nearly 90 percent of the world's total.

The educational implications are immense. In the short run—which, in contrast to the business world, may be five to ten years for educators—the response will be "more." Indeed, partly resulting from our work in *Global Stakes,*¹⁰ the U.S. Congress has passed legislation that will authorize up to $60 million to the National Science Foundation for matching grants to bolster education for science,

Figure 2–3. Global Science and Technology. Number of R & D Scientists and Engineers per Million Population by Region (1978 Estimates[a]).

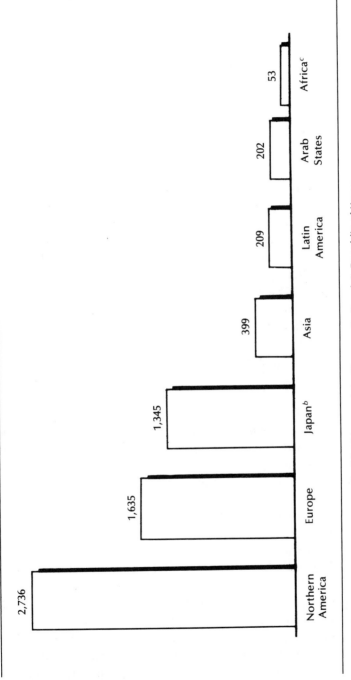

[a] Excluding the USSR, China, Mongolia, Viet Nam, and the Democratic People's Republic of Korea.
[b] Including Oceania.
[c] Excluding Arab States.

technology, and engineering. Certain programs in management education are also eligible. But in the long run, education in the social sector is most in need of innovation. New technologies may help, concepts of lifelong learning and cooperative education are good, and new emphasis on self-directed learning are all moves in the right direction. Even more fundamental changes in the goals and roles of education, however, will need to induce innovative learning rather than information absorbing.

Management Style

The most significant factor that affects competitiveness is management's willingness to promote innovation and absorb new technologies. Wherever the old ghost of Taylorism maintained its influence, innovation seemed stifled. From the present perspective, Taylor's Scientific Management is a bankrupt philosophy, although it has taken sixty years to uncover its liabilities fully. It has lost its punch, both with regard to efficiency and to cost, primarily because it failed to take into account the human side of the equation—the fact that humans are capable of far more than routine tasks. Ultimately, people revolt when their skills are underutilized and their jobs are boring. When demotivated by the nature of work, efficiency drops, quality erodes, and costs escalate. Employees only want to understand the name of the game and the rules by which they play. When they do, there is an incredible reservoir of skill and motivation that is drawn into the work process.

The Emhart Corporation, headquartered in Hartford, Connecticut, is what industrial analysts would call a "mature" business. Two of its important divisions produce machinery for making glass bottles and for making shoes (the latter is the old United Shoe Machinery Company). Until recently, both divisions were making products in ways reminiscent of the 1936 Charlie Chaplin movie, *Modern Times*. Starting in 1979, Emhart "went high tech" and began a program of innovation whose backbone was the adaptation of old processes and products through the introduction of new technology. The lessons on how to initiate and manage innovation come from three sources—what the top corporate managers did, what the glass plant did to be successful, and what the shoe plant did not do and consequently met only partial success.

Corporate management did the following significant things. The key was to form what I nickname a "GALT"—Gang of At Least Three. In this case it was the chief executive officer (Mike Ford), the vice president for research and development (Wally Abel), and the vice president for productivity (and later technology, John Rydz). Together they represented power, vision, and implementation. The power figure instituted a company-wide audit to identify products and processes for upgrading. The visionary developed a strategic plan for technology, and the implementor crafted an action plan to implement it.

A major goal of the Gang of At Least Three was to get everyone involved. Rydz created a staff of specialists to monitor twenty different technologies. A quarterly technology review was started and circulated widely in the company. Ford instituted a technology committee at the board of directors level. Abel created a center for technology innovation located at the USM plant and signed a contract with a nearby technical school, Worcester Polytechnic Institute, to investigate robotics and training of robotics operators. The sum total of these actions sent a clear message to the organization, which Abel expressed as "innovate or go down the tubes"!

The divisional managers in glass bottle machinery got the message. They identified a first step with strategic payoff. Automating the "gob forming" part of the line would translate into captive sales of $100 million. They identified the most likely source of innovation—their R & D facility in England (so much for U.S. policymakers). They involved lots of people, shuttling them back and forth across the Atlantic. They shared proposed changes early on with marketeers, salesmen, and selected clients. They started changing the composition of the work force to take on electrical engineers with knowledge of glassmaking (a rare but trainable human resource). And they rewarded the innovators—at company ceremonies, mention in their own press, and financial awards. The result after only two years is what the technicians call the "1:2 vertical blow mold triple overlap with added reheat machine for quad gob." To the financiers, it is a $100 million success story.

The shoemaking machinery division fared less well, though not for lack of trying. The division managers were faced with a unionized labor force and with a line of mechanical gear-driven, pully-drive machines that so far have proven nearly impervious to computers and electronics. They could not identify a first step without citing a radical rethinking of the whole production line, which would mean a financial risk that no one could justify. One internal study showed that productivity gains in the range of 300 to 800 percent were needed, which meant not incremental changes but radical innovation. They put in a welding robot and trained a young union member with great success. His success, however, made older union and middle management officials feel uncomfortable. Rather than reward the innovators, it seemed better to keep them under wraps for fear of ruffling otherwise calm union–management relations.

The division did succeed in building a computer-controlled stitching machine used to sew complicated patterns on cowboy boots. Previously done by inexpensive Mexican labor, these jobs have now moved back to the United States with the automated stitcher. But the payoff is small. Fancy cowboy boot patterns are not the heart of the market. Now the divisional management is cautious. "Our tactic has been to move ahead only on those technological innovations proven to be cost effective. It is difficult to justify costly automated equipment."

The case illustrates both the prospects and the problems in innovation. On balance, this company is making a significant turnaround due largely to the foresight, attitudes, and follow-through of its top management. But the more radical the innovation required, the more factors beyond the immediate management purview come into play.

Research and Development

One of the higher level factors is research and development (R & D) policy. Research and development is critical to a country's innovation ability. Figure 2–4 shows an international comparison. Here you can see that the United States is

Figure 2–4. International Research and Development.

Technological Strengths—R & D ($) × Quality of People

| Industry | R & D Spending (percent) | | | |
	Japan	U.S.A.	W. Germany	England
Chemical	17.6	10.9	26.3	16.6
Ceramics	2.5	1.0	0.6	1.3
Steel	4.7	0.9	1.4	2.1
Machinery	7.0	13.2	11.7	5.5
Electric/electronics	25.3	19.8	25.2	23.6
Automobile	14.5	11.0	11.1	6.6
Precision machinery	3.0	4.7	2.0	1.6
Aerospace	–*	23.6	9.0	21.8
Civilian R & D (percent of GNP)	2.3	1.7	2.5	1.5
Federal R & D (percent spent on economic development)	76.0	13.0	–	–

strong in aerospace, Germany in chemicals, and Japan in automobiles. The most significant numbers are that, while we still spend more on R & D than all other OECD countries combined, the United States is slipping as a percent of GNP when military spending is removed. The United States spends only 13 percent of its federal research budget for economic development compared to 76 percent in Japan.

The Defense Department's Advanced Research Projects Agency (DARPA) has had a positive impact on generic information processing technology development and, therefore, helped the commercial/civilian sector. However, this is no longer true of the vast military R & D budget in the United States. Military budgets for pure research gave birth to the semiconductor industry in the 1950s, but by the 1980s, only $800 million of the $21.6 billion military budget went for basic research. The rest is in weapons development, which means modifying existing products to meet military specifications.

An important area for attention concerns this balancing of national priorities in research and development. Presently we are heavy on defense and health. In comparison to other countries, we are light on research for industrial development. The federal government is presently the largest source of research funds. How these funds are deployed will have a significant impact on future innovations.

Capital Costs

Innovation costs money. Whether the funds are used for education, R & D, laboratory or process equipment, the high cost of capital can put a damper on innovation. A recent report by George Hatsopolous, president of Thermo Electron, shows that the cost of capital in the United States is three times higher than in Japan. The Semiconductor Industry Association came to a similar conclusion. The significance is what Hayes and Abernathy called "managing our way to decline." The higher the cost of capital, the shorter a manager's time horizon. Everyone complains about the shortsightedness of American management. The best way to raise their sights is to enable them to afford the long term.

Notes to Figure 2–4

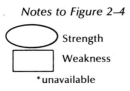

Strength

Weakness

*unavailable

Sources: Kenichi Ohmae and National Science Foundation.

CENTERS OF TECHNOLOGICAL EXCELLENCE

The most exciting development in the United States concerning innovation is the proliferation of university–industry consortia. In the Semiconductor Research Collaborative nineteen companies provided $5 million to eight universities in Research Triangle in North Carolina; in the Microelectronics and Computer Technology Corporation twenty companies have set up shop abutting the University of Texas. There are many more — for example, the Industrial Technology Institute in Michigan and the Michigan Biotechnology Center, financed by foundations with participation from state government and industry. Another is the polymer center at the University of Massachusetts. The Emhart Corporation is a major supporter of Worcester Polytechnic's Manufacturing Engineering Applications Center (MEAC), where process engineers test new ways to use new robots.

I disagree with those who want to create an industrial policy in the United States. My recommendation is for a strategy that is decentralized and focuses on university–industry consortia. The U.S. government should match and leverage industry dollars to support many "centers of technological excellence." This proposal is analogous to our own historical precedents when one hundred years ago Justin Morrill created the Land Grant Act. Just as we revolutionized education and research for agriculture then, our strategy today should be the same for new technologies that interact with mature manufacturing and service industries. This could be done through an updated Morrill Act or through funds of a department of commerce or trade.

The people who create, direct, and manage these centers of technological excellence are rapidly becoming "the new strategists" of our changing economy in at least three ways. The first is in terms of education policy. Close links between business and university are still a controversial subject, from both perspectives. Does such cooperation subvert the mission of a university? Is it good or bad to link real world concerns and the world of work to the more reflective and isolated campus concerns? Are these long-term linkages on which universities can depend for financial support or will companies withdraw their funds — as the federal government did in the late 1960s — leaving educational institutions to fend for themselves? As these questions are resolved, new possibilities open up for educators to fashion novel learning experiences for their students.

The second area concerns corporate strategy. If the global economy is indeed at a turning point then progressively more radical innovations will be necessary. This, in turn, implies going outside of day-to-day corporate boundaries for new ideas going closer to creativity and sources of innovation. One such source is the university laboratory where good ideas are abundant but an ability to move from lab to line is limited. Companies are seeking to shorten the time line from invention to implementation, and the bet is that a university business connection can help. So far, this strategy is being tested mainly in North America, where business–university consortia now number in the hundreds. Japan and Europe have variations on this theme. Tiny Singapore, again, has six well-developed, highly visible, and successful such partnerships. (One of them is in the management of technology at the Institute for Systems Sciences at the National University of Singapore, in joint venture with IBM.)

The third element of strategy concerns public policy and the role of government. Of course, the federal government is important, but the reality is that state government is probably more so—either by its presence or its absence. Many states, like North Carolina, have set up industry–university microelectronics centers. New York has a detailed strategy for eight such centers, each in a different technology and each at different private and public universities. New Jersey has proposals for four centers, including a ceramics venture at Rutgers University. Virginia announced its $30 million center at Virginia Polytechnic Institute in September 1984. Two Michigan governors teamed up with the Kellogg Foundation to start institutes in robotics technology for auto suppliers and biotechnology for their food and forest industries.

What makes no sense is for all fifty states to "go high tech." What does seem to pay off, however, is carefully identifying a region's already existing base and evaluating whether joint business–university centers can make a contribution to upgrading old businesses with new knowledge-intensive technologies.

NOTES

1. See Dan Dimancescu, Ray State, and James Botkin, *The Innovators: Rediscovering America's Creative Energy* (New York: Harper and Row, 1985).
2. *Industry Week,* 3 October 1983.
3. Personal interview, November 1983.
4. Nolan, Norton & Company, Lexington, Mass., adapted by J. Botkin.
5. Robert Ronstadt and Robert J. Kramer, "Getting the Most Out of Innovation," *Harvard Business Review* (March–April, 1982).
6. See Gene Gregory, "Japan: New Center of Innovation," in Speaking of Japan, Keizai Koho Center, Japan Institute for Social and Economic Affairs, Tokyo, Japan, June 1982.
7. MITI report, *The Vision of MITI Policies in the 1980s,* March 1980: 153.
8. Rustom Roy, testimony before the House of Representatives, 19 May 1983.
9. Personal interview, October 1982.
10. James Botkin, Daniel Dimancescu, and Raymond Stata, *Global Stakes: The Future of High Technology in America* (Cambridge, Mass.: Ballinger Publishing Company, 1982).

Chapter 3

ORGANIZATIONAL REALITY AND PSYCHOLOGICAL NECESSITY IN CREATIVITY AND INNOVATION

Abraham Zaleznick

A creative act depends upon the ability of talented people to break out of traditional modes of thinking, to see the world in new ways, and to arrive at a novel synthesis. This synthesis may be theoretical, technological, and even ideological, but regardless of content, it reflects a major shift both in the definition of problems and in the approach to their solution. Could such activity occur in a business organization? I would tend to say no, but that negative response leaves me uneasy and discontended.

Creative activity is essential in the current competitive business environment. The pressure to adapt to swift-moving changes that arise from social, political, and economic upheavals demands creative responses. The ego ideal of the scientist, for example, establishes creativity as the desired level of achievement and a requirement for self-esteem. The presence of this ego ideal in business becomes a force for abandoning traditional ideas and methods. One urgent desire is for new ways of thinking, including new ways of organizing creative work.

The importance of creativity has become so obvious that we tend to forget that preoccupation with the idea itself is modern. In fact, it did not surface until rather well into the period of social changes that modernization has produced. The early editions of the *Oxford English Dictionary* had no listing for "creativity." The 1933 edition gives a fifth definition of "creation" as "an original production of human intelligence or power, especially of imagination or imaginative art," and in the appendix to the *OED* of 1933, "creativity" finally appears defined simply as "creative power or faculty; ability to create." Two of the three illustrations of its use are taken from Alfred North Whitehead's 1926 book, *Religion in the Making.*[1]

The idea of creativity began with religion, moved into art, and then, in the modern period, found a home for itself in science. In its evolution, the idea of creativity maintained a striking continuity as it moved from religion to art, science, and now the world of practical affairs. The continuity is in man's effort to understand and possibly to control his environment. Michael Walzer explains Calvin's doctrine of predestination as being a response to the chaos, disorder, and threat of the world in which Calvin lived.[2] Science became for its practitioners during the seventeenth century a means for imposing order on the chaotic and seemingly irrational world in which they found themselves. The artist's work, from the time of the caveman to the present, has expressed a yearning to master the unknown as represented in the problem of man's separateness and estrangement from nature and his fellow man.

One of the consequences of modernization is the movement toward egalitarianism, which has affected the idea of creativity as well as the possibe linkage of life-style and individual choice. Creativity in recent years has become an ideal of democratic living and institutions. Fueled by the writings of Maslow, Rogers, and other humanistic psychologists,[3] this desire to stimulate creativity at all levels of society, including in particular the work force, has taken form in existentialist movements, encounter groups, T-Groups, and other activities that fall somewhere between education and psychotherapy. The assumption behind these movements is that all people have creative potential. The problem for society is to develop methods for tapping and releasing this potential, which usually include some means for converting authority into a benevolent instead of a repressing force.

This egalitarian thrust overlooks an important idea: that creativity depends in large measure on the presence of individual talent. While authority may repress the expression of talent in creative work, it does not have the power to put talent in where it does not exist in the first instance. There is much that is mysterious in understanding, let alone explaining, talent. Even for a deep student of human nature like Sigmund Freud, talent evoked a sense of awe. He wrote in *Dostoevsky and Parricide,* "Before the problem of the creative artist, analysis must, alas, lay down its arms."[4]

Innovation is also a topic in this paper. However, it has been necessary to explore some aspects of creativity first because I consider that creative work has precise qualities that distinguish it from innovation. The most obvious distinction arises from the fact that creativity is scarce while innovation is, or should be, plentiful.

Webster's Dictionary defines innovation as making changes or introducing something new, citing specifically new customs, manners, and rites, As this defi-nition suggests, innovations are intrinsically related to membership—advances that are possible when individuals, steeped in the traditions of a craft, activity, or organization, apply collective knowledge to making things better. The French call this kind of work *bricolage,* or tinkering. The person who does this kind of work is a *bricoleur,* or handyman.

Lest one gain the impression that innovation is debased by being linked to *bricolage,* let me hasten to assert that the art and craft of the handyman enjoys a special position in the social sciences, thanks to the work of Claude Levi Strauss.[5] In his theory of myth, this extraordinary anthropologist likens the con-struction of the myth and its existence in a social structure to the efforts of a society to solve a problem, usually very profound, by adapting the materials at hand. *Bricolage* done well is important whether applied to the major causes of anxiety in primitive cultures, to the normal anxieties connected with keeping the plumbing in working order, or, in the case close at hand, performing work in organizations.

Bricolage or innovation is largely traditional and grows out of the accumu-lated knowledge existing within a social system. The key to understanding in-novation, or more importantly, its absence, is to discover the circumstances in which the knowledge of the *bricoleur* becomes either forgotten or suppressed. The same analysis cannot be applied to creativity, because the organic deriva-tives from society's lore, wisdom, and understanding do not apply to the cre-ative act. Writers with widely differing backgrounds, such as the scientist Ilya Prigogine and the humanist Arthur Koestler, believe that creativity requires a mental act, or state of mind, that frees the individual from the boundaries of common knowledge. Whereas the knowledge required for innovation is con-tained within the social structure, the work of the creative individual has to be freed of its ties to social structure.

At specific crossroads in its history, society undergoes massive revisions of its accepted view of the world. To think today what was unthinkable in the past requires a revision in the elements of consciousness constituting "conventional wisdom." Socially, the creative person is not an isolate who remains withdrawn from the currents of thinking in society. While the creative individual is seldom limited by the definitions of himself that society and organizations offer as an identity, he is still affected by the range of the possible and especially by cur-rents of changes both evolutionary and sometimes revolutionary.

In his book *Order Out of Chaos,* Ilya Prigogine analyzes the changes in thinking that accompanied various theories in the physical sciences.[6] Broadly speaking, between the seventeenth and twentieth centuries the change was from a so-called closed and deterministic system to a so-called open and irreversible system in which nature, or at least the part we understand, changes with the passage of time. In the ideal of Newtonian physics, everything was given and it was only man's ignorance that prevented all things from being known. Since the laws of motion are "reversible," which is to say that a film of an object in motion can be run backward and appear exactly the same as when run forward, the concept of time was inconsequential. Scientific discoveries later challenged this deterministic view, and by the 1920s, the excitement in science and philosophy was centered on the concept of the open system and irreversibility in nature.

Prigogine perceives a development in the human sciences, particularly psychology, that appears to be similar to the changes that have occurred in the scientific world view. "Classical psychology centered around conscious, transparent activity; modern psychology attaches much weight to the opaque functioning of human existence. Remember Oedipus, the lucidity of his mind in front of the sphinx and its opacity and darkness when confronted with his own origins."[7] Prigogine concludes this analogy with the observation, "Perhaps the coming together of our insights about the world around us and the world inside us is a satisfying feature of the recent evolution in science that we have tried to describe."[8]

Unfortunately, in *Order Out of Chaos* there is little hint about the nature of the creative individual who, in a sense, both causes and is affected by the sweeping changes in world view that accompany progress in science and philosophy. Fortunately, we have some clues that can, at a minimum, outline possible connections between the major alterations in world view and the creative act examined, as it were, under a microscope.

The creative act, whether in art or science, destroys certain habitual modes of perceiving and thinking. In Arthur Koestler's terms, the creative act is "an act of liberation — the defeat of habit by originality."[9] The process might be likened to taking two pictures, overlaying them, and seeing a third picture that in essence destroys the validity of the two originals. This intersection of two pictures from which a new synthesis is derived involves a mental function which Koestler called "bisociation" to describe the escape from routine, habitual thinking. This mental function draws on unconscious activity.

For most of us, the ability to see things in new ways requires some flirtation with absurdity and humiliation, which ordinarily demands we tolerate potentially painful feelings. Most mortals defend against such exposure. For the creative individual, the exposure is a necessity. Indeed, it goes beyond tolerance to the active use of what lies behind the potentially absurd and humiliating. If one asks a question that takes us beyond conventional wisdom, the risk is isolation from our fellow man, to be perceived a fool and, what is worse, like a person who is asking that we not take him seriously. Tolerating this state of isolation, even though it may be temporary, assumes that other aspects of mental function act in a compensatory manner.

Compensation appears directly from the mental state that accompanies discovery. This mental state has been described, variously, like an oceanic feeling or union with a loved object once lost. Most of us experience this feeling in connection with humor. For example, Koestler borrowed the following story from Freud's essay on the comic. A marquis at the court of Louis XIV enters his wife's boudoir and finds her in the arms of a bishop. The marquis walks calmly to the window and goes through the motions of blessing the people in the street below. When his anguished wife cries out, "What are you doing?" he answers, "Monseigneur is performing my functions, so I am performing his."[10] The humor derives from the juxtaposition of a number of conventions that are rendered absurd. The most important is that of taking authority figures from their lofty positions and rendering them as absurd as the rest of us. The release of laughter comes from the momentary unity one has achieved when a wish to debase authority is freed from the restrictions we all experience in doing just that. In art and science, the comparable experience is, when after having labored diligently, there then comes the moment of awe when one feels he or she has received a gift. This gift is so special that it heals, at least for the moment, whatever breach exists between the self and its relation to the object world.

In his excellent study of cognition and creativity, Howard Gardner emphasizes the risks the creative person faces in observing that, "Despite the pleasure that individuals obtain from their work, they are typically embarked on a solitary voyage, where the chances of failure are high. To pursue this risky tack, they must be courageous and willing to deviate from the pack, to go off on their own, to face shame or even outright rejection. It requires a strong constitution to go it alone in creative matters." Under these circumstances, creative people "experience a strong need for personal, communal, or religious support."[11]

Gardner also tries to express the quality of the creative person's attachment to his or her work, describing an emotional involvement that is sensuous in its attraction.

> The individual experiences a strong, almost primordial tie to the subjects of his curiosity. Einstein, Darwin, Piaget—all felt a special intimacy with the natural world. In each case, a loving dialogue with nature, dating back to childhood, was transformed into a scientific journey. The creative individual comes to love his work—indeed, cannot thrive without it. And, the kind of pleasure he derives from making scientific discoveries, from solving a puzzle of nature, or from completing an artistic work can be compared in a nonfacetious way with the kind of pleasure most individuals gain from sexual involvement with someone they love."[12]

Gardner's "nonfacetious" comparison deserves serious consideration. What Gardner omits from his comparison is the notion that both in creativity and sexuality, the individual is in a regressed mental state. The problem this regression poses is to develop the sense of trust that enables this state to be sustained through the realization that one will not be lost, that rationality will be restored in due course. This type of regression, in the service of the ego, may become the vehicle for the uses of talent that would otherwise remain dormant.

Earlier in this paper, I suggested that there is a marked difference between creative and innovative work. Creative work disrupts the habitual ways of thinking. Innovative work utilizes habit, tradition, and culture to arrive at new ways of doing things. The steps in innovation are incremental and do not involve breakthroughs of the kind we hear about in fundamental research and, in particular, in the natural sciences. Innovation is needed to deal with problems that interfere with the achievement of commonly held objectives. Innovators are usually an integral part of the social structure and usually rely on the ideas and materials at hand to evolve solutions. Innovation is, therefore, traditional and often easily accepted within the social structure. In many cases, innovations are the result of memory: someone remembers a solution that had once been applied and perhaps had been forgotten. This memory, perhaps with variations, is brought forth to meet current needs.

Innovation then, unlike creativity, is a highly socialized activity. The handyman as innovator works at the point where problems are perceived. His identification with his craft and organization motivates him to find solutions using the well-established principle of efficiency: the best solution provided by the least effort. Because solutions are often both elegant and practical, the innovator takes pride in his accomplishment.

Recently a book, *In Search of Excellence,*[13] has sold over one million copies in its hard-cover edition and seems just as popular in a paperbound version. What accounts for such success? Of course, the recent awareness of America's competitive problems, the comparison between productivity in the United States and Japan, and hard times facing America's smokestack industries, and the fall from grace of the American automobile as the symbol of this nation's abundance and productivity have stimulated interest in learning what went wrong and what can be done to correct contemporary problems in business. All of these concerns laid the groundwork for the success of *In Search of Excellence.* In addition, however, the message of the book appealed to, while making explicit, the discontents people have been feeling for a long time in their experience with organizations.

Further, *In Search of Excellence* reveals that *bricolage,* the traditional means of innovating in business, has fallen to a very low level. The book calls for its revival. This craft of solving problems can be applied to all levels of an organization, but the value assigned to *bricolage* depends upon the example of leaders at the top. The book criticizes modern organizations for failing to build and maintain an environment in which problem solvers can perform. Organizations lack the cohesiveness that enables people to maintain their identity in and with an organization. Under these conditions, people forget or suppress their ability to solve problems because they do not maintain the state of mind that equates what they do and where they are in an organization with any visible outcome.

Innovation grows out of membership and the sense of responsibility people feel for their work and the organizations that employ them. Creativity, on the other hand, depends upon the presence of gifted people who are capable of escaping from the channels of thought that are habitual and intrinsic to the culture of organizations. Creative people tend to be disruptive, while innovators support the social structure upon which they depend. Yet, the fact remains that, with the exception of writers and artists, creative people work in organizations. The recent listing of the Nobel awards in science for 1984 referred to the institutes, universities, and laboratories that employed these distinguished laureates. Most scientists today are absorbed in the frenzy of competing for grants, of publishing papers in prestigious journals, and of serving on committees that decide who gets money and whose paper will be presented at scientific meetings and later published in the journals. This activity suggests that creativity, along with innovation, is fast becoming an outcome of organizations that require the contributions of membership and the psychological readiness to participate in coordinated human effort.

Organizations fulfill different needs for creative people and for innovators. The most important difference in the case of creativity is that organizations are required to support a fairly deep level of regression occurring in the course of the gifted individual's work. The movement in thought processes is vertical in creativity, from highly structured and disciplined activity to loose, associative, and symbolic thinking. The vertical movement is from secondary process thinking, which is sequential as well as logical, to primary process thinking, which is characteristic of the unconscious.

The innovator applies horizontal modes of thinking. While horizontal thinking uses analogies and depends upon remembering past experience, it depends on a limited number of styles of thinking, the most predominant being linear reasoning and successive trials. Because this mode of thinking involves limited or almost no psychological regression, we are generally dealing with low levels of emotion and, in particular, little anxiety.

An illustration of vertical and horizontal types of thinking perhaps will clarify the distinction I am drawing between creativity and innovation. My illustration comes from examining the work and life of Frederick Winslow Taylor, who has rightfully been called "the father of scientific management." An individual much maligned in his time and even today, his life and work deserve careful study not only for the contribution he made to industrial management but also because he embodied both creative and innovative approaches in his pioneering efforts.

Taylor was both innovative and creative as I am using these terms in this paper. An example of innovation is the work leading to the publication of his pamphlet "On the Art of Cutting Metals,"[14] which investigated the relationship among several variables involved in cutting metals. This pamphlet resulted from painstaking labor that proceeded in a rigid empirical fashion. Such empirical work epitomizes horizontal thinking within a limited but nevertheless significant range of mental effort. On the creative side, Taylor perceived a fundamental problem in the relationship between management and workers. In Taylor's view, authority relations were poisoned by the irrational conditions in the factory. No one knew what constituted a fair day's work for an equivalent fair day's pay. The absence of these standards in the minds of either management or labor meant that the definition of justice was a matter of choice, subject to arbitrary determination by the adversaries in the workplace. Taylor's vision for scientific management was industrial harmony. By removing arbitrary definitions of justice, people in authority relations could agree on standards of equitable returns for effort expended and thereby eliminate arbitrariness by management or labor as the cause of conflict. Although depersonalization limited freedom of action, it maximized freedom in another sense because everyone was bound to the same standards. If people acted in accordance with these standards and expectations, they were free from personal tyranny and could develop self-expression and individuality during their leisure time.

According to my understanding and definition of creativity, Taylor's solution to the problems of authority in organizations clearly belongs to the category of creative work. In Taylor's work with metal cutting, he proceeded from order to order; in the case of his contributions to authority relations, he proceeded from chaos to order. The chaos, however, coexisted on two levels — the personal and collective — and both interacted in his creative solution.

On the personal level, Taylor suffered from an obsessional neurosis that from all indications began early and plagued him throughout his life. Like most obsessional neuroses, Taylor's consisted of an inability to tolerate his own impulses, particularly his aggressive urges, which he defended against by compulsive work habits, the distraction of establishing rigid routines, and the displacement of his anger onto authority figures who appeared distant, abstract, and even in his eyes somewhat effeminate. When his defenses crumbled under the pressure of hostile relations with authority figures, he became depressed and had to withdraw into a form of therapy that he devised. He would return to an old boss who ran a machine shop, the Midvale Company, and engage in routine experimentation with methods of work. This was solitary work and served as a return to a base line of activity and routine under the care of a man who had been a father figure to him over a period of many years. Through this self-devised therapeutic regimen, Taylor was able to restore his defenses and overcome the worst ravages of his depression.

At the collective level, Taylor considered the workplace a chaos of self-interest, power struggle, and moral failure by both management and workers who were unable to establish, and live by, a just system of work and compensation. In his later years, Taylor became a prophet of a new industrial utopia in which authority no longer revolved around personal relations of superior and subordinate. Instead, all participants in factory work subordinated themselves to a system called scientific management. Through this common subordination, all men were equal. This utopian vision ultimately failed to produce the results Taylor had envisioned, but despite this failure, the utopian ideal persisted. It took on many variations in actual practice, but the central ideal of common subordination to a system persisted and lives on in the ideology of modern management. Through measurement, control is established so that rampant emotions may be contained, freeing the individual from the anguish of anxiety generated from within and without in the attachment to power.

It is important to recognize, in the case of Frederick Winslow Taylor, his inability to work in organizations. His most productive episodes occurred when he worked in the Midvale Company, which was operated by William Sellers. Taylor found in Sellers a benevolent protector who was instrumental in Taylor's creative effort. A closer examination of the needs of gifted people can help us understand what organizations must provide, for in failing to so provide they cause the shortfall between goals and outcomes in the case of creative work.

From my own investigation of gifted people, along with reading biographical studies, I find a recurrent theme that corroborates the interpretations I have made in the Taylor case. Gifted individuals often embark on a course of work that simultaneously attempts to resolve personal conflict while solving objective problems in a unique way. To carry out this complicated psychological effort requires considerable emotional support, resembling in many respects the support necessary to undertake investigation of unconscious motivation. In psychoanalysis and some forms of psychotherapy, this support is sometimes called the therapeutic alliance, but for the type of problem we are concerned with, a more apt description is the "holding environment." A matrix of support evolves in the treatment, with the patient playing an important role in erecting this psychological structure on his or her own behalf. Within the holding environment, an individual can venture into vertical thinking being assured he will not get lost in deeper levels of motivation and psychological conflict.

Generally, gifted people also require a holding environment in order to proceed with their work, involving as it does the vertical form of thinking. While it is true that not all vertical thinking is by its nature or outcome creative, all creative work may require vertical thinking. In some cases, gifted people provide their own holding environment by maintaining an inner connection with benevolent figures from their past through the psychology of introjection and identification. Where the benevolent inner world cannot exist because such figures in the past are absent, it becomes crucial for the individual to find himself in a situation that can erect this holding environment. This occurs, if at all, in an intense personal relationship that has popularly been called the mentor relationship. If such a relationship is successfully established, then the structure, process, and substance of the organization in which the relationship develops may make little difference. The holding environment is intact and relatively insulated from the strains of the larger organization in which it is imbedded.

Such relationships are more easily established in universities and other organizations in which authority can be made personal and human rather than abstract and solely institutional. Organizations that do depend on abstract and institutional forms and processes often segregate gifted people into relatively insulated structures that can encourage the formation of personal relationships and the simulation of the holding environment. Bell Laboratories, for example, was developed apart from the institutional structures of AT & T. Evidently, companies like AT & T that use this approach have discovered how to deal with transferring creativity from the laboratories to the institution, with its requirements for standardization, routine, and habitual practices in the work force. Whether these same companies recognize that within the institutions attention must also be paid to the problems of connecting the organizational reality with the need for innovation is another problem.

So far as I can judge, institutions are attempting to solve their lack of innovation by involving an abstract principle and using an interactive method. The abstract principle is to secure a just environment that meets the standards of equity and due process. This encourages a belief in the organization's rationality and the willingness to exchange one's best efforts for the mix of compensation that an organization provides contractually. The interactive method for encouraging innovation is to make it easy for participants to meet, exchange ideas, and in other ways to deal face-to-face in solving problems. The interactive method also has a rational foundation: individuals and groups have only partial access to information and ideas, and by bringing the most important participants together, limitations of partial information can be more readily overcome. Along with implementing interactive methods, organizations also often provide training to help people improve their abilities to solve problems interactively.

In my view, both the theory of justice and the method of interaction as the solution to institutional problems of innovation have not been studied or analyzed carefully enough for me to venture a solid opinion about their efficacy. I would only point out one of the endemic problems of institutions that others have called "the bureaucratic malaise." Bureaucracy tends to produce power struggles, displacement of goals, and "trained incompetency," along with equity, due process, and practical rationality.

These bureaucratic problems cause the skills and energy of the *bricoleur* to become repressed and suppressed, where just the opposite should be occurring to stimulate innovation in organizations. Very often, deficiencies in organizations arising from bureaucratic effects are recognized, but often solutions to the problem exacerbate rather than remedy the "illness." More process may be added to solve problems that themselves have arisen from either too much process or the wrong kind of process.

Innovation calls for the rediscovery of intuition, judgment, and fruitful trial and error. The formalization of these activities often goes against the instincts for work that are the foundation for innovation. The work of innovation is extracting from memory and habit those techniques that solve problems gracefully as well as efficiently. There are certain rituals connected with innovation. The rituals bring the individual closer to the organization. In contrast, bureaucratic forms tend to alienate and, ultimately, to suppress intuition, judgment, and trial and error.

Can the psychological need for both creativity and innovation be met in one organizational reality? The theory of open systems would seem to hold promise for an affirmative answer. The theory envisions an open system as one that is responsive to information from its environment, that utilizes its resources and seeks to influence its environment rather than merely to adapt to changing circumstances. Out of the flux resulting from interaction and from heightened sensitivity to information emerges new forms and processes that potentially support both creativity and innovation. If progress in science is measured by the distance between deterministic and irreversible models of nature, the same scale should be applied to organizations as closed and open systems.

Unfortunately, this solution collides with facts about human nature. It changes only slowly and, being rooted in biology, resists verbal solutions to fundamental human problems.

NOTES

1. *Oxford English Dictionary* (Oxford: At the Clarendon Press, 1933).
2. Michael Walzer, "Puritanism as a Revolutionary Idealogy," in S.N. Eisenstadt, *The Protestant Ethic and Modernization* (New York: Basic Books, Inc., 1968), p. 121.

3. Albert Rothenberg and Carl Hausman, eds. *The Creativity Question* (Durham, NC: Duke University Press, 1976).

4. Sigmund Frued, *Dostoevsky and Parricide,* in James Strachey, ed., *The Standard Edition of the Complete Works of Sigmund Freud* (London: Hogarth Press, 1966–74).

5. Claude Levi-Strauss, *The Savage Mind* (Chicago: University of Chicago Press, 1966).

6. Ilya Prigogine and Isabelle Stengers, *Order Out of Chaos* (New York: Bantam Books, 1984).

7. *Ibid.,* p. 312.

8. *Ibid.*

9. Arthur Koestler, *The Act of Creation* (New York: The MacMillan Co., 1964), p. 96.

10. *Ibid.,* p. 33.

11. Howard Gardner, *Art, Mind, and Brain: A Cognitive Approach to Creativity* (New York: Basic Books, 1982), p. 355.

12. *Ibid.*

13. Thomas J. Peters and Robert H. Waterman, *In Search of Excellence* (New York: Harper and Row, 1982).

14. Frederick W. Taylor, "On the Art of Cutting Metals," (New York: The American Society of Mechanical Engineers, 1907).

DISCUSSION

George Kozmetsky

Bert Brown: What about music and the arts? Have we ignored half our brain in this book, concentrating on the analytical left side and ignoring the artistic right side? Are we fundamentally flawed by not having an open discussion of the arts as well as the sciences and management?

James Botkin: In the courses and seminars we conduct for executives in corporations, we find that some music or art or dance does promote creativity and innovation, even if we are dealing with high technology and computers. Yet it is difficult to bring the arts into an industrial setting. If I tell the chief education administrator at Aetna that we are going to have a string quartet open our two-day management seminar, the chances of the sale are fairly limited. Yet it is precisely this kind of thing that is needed for creativity.

Abraham Zaleznick: The absence of the arts has much to do with the problems of people in industrial organizations who are notably unable to undertake regressions that are acts of renewal. Some of our executives are extraordinarily limited in their capacities, and, as a clinician, I can tell you that when a breakdown occurs because of this overly rigid adherence to certain forms and structure, it can be caused by this absence. We must recognize the importance of vertical thinking—that is, being able to appreciate the full spectrum of thinking, from rational and structured thought forms to those loose and free form—and to be able to be very comfortable in such diverse dimensions. Most people, I think, are horizontal thinkers.

53

Question: In characterizing creativity, you focus on *visual* creativity, and I'm wondering if true creativity is different, closer to innovation?

Abraham Zaleznick: Let's not put creativity and innovation on the same continuum, because we'll lose something in the process. We will lose the value, at least for analytical purposes, of understanding the distinction, just to see where it takes us. I don't honestly know if it is real, but it is a useful thought experiment to make creativity and innovation discrete, putting them on separate levels and watching what happens.

Question: Can creativity be a group process?

Abraham Zaleznick: I don't believe it. Any distinction is a mere observation, because we see a peculiar form in which group activity depends on instituting certain kinds of rituals. Defense mechanisms are taken up to a new level in which certain rituals are extremely important. But for creativity, it works in a very different way. It involves the regressive states. Now when I say creativity does not go on in groups, I don't mean that creative people are isolates; to the contrary, they are not isolates. They are susceptible and much influenced by the currents of thinking. But what creative people need in their relations to the world is what I call a "holding environment." This is a kind of matrix that will allow them to take personal risks and sustain themselves in the course of that work. Group psychology operates at a totally different level; in fact, when regression occurs in groups, what happens is catastrophic. There is something about groups that reduces creative ability. Chester Barnard was so frightened of the human psyche that he viewed constituted organizations as the civilizing influence. It was that which would prevent people from becoming the kind of anarchists and murderers that, I assume, he felt they really were underneath. For me, it is the opposite. I believe that the human psyche is infinitely fascinating and the only terror that arises is when people band together. Groups take away civilizing influences. It is in groups that you will find horror. Nazi Germany was a group phenomenon. When a journalist interviewed one of the convicted gas chamber executioners, what did she discover? The man loved his children. He had the most socialized attitudes about life. What was it, then, that mutated this monster? The group effect.

Question: Could you develop your concept of regression?

Abraham Zaleznick: I stress the concept of the holding environment, so that when these regressed states begin to occur, the individual is not afraid because there is what Ericson called "trust." This is a sense of confidence that one will have ultimately achieved control and therefore there is nothing to fear. The concept of the holding environment comes from a brilliant psychoanalyst named Winicotte, who worked primarily with children. He saw their struggle against terror and concluded that unless they found ways of controlling it, they were going to be lost. Winicotte developed the concept of the holding environment —which provides a bedrock of security to the individual, so that one knows that one can always come back and be able to reconstruct logic in one's thinking.

In groups and in organizations, things do not operate at this fundamental level. The operative principle in organizations is justice and equity—and that's a different category of ideas. People get extremely upset if they perceive an unjust world or an unjust organization.

James Botkin: I am not prepared to give up the notion of group creativity. One of management's tasks today is to create "holding environments" where the possibility of group creativity exists. Why? Because one of the differences in the revolution of technology that is going on today is that many creative acts are needed. Not just one single one. It wasn't Bob Noyce alone who invented the process for making microchips; it was, in fact, groups of people, who were interacting with one another. Noyce was just the one singled out. There is something in our western culture that seeks to glorify the single individual creative act; that has been our history and social sense. We like to identify the creative act with isolated individuals. Yet today is different. We need a new mind set. Even with modern music—with large orchestras and synthesized music—creativity is becoming a collective process. There's a whole social infrastructure of creative people operating in groups that generate creative solutions to complex problems. Creativity *can* happen in groups.

W. W. Cooper: Consider the organization that knows where it wants to go and makes sure that everything is put together and everybody is in tow. In that kind of organization creative people are not going to be very happy.

Abraham Zaleznick: Creative people are not isolates, and they internalize a concept of the company; they take into their minds some image of the organization or the society. Creative people internalize certain aspects of the culture. That is why, for example, when repression is expressed by painting, it develops into schools of art; similar patterns occur in certain forms of music and science. It is not that the artists must talk to each other; they are simply internalizing in approximately similar fashions and therefore their psyches are affected in similar ways. The biggest difficulty with organization theory is that it does not understand what internalization is about. Consequently, these theorists try to make an organizational artifact out of what is essentially an act of individual internalization. The individual incorporates into his or her mind an image of the society or the organization; the individual not the organization drives the creative process.

Question: What is the emotional content of institutionalizing innovation?

Abraham Zaleznick: This certainly brings the concept of *power* to the forefront. We have to consider seriously the nature of power in organizations, the nature of organizational forms or practices in the development of change and innovation.

James Botkin: We've identified three particular things needed for innovation: *power, vision,* and *implementation.* I focus as much on vision as I do on power. The two are closely related. If there is no vision to remove the blind spots, there is no innovation. And if that vision is not backed up by power, forget it; there's nothing you can do—except change the power structure.

Part III

MANAGING CREATIVITY AND INNOVATIVE ACTIVITIES

Chapter 4

A PERSPECTIVE ON MANAGING ENTREPRENEURIAL ACTIVITIES IN AN ACADEMIC ENVIRONMENT

W. Arthur Porter

Academic environments traditionally inhibit entrepreneurial expression. This paper focuses on aspects of an academic environment that can support entrepreneurial activities and the exciting challenges of implementing, nurturing, and managing such programs. A real-time example is presented and discussed.

It is well known that in times of national emergency our academic communities have been capable of developing creative and innovative solutions to critical problems. There are certainly powerful examples associated with the World War II period. The need for radar, stronger weapons, and better communications systems was unquestionably in the national interest. During that period the talents of faculty and students were used to develop creative solutions. On the other hand, when the clear priority of a national emergency is lacking, universities are well known to be hesitant, if not resistant, in responding to a problem outside of expected academic interests. Former Secretary of Health, Education and Welfare, John W. Gardner, wrote only fifteen years ago:

> As things stand now, modern man believes—at least with half his mind—that his institutions can accomplish just about anything. The fact that they fall very far short of that goal is due, he believes, to the prevalence of people who love power or money more than they love mankind. To my mind there is an appealing (or appalling) innocence to that view. I have had ample opportunity to observe the diverse institutions of this society—the colleges and universities, the military services, business corporations, foundations, professions, government agencies and so on. And I must report that even excellent institutions run by excellent human beings are inherently slug-

gish, *not* hungry for innovation, *not* quick to respond to human need, *not* eager to reshape themselves to meet the challenge of the times.

Gardner continues:

I am not suggesting a polarity between men and their institutions — men eager for change, their institutions blocking it. The institutions are run by men. And often those who appear most eager for change oppose it most stubbornly when their own institutions are involved. I give you the university professor, a great friend of change provided it doesn't affect the patterns of academic life. His motto is 'Innovate away from home.'

The theme of this volume is creative and innovative management, yet I am struck by a contradiction in objectives and terms, particularly if the classical definition of management is applied. Creativity and innovation are processes that must be encouraged and permitted to happen, not projects or products that can be predicted, controlled, or "managed." The creative process proceeds best when there are no constraints on the thought process, no planned or controlled format that must be used, and no established laws, theorems, or assumptions that cannot be questioned. From this creative process, which tends to occur when and where it can, comes innovation.

This innovation point is the pivotal moment when talented and motivated people seek the opportunity to act on their ideas and dreams. The academic community has almost always been thought of as a bastion for supporting the creative process, a place where innovative solutions can be theorized and defined. Yet today there are questions. The substantive academic issue in our society today is: What further role should our universities play in supporting the active process of testing, implementing, and nurturing creative and innovative ideas and people to further strengthen the economy of our nation?

Where have many innovative and creative processes occurred and how have they led to meaningful ideas, solutions, and products? In the book *The Sources of Invention,* by John Jewkes, David Sawers, and Richard Stillerman, two classes of inventions are defined. An *individual invention* is described as one for which "an individual chooses the field of ideas in which to work, employs his own resources or acquires them from others who exercise no control over his work, stands to gain or lose directly from his inventive success or failure, works with limited resources and with colleagues subject to his guidance and leadership." On the other hand, if an invention has emerged from "the laboratory of a firm where the research workers have been engaged on a 'set' problem and are salaried employees who would not normally gain directly from the invention, where the cooperation of a team has been involved and where considerable sums have been made available for the research," the authors have categorized it as an "*in-*

stitutional invention." More than one half of the cases they studied were ranked as individual inventions.

Xerography, jet engine, ball-point pen, penicillin, safety razor, and titanium are examples of individual inventions. Float glass, the crease-resisting process, and semi-synthetic penicillins are institutional inventions. In the case of the ball-point pen, several innovative people working individually contributed to the pen's development; however, the most meaningful improvement was not in the mechanical design of the pen but in the later improvement of the ink, incorporating a chemical change that produced a self-sealing property to prevent leaking. This development led to the Papermate pen. The stories vary from product to product but the thread of consistency for management purposes is clear: we know so little about how to control or encourage the creative and innovative process that there is great danger in trying too hard to "manage" it.

I suggest that the greatest ally the creative and innovative processes have is competition. As we conduct studies on managing the creative process, we must be careful not to block competition—we must avoid destroying the very process we are trying to understand.

In coming to the program example in academia, I focus on the most critical aspects of a "managed environment" that can support the creative and innovative process. The most commonly asked question of a successful individual or institutional inventor is: How did you do that? Everybody wants the recipe. How to specify and quantify the process of managing such programs and processes? The key elements are people and program priorities.

To support the innovative and creative process, an institution must not only be interested in recruiting acclaimed and talented people from external sources but must also place at least equal emphasis on nurturing and supporting the development of internal talent—each "creative" institution must learn to "grow" and stimulate its own leaders of change. This nurturing occurs through trust, support, and the commitment to reward success—without punishing failure. In other words, risk taking must be supported and encouraged. My single piece of management advice relative to this process is to remember that institutions do not make discoveries, people do. Institutions can at best support the process and encourage the people.

Now to program priorities. Institutions can and must set program priorities. Resource allocations usually reflect the priority, but it is my experience that the creative people who must work on the problems, particularly in a university research environment, will do so with about the same enthusiasm and regularity as the institution responds to the researcher's own priorities.

Let me go now to the real-time example. Two years ago the Texas Engineering Experiment Station at Texas A & M University created a program called INVENT

(Institute for Ventures in New Technology). The purpose of INVENT is to make the talent on the university campus available to creative and innovative people by providing technical and/or business expertise in the commercialization of new products, and thus new businesses. INVENT is intended to be a source of intellectual seed capital made available at the pre-venture capital stage of a potential business. It also provides that most difficult to find seed money for research in both the technical and business aspects of a potential company prior to the venture capital stage — and takes a future royalty return for its contribution. While the program is still young and evolving, over 600 ideas have been brought to INVENT, a few businesses have been created, and several more are in the final stage of our four-stage process. It is also worth noting that the seed resources available to INVENT are appropriated by the Texas legislature, a good example of university–industry–government cooperation and interaction.

The critical operational and management questions relevant to this volume arise, however, when the traditional roles of a university or university professor are compared to the roles that are played when working with INVENT. The format is changed, and the objectives, or at least the stage of the objectives, are different. There are complex contribution valuations and nettlesome financial participations to consider. There are real conflicts that arise. Teaching and learning are occurring, but not in the traditional manner. Rather, there is a closer academic interaction with the public.

Is it desirable or destructive to permit this type of activity to occur in an academic environment? Is it possible for a university student and/or professor to be productively involved in the INVENT type of research or to be responsive to the public good? Does that involvement enhance the professional reputation of the institution or individual? Should INVENT only respond to those creative and innovative people whose ideas involve technical problems of sufficient scope to enhance a university professor's professional reputation? Should the academic community be willing to work on a ball-point pen problem? If so, how can the quality of the performance be measured? The traditional process of publish or perish is difficult to apply. Possibly the answer is that both activities can and should be accomplished by the researchers and that the more trivial problems can be handled by the students. (But often, as any businessperson knows, solving the "trivial" problems generates the highest return.)

Other questions can and will be raised as our nation seeks improved management of its resources and institutions, but the fundamental questions for academia still remain: To whose problem does the university community respond and to what end or purpose? These questions are the critical ones facing our leading institutions of higher education as we look for creative and innovative ways to manage our resources. We must keep our nation strong, leveraging and networking our talent in support of a strong economy and healthy future for our citizens.

I have struggled with the unknowns associated with tying our universities too intimately to our short-term national needs, or, on the other hand, in being too far removed and aloof from our long-term national goals. In the current stage of evolution of our country and its higher education system, however, I am more comfortable in risking to err on the side of national interest. I agree with the spirit of Thomas Jefferson and the view held during the period of creation of the land-grant colleges as expressed by Alfred North Whitehead: "Celibacy does not suit a university. It must mate itself with action."

Our nation needs the action of our universities more now than at any other time in our history, and our students want to be involved in the business of our world and are looking to our campus to provide them with the tools of competition. Academic traditions do not naturally germinate creative and innovative university programs in support of our state's and nation's needs, and hence those that try are indeed challenged in implementing and managing them.

In closing, I again quote John W. Gardner on facing the challenge before our nation's universities:

> I would not wish anything to alter the character of the university as a haven for dissent and for creative, scholarly work. That must be preserved at all costs. But I believe that those parts of the university which are already involved with the larger community are going to have to take that relationship more seriously than ever before. Some academic people—including close friends of mine—are advocating precisely the opposite position: less rather than more involvement. I respect their motives; I see the point of their arguments; and it grieves me that they should be so wrong.

In summary, then, the key points to keep in mind when "managing" creative and innovative people or projects are:

1. Support competition.
2. Reward success but do not punish failure.
3. Permit, indeed encourage, all assumptions to be questioned.
4. Challenge tradition and seek new perspectives.
5. Invest in people, recruit talent, and encourage its development and growth.
6. Seek new processes of reward and recognition in the academic environment.
7. Challenge academic to mate itself with action in addressing the nation's needs and to provide its students with the tools of competition.

Unless we respond to the challenge, universities run the risk of quite literally going out of business. Only by taking charge of the process, by pioneering inter-sector relationships, and by instituting creative and innovative management will universities maintain their historical perspective and social leadership.

Chapter 5

SEVERAL DILEMMAS FACING INNOVATIONS MANAGERS

Gerhard O. Mensch

One evening on a major TV network's business report, the commentator made a quip about management education and training as provided by major business schools and leading consulting companies. In essence, he said that Peters and Waterman may have thought they found excellent management in the high performance companies they had studied, but since so many of them showed a slump in performance this year, he concluded, shouldn't TV viewers call their librarian "in search of a refund?"

This wisecrack highlights the risk and ridicule pioneers are often exposed to when pushing a frontier. As the saying goes, a pioneer is a person with mud on his face and an arrow in his back. Like us, Peters and Waterman are pushing frontiers in management practice, which is the same frontier we want to expand and break through. They now have their unfair share of mud, and we should sympathize with them.

That commentator's remark illuminates three salient aspects of excellence in management that need to be considered in regard to creativity and innovation. Firstly, it illuminates an important aspect of *corporate culture* —namely, the failure component in creativity, people's resistance to change, and an inclination to punish the change agent. Secondly, the episode helps us see the *relativity of practical standards of excellence* —namely, the contingent nature of creativity and innovation. Thirdly, it sheds light on the *bounded rationality of the pursuit of excellence*. These three points form my framework.

CORPORATE CULTURE IN TRANSITION

That TV commentator blundered. He made an error in logic when he insinuated that a drop in performance of some of the companies in the sample indicates a sudden lack of excellence. That is, of course, a wrong conclusion. He blundered even worse when he implied a default in the scholarly deductions. Deductions do not suffer from drop out of data but from contrary data only if it were included.

The error must be regarded not as a one-time slip of a talented and highly educated person but as a symptom of populist pressure on a person in that spot. So strong is the pressure to please the public that TV commentators do not shy away from poking fun at outstanding performers even if the joke is based on false thought. Show-business knows its customers' wants. It knows the average man's hidden desires for tearing down institutions, for getting even with his heroes and benefactors. In our culture, creators and innovators have NO RIGHT TO FAIL.

Do you recognize the paradox? While institutions strive to create and innovate, there are many countervailing forces at work, often well hidden. In systems theory this paradox is described as equilibrating forces nullifying a creative disequilibrium (the LeChatelier principle). In behavioral quarters in Anglo-Saxon countries it is known as Gresham's law of excellence: low performers will try to overexpose and then undercut the high performers. The average drives out the best. Warren Bennis thinks this hidden conspiracy is a general phenomenon and the reason why leaders cannot lead. The French call it the champion-effect.

This is a time when corporate culture is changing—prompted by necessity. In the past, creativity and innovation was an individualist, even *elitist phenomenon*. It is most often described by some version of the so-called "hero theory." Most of the literature on creativity and innovation adheres to some sort of hero theory. *In Search of Excellence,* of course, fits that category but also breaks away from it. It overcomes some of the hero theory's limitations.

In modern times, innovation is organized creativity. It must become a *populist phenomenon* if we want to stay ahead in world markets. Elitist conduct needs a broader base. "Teamwork is the lifeline of genius," Dr. James Botkin states. Instead of a "hero theory" we need a "team theory" of creative and innovative management, one that incorporates leadership and cooperation. We also need an implementation strategy that reckons with Gresham's law of excellence as a countervailing force.

Appealing to managers to become more creative, more innovative, is just not enough. Our managerial theory must realistically reflect the cultural and social impediments to risk taking. As long as we let the spokesmen of mediocrity get away with making those jokes, creative and innovative management will be an unlikely choice of most junior and senior managers.

RELATIVITY OF PRACTICAL PERFORMANCE STANDARDS

Creative and innovative managers are up against even stronger forces than cultural walls and personal resistance. Reality is more brutal than mere subjectivity. In most companies strategic business units are operating in competitive environments, struggling with technological imperatives, and facing adverse financial circumstances that severely limit their maneuverability. Managers face objective difficulties. What they can do is contingent upon those limitations.

These objective limits on creativity and innovation are no static constraints. They are mobile barriers that change over time. In fact, most innovations aim at stretching, moving, and piercing those constraints. Excellence has to be judged against what is possible under the circumstances. The possibility frontier is a moving standard. What can possibly be accomplished depends on the situation that is in motion. The TV commentator failed to honor this fact of life. He bruised over the simple truth that excellent, creative, or innovative managers do not all of a sudden become non-excellent, noncreative, non-innovative if the firm plunges into a cyclical slowdown, or suffers a dip in output that has nothing to do with the subjective performance of managers but everything to do with the objective developments in the industry.

It would help our quest for creative and innovative management to report some conclusions that have emerged from our field research and that address a) the fundamental factor common to all the objective difficulties managers are facing, and b) the most frequent difficulties, in particular.

Innovations Management—A Difficult Battle at Multiple Business Frontiers

The basic proposition suggested here states that management is a multifrontier struggle: customers, competitors, suppliers, workers, banks, the government—all want a bigger share. Innovations management, specifically, is troubled with the additional complication that all these frontiers constitute interfaces where the established old practice rivals the emerging new. Each of these frontiers constitutes a dilemma for innovations managers, who are thus entangled in a web of multiple dilemmas.

Viewing the many frontiers of creative and innovative management as a web of dilemmas allows us to fall back on the wisdom of great management scientists. First is Chester Bernard, whose *Function of the Executive* treats increasing efficiency in the inner environment of the corporation and increasing effectiveness vis-à-vis customers, suppliers, and competitors. Secondly, owing to Herbert Simon, we now comprehend such multidilemma situations as causing bounded rationality, which may lead to muddling through. Of course, bounded rationality implies optimizing behavior within given constraints. It is consistent with the theory of second best. Thirdly, going on to flexible constraints, we appreciate Charnes and Cooper's seminal work on chance constraint programming. It leads us to analytical concepts of planned extensions of movable frontiers of business, thus providing a foundation for innovation planning. Fourthly, Bela Gold's productivity network approach to multiple frontier management generates a heuristic methodology for dealing with webs of dilemmas.

The Three Dilemmas of Time, Track, and Turf

Of the many practical dilemmas facing the innovations manager, I comment on only three. According to our field studies with innovating companies in West Germany and the United States, objective forces render these three dilemmas especially hard to manage. Here is a capsule summary of the managerial dilemmas caused by "time," "track," and "turf":

- *Dilemma I:* In mature businesses, the shortening of product life cycles in the market clashes with the long *time-to-market* of any nontrivial innovation. Consequently, "trivial pursuit" has become the game plan for many companies.

- *Dilemma II:* Nearly all technical fields can be viewed as technological trajectories (R.R. Nelson), as turnpikes for technological advancements. In a *track (or series) of innovations,* many ideas are called as candidates for the next step, but few are chosen to be winners.

- *Dilemma III:* True innovation does not respect managerial territories. It penetrates the formal lines of authority in corporations; it intrudes on someone's *turf* but is resisted. That's life.

OBSERVATIONS ON TIME, TRACK, AND TURF

Over the last ten to fifteen years, a large number of industries have been maturing, without an equal number of new industries coming into existence to offset the overall maturation. This trend has had a profound effect on business conditions and managerial attitudes.

During the academic year 1983/84 the Innovations Management Research Team at Case Western Reserve University surveyed Northeast Ohio industries (106 responding managers representing forty-six companies with one to over fifty strategic business units.) We concluded that about 85–95 percent of the participating businesses are in the mature state. We have derived these figures (as lower bound and upper bound estimates) from data on the age of technology embodied in the products and processes of these businesses. The data is given in Figure 5–1.

We defined as mature industries those companies in which 50 percent or more of output was produced with plant and processes that are five years or older, or in which 50 percent or more of revenues was derived from products five years or older.

- 88.7 percent of the participants responded that more than 50 percent of the firm's output produced in 1983 was with plant and processes five years or older (sum of the three "process" bars on the right-hand side of Figure 5–1).
- Only 5.7 percent of the respondents represented businesses where at least 75 percent of sales was accrued from products younger than five years (the "product" bar on the very left of Figure 5–1).

In short, over the past fifteen years, innovation possibilities have shrunk in most branches of industry. It became more difficult to innovate in a growing number of industries.

Observations on "Time"

When an industry matures, technology settles in. While it is settling in, the limits on technological innovation get tighter. Consequently, a gap in timing develops.

- On the one hand, significant improvements become less often available, and the lead time from inception of an R & D idea to the implementation

Figure 5–1. Age of Product and Process Technology.

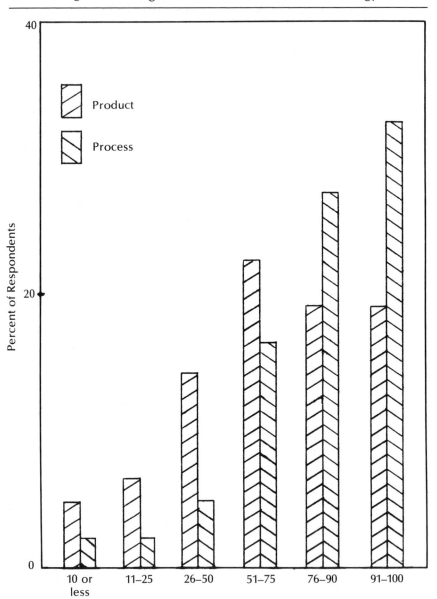

Percent of Sales Accounted for by
Products/Processes.5 Years or Older

of a new product increases. Field studies with West German and American companies confirm an average lead time of five years in maturing companies.

• On the other hand, the market cycle of mere incremental changes and product variations shortens during settling-in. The product life cycle once was four or five years when it was stimulated by significant improvements. The cycle shortened when it was fed minor modifications only. In many mature industries now, the life cycle approaches one year, which is the duration of the fashion cycle.

The managerial reality in business where technologies are settling in can be characterized by tougher deadlines, falling out of step, hectic patch-up work, improvisation, quality decline, and decreased efficiency. Everyone has reasons for getting angry. Things do not get done in time as they used to.

This reality is the consequence of a scissor effect—namely, the speeding up of the life cycle and the slowing down of the development process. This "time" dilemma is illustrated in Figure 5-2.

The task of creative and innovative management in these situations is to bring the business back into lock-step with the market rhythm. Figure 5-3 depicts the target area for efficiency gains in innovations management.

Observations on "Track"

Track denotes the fact that industries evolve within technological boundaries. Like drivers on a turnpike, innovations managers are locked in, or constrained by, these technological trajectories.

The dilemma facing the innovations manager is that he is usually well aware of possibilities for minor incremental innovations as well as potential for major breakthroughs. Both sets of opportunities would require additional work and risk taking. However, the rewards for incremental innovation are less uncertain. At the same time, the manager suspects that if his company elects the conservative route of incremental change, some competing firms may elect to introduce a radical innovation that may disrupt the pattern of doing business. In other words, he must fear "hidden foot feedback" (Burton Klein).

We have ample information now on managerial perceptions and realities in the heartland of American manufacturing (Northeast Ohio) and of West German manufacturing (West Berlin). The situation can be characterized as being dominated by incremental innovation, seasoned with respectable efforts made at breaking through the technological walls of mature businesses.

Figure 5–2. "Time" Dilemma.

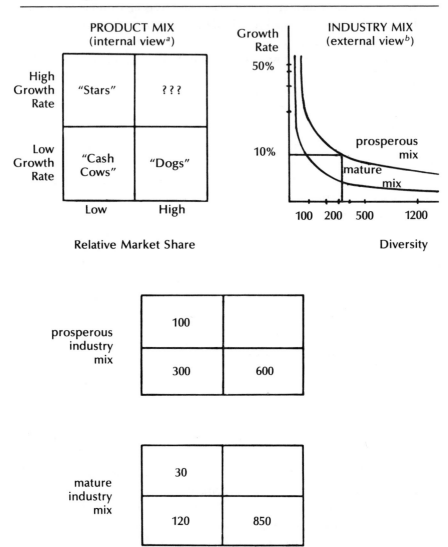

a Looking at a set of markets from a company's point of view (portfolio approach).
b Looking at a set of markets from a stakeholder's point of view (incidence method).

Source: Gerhard O. Mensch.

Figure 5–3. The Shifting Product Portfolio (According to the Imbalanced Technical Change Hypothesis)

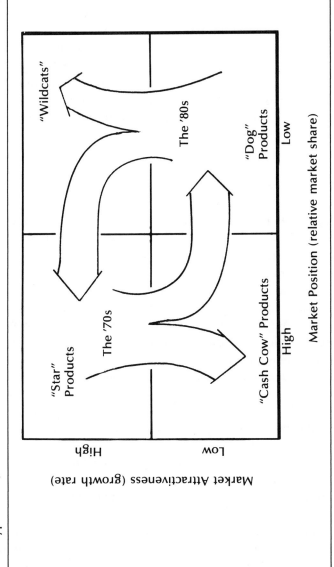

Major Trends in Industry Mix
1. Maturation during the 1970s; experience.
2. Innovation during the 1980s; expectation.

Source: Gerhard O. Mensch.

Figure 5–4 depicts the distribution of innovative expenditures targeted at product innovation, process innovation, and service innovation in our sample. The remarkable point is that the distribution is Pareto (60 : 30 : 10), indicating prevalence of the law of large numbers. This law applies to small increments of change. In other words, the observed pattern of innovation reveals that most of the innovations are incremental.

However, several firms concentrate significant resources in the pursuit of disruptive, radical innovation (see Figure 5–5). Several small companies (up to $6 million in sales) and medium-large companies ($50–500 million in sales) stand out in frequency of trying a disruptive innovation, while medium ($6–50 million in sales) and large companies seem less inclined to take such a high risk. Obviously, technological risks are evaluated contingent upon thresholds of opportunity for growth within the track.

Observations on "Turf"

Incremental innovation usually respects established organization boundaries within the firm. It also stays within the bounds of the served market. Radical innovation reaches beyond. It does not respect the traditional territory of incumbent managers in the corporation. It intrudes and it invades. Our innovations management survey reveals that many managers feel the wind of change. The incrementalism that allowed their business to mature and settle in is becoming unsettled. Advances in technology threaten the competitive advantages of established technology. In many mature businesses, strategies become more oriented toward "innovation by invasion."

We have distinguished three types of product innovations by degree of radicalness:

- Incremental improvement: improvement of an existing product in the market served to date.
- Radical improvement: development of a greatly modified product for the same market.
- Radical breakthrough: totally new product for a new market.

Figure 5–6 depicts the frequency of incremental and radical innovation projects in our 1983 Northeast Ohio survey. It differentiates the frequency by degree of focus of innovation effort as measured by the portion of innovation expenditures dedicated to the project. The two most striking observations are that there

Figure 5–4.   Percentage of Respondents Allocating More Than Y% of Total Innovation Expenditures to Product, Process, and Service Innovations, Respectively.

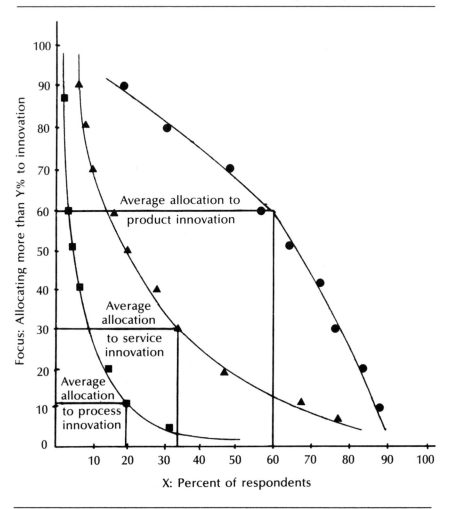

A horizontal line from any given Y% projected on the X axis from the corresponding curve shows the percent of respondents that allocate more than Y% to the relevant innovation activity category.

● Product innovation
▲ Process innovation
■ Service innovation

Source: Gerhard O. Mensch.

Figure 5–5.   Efforts Directed at Product Innovations
(Measured by Expenditures as Percent of Sales in Four
Size Classes).

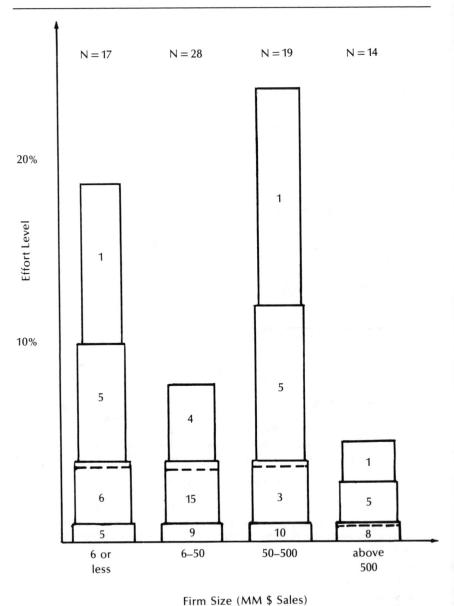

Source: Gerhard O. Mensch.

Figure 5–6. Frequency of Incremental and Radical Innovation Projects (1983 Northeast Ohio survey).

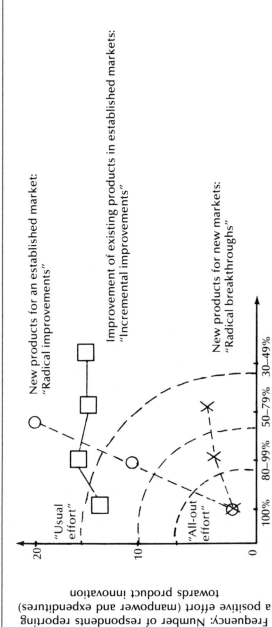

Source: Gerhard O. Mensch.

are several all out efforts at radical innovation represented in our sample, and that efforts made at incremental innovation are not correlated with focus.

In other words, we find striking differences in strategic focus and posture. On the one hand, there are those stagnant companies that muddle through. On the other hand, there are the carefully focused companies where creative and innovative managers know precisely what they are doing.

BOUNDED RATIONALITY IN PURSUIT OF EXCELLENCE

This brings us back full circle to the initial point. The TV commentator's quip exemplifies that failure component: outstanding performers are in greater danger of being ridiculed and blamed if they fail with a daring venture than are the average performers who stick to their knitting. Even so, sticking to one's knitting today means undertaking some incremental innovations, at the very least.

Cultural and social forces make innovating an unnecessarily lonely and burdensome initiative. The objective difficulties described as the three dilemmas of time, track, and turf make the job even harder.

The upside rewards for winning and the downside costs for losing are out of balance as society behaves unfairly to those who try and fail. Hence, as long as those discouragements prevail, many managers will opt for second best. They will probably make a conservative shift toward no innovation, imitation, or simple improvements, rather than make a risky shift toward focused radical innovation that aims at new business.

What we can accomplish here is:

1. Emphasize the social and economic value of reaching beyond the conventional boundaries of average practice.
2. Laud the practitioners who have stepped forward and have moved the best practice frontier.
3. Explain how the boundaries are shifting anyway, as a result of cyclical and structural change in the industrial base of leading industrial nations, thus facilitating the difficult task.

OUTLOOK

My message to innovation managers is that past experiences should not darken expectations. While in most maturing industries the going has been hard, prospects are becoming better. I see facilitating factors coming to the innovator's aid. There is a favorable drift in the side conditions.

Present economic conditions are such that in many mature industries the probability has increased for the adoption of radically different production technologies. Furthermore, many novel product technologies are now ready for implementation. They will establish new branches of industry. The economy has reached the macroeconomic state that I call "the state of structural readiness for clusters of basic innovations." It is a situation where the time is ripe for breakthroughs because of structural readiness.

Chapter 6

CREATIVITY AND CONTINGENCY IN STRATEGIC MANAGEMENT

Maurice Saias

Previous papers have shared certain points and diverged on others, inciting us to clarify definitions and options. Apparently "to manage creative and innovative activities" seems, to some, a contradiction in terms. My view is different; not only do I maintain that creative and innovative activities can be managed, but I also hope to show that they *must* be managed. Perhaps the argument comes from the expectations one has about the act of management. What do I mean by management? Quoting Webster, "the judicious use of means to accomplish an end"? Or, quoting Abraham Charnes and William W. Cooper, "Making things work successfully is the old and abiding task of management.... Finally, it is the ability to induce these [kinds of] activities in others in an organized way that makes it an act of management rather than only the act of an individual."[1]

Agreement on terms is important. It is not a semantic exercise, if we wish to advance the objectives of this book. It is my guess that most would agree with these definitions—even Dr. Arthur Porter, who seems to reject the desirability of managing creative and innovative activities. (In my opinion Professor Porter's paper refers to *acts* of management.)

Consensus appears stronger when it comes to creativity and innovation. Although everyone does not agree that they are essentially different, one wishes to separate them totally in an organizational context; obviously, the Schumpeterian mark is still strong. Creativity and innovativeness are not limited to high technology sectors; they are needed and can be found everywhere from service to smokestack industries. They must not be limited, either, to the technical aspects of business but must cover equally the managerial side of our activities.

Being a French national, I cannot end this short discussion on definitions without pointing out the necessity to avoid confusion between innovation and *bricolage*. According to *Le Petit Robert*, a French dictionary, *bricolage* is the act of *bricoleur* and *bricoleur* means "to repair something in an unskilled manner, the repair is not made to last." In professional circles, *bricoleur* has a negative connotation. *Bricolage*, in this sense, has been so widely spread over most European nations that they are in deep trouble today. "Renault," the largest French car manufacturer, has been so good, and for so long, at practicing the art of socioeconomic and technological *bricolage* that it slid from first to sixth place in Europe and lost one billion dollars in 1984. Other examples can be found all over Europe as well as in the United States.

Another side of creativity and innovation is the British. The British have a good reputation in R & D. As a matter of fact, many American corporations go into the United Kingdom to "round up the doggies" (i.e., British engineers in biotechnology, electronics, and computers) and bring them back to the United States. Amazingly, the British seem unable to go from lab to production line. What does this suggest about creativity and innovation? It must be managed.

Hypercompetition, to use Dean Kozmetsky's word, and market globalization make creativity and innovation compulsory for economic success. Business organizations particularly cannot allow creativity and innovation to wander without guidance; they must be targeted to be efficient and effective. The kind of creativity and innovation that is needed varies extensively according to the competitive environment that corporations have to face in their different industries. Creativity and innovation requirements also differ in relation to the strategic positioning of a business within a given competitive environment. This is a *contingent* view of creativity and innovation. Everybody understands why a corporation involved in telecommunications will not spend a large proportion of its creative and innovative resources to grow peanuts in Latin America. Similarly, one must understand why program priorities must be congruent with the competitive systems or the strategic positioning of a business.

Professor Mensch's paper deals with what can be called strategic endogenous contingency—i.e., with the creative and innovative activities connected with the strategic positioning of a business in a particular competitive environment. The competitive system that has been chosen is the one described in the famous BCG market share/growth matrix. The construction of this particular portfolio technique rests on three hypotheses:

1. Thanks to the experience and scale effects, market share dominance insures a strong competitive advantage.
2. Cash requirements are related to market growth.
3. Cash performance is a function of market growth and relative market share.

When one of these hypotheses is not validated, the use of the BCG matrix can lead to major strategic mistakes. They may include the creative and innovative moves covered in Professor Mensch's survey; moves to reduce costs, launch new products, or increase market share lead to success in certain competitive systems and to disaster in others. We would like, therefore, to broaden our perspective and replace the market share/growth portfolio technique in the larger context of competitive systems analysis—that is, the exogenous strategic contingency.

Following a more recent BCG approach, competitive systems can be characterized by two sets of factors. The first set deals with the importance of competitive advantages; the second with the number of potential ways to achieve them.

Successful businesses are based on a strong competitive advantage. Their strategic value depends upon the importance of the leader's advantage over its challengers. When and where costs are similar and differentiation is not possible, returns can barely pay for the required growth. Significant long-term profitability requires a well-established competitive advantage.

Equally important is the number of ways in which a competitive advantage can be obtained. If many sources of differentiation do exist, several competitors can adapt their offerings and cost structure to the specific demands of various strategic segments. If the differences they have created can be defended, their business will be profitable even when facing a much larger competitor. If the advantage, however, is not defendable and if diseconomies of scale prevail, the name of the game is fragmentation.

The two variables—potential size of the competitive advantage and number of approaches to achieve it—can be combined in a matrix form (Table 6–1).

Table 6–1. BCG. Competitive Environments.

Potential Size of Advantage	Number of Approaches to Achieve Advantage	
	FEW	MANY
SMALL	Stalemate	Fragmentation
LARGE	Volume	Specialization

Source: Maurice Saias.

Creative and innovative activities are quite different in the four competitive systems described in Table 6–1. Creativity and innovation are *contingent* and should be geared to the key success factors associated with each competitive situation.

Volume businesses require overall cost leadership; the emphasis should be on process technology, product design for ease-in-manufacture, low cost distribution system, cost minimization and control. Specialized businesses require focusing and cost leadership in segments; the emphasis should be on creating something that is perceived industrywide or for a particular segment as being unique. It can take many forms: design or brand image, technology, features, customer service, dealer network, and so forth. Product engineering, flair, marketing and R & D capabilities, functional coordination, and control systems are some of the domains where creativity and innovation will apply.

If, for the sake of argument, imagine that the creative and innovative actions required by specialized businesses are applied to the "volume" environment, or vice versa, we can see the consequences. This is precisely what must be kept in mind when talking about the management of creative and innovative activities. In business, at least, creativity and innovation are badly needed, but they must be directed towards certain ends. The third and fourth competitive systems will stress this need for directed strategy even more. When large corporations get trapped in fragmented environments, all their creative and innovative capacities must be geared to operating in small units in order to maximize differentiation and operational efficiency. Indeed, diseconomies of scale is the most pertinent characteristic of fragmentation. Using one's creativity for market share gains or cost reduction in that environment will not lead anywhere; using one's creativity, however, to move out of fragmentation and change the rules of the game (as McDonalds did to transform a fragmented business into a volume one) does pay. The situation is very similar in stalemate industries where creativity should be directed to find solutions to move into a different environment.

In this context of strategic exogenous contingency, creativity and innovation must be managed because the various competitive forces at play leave no room for major mistakes and waste of resources. Each competitive system has its own requirements in terms of creative and innovative activities, the least of which are the involvement of creativity and innovation to change the rules of the game and move one business from one strategic environment to another.

NOTE

1.   A. Charnes and W. W. Cooper, *Creative and Innovative Management* (Cambridge: Ballinger Publishing Company, 1984), p. xvii.

DISCUSSION

Maurice Saias

Robert Kuhn: Do we have a problem here? Given the high cost of failure, can only the rich afford to be creative?

Gerhard Mensch: Your observation is correct. Yet I see pockets of change where this universal tendency is reversed, where the odds of failure have been shifted, where the tightness of constraints change. These constrictions may be capital, cognitive or cultural; they may be technological or organizational. We have the methodology; there seems to be a general easing of constraints, making creative things easier to do.

Question: How can high-risk ventures flourish in a large bureaucratic organization? What can managers do?

Arthur Porter: That's your job and your risk. Good managers spot potential better than managers that are not so good. No manager can afford not to take the risk of identifying top talent. If you're worried that you're going to pick the wrong person, and hence decide not to make the bet, you're going to lose anyway. Get up your own guts and make your own call.

Part IV

ORGANIZATIONAL DESIGN FOR IMPROVING CREATIVITY AND INNOVATION

Chapter 7

"BIG BANG" MANAGEMENT

Frederick W. Gluck

In a 1984 article, *Fortune* identified eight companies—3M, Apple, American Airlines, Campbell Soup, General Electric, Intel, Merck, and Philip Morris—as leaders in innovation. Certainly these companies are among the most successful and innovative in the United States. The author, Gene Sherman, put his finger on a number of important aspects for creating an innovative environment: the notion of controlled experimentation; the obsession with meeting customers' needs; the importance of a strong culture; the looseness in the idea generation stage; and the disciplined assessment of these ideas in terms of commercial viability.

The article left me with a sense of frustration, however. There is a sizable gulf between the kind of innovation represented by the Apple Computers and the Intels of the world and that represented by Philip Morris and General Electric. Of course Mr. Sherman recognizes that innovation runs the gamut from product line extension to the creation of new businesses. But for a consultant with a "What am I going to do Monday morning?" orientation, simply noting the fact that innovation covers a multitude of sins is not enough.

We need to understand the significance of the difference between what might be called, at one end of the spectrum, "suggestion box" innovation (i.e., product line extensions, cost reductions and the like)—in other words, incremental type of innovation—and, at the other end of the spectrum, the "big bang" type of innovation that Apple Computer represents. If we are really looking for lessons about innovation, creativity, or entrepreneurialism—three very popular words these days—we need to understand what we are talking about.

The *Fortune* article is replete with examples of innovation that cover that spectrum: Apple and Intel, new start-ups that knocked the big boys out of the box; 3M's long history of sheltering individual entrepreneurs under the umbrella of an understanding and supportive culture; Philip Morris systematically incrementalizing and executing its way to a dominant position in cigarettes and courageously attempting to revolutionize beer and soft drinks; American Airlines, Campbell Soup, and General Electric changing their strategic course by reshaping their management approach; Merck investing in research to stay ahead.

Each of these very successful corporations has responded to its particular situation in a way that has led to success. There is a problem, however, hidden in these success stories and in the untold stories of the many not-so-successful companies that failed to make *Fortune's* list. Undoubtedly, this problem prompted *Fortune* to refer somewhat disparagingly to the heads of major corporations who "used to be known as captains of industry." It is this unspoken problem that needs to be addressed if we are to have truly creative and innovative large corporations.

The problem is this:

> Very few of our largest and most successful corporations have really solved the problem of how to renew themselves when *major* shifts in the environment occur. When the fundamental nature of competition in their industries changes, or new market opportunities open up, they do not seem to be able to rethink—from ground zero—the way in which they do business.

This inability to rethink was true of General Electric and most of the other post-war electrical giants in computers and integrated circuits, and even consumer electronics. It was true of 3M in copiers—remember when Thermo-Fax was the best game in town? It was even true of IBM—inexplicably left off *Fortune's* list—in minicomputers. One only has to look at the difficulties of giants such as General Motors, AT & T, U.S. Steel, International Harvester, Caterpillar—and an endless list of European companies—to find ample evidence in industry after industry. I believe that there is a fundamental reason for this problem: there is a substantial difference—both culturally and conceptually—between what it takes to pursue suggestion box innovation successfully and what it takes to pull off a big bang innovation.

When the context of your business—competitors, suppliers, distribution networks, markets, and so on—is stable, the search for competitive advantage is essentially an information-processing exercise. There is usually lots of history, lots of data, and some well-understood rules. Frequently, industries like these behave like oligopolies, and the situation is so stable that active, alert monitoring may be all that is needed. Management may simply mean fine-tuning. Innovation in industries like these is still necessary, but it is generally incremental, largely based on analysis of operations. Consequently, it is not very disruptive or, frankly, very innovative.

Suggestion box innovation generally requires a great deal of highly specific information on a particular aspect of a business, such as a function or a market. The new insights are usually limited to small, incremental improvements in that function. In other words, suggestion box type innovation produces changes that can be carried out in a reasonably contained way and with relatively little disruption to the organization.

Even if one whole aspect of your industry is changing—for example, manufacturing technology—incremental innovation is generally still the order of the day and disruption is limited to a single function with some ripple effects. But when your entire business concept is threatened through radical technological change, globalization, deregulation, or the like, you have a different problem. History may be nonexistent, data contradictory, and rules yet to be invented. You cannot analyze all that well because you cannot find all that much to analyze. What you need do is to "tamper with the mainspring." In short, you need a big bang innovation and the institutional courage and skills to pull it off.

Big bang innovations generally require information that goes beyond the province of any function and, in many cases, beyond the ken of general managers. They are generally *very* disruptive. People are made obsolete, facilities made redundant, and large investments rendered unproductive. But most importantly, the culture or organization—"the way we do things around here"—may be torn apart. It is the business equivalent of political revolution.

Since most large organizations view change not as an opportunity but as a problem, it is not surprising that they back off from this kind of change except as a last resort. Unfortunately, that is often too late!

The steel companies, for example, failed to see the need for reinvestment in more modern equipment until very late in the day. They did not feel the pinch of European and Japanese imports until response was difficult. They kept inefficient, outdated capacity open too long. They failed to anticipate the impact of minimills. True, the U.S. steel industry has come a long way up since it began reckoning with these problems in the late 1970s. But here is a classic case where adaptation was not enough. Innovation—in the fundamental way in which they both thought about and conducted their business—was required.

This is the real dilemma for our captains of industry. At what point do they forsake suggestion box innovation and go for the big bang? And how do they do it without destroying all that is good in their organizations? The answers to these two questions are at the heart of the challenge facing those who aspire to be creative and innovative during a period when major change seems to be the order of the day.

The subject of creativity and innovation, and how they relate to organization design, has preoccupied McKinsey & Co. for years. It has been at the heart of our research into excellent companies and strategic management. How do we make companies more innovative? How do we help them create their futures? There are endless debates in our firm as to whether there is a difference between being entrepreneurial and being innovative and creative—and whether analysis or culture should dominate. I myself have been on all sides of the debate.

I can make the distinctions or convince myself that they are all the same or all different; I can think of instances where the rational model ought to dominate, where organizational dynamics needs to take precedence, and where they ought to be considered in tandem. But about one thing I am sure: I know innovation when I see it. And whenever I see it, I know that somewhere in the background are the entrepreneurial instinct and the creative process.

What about the specific question of creativity? We have tried to pinpoint the characteristics of a creative person, a creative process, a creative organization, and have compiled a variety of specifications. Generally, when we talk about a creative person, we paint a picture of someone aggressive, imaginative, single-minded, knowledgeable, talented, and energetic. But after much debate, I have concluded that there are *only two things that really distinguish the creative person: the possession of a tremendous store of raw information, and the ability to combine, order, or connect this information in a novel and better way.*

True, creative people are also energectic and single-minded. But I also know many single-minded people who are incredibly pedestrian and many energetic people who are incredibly ordinary. However, I do not know any people who have a wealth of information about a subject, and the ability to combine, order and connect it in better or novel ways, who are not creative. And I believe the same is true of organizations, regardless of size.

If we accept this hypothesis about creativity, we can begin to explore the question of how to design the creative organization. To begin with, of course, we have to be working with people who have the capacity to be creative. Without the proper people, nothing is possible.

The lifeblood of the creative organization is uncategorized, unanalyzed, undigested, messy information. It is the raw material of creativity. How far would Watson and Crick have gotten without an encyclopedic knowledge of what was already known about genetics? How far would Mozart have gotten if he hadn't understood music? Steven Jobs did not simply walk out to his garage one day and invent the Apple computer. Most creative people I know have vast memories and aren't too quick to categorize their knowledge. They want to know every-thing there is to know about their subject. They get the information first and figure out what is important later. Efficiency in the information acquisition pro-cess is not a high priority for them. They use all the sources they can get their hands on. They accept lots of redundancy. They have little patience with other people's digests of what's going on.

So the first requirement for a creative organization is a method or approach to information acquisition that puts a great deal of raw information in the hands of many people—planners, market researchers, designers—but most importantly, line managers, because they are the ones most likely to make things happen.

If information is the lifeblood of the creative organization, then the decision-making process is its heart. There is no need for me to recite for you the litany of brainstorming or synectics—a great deal is known and has been written about creative decisionmaking processes. They are unstructured, playful, contentious, and rambling.

And so the second requirement for the creative organization is to have its de-cisionmakers involved in the unstructured, playful, contentious, and rambling process of discerning patterns and meaning from raw, undigested information.

Understanding the fundamental design requirements for a creative organi-zation only gets us halfway there, however. New ideas, even good new ideas, are not innovation. To truly have an innovation, you have to make something happen.

So the third requirement—what enables an organization to convert creativ-ity into innovation—is the ability to execute. That means functional skills and the kind of culture identified in the McKinsey research into excellent com-panies that has been reported by Tom Peters and Bob Waterman in *In Search of Excellence*.

Against this template of three requirements for a creative, innovative orga-nization, let us examine the really interesting question, how top management makes the call between incremental and big bang innovations. To begin with, the leadership of the organization unit that needs the big bang—whether it is the whole corporation or simply a major division—must be dealing with raw information in a way that makes ordering it in new ways possible. What does this mean? First of all, I am not talking about financial information. Financial information is a highly digested summary of what has either happened or might happen. As an historical fact, it has relevance; however, as a future indicator, it has little.

Many other types of information suffer from the same flaw. Most forecasts, for example, are simply the past dressed up with future phrases. Remember, experience curves, most growth share matrices, economic value calculations, and the like are essentially forecasts that may be useful for raising danger signals but are totally useless for helping executives figure out how to make a big bang innovation. The raw materials for the big bang are detailed understanding of customers, competitors, markets, technologies, and the implications of how they are all interacting and changing. Equally important are the forums that provide management the opportunity for wide-ranging debate, the kind that promotes different interpretations of these facts in order to arrive at creative solutions.

Many, if not most, captains of industry are distant from the kinds of raw information that we are talking about, and spend very little of their time in the types of debate I have mentioned. They view change as a problem, not an opportunity. I am not criticizing. They almost have to. The demands on their time are monumental. They cry out for digested information and all too frequently embrace tools and methodologies that give the appearance of precision and insight but are simply highly digested summaries of the status quo. They do not view themselves as having time to view undigested information or to deal directly with customers and technologists. They want clarity. They do not think that they have the time to tolerate contradictory and ambiguous information. They tend to get information from a few sources rather than many.

In fact, the reason why so many organizations are so layered, choreographed, and procedure-ridden is the fear of being overwhelmed by raw information. But the genius of an IBM top management team or a Lee Iacocca or a Jack Welch is that, despite the threat of raw information, they have found ways to deal with it and make leaps of faith based on their convictions about its meaning.

About ten years ago, when John Opel first took over as president of IBM, he and I were discussing the use of financial estimates and forecasts in making decisions about R & D investments. He told me, in effect, "The financial numbers are abstractions and are of no use to me. If I can't personally justify to my marketing, R & D, and manufacturing people my decision to bet on, say, monolithic versus MOS technology — based on my own assessment of what it will mean in terms of the relative value we will be delivering to customers in the competitive market place — I will simply lose my ability to lead this company."

The genius of IBM top management in the case of personal computers (PCs) was not the conception of the independent business unit. It was in the more basic conclusion that PCs were not simply a product line extension but the harbingers of a different way of doing business in computers and that a big bang innovation was required. That kind of conviction came from first-hand knowledge that nothing less than a radical departure from their tried and true success formula in mainframes would get them where they wanted to go.

IBM had seen its share of the computer market drop from 60 percent in 1967 to 31 percent by the early eighties, largely because it stuck to its mainframe approach to the market and missed the minicomputer wave. It was determined not to make a similar mistake in personal computers. Now IBM has long had the reputation of being conservatively run, highly analytical, and maybe just a bit too orthodox for its own good, a characterization that does not bode too well for big bang innovation. But when management decided to go after the personal computer market, it jarred itself loose from "the way things are done around here." It set up an independent business unit to develop the personal computer and gave the manager in charge, Don Estridge, lots of latitude. The PC group sourced microprocessors from Intel instead of using internally developed circuitry. They used some outside software suppliers. They built an automated factory. And they ventured into distribution channels unfamiliar to them previously. Today they are a major force in the market, to say the least.

I am not sure IBM could have invented the PC concept—they probably could not have done what Jobs and Wozniak did at Apple. They showed, however, tremendous flexibility and changed some very fundamental ideas about how to succeed in the computer business. And they continue to follow up on the big bang. The recent moves we have been reading about in the press—the entry into the software market, the investment in MCI, the new products and services they will be developing through joint ventures with British Telecom and Matsushita, the acquisition of Rolm—are all indicative of IBM's determination to capitalize further on their big bang move and to reshape their way of doing business.

Not long ago I was talking with the head of the computer division of one of IBM's erstwhile competitors. After an extended discussion of what was going on in the PC market, I asked him, "Well, how are you treating this market differently from the way you conduct your mainframe business? You know, how are you doing the R & D, the sourcing, the manufacturing, the selling?"

He thought for a minute and said, "Why, exactly the same way—each department has its responsibilities to get the job done." In other words, he was viewing the PC as simply a product line extension—business as usual.

The amazing thing to me was that this discussion took place long after IBM had shown its hand. "The way we do things around here" dies hard.

These observations have, I think, some sobering implications for those corporations that seek to be creative and innovative.

First of all, they raise serious questions about the desirability of using tools and techniques for digesting information when things are changing fast. I do not question the need for digestion; I simply call attention to the fact that it must be done with great circumspection. And it must be done by people with a broad understanding of the factors that challenge the corporation and who are in a position, and have the responsibility, to do something about meeting the challenge.

Secondly, we ought to challenge many of the traditions that have grown up around planning — the tendency to treat planning as a process done by planners; the tendency to want to make strategic planning flow gracefully into operational planning without any disruption; the desire for buttoned-up detail about action steps, and so on. This is not to denigrate the importance of good operational planning or attention to detail. But we cannot afford to forget that the level of uncertainty surrounding major changes militates against programmed decision making and excessive detail.

Finally, the notion of big bang creativity with its need for radical departures from conventional wisdom and "the way we do things around here" calls into question whether existing management teams can see such programs through. The sad fact is that existing management at several levels may not respond well to, or be comfortable with, the kind of creativity and innovation we are talking about. The CEO may be put off by the drain on his time, the affront to his experience, and the confusion raw information represents. The planner may view analysis — the digestion of information — as his stock in trade rather than creating forums for wide-ranging discussion. And the business unit manager may often want to concentrate simply on incremental innovation and therefore very carefully parcel out the information he has on future threats and opportunities.

It is fair to point out that there are instances where innovation is at odds with corporate goals. Pan American and British Airways could not have followed Freddie Laker's entrepreneurial idea without starting a fare war. As it happened, Laker started one anyway. IBM could not have done what Gene Amdahl did without eroding its price structure. There is a whole class of innovative, entrepreneurial things like this that corporations probably should not undertake. But the large corporation that would renew itself must seek hands-on leadership from the very top — hands-on leadership from people with a sense of what the future holds and the courage to act on it.

In sum, I see large corporations placing three demands on those who are concerned with creativity and innovation:

1. *We need to discover better ways of both sensing and, even more importantly, communicating, "early warning signals" of impending change to top management.* The only satisfactory way to do this is to immerse them in: the specifics of how customers are viewing the value they are receiving; the way in which different groups of customers are segmenting; the details of competitive cost position; and how all these things are likely to change in the future. We all know, only too well, that early warning signals that are sensed and felt by

corporate planners or middle managers are not necessarily embraced by top management decision makers. It is very hard to overcome years of successful experience and accumulated wisdom simply through analysis or the occasional briefing. More hands-on approaches are necessary—the external equivalent of "MBWA," management by walking around.

2. *We need to create better forums where new big bang ideas are more easily expressed and new leadership can begin to emerge.* The annual planning review is useless when dealing with big bang innovation. The excessive choreography normally associated with such exercises and the very limited amounts of time devoted to real interaction is counterproductive to the kind of innovation we must seek. Large amounts of top management time must be set aside to continually grapple with the uncertainties of the competitive marketplace as they unfold. Decisionmaking based on somebody else's analysis of the situation is simply too risky and cannot lead to bold initiatives. Top management has to spend time speculating about the way things might be, rather than simply listening to analyses of the way they were. And this type of interaction requires that new voices of innovation be heard no matter at what level in the corporation they may reside.

3. *We need to choose "captains of industry" who view change as opportunity, rather than as a problem.* M.J. Kirton has published some provocative work on the differences between adaptive and innovative personalities and their behavior in corporations (as has Abraham Zaleznick). The large corporation in search of a big bang innovation must ensure that a good sprinkling of its top management leadership are "innovators" or "leaders" because, in the end, it is people who innovate.

John Gardner, in his book *Self Renewal,* expressed the thought more eloquently: "Institutions are renewed by individuals who refuse to be satisfied with the outer husks of things."

The bad news is that disorder creates losers. The good news is that it also creates winners. If it is seen as an opportunity, then the greater the rate of disorder, the more opportunities to win there are.

Jeremy Campbell, the British science writer, recently published a rather ambitious book, *Grammatical Man,* in which he attempts to synthesize what has gone on in the last few decades in information theory, thermodynamics, genetics, and linguistics. One of the his major themes is the importance of uncertainty to create the potential for innovation. His description of Norbert Wiener, the father of cybernetics, best captures the essence of the idea: "As his mathematical horizons expanded, he came to realize that the power to create the new out of the old cannot exist in any proper sense in a world where everything is necessary and nothing is uncertain."

Chapter 8

ROUTE TO THE TOP

Gerard Roche

My job is to find presidents of institutions. I have been responsible for the "searches" that have placed the presidents of CBS, RCA, GTE, International Paper, Allied, and Apple Computer into their present positions. I placed Tom Vanderslice as the new CEO of Apollo Computer. I have also been involved in finding and placing the heads of Sloan–Kettering, Brown, Colgate, Cornell, SMU, Cal Tech, Southern California, and Case Western Reserve, and am now in the process of searching for the presidents of two other major universities.

The reason I am sharing this information with you is to let you know the nature of my function, the level at which I'm active, and the basis for what I'm about to say. I am not—I repeat, I am not—a specialist in creativity and innovation, but I can speak with some authority on finding heads for major institutions.

I'll begin by saying that in my twenty-one years of looking for presidents, I cannot recall ever being asked first and foremost to come up with a creator or an innovator. Certainly, that may be critical to many searches, but don't get the impression that creativity is the main attribute my clients are looking for. Let me tell you what they do ask for in candidates, and then I will relate that to how creativity and innovation may play a part in the selection process.

The most important requirement for any new president is a successful track record. We can argue all we want about the wisdom or flaws inherent in that kind of reasoning, but I can absolutely assure you that the names of the people who took International Harvester, Atari, and Itel "down the tubes" will not appear on the short list of any search firm looking for a new CEO. On the other hand, the names of general managers coming from General Electric, 3M, Hewlett Packard, and IBM will appear on those lists. You can dispute the causative relationships of these track records but not the reality of CEO selections.

Each of the other factors that I am about to discuss is a subset of the requirement for a successful track record. Foremost among these factors are the following categories of experience:

Profit Center Management. My clients want people who have had bottom line profit responsibility. In some rare cases, staff personnel can get the nod, but almost always my clients ask for a successful line profit center track record.

Functional Background. Demands for a particular functional background may vary, depending upon the economy and related business trends. During a period in the sixties, marketing types were the hue and cry. In the early seventies, manufacturing, operations, and research and development backgrounds were in heavy demand. In the late seventies, the financial function was most intensive. Predictably, the recent recession made those who had track records in asset management, budget control, and cost cutting the rage. Currently, an enormous amount of attention is being focused on those who have experience in mergers and acquisitions and in corporate development.

Industry Background. I will not spend much time discussing this factor, since all of us are aware that high tech, information, and the broad service industries are now dominant. The result is great demand in the computer, telecommunications, biomedical, and related industries. Yet even in these fields, diversified product backgrounds are more desirable than monolithic or vertical product backgrounds, unless the job is for a toe-to-toe competitor. Still, even in these cases, breadth, flexibility, and adaptability are key determinants in the selection process.

Education. The question of education varies with individual searches, but most clients recruiting presidents treat education as a secondary aspect. Their typical comment is: "The person we're after should have established a successful record by this time, and the extent to which school contributed to that success is not important". Make no mistake about the fact that a good, sound Ivy League liberal arts or high tech degree, blended with a top-tier MBA, is a distinct plus, but it is not a sine qua non.

All of the criteria I have just mentioned are important and give us guidance and direction in charting the course necessary to complete a search. To a great extent, they represent the skills required to "make the team." Once these credentials are established, the question becomes, "Who gets to play the game?" Or further, "Who plays quarterback?" At this level, the determining factor in who wins the key position, and who does not, is almost always based on "personal characteristics."

As I thought about this presentation, I considered a list of CEO attributes or characteristics that are in demand. I immediately encountered an obstacle in that they differ depending upon whether you are working for Bill Paley or Thornton Bradshaw or Steve Jobs or Steve Ross. Yet I was able to come up with a general list that includes leadership, command presence, bearing, and stature. Overall, what we may be talking about here is an indefinable factor—the unknown "X" component. We know when it is there, and we know when it is not.

When I thought about this list again, in relation to the topic of creative management, I realized that these same attributes appear and reappear in any theoretical or practical treatment of the subject.

Human Sensitivity

The very definition of management is achieving objectives through the efforts of others. If a leader cannot understand or be understood by others; if a leader is not aware of what makes a management team tick or how to motivate, stimulate, measure, and compensate people—he or she does not have a prayer as a CEO. That is why it never ceases to amaze me that Harvard, Stanford, and other MBA schools, do not have required courses in human sensitivity, along with their statistical analysis and corporate finance curricula.

What does this sensitivity have to do with creativity and innovation? The answer is simple. It is human sensitivity—an acute awareness of others—that enables a leader to recognize creativity in others, to encourage and nurture that creativity, and to turn creative ideas into innovative action.

Communication

How does the creative leader who has this sensitivity demonstrate it? Through communication. Nobody has made it to a position of top responsibility without being a good communicator. By communication, I don't mean writing only; I also mean verbal, group, one-to-one, and body language communication. Once again, I don't understand why the business schools don't have compulsory courses in communications. The most popular speaker at the Young President's

Organization is not a business person but Dorothy Sarnoff, who teaches presidents how to communicate. What does that say about our business school curricula?

Value Structure

Regardless of each client's corporate culture, top candidates must have strong value structures. Most CEOs are individuals who have a deep sense of value and who see beyond immediate, material gain to a deeper appreciation of what life is all about—or at least their business and its place in society. Included in that value structure is a given quality—integrity. No candidates from "Indecent Exposure" make the short list of the client companies I have served.

Again, what does a value structure have to do with creativity and innovation? I believe a broad-based value structure is the foundation from which creative thinking emerges. It is the mental environment that enables a CEO to, in Arthur Koestler's terms, bisociate or bring together seemingly incompatible frames of reference. After all, it's hard to be creative when all you have to draw from is business and business!

Flexibility and Adaptability

Boards of directors look for the nimble manager, not one who exhibits the rigid, hard-bound "here's the way we did it at IBM" attitude. As a matter of fact, I mentioned IBM, GE, and P & G as being good places to get executives. The ideal concept is to take people from those organizations and then give them at least one other company that can serve as a "decompression chamber" before they meet the real world. By "real world," I mean organizations that lack staff and internal support and the committees, consultants and task forces that can aid them in their efforts.

As to how this concept ties in with creativity and innovation, it is actually flexibility in a new situation that opens the doors for these processes to take place. Without flexibility in thought and action, creativity and innovation cannot occur.

A Visionary

With this attribute, I finally thought, "Ah, maybe we're getting close to the center of the topic." Selection committees want someone with an eye, ear, and nose for the future. They want someone who has a sense of what will be happening, not just an understanding of the next quarterly report or what is immediately visible. The true top executive is both a doer and a planner. And planning involves a disciplined approach to handling the future. That includes working with markets, monies, people and governments. But projections for the future are made within constraints imposed by reality. This truth provides the parameters for planning. Here's where creative thinking comes in. You cannot do planning in a vacuum, and planning requires innovative solutions to present problems — always with an eye toward future developments.

A Risk Taker

Another key ingredient inherent in the character of successful CEOs is closely allied to being a visionary. CEOs are risk takers. Every time we let our minds run astray from the norm — when we creatively start relating seemingly incompatible things — we are risking failure. We have often heard that any virtue taken to an extreme can become a vice. That is certainly true in this case. But very few corporate selection committees want a cautious, conservative individual who is afraid of taking a foot off first base before trying to steal second. Particularly of late, the ability to think in an entrepreneurial fashion has been gaining more weight in the selection process. To prove what I mean, twenty years ago Jack Welch could not have become CEO of GE nor Ed Hennessy the head of Allied Corporation. But today, these boards consider this characteristic an absolute necessity for their CEOs. And both these men are extremely successful.

I could continue my presentation and consider other characteristics. But that would serve little purpose, since the characteristics we have considered are the dominant ones that consistently come through on search requests. Now you may ask again, "What part do creativity and innovation play in what is described?" My answer is that the need for innovation and creativity can be found in every one of the characteristics that I have mentioned. They even run through the functional and industry requirements I covered earlier. Companies who want someone with a financial background want that person to add a creative aspect to their financing programs. The same is true for acquisition skills and for the marketing and manufacturing functions. But to isolate creativity and innovation as a separate requirement is unrealistic and does not happen. They don't exist by themselves and are only present when found operative in the areas mentioned.

When we consider personal characteristics, the ability to be a leader in an innovative, creative, imaginative way is a necessity. Creativity and innovation must be present in all of the aspects I have mentioned. Plato, in his dialogue, the *Symposium,* describes creative people not according to the fruits of their labor, but according to their effect on reality. In this viewpoint, creative people enlarge human consciousness and, in so doing, give birth do some new reality. If we update this concept to the reality of the "bottom line"—when a selection committee demands an answer to the question "How is his bottom line performance?"—you can be sure than creativity and innovation are forces interwoven in the decisions and actions that lead to any bottom line performance.

DISCUSSION

David Bendel Hertz

David Hertz: How do you organize institutions to implement creativity and innovation? Allow me to be a bit more provocative. The world of science has long known the necessity to accept failure in order to achieve success. No scientists would deny that in order to find out how to do something well or to find out something about the nature of the universe, you have to experiment; and if the experiments are not in some sense failures, you really haven't learned anything. You knew it before you started. Now, Fred Gluck, as an outstanding management consultant, knows perfectly well he wouldn't even have a job if there weren't a lot of failures. He wouldn't have a continuing job if he could make everything successful — which, of course, he can't. Gerry Roche knows that the reason companies recruit new executives at top management levels is because boards of directors think they need somebody who is better than the last man — who either failed or at least who didn't do as well as he should have. If, in fact, Gerry was able to put in an indefinite series of successful people, he also would probably not have a job. So, in the long run, designing a creative organization means designing an organization that has some in-built mechanism that will allow somebody to do something wrong with that organization. If not, I don't think that there's anything scientific or even interesting about creative and innovative management.

Question: Why do most corporations opt for only incremental changes?

Fred Gluck: There are sometimes good reasons why large corporations do not big bang. For one, it is not always in their best interest. For example, when Amdahl undercut IBM's prices, they chose not to match them because it would cost them too much money. And there are other reasons why companies do not make radical changes in strategy. Large organizations will not do a big bang innovation except under threat. It was such a threat that really galvanized IBM to go into personal computers after they had flubbed so badly with minis.

Question: What are some big bang examples?

David Hertz: The 747 airplane for Boeing and the 360 computer for IBM. In both cases they bet the company.

Fred Gluck: There are lots of big bangs in start-up situations. Apple was a big bang; Intel was a big bang. But this is the problem. When most established corporations are faced with fundamental external shift they do not have the capacity to do the creative thinking or make the innovation because of the way the organization is designed.

Comment: When General Electric divisionalized and set up its management education centers, that was a big bang. But big bangs are rare.

Gerard Roche: I hate this play on words, but I can't resist it. The Manhattan project was a big bang.

David Hertz: My hunch is that big bangs come when somebody or some organization sees a crisis, not necessarily an opportunity.

Fred Gluck: Many large corporations are now faced with the need to big bang or atrophy. And some of them are atrophying badly. Chrysler, on the other hand, is certainly a big bang. So is what Walter Wriston did at Citibank.

David Hertz: How do you organize the big bang?

Robert Kuhn: Large-scale innovation or radical innovation occurs when there is a concentration of power. That concentration should come from two sources. One is a pulling together as a consequence of crisis. The other one is when there is enough centralized power in a major league company, such as the case of Tom Watson, Jr. when he chose computing as the way to outdo what his father had done in tabulating at IBM.

Fred Gluck: The question of power is an important one. There are many situations—U.S. Steel, for example—where there was a concentration of power and nothing happened. I don't think a big bang can happen without power, but it is not sufficient by itself. What is sufficient is the gut feeling and visceral understanding on the part of the people with the power that unless they act something very bad is going to happen very quickly. Yet because of the way many companies are managed, senior executives rarely get the information allowing them to dvelop this gut feeling.

David Hertz: Here's the "big bang" question. Companies are managed so that top mnagement rarely gets proper information. Fred, you are a management consultant: Tell us how to organize a company so that it does have that power or can use that power to create a big bang.

Fred Gluck: The IBM model is about as good as you can get. The managing committee of IBM is intimately familiar with their competitive position in every product line throughout the world. They are also intimately familiar with how the needs of their customers are changing and are likely to change. Those are the two key input ingredients—competitive position and customer needs—needed in an organizational information system. Information about your competitors and what they're doing and information about your customers and how their needs are changing are vital, and the impact of technology on both is important. IBM's top management spends most of their time talking about these things. They don't spend their time dealing with financial reporting or what I call "how you digest it information." Here's a little test I use sometimes when I'm talking to a top manager about strategy development. I'll say, "Mr. Jones, why don't you describe for me what you think is happening with your XYZ competitor and why he's doing what he's doing." And if he says, "Let me get you my strategic plan," I know I'm wasting my time, because he's depending on other people to do his job.

Understanding the fundamental forces that are likely to undermine the company's position in the competitive marketplace is the heart of CEO responsibility. Hence my prescription. Companies must have their decisionmakers intimately familiar with the raw information about the competitive marketplace and customer needs, and they must spend substantial amounts of their time doing so. (This, by the way, is somewhat contradictory to Dr. Zaleznick's notion of creativity as solely an individual act. Executives must discuss together what the information means and discern together new patterns that might emerge, leading them to action.) About three or four years ago I was appalled when the chairman of General Motors said that General Motors had a $1,500 cost disadvantage at the low end of the car market with respect to Japan, and he cited as his source the Interstate Commerce Commission. It was mind boggling to me, but that's the problem. Senior executives are too concerned about financial matters and insufficiently concerned about competitive markets.

David Hertz: What you're saying is that top management must make the collective function of $x + y$ greater than the individual functions of x and y. This is basically a scientific dialogue. It's like saying that physicists are not going to discover new ideas in physics without knowing and talking to the people who know about the current ideas in physics. Now that's not so easy in companies.

Fred Gluck: I'm also saying that professional management—which developed as a methodology of management—really falls apart in the face of substantial change. And because many of our corporations have been designed to be operated by professional managers, they can easily find themselves in trouble when major shifts or discontinuities occur.

David Hertz: Gerry Roche, let's talk about executive search and creativity. I think that you inadvertently defined your view of creativity quite clearly—selection by board-of-directors jury of the right chief executive who himself is not creative but whose organization becomes creative because of the characteristics he possesses. I might question some of those characteristics—especially the priorities—but I don't think it's a bad idea. To recruit a new CEO, you pick how many objectives before brains?

Gerard Roche: Six.

David Hertz: Six before brains? And you put some bottom-line executive in charge of an organization hoping it will become creative?

Gerard Roche: These CEO characteristics are not mine. I did not come up with them. There are reflections of what my clients want; they are objectives set by the search committees of corporate boards. Furthermore, I am not dumping on brain power. The brighter you are, the better you are. I'm just saying, sorry: smarts don't come first, folks.

W. W. Cooper: Here's a research question: When do you need a big bang, and what are its effects on corporate creativity and organizational structure—using before and after comparisons?

Fred Gluck: I would make three suggestions for research: 1) what kind of information needs to be placed in the hands of decision makers in order for them to anticipate and implement big bang innovations; 2) what type of interactions do we want with this information to make sure that new patterns emerge; 3) how do we get more innovative leaders into top management of major corporations (which appeals specifically to Gerry Roche's notions). In terms of whether the organization is more creative after than before a big bang, I think the answer is unquestionably more creative after. Chrysler, for example, which was a big bang, continues to be a much more creative organization following its renaissance. I think AT & T, if it survives its big bang, may end up as a more creative organization than it was beforehand. In many ways, the company was resting on past laurels. (I worked ten years as a scientist for Bell Labs.)

Comment: We have a paradox here. Corporations demand a consistent track record as the first qualification for a new CEO. I think it's time to change that. You can't have a truly creative person maintaining an organizational mold for twenty years without having been beaten down and fallen into a sewer several times. It's all contradictory. You can't measure creativity using traditional yardsticks.

Gerard Roche: Well said. Any virtue taken to an extreme becomes a vice. Any corporation that makes judgments solely on quarterly reports and track records is asking for trouble. Conversely, any corporation that does not have some kind of punishment system for consistent failure is also asking for it. What we need is balance.

Question: Don't different kinds of strategic situations demand different kinds of managers?

Gerard Roche: Sure. I hear it all the time. For example, there are maintenance-type managers that might come out of, say, a GE where they've never had to turn around a bad situation, where they've never had to come up with anything spectacular, where they've always been running the bulb division with a consistent share of a consistent market. Those are not the managers you would throw into Wickes or Chrysler or Continental Bank to turn those companies around. Different corporate situations call for different CEO characteristics and different track records. Every CEO search I do is not done with the same profile. Yet what I presented were the common denominators. One final point: maybe I'm overreacting, but if readers come away without feeling a need for greater emphasis on human understanding and communications, then I've wasted my contribution.

Question: Does the size of corporate boards affect the CEO selection process?

Gerard Roche: When you have a twenty-person board, the issue becomes not who is the best CEO candidate but who can get through twenty different people. On the other hand, when you have a de facto board of one (e.g., a Bill Paley at CBS), when that one finds the blue suit he wants, you pull him in.

David Hertz: Organizing is a universal activity of the living world from ants to humans. Organizing is a managerial function that takes finding people (which Gerry Roche does); it takes putting structure together (which Fred Gluck does). Creativity in organizations means putting proper people in proper structure so that individual and collective creativity can flourish.

Part V

ORGANIZATIONAL CREATIVITY AND INDIVIDUAL PERSONALITY

Chapter 9

CREATIVITY AND COMMITMENT
Modeling Meaning and Mission for Individuals and Institutions

Robert Lawrence Kuhn and George Thomas Geis

Creativity is the explosive energy erupting from individual initiative. Commitment is the psychic knot tying together individuals and institutions. It is our thesis that individual creativity must be linked with institutional commitment in order to generate novel thinking and productivity in organizational environments.

We have developed a working model of commitment by analyzing the link between personal meaning and organizational mission in ecclesiastical settings and applying the results in commercial settings.[1] In this chapter, we build this commitment model inductively and then apply it deductively. Our thesis, remember, is that individual creativity is directly related to organizational commitment.

Commitment is a primal force driving employees to work for organizational goals, and it is our view that such commitment is linked closely with the presence of organizational creativity. The purpose of this chapter, in addition to developing the commitment model, is to shed light on at least two areas of the creativity–commitment connection.

First, building and maintaining the commitment of people almost always involves a creative, even artistic, effort on the part of organizational leadership. To build commitment, managers must not only understand the needs and goals of employees but must also be exquisitely sensitive to how their particular organizational society (culture) influences each individual's level of commitment. Commitment is both vital and delicate, and care must be taken in its development.

Second, we suggest that there is a direct connection between the level of employee commitment and the extent to which an employee is willing and able to engage in creative efforts on behalf of the organization. Creative acts clearly demand a level of energy expenditure that is not commonly given by one who is only "routinely" attached to an organization. Personal creativity is proportional to company commitment.

We seek to promote the focused efforts of organizational leaders in building employee commitment — which, in turn, is hypothesized to increase employee creativity. Our approach is to employ the model designed to explain the dynamics of the commitment building (or breaking) process. We readily acknowledge that the comprehension of any model is not sufficient condition for commitment building (or breaking) to take place. However, we feel that our model does provide insight as to how employee commitment is built (or broken). It is our contention that such insight can facilitate an intuitive and pragmatic understanding of the nature of commitment and that this practical application of the model, used properly, can enhance commitment building and retard commitment breaking.

One point of reference. "Creativity" in this paper does not mean the independent creativity of the artist; the lone creations of solitary geniuses are not our subject here. Whenever we discuss "creativity," we mean creativity in *organizational* environments, more specifically *productive* creativity intended to further organizational objectives. It may well be possible that creativity and commitment are directly related only in *organizational* settings. For example, the building or breaking of commitment and the resulting enhancing or inhibiting of creativity may only reflect what happens in groups, institutions, or corporations. (Solitary creative artists, quite to the contrary, are often energized by broken commitment to organizations.)

ASSESSING COMMITMENT

Commitment draws us all; we are attracted by its mental magnetism. But what, really, is *"commitment,"* an ordinary enough word with common-sense understanding?

As human beings we belong to various groups. Whether economic, political, social, or religious, these groups compete constantly for our loyalty and our attention. Which groups we choose, and how we allocate energy to each, affect our lives intimately. Little else makes such matter. The power of groups is immense.

How do people go about making these allocation decisions? Why do they exert effort to support company policy? Why subjugate individual desire to collective need and make sacrifices for nonpersonal goals? What considerations are given, what points weighed? What are the factors that build organizational ties? What are the antecedents of commitment and how do they perform their magic? Neither financial considerations nor social conventions, however influential, explain everything. The formula for organizational glue has other essential ingredients.

What is this bond between people and groups? What is it about human nature that extends the boundaries of self beyond self, stretching one's skin to encompass others, merging individual identity into amorphous mass, melding *I* into *we* and ego into crowd? What is the subtle and complex interplay between organizations and members?

Our focus is managers—of all kinds, at all levels, in all groups—and we view them on both sides of the organizational lens. On the one side, these administrators have the authority and responsibility for building corporate strength and employee cohesion; and on the other side, they themselves feel the pressures and tensions of company association and career ambition. Being creative managers and managing the creativity of employees are two sides of the same coin.

What makes people give all, putting out to accomplish company programs? Why strain to work in concert with others? These are fundamental executive questions. To give subordinates such stimulation is to move the company aggressively forward. This directed thrust develops a firm's competitive capacity. To build strong market position in a turbulent industrial environment, a tight, tough team is essential. Creative management is the new weapon in the managerial arsenal.

Just how sensitive to commitment are business effectiveness and production efficiencies? If effectiveness involves "doing the right thing," what role does personnel commitment play in influencing company goals? If efficiency involves "doing things right," what is the value of employee commitment in improving company performance? Finally, how can commitment dynamics be focused for developing personal creativity and company productivity? What can an organization do to maximize individual commitment and mobilize it to accomplish collective purpose?

Defining Commitment

Scholars studying organizational commitment have not always agreed on definitions, much less measurements.[2] Some writers frame commitment in terms of "strength of individual involvement" with a given organization, stressing acceptance of values, willingness to allocate effort, and desire to maintain membership. Others view commitment in terms of "intent to maintain the group," targeting the impulsion to support the organization because it provides what the person needs. Still others see commitment as emotional, a sensate attachment to an organization, an affective allegiance to its goals and values—totally apart from any material gain or worth that an individual may drive from the association.

We propose a structural definition. *We define commitment as the link between personal meaning and organizational mission.* Commitment is the emotional lines of force that attract individuals to institutions, the psychic energy that maintains physical presence and mental membership. It is the strength of the meaning–mission link that determines the power of the attachment.

Metaphors for commitment come easy: the interpersonal glue that produces group stickiness? The master knot that ties together independent strands?

Commitment can be described as "purpose with action," an internal compulsion of the individual to achieve an external objective of the group. It is the "strong force" that holds people in the organizational nucleus. It is the human essence that endows groups of people with centripetal focus and agglutinizing strength. The coherent commitment of individuals generates the cohesive attraction of groups.

Commitment signals emotional attachment, and the continuum runs the gamut from extreme self-sacrifice through blasé detachment to fierce adversarial attack. All ranges of personal meaning can be present, including nonmeaning.

In examining commitment we analyze three general categories of antecedents: personal factors, organizational facors, and experiential factors. All are analyzed as they influence commitment, and as a result, creativity.

PERSONAL FACTORS INFLUENCING COMMITMENT

Creativity cannot be coerced. Innovation must be nurtured, not enforced. Encouraging the creativity of employees involves understanding and meeting their changing needs. As these needs evolve throughout the life cycle (and work span) personality variables shift in relative importance. Managers must understand what brings meaning to an individual employee in order to generate optimum creative effort.

Classifying people is the easiest thing to do fast and the hardest thing to do well. Psychologists like to devise systems to help us, to make personality assessment snappy, to put people into simple boxes we can understand. It is said that there are as many theories of human personality as there are theorists (and maybe more, since theorists often change their minds).

The touchstone of truth has long been sought. Freud looked to unconscious processes and biosocial instincts of self-preservation and sex. Neo-Freudians kept Freud's basic picture of human personality as a battleground between primal instincts and social values. Some, however, proposed different candidates for the critical instincts. Adler posited the need for superiority as a primal force, thus popularizing the inferiority complex. Jung, drawing heavily from physics and mysticism, saw the libido or primal force as a general life energy that socially binds individuals to the whole of the human race. (Jung also developed the introvert–extrovert scale.) Frankl emphasized the search for meaning, claiming ultimate answers are the root motivation of man. Erikson proposed a life-cycle approach, with distinctive "psychosocial crises" at different stages of one's life.

Humanists, such as Maslow and Rogers, emphasized individual growth motivation and stressed the importance of self-actualization. Behavior theorists, such as Skinner, saw human personality resulting more from environmental factors than psychic events. Human personality can be analyzed, they proclaim, only in terms of the interplay of human action and environmental consequences.

Enough of personality theory. There are others, of course, but enough. Human personality is complex, that's clear. Although each theory has something to tell us, none has a monopoly on truth.

Our interest in human personality is more focused. We center on aspects of personality that an individual brings to an organization and how these personal traits influence the style of commitment and degree of creativity.

Desire breeds motivation. If we want nothing, we do nothing. For the want of water, food, or sexual partners, rats will traverse electrified grids until their feet run raw. For want of things similar in character, people will do just about anything.

Different people desire different things. In building a model of commitment, in establishing a pragmatic union between individuals and institutions, we must understand the human side of the linkage.

Following are some categories of human desire. All compete constantly for our attention and control, and all are involved in building and breaking the firm bond.

Our approach is to look at ourselves in various ways, from various perspectives. It is the composite, we stress, not the components, that really turns us on.

The list of personal factors that influence organizational commitment is neither exhaustive nor infallible. All variables relate to commitment and, by extension, to creativity. We define three classes of variables describing personality: *meaning-related* needs; *security-related* needs; and *other* personal variables descriptive of the individual.

Meaning-Related Factors

Transcendence: The need to go beyond the corporeal limitations of individual humanness; a deep interest in an ideal world and how to create it; a profound concern for the nature of ultimate reality. Companies that match corporate objectives with executive ideology optimize commitment. Such coherence is more easily obtained in not-for-profit institutions such as religious organizations, charities, hospitals, foundations, and the like. Some innovative firms—often high tech—offer excitement in company products and flexibility in company structure. Employees who believe in some higher order will often be more dependable on the job (though "head in clouds" can sometimes lift "feet from ground").

Autonomy: Independence from authority and external control; the capacity to do what you want when you want. Entrepreneurs would rather work sixty hours a week for themselves with less pay than forty hours a week for someone else with more pay. Creative and innovative types, increasingly important in an information and science-based society, demand autonomy and freedom in work conditions, and managers must find ways to accommodate and encourage them.

Achievement: The desire to complete tasks and reach goals, whether assigned by another or set by oneself. Accomplishment carries its own reward—and it can dominate all others, irrespective of other benefits no matter how large. Job satisfaction can correlate more with finishing work than with increasing pay. Entrepreneurs as a group are motivated far more by achievement than by power or money; they would rather finish the job in an old garage than direct operations from an eight-window corner office.

Esteem: A sense of personal worth; prominence and recognition among friends, respect and admiration among peers. Some people will do anything for accolades and acknowledgment. The craving for fame can be an addiction (so much so that when celebrities are forgotten, they can become suicidal). Star status fascinates us, epitomized by the line, "I don't care what newspapers say about me as long as they spell my name right." Creative types like acclaim.

Power: Control and authority over people, groups, and things; the capacity to influence ideas and dominate events. Political leaders, government officials, military generals, newspaper editors, university presidents do not earn high salaries by today's standards; though many are motivated by lofty ideals, others trade off materialism and wealth for power and influence.

Security-Related Factors

Affiliation: The social sense of belonging; the desired association in organizations and groups. Club memberships; fraternal societies; common interests drawing people together. Many men and women live for their avocation, whether active or spectator sports, card games, recreational activities, or simply socializing with friends at the "club." Acceptance is important here; whether it be the Blue Bloods of Boston of the Bowling Boys of Brooklyn, belonging to groups can be serious business.

Stability: The comfort of calm; maintaining routine; keeping of the status quo; staying the course. The elimination of surprise and the attenuation of change. Some people value constancy and surety above all else; they are risk averse and would never switch jobs for a 50 percent increase in pay if there were even a 5 percent chance of getting sacked. Few creatives found here.

Structure: Dependency on others; looking beyond self for solutions to one's problems, answers to one's questions, and provisions for one's needs. Where one fits in the social order is of primary concern. The need for organizational position, ratified by title and benefits, is common in large companies. Some are uncomfortable with new forms of governance without clear lines of authority.

Materialism: The desire for wealth; the security money can bring, the things money can buy. Bonds in the bank and stocks in the safe. Homes, cars, furniture, clothing, jewelry, electronic toys, and the like are things that we have; trips, travel, shows, dinners, entertainment, and the like are things that we do—all are in the spirit of materialism and represent the trappings of wealth. A doctor who buys exotic cars may well be more motivated by materialism than a corporate president who builds his business.

Other Personal Factors

Educational Level: The nature and extent of formal education; the quality and quantity of academic experience. Research findings have shown that, other things being equal, individuals with higher levels of education tend to be less committed to organizations and more committed to professions.

Generalized Sense of Loyalty: A desire to continue supporting groups with which one is associated; a "sticker," not a "quitter." This variable has roots in one's cultural and family background, with a good dose of individual temperament thrown in.

Locus of Control: Whether one's behavior is determined internally or externally. People with an internal locus of control see themselves as active "origins," feeling that they direct personal events from within. Those with an external locus of control see themselves as passive "pawns," feeling that chance, powerful people, and forces beyond their influence determine individual occurrences and life course.[3]

ORGANIZATIONAL FACTORS INFLUENCING COMMITMENT

Creative organizational design is essential for building strong organizational committment—and hence, completing the circle, strengthened organizational creativity.

We now deal with the institutional side of the individual–institution bond. What characteristics of the organization affect member commitment? We set the factors into two classes: mission-related and other.

Mission-Related Variables

Goal Structure: The nature and essence of group goals, whether visionary or pedestrian, comprehensive or limited, theoretical or practical, attainable or illusory. What is the planned position for an organization, its grand design, its purpose, its mission?

Permeability: The openness of group boundaries; the ease of passage inside out and outside in; the degree to which an organization desires members to interact with external elements. Does the group maintain a life-style different from general society, and does it shield members from interference?[4]

Leadership: The character and strength of senior management, whether sharp or bland, individual or collective, democratic or dictatorial, logical or emotional, permanent or transitory. The style of the chief, the charisma of the boss. How dominant is the organization's leader, and what would be the impact of change?

Progressiveness: The presence or absence of forward motion; the dynamic sense of momentum, whether the group is growing or holding, moving or stuck. The innovative character of the organization, the willingness to explore and take risks. Is the group going ahead, and at what pace?

Other Organizational Factors

Cohesiveness: The strength with which an organization adheres together; the unity and coherence of the group. Whether the agglutinizing force is internal or external, desire or coercion. How strongly does the organization pull together; how tightly do members support group goals?

Organizational Esteem: The internal sense of organizational worth, whether appreciated by outsiders or only by insiders; the collective confidence in intrinsic value; the degree to which members feel proud of group association. Do members boast or hide their affiliation?

People Valuing: The extent to which people are recognized and treated as organizational assets (to be maximized and developed) and not as organizational expenses (to be minimized and eliminated). What is the group's attitude toward members?

EXPERIENTIAL FACTORS INFLUENCING COMMITMENT

The interaction between personal and organizational factors help generate institutional commitment — and therefore enhance individual creativity. Creative mechanisms for achieving organizational uniqueness, creative structures for providing support to key people, creative company events that build a sense of emotional identification (conditioning), and creative strategies getting employees to invest in (bet on) the firm all contribute to an organization increasing its receptivity for creative expression.

In the previous two sections we examined the impact of various factors on individual commitment: pure personal variables and pure organizational variables. Now we look at the melding of the two: these are the factors arising out of the intricate interaction between individuals and institutions. The thrust, remember, is our working definition of commitment, the firm bond between personal meaning and company mission.

Rewards and status are examples of variables that are generated in the intimate interplay between employee and company. These are factors that do not exist independently but *emerge* as the product of what is almost a chemical reaction. The elements that go into the test tube of organizational experiences — the pure personal and organizational factors — may be very different from the compounds that come out.

Those variables emerging out of the interaction between individual and institution we label "organizational experience." We set two classes: meaning/ mission related variables and other organizational experience variables important in the determination of commitment.

Meaning/Mission-Related Factors

Meaning/mission-related factors result primarily from the direct interaction between meaning-related factors (individual variables) and mission-related factors (organizational factors).

Importance/Uniqueness (Perceived): The relative importance of the organization, whether real or perceived; the differences between this organization and all other organizations in the mind of an individual. How special does the member consider the group?

Support: The extent to which the organization provides an individual with freedom and help to do a job; the amount of collective aid in all facets of group membership or company employment. How much can the individual rely on the organization for physical and mental sustenance?

Reality Congruence: The correlation between what the organization professes to be true and what an individual believes to be true (opposite: credibility gap). How accurate are organizational pronouncements; more important, how much are they believed?[5]

Status: The personal position of an individual relative to others in the organization; the degree to which a person is recognized in the organizational culture. How prominent is the employee, and what does that prominence connote in the company?

Task Identification: The degree to which an individual enjoys a specific job or responsibility; whether one invests ego as well as effort in fulfilling the position. How much does the person like the job compared to other possibilities?

Other Organizational Experience Factors

Emotional Conditioning: The affective, nonrational aspect of an individual's commitment to an organization. The general feelings of a person toward the organization, independent of specific factors. How strong is the tie between member and group, and how difficult would it be to break?

Rewards: The psychic and/or financial improvement of an individual's condition as a direct result of specific organizational action. What does the individual get, how meaningful is it, and how important compared to other possibilities?

Role Strain: The amount of stress experienced by an individual when having difficulty complying with role expectation. The tensions of playing parts cast by others; the conflicts between competing aspects of life (as between job and family). How does one cope with uncertainty in an organizational position?

Investment: The degree and quality of ego and effort sunk by the individual into the organization (prime examples are time, money, and reputation). How much of yourself has been invested in your company, and what would it take to walk away from it?

COMMITMENT STRENGTH TYPES

Commitment in total organizations is neither constant nor consistent. In fact, the pure-form magnification[1] reveals more levels and nuances than can be appreciated in normal organizations. Figure 9–1 presents six types of commitment strength. They are arrayed linearly in descending order.

Partisans radiate maximum commitment. These are dedicated and persistent, the proselytizers, the backbone of total organizations. Unshakable in mind and deed, zealous in fervor and intensity, they are ready to sacrifice their lives, figuratively or even literally, for the assumed good of the organization. Wholehearted belief, irrespective of personal benefit, is the key characteristic of a partisan. (There is high correlation between our "partisan" and Eric Hoffer's "true believer.")

Adherents are motivated to promote and protect the organization. Their

Figure 9–1.   Commitment Strength Types.

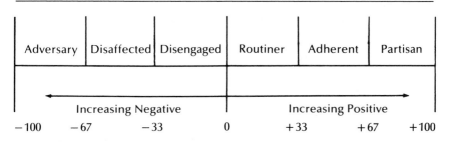

Source: Robert Lawrence Kuhn and George T. Geis, *The Firm Bond: Linking Meaning and Mission in Business and Religion* (New York: Praeger, 1984). Reprinted with permission.

motivation is typically a blend of internal and external elements. They behave proactively to support the system. Positive organizational action is important to them, although the basis of the importance is often enlightened self-interest. Building the organization of personal reward is the essence of an adherent.

Routiners are a shade more positive than neutral, requiring direct external motivation to fulfill organizational expectations. Work is done but action is passive, and consequences are of little personal value. Keeping the status quo is all a routiner wants.

Disengageds are psychologically retired, slightly more negative than neutral. Jobs are done and tasks are accomplished, but barely within the allowable range of organizational acceptability. There is no personal interest. Their passive presence can produce a deleterious effect on other workers, depressing motivation and dedication. Dragging an organization down is the contribution of the disengaged.

Disaffecteds may or may not be connected with the organization. If they departed, it was probably due to some disparity between personal expectations and organizational realities. Whether within or without the organization, they work to hinder or destroy it, especially when doing so will serve their own benefit. Personal profit from hurting an organization is what the disaffected seeks.

Adversaries are energetic foes of the organization, operating actively and maliciously either from inside or outside. They seek, at the least, dramatic change in the organization's goals, policies, structure, or leadership, and often nothing less than the overthrow of the system will suffice. Destroying an organization, irrespective of personal benefit, is the mission of an adversary.

These six types of commitment strengths reflect varying degrees of willingness to exert personal effort to support (or hinder) organizational goals.

Organizational commitment profiles representing the frequency of members/employees in each commitment type can be drawn. Figures 9–2 to 9–7 present sample profiles for vibrant total organizations; total organizations in schism; start-up companies; growth companies; mature companies; and bankrupt companies.

We can use the commitment scale to assess creative contribution. Creativity on the job is likely to increase in *both* directions away from "0," toward the Partisans on the plus side and toward the Adversaries on the negative. (Compare, from the New Testament, the similar degree of creative efforts put forth by the Partisan Paul and the Adversary Saul.) Routiners and Disengageds will not be likely to expend the physical effort or psychic energy necessary for creative development; the other four categories will do so, putting out creative effort relative to their level of commitment.

Figure 9–2.   Commitment Profile for Vibrant Total Organization.

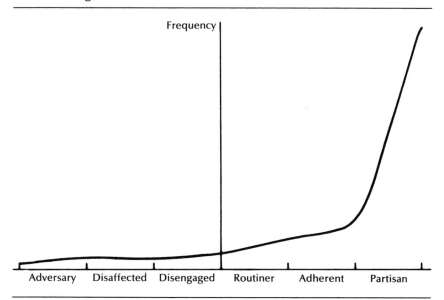

Source: Kuhn and Geis, *The Firm Bond.*

Figure 9–3.   Commitment Profile for Total Organization in Schism.

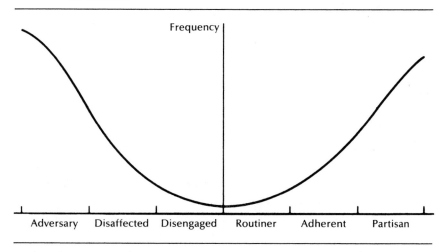

Source: Kuhn and Geis, *The Firm Bond.*

Figure 9–4. Commitment Profile for Sample Start-up Company.

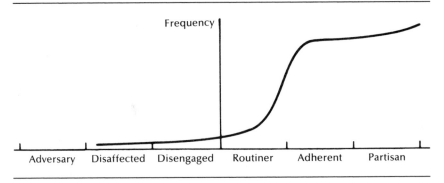

Source: Kuhn and Geis, *The Firm Bond.*

Figure 9–5. Commitment Profile for Sample Growth Company.

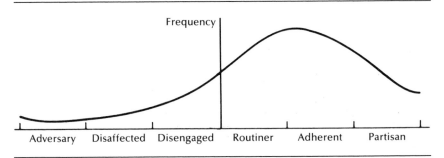

Source: Kuhn and Geis, *The Firm Bond.*

COMMITMENT STYLES

Commitment Style I: Core

Our commitment model postulates three styles of commitment strength: core, calculative, and cog (Figure 9–8).

Core Commitment involves profound personal belief in organizational goals and their melding into one's own identity. It means that an individual wholly accepts organizational ideals and values and has internalized them. When the aims and mission of the group have been incorporated into a person's psyche,

Figure 9–6.   Commitment Profile for Sample Mature Company.

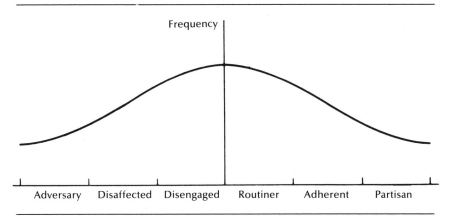

Source: Kuhn and Geis, *The Firm Bond.*

Figure 9–7.   Commitment Profile for Sample Bankrupt Company.

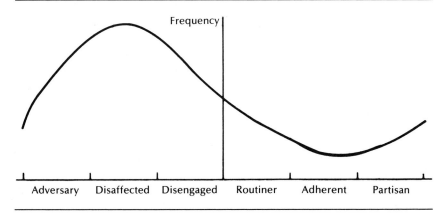

Source: Kuhn and Geis, *The Firm Bond.*

we call this commitment "core positive" — core(+). Such a person will adopt and reflect the style of the organization, the culture of the company, and the attitude of the group. An individual with core(+) commitment has the organization's welfare at heart; building the institution is the key consideration — perhaps even the starting point — in deciding general behavior and specific action. Individual creativity is motivated here, at least in part, by seeking collective

Figure 9–8. Styles of Commitment Strength.

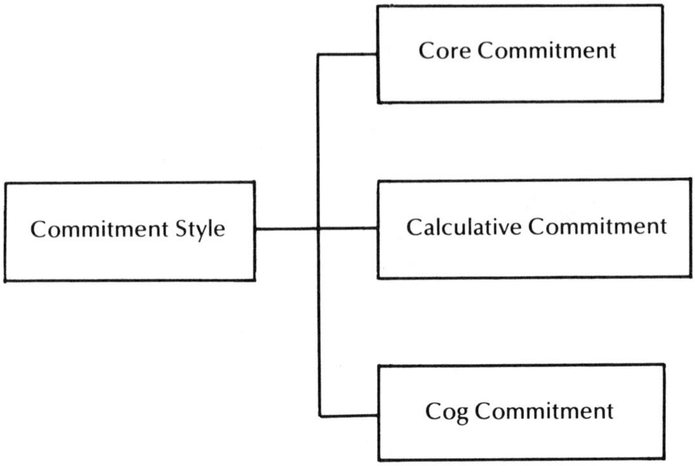

Source: Kuhn and Geis, The Firm Bond.

benefit. This is the arena where personal creativity increases organizational productivity most effectively and efficiently.

"Core negative" — core(–) — commitment is present whenever an individual is an active enemy of the organization. The person is staunchly opposed to the group's mission and values, and this adversarial position is the central purpose of life. A true core(–) seeks to destroy the organization irrespective of personal gain.

Commitment Style II: Calculative

Calculative Commitment starts with the individual, not the organization. The prime consideration is personal gain. How effectively are one's total needs being satisfied? How does the individual benefit from the organization or from personal creative achievement? How much is one making — "making" in the broadest sense? What has the company done for me lately? Calculations, measurements, are important here. What is one's total net income — financial and psychic, now and in the future? Comparisons are part of the picture. The total net income one could derive elsewhere is determined and comparisons are made.

"Calculative negative" — calculative(–) — occurs when it is in one's best interests to work against the organization. The motivation is purely personal benefit; meaning or conviction is completely irrelevant. Examples of calculative(–) include selling stocks short, spreading bad rumors about a love-rival, and mercenaries/bounty hunters/hired killers. (Note that we use "core" and "calculative" without " + " or " – " to mean positive.)

Commitment Style III: Cog

Cog Commitment is present in an individual when work is seen only as a necessary routine. Little meaning is present, little emotion felt. In cog(+) commitment, the teeth of the personal-organizational gears are normally engaged, although it is the organization that provides the energy for motion. The job gets done, but externals are necessary for motivation. As for real creativity, forget it for cogs.

"Cog negative" — cog(–) — occurs when the individual hopes that the teeth of the personal-organizational gears are in contact a minimum amount of time. That person will try to limit activities with the group. When engagement is forced, cynical comments about the organization are common. The individual may be present physically but is absent mentally.

The Parallel Universe

Though we are presenting commitment as one-dimensional and flat, it is more properly portrayed as two-dimensional and folded. The continuum of commitment strength is like a parallel universe. Low, medium, and high levels of commitment in the positive direction all have mirrors in the negative (Figure 9–9).

In fact, it is often a quick crawl through a "worm hole" to get to a corresponding commitment style of equal intensity, but opposite force. Thus at the extreme ends of the scale, Sauls become Pauls, and Vaders cross over to the

Figure 9–9. Parallelism of Commitment Styles.

Commitment Valence		Commitment Style		
		Core	Calculative	Cog
	+	Partisan	Adherent	Routiner
	–	Adversary	Disaffected	Disengaged

Source: Kuhn and Geis, *The Firm Bond.*

Figure 9–10.   Commitment Types, Styles, and Strength.

TYPES	STYLES	STRENGTH SCALE	MISSION CONTRIBUTION VARIABLE
Partisan	Core (+)	100	
		67	
Adherent	Calculative (+)		
		33	
Routiner	Cog (+)		Commitment strength
		0	
Disengaged	Cog (−)		
		−33	
Disaffected	Calculative (−)		
		−67	
Adversary	Core (−)		
		−100	

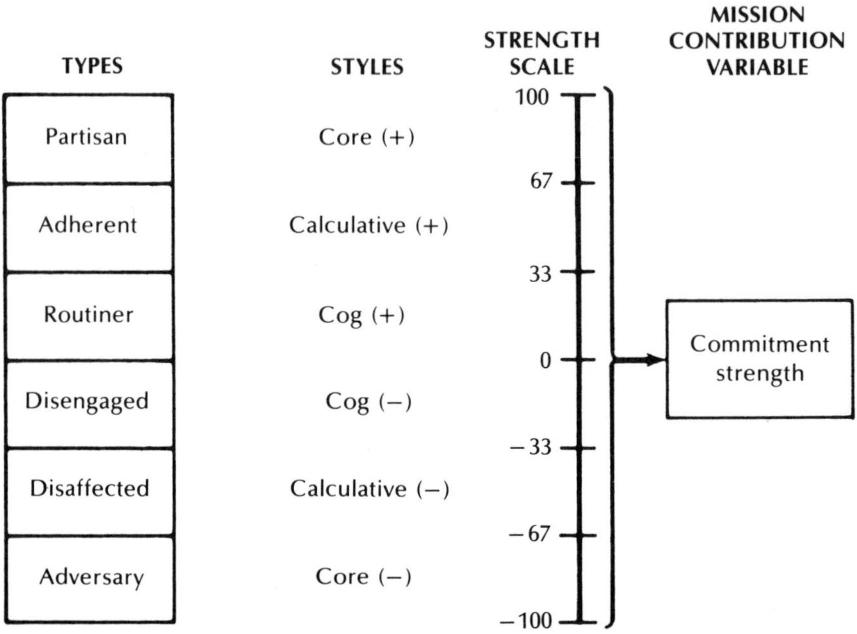

Source: Kuhn and Geis, The Firm Bond.

"dark side" (and perhaps even return to "Jedi heaven" in the end). Crossovers at lower levels of commitment strength are also common. A comprehensive diagram — integrating commitment types, styles, and strength measure — is provided in Figure 9–10.

Aspects of core, calculative, and cog commitment can be found in most every individual. One style, however, usually dominates. This is especially true with respect to an individual's commitment style in response to organizational mission. At different moments in one's career with an organization, the style of commitment may shift. To cross the boundary into a new predominant style is often not without trauma.

THE ANTECEDENTS OF COMMITMENT

The commitment styles relating individuals to institutions were derived from personal histories.[1] Whether core, calculative, or cog, each style is founded on

Figure 9–11. Antecedents of Commitment Type (and Strength).

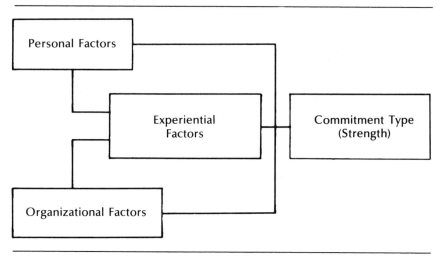

Source: Kuhn and Geis, *The Firm Bond.*

past experience. There is a series of antecedents that lead to the growth and formation of each commitment mode.

In previous sections we introduced three primary classes of antecedent variables (see Figure 9–11):

Personal Factors: Individual needs as well as other personal variables influencing commitment, independent of any organizational association.

Organizational Factors: Key factors of the organization affecting member commitment, independent of any personal association.

Experiential Factors: Those elements that emerge from the interactions between individual and organization, the experiences that develop from group association.

Let's review the variables in each of these classes in preparation for assembling the full model.

Personal Factors (see Figure 9–12)

Meaning-Related Variables

- *Transcendence:* Beyond self; interest in ultimates.
- *Autonomy:* Independence from authority.

Figure 9–12.   Personal Factors Influencing Commitment.

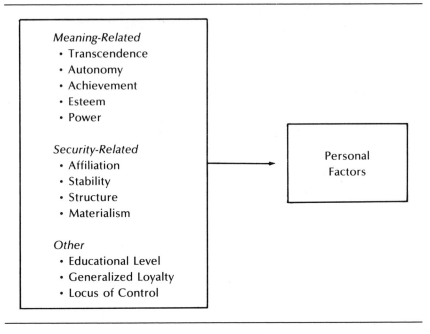

Source: Kuhn and Geis, *The Firm Bond.*

- *Achievement:* Fulfillment in completing tasks.
- *Esteem:* Sense of personal worth.
- *Power:* Capacity to influence.

Security-Related Factors

- *Affiliation:* Sense of belonging and association.
- *Stability:* Comfort of routine and status quo.
- *Structure:* Dependency on others.
- *Materialism:* Money and wealth.

Other Personal Factors

- *Educational Level:* Amount and kind of schooling.
- *Generalized Loyalty:* Desire to belong; sense of duty.
- *Locus of Control:* How life is directed—internally or externally.

Figure 9–13.   Organizational Factors Influencing
Commitment.

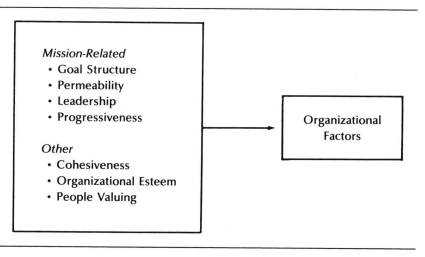

Mission-Related
  • Goal Structure
  • Permeability
  • Leadership
  • Progressiveness

Other
  • Cohesiveness
  • Organizational Esteem
  • People Valuing

→ Organizational
Factors

Source: Kuhn and Geis, *The Firm Bond.*

Organizational Factors (see Figure 9–13)

Mission-Related Factors

• *Goal Structure:* Group mission, purpose, grand design.
• *Permeability:* Degree of flow between group and society.
• *Leadership:* Nature and character of the boss.
• *Progressiveness:* Degree of forward motion; momentum.

Other Organizational Factors

• *Cohesiveness:* Group coherence; internal attachment.
• *Organizational Esteem:* Sense of group value and worth.
• *People Valuing:* Degree to which employees are treated as assets.

Experiential Factors (see Figure 9–14)

Meaning/Mission-Related Factors

• *Importance/Uniqueness:* Distinguishing the group from others.
• *Support:* Group sustenance and help.

Figure 9–14.   Experiential Factors Influencing Commitment.

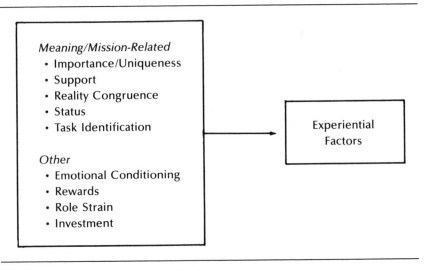

Source: Kuhn and Geis, *The Firm Bond.*

- *Reality Congruence:* Confidence in group pronouncements.
- *Status:* Personal position in the group.
- *Task Identification:* Enjoyment of job.

Other Interactional Factors

- *Emotional Conditioning:* Affective, nonrational elements.
- *Rewards:* Psychic and financial benefits.
- *Role Strain:* Job-related stress.
- *Investment:* Degree of ego and effort sunk into the group.

These three classes of variables provide the framework for our examination of commitment. We ask two questions: How do these factors determine the style and strength of commitment? And how can they be used to encourage creativity for the ultimate good of individuals and organizations?

We tighten our focus. Our primary interest is the nature of personal meaning and company mission—linking individuals to institutions in our definition of commitment. Thus we give certain variables special attention: meaning-related personal variables; mission-related organizational variables; and meaning/mission interactional variables (reflecting organizational experiences). Here we find the breeding ground of core commitment, and the fertile soil in which creativity can bloom.

Figure 9–15.   Relationship of Commitment Strength to Mission Contribution.

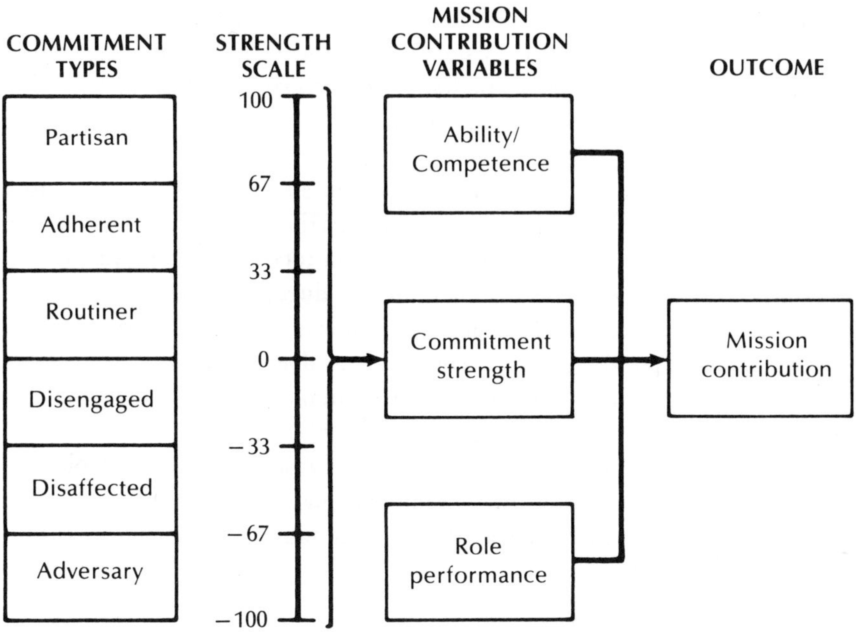

COMMITMENT TYPES	STRENGTH SCALE	MISSION CONTRIBUTION VARIABLES	OUTCOME
Partisan	100	Ability/ Competence	
	67		
Adherent			
	33		
Routiner		Commitment strength	Mission contribution
	0		
Disengaged			
	−33		
Disaffected			
	−67	Role performance	
Adversary			
	−100		

Source: Kuhn and Geis, *The Firm Bond.*

MODEL OUTPUT: MISSION CONTRIBUTION

Commitment strength is a central element determining how much an individual contributes to the goals or mission of an organization (see Figure 9–15). It can be assigned numerical weight (strength scale), a function of commitment type. Other things being equal, the more willing employees are to exert effort on behalf of a company, the more extensive their contribution will be, and the more creative they will be.

Other things, however, are rarely equal. In Figure 9–15 we see that, in addition to commitment strength, elements such as individual ability/competence and role performance must also be considered. ("Ability/competence" defines the general capacity and specific ability of people doing their jobs. "Role performance" refers to the vitality of individual responsibility and the extent to which it can be exercised.)

"Mission contribution" is the model's ultimate output. It is what all employees bring to the corporate table, what they deliver to the party. Mission contribution answers the critical question: *How much is an employee doing to help the organization?* The quality and quantity of work output is what the model assesses. The application to creative productivity is direct.

The mission contribution of an individual can be estimated in a quasinumerical manner. Simply multiply measures of the three critical variables: ability, commitment strength, and role performance (see Figure 9–15). The result is a reasonable estimate of employee contribution and worth, and, by extension, to the degree of creative output.

The model enables us to go further. We can estimate how well the entire organization is accomplishing its goals, the direction it is going, the energy it has. If we assume that the company is the sum total of all employees (in an atomistic sense), we can assess its total mission-directed strength by summing the mission contributions of all individuals interacting with the organization. Individuals with positive commitment strength will enhance this "mission contribution index"; individuals with negative commitment strength will depress the index.

In affecting performance of an organization as a whole, the commitment strength of senior management weighs most heavily. Nothing is as critical for the achievement of organizational goals than the commitment of the chief executive.

Assembling the Model

The full commitment model is pieced together in Figure 9–16. The flow is from left to right. The three primary drivers, the energizing inputs to the model, are personal factors, organizational factors, and experiential factors (organizational experiences)—the first two are independent, the latter is the product of the previous two. All activate the model.

Commitment types form the central structure (or backbone) of the model, which, at its output end, yields "commitment strength." Commitment strength then generates the final output—mission contribution—with modulations by ability/competence and role performance.

The model is designed to represent reality and clarify thinking. It can be used as a template for understanding personal creativity and company productivity as individuals interact with institutions.

COMMITMENT BUILDERS

Out of the elements of personal meaning, organizational mission, and meaning/mission variables, we synthesize "builders" and "breakers," the compounds of commitment. Some compounds are relatively simple blends of inputs; others

Figure 9–16. The Commitment Model: Antecedents, Types, Strength, Contribution Variables, and Output.

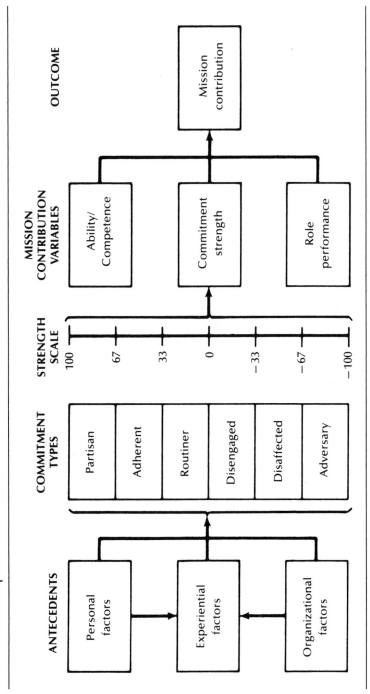

Source: Kuhn and Geis, The Firm Bond.

Table 9–1. Commitment Builders: Where They Come From.

Building Compounds	Personal	Organizational	Experiential
		Elements/Factors (Antecedents)	
Identification	Transcendence	Goal Structure	Importance/Uniqueness
	Esteem	Leadership	Support
	Generalized Loyalty	Cohesiveness	Task Identification
	Materialism	Organizational Esteem	Investment
	Education	Permeability	Emotional Conditioning
Confidence	Affiliation	Leadership	Reality Congruence
	Stability	People Valuing	Support
	Structure		Role Strain
	Materialism		
Momentum	Achievement	Progressiveness	Reality Congruence
	Esteem	Leadership	Importance/Uniqueness
Responsibility	Power	Goal Structure	Support
	Autonomy	Leadership	Status
	Achievement	Cohesiveness	Rewards
	Locus of Control	People Valuing	Role Strain
	Transcendence		
Accomplishment	Achievement	Goal Structure	Rewards
	Esteem	Progressiveness	Importance/Uniqueness
	Transcendence	Organizational Esteem	Task Identification

involve more complex reactions. All become primary prescriptions for building or breaking the firm bond.

We focus on five mechanisms for building commitment, five descriptions of an ideal relationship between organization and employee. Each enhance individual creativity in group settings. There are other builders, of course, but these are some of the best. Each is powerful in its own right, and although in real organizations many would be working in concert, each will be discussed by itself.

Antecedent elements from our commitment model are suggested in Table 9–1. These are the ingredients from which we distill the five building compounds. Note that in accord with our definition of commitment (being the link between meaning and mission), most antecedents relate to these elements. (Others included are "catalysts" to the reactions.)

Identification: The melding of interests between person and group; the extension of personal ego to include organizational essence; the expansion of empirical self. Related concepts: meaningfulness, the sense that group membership is important in some larger (perhaps transcendent) way; participation, a personal stake in organizational ownership, whether literally or figuratively.

Confidence: The belief that the institution can be trusted in its stated policies and public pronouncements; a relaxed conviction that the organization is concerned with the welfare of the individual, that the group cares for the member. Related concepts: integrity, the honesty and fidelity of the organization; solidity, the consistency and reliability of the organization; fairness, the record of the organization in dealing evenhandedly without bias or prejudice.

Momentum: The forward motion of the organization; the energetic impulsion of growth and advancement; the sense of electricity and excitement generated by dynamic movement. Related concept: innovativeness, the pioneering of process and content, a venturing spirit, the intent to be in the vanguard.

Responsibility: The position of the individual in the organization; the degree of organizational trust given to the person; the expectational level of job performance. Related concepts: respect, the social standing of the individual; knowledge, how much information and feedback the organization gives the individual.

Accomplishment: The person's sense of reaching and attaining a broad and noteworthy goal, generally after significant effort. Related concept: fulfillment, the specific sense of task completion and a job well done.

Identification

What makes an individual allocate ego to an institution? Why do people exchange personal freedoms for organizational roles and exert private effort to achieve common objectives? Why create for someone else?

If the reasons found are ones of necessity, whether financial requirements or administered coercion, then the commitment can only be calculative or cog and the creativity can only be weak.

Most organizations have clusters of partisans and adherents. To build core commitment, to rouse partisans, it is necessary to form deep structural linkage between individual psyche and institutional essence. Individuals must extend themselves to embrace the organization. Identification is a merging of individual meaning and organization mission, and creativity flourishes in such an environment.

Identification comes in many forms. Most root for athletic teams, and when the spirit becomes strong, the rooting becomes strange. Sports fans in New York, for example, are not known for their lackadaisical reaction when their baseball or football teams blow a game; and soccer fans in South America have rioted in the wake of international championships. In the Olympics, Americans identify with American teams, as do citizens of other countries with their teams. In the best of circumstances, these feelings should not be unlike those between employees and companies.

Identification is amplified if importance or uniqueness is attributed to the organization. It is difficult to identify with an organization or corporation if the individual does not perceive the presence of something salient. Identification requires significance, a resonance with what is important to the person, even if that significance is simply to be on a winning team.

Identification is also related to participation, especially to a group that is cohesive. People will relate to an organization in direct proportion to their involvement. A high school student dropped from the football team will lose identification with the team and probably the school. Conversely, the surprise election of a new student to the governing council will increase that student's identification with the school.

When members identify with an organization's overall purposes, more is helped than just the organization. The process of transpersonal expansion, of sending ego out from self and joining with others, has an invigorating influence on the person. People fired up by causes are people energized for life.

Confidence

Nothing promotes creativity more than confidence. Nothing holds the firm bond steadier than the anchor of trust, the internal comfort of knowing that your organization will promise what is right and will do what it promises. Confidence underlies all elements of commitment and without it all else is for naught.

For a company to build confidence in its employees, it must be stable and consistent, predictable in its policies and fair in their administration. The company must treat all employees by the same standards. Nothing is more demoralizing than uneven compensation arrangements or overt favoritism irrespective of performance or seniority.

The company must also establish an image of integrity; in this manner personnel will believe what they are told and will act on what they believe. Leadership must establish a reputation as dedicated and forthright. When top management is suspected of softness or sluggishness, employee commitment follows suit. Confidence in the boss is confidence in the company.

Stability and consistency, we should note, does not mean stagnancy and torpidity. Creative companies can be stable, and innovative ones can be consistent. A firm that brings out highly original products radically unrelated to previous ones can certainly generate confidence among employees. The excitement brings its own consistency, and the new introductions its own stability. (Needless to say, these kinds of stability and consistency are more difficult to maintain.)

Confidence is easy for a company to keep when present but difficult to regain when lost. Employees have a natural tendency to believe the best but become most suspicious once fooled. Confidence of employees is something that companies must not take for granted. It should be developed actively and monitored constantly.

Momentum

Forward movement is exciting; the thrill of high growth can energize company creativity. Momentum is what happens when inertia is overcome through the application of constant force. Once started, it is hard to stop; once stopped, it is hard to restart. Corporate momentum is the exhilarating sense of company growth, with the payoff to employees coming in bonuses, promotions, and the personal pleasure of being a winner.

Progressiveness is more attitude than action, more a general state of corporate mind than a specific expression of company growth. A progressive company is always on search for better products to market, more efficient ways to manufacture and distribute the product, more effective systems of internal control, better programs and benefits for managers and employees. A progressive company always wants to stay out front — if not number one in its field, at least very close to it.

Momentum and progressiveness are usually related, but either can be present without the other. Momentum without progressiveness will still stimulate employees into high commitment but runs the risk of running wild. Progressiveness without momentum can also engender commitment, but it is only a promise of things to come and will falter unless those promises are eventually fulfilled. There is little warning in the former and little energy in the latter.

Responsibility

Responsibility is personal burden. It is being accountable for something within one's power. People react to responsibility in different ways. Some enjoy it — they like the power to do and the capacity to accomplish, and they like control over their personal path. Others do not enjoy it — it is weighty and onerous and taxes their freedom. In either case, however, when responsibility is given, commitment increases.

It is a curious thing, this responsibility. It carries with it more work and anxiety, and all it can assure is more fear and more danger. If one does not have responsibility, there is no way to fail. Yet people seek it and pursue it with passion and fire. Why?

Responsibility pulls one into many; it assumes a high degree of group trust and requires confidence on both sides of the bond. Responsibility heightens the exhilaration of achievement. Achieving something on one's own, however rewarding, usually means a smaller scope than achieving something with a team. Preparing a succesful business plan is one thing: running a successful business is something else.

Commitment is built by knowledge and feedback. The more employees know what is happening, the more they feel part of the action. This applies to all employees, at all levels of an organization.

Responsibility is a recognized facilitator of creativity in organizational environments. Being responsible for a program or project triggers greater creative efforts; the ego is energized and the psyche freed.

Accomplishment

Accomplishment, the concluding of noteworthy work, is the fulfilling of achievement, one of our meaning-related personal variables. It is completing tasks of personal significance, and the process itself carries its own reward. A more formal definition of accomplishment might be "bringing meaningful assignments to successful conclusions." Often it requires great effort and the overcoming of large obstacles. Accomplishment is more mental satisfaction than physical reward. It is the act of fulfillment itself, irrespective of benefits derived, that generates joy. Accomplishment is the goal of creativity.

Doing things right gives intrinsic kick. We all exalt in the feeling of a job well done, even if we are the only ones who know it is done. This is especially true for creative jobs. In many situations the reward can be eliminated without diminishing the feeling of triumph. (Take, for example, videogames at arcades; rewarding high scores with free games does little to increase playing or paying.)

Studies have shown the uniqueness of achievement as a mental phenomenon. Its independence from other desirables such as power and possessions is well established. Achievement, like creativity, is desired for its own worth. Though financial compensation can be an "achievement," achievement per se is not dependent on financial compensation. Achievement is more than money or wealth. Achievement touches the human psyche deeply; it is part of what makes us tick.

Entrepreneurs as a class are the personification of achievement. They have a great need to see jobs completed and goals accomplished, and have little need for power or position.

Entrepreneurs are task driven and goal oriented. They are immersed in their work, yet can keep a critical perspective. They remain distant enough to see the forest for the trees and yet are close enough to get hands on any of the wood. Entrepreneurs are creatives.

Achievers are dedicated to finishing their work, which is often self-assigned and self-motivated. Achievers are compulsives, beset by self-generated passion to perfect and complete. Nothing makes them happier than to see the tough task done—but then again, they are not happy unless they are working on tough tasks. Ditto for creatives.

COMMITMENT BREAKERS

Breaking commitment seems easy. It is not—it's just that organizations work so hard at it.

Commitment is broken by disturbances between individuals and institutions; the firm bond is severed by disruptions between personal meaning and company mission. It does not matter which side triggers the disturbance or causes the disruption. What is broken and severed on one side is broken and severed on both sides.

You would think that breaking commitment must be a high art, at least from the effort many groups devote to it. It is surprising the frequency at which reputable firms frustrate the strengthening of commitment. (One might assume that Nobel Prizes were awarded for crippling relationships between employees and companies, or, better yet, tax credits.)

In this section we pull the previous one inside out. What, we ask, are the mechanisms for *destroying* commitment, for shattering the bond between individual and institution? Though commitment is undermined gradually, the impact can emerge suddenly.

The commitment of employees, we should remember, is something an organization usually begins with; the firm bond normally starts out tied with some strength. For openers, commitment is a given, almost like having products to sell. Commitment, at least at the calculative level, is something for companies to *lose,* not win.

We will look at five ways that commitment is broken. Each retard individual creativity in group settings. They are not the only ways, but they *do* work — and they are certainly tried often enough (Table 9-2).

As with the "builders" of the previous section, these "breakers" are compounds distilled from the inputs to our commitment model — personal factors, organizational factors, experiential factors (organizational experiences). Breakers are formed by combining and reacting these driving variables. Of course, when it comes to the formation of breaking compounds, the elements come together in unproductive, unmeaningful, or even damaging ways. (Note that several of the breakers are almost direct opposites of several of the builders. This was not intended; no effort was made to generate parallelism — but since both were derived from the same concepts, a few worked out that way naturally.)

Alienation: The social separation between individual and institution, the estrangement between member and group; the feeling that organization and individual are moving in opposite and contradictory directions; the active rejection of organizational goals, values, essence, and substance. Opposite: identification.

Powerlessness: The belief that organizational events and outcomes are determined by forces beyond individual control; the feeling that what will happen to people is unknown and unknowable and they cannot change or influence future events. Opposite: responsibility.

Meaninglessness: The sense that nothing about the organization has any import or interest for the individual; the feeling of emptiness, the absence of significance in everything the organization is doing. Opposite: import and significance.

Worthlessness: The sense that a person is engaged in organizational activities devoid of benefit or reward of any kind; a depressed image of self and group. Opposite: esteem and pride.

Table 9–2. Commitment Breakers: Where They Come From.

Building Compounds	Personal	Organizational	Experiential
		Elements/Factors (Antecedents)	
Alienation	Transcendence Esteem Generalized Loyalty Affiliation Structure	Goal Structure Leadership Cohesiveness People Valuing Permeability	Support Task Identification Importance/Uniqueness Emotional Conditioning Rewards
Powerlessness	Power Autonomy Achievement Locus of Control	Goal Structure Leadership People Valuing	Status Support Task Identification Rewards
Meaninglessness	Transcendence Achievement Esteem Education Autonomy	Goal Structure Organizational Esteem Progressiveness	Importance/Uniqueness Reality Congruence Investment Task Identification
Worthlessness	Esteem Materialism Education	Progressiveness People Valuing Organizational Esteem	Support Status Emotional Conditioning
Anxiety	Stability Structure Locus of Control Autonomy	Leadership People Valuing Cohesiveness	Role Strain Support Reality Congruence Investment

Anxiety: The uneasy feeling caused by apprehension of trouble, danger, or personal misfortune; an unsettling expectancy of future events, a foreboding uncertainty about what might happen. Opposite: confidence.

In the examples to follow, we watch each of the above breakers fracture the firm bond and destroy both commitment and creativity. The point for managers is to note the signs and avoid the path. In every case, options are discernible and alternatives available.

Alienation

Alienation was the buzz word of the 1960s. It was, we were told, what all institutions of society—government, corporations, universities—were doing to us. It was a conspiracy, some charged, and others echoed the cry.

Alienation implies distance and disruption. As with many of the breakers in this section, it can be more easily defined in the negative. Alienation is the absence of identification. It is what happens when there is no positive relationship between organization and member, and it implies active rejection of all aspects of organizational essence.

When employees are alienated, they feel isolated and apart. The culture and society of the company become, in a very real sense, an alien world, a foreign territory in which people neither have nor want a part. Overt antagonism to goals and values is common, and ridicule of executives and managers is frequent. Alienated personnel—adversaries or disaffecteds—are a hard-bitten bunch to turn around, and never expect positive creativity from them.

Organizations do not have to be evil to turn off employees. In most situations, a part taints the whole. It is not that a middle manager at an oil refinery suddenly sees the entire company as rotten. It is more that he was not promoted or respected or given proper attention. Alienation usually begins as a small seed, but it is virulent and contagious and can grow anywhere.

Powerlessness

Powerlessness as a commitment breaker is not the opposite of power as a meaning-related personal variable. Nor is powerless, in this context, the mere absence of power.

Having power is the capacity to command, alter, or influence the behavior of people and the course of events. If we choose to define powerlessness as the negative of power, then there is more here than common connotation.

Power per se is not a prime commitment builder. Power motivates inwardly, feeding the ego. Powerlessness goes beyond an individual's lack of capacity to command, alter, or influence people and events. Powerlessness describes the *helplessness* of a person within an organization; it is the inability to make any dent whatsoever in matters of personal concern, especially those within one's own sphere of influence. Powerlessness for, say, a quality control supervisor in an electronics assembly plant is not the fact that he cannot change market strategy or affect compensation policy; it is the fact that he cannot make his job more effective or his procedures more efficient. His suggestions are requested but never heard. Creativity wilts under such pressure.

Powerlessness is that airy, aimless sense of no control when organizational forces dominate directly. Powerlessness is real when it is specific, personal, and close. Events seem to swirl around like a tornado without awareness or concern for the individual. (It is like the feeling one gets of trying to play a video arcade game when no money has been deposited. Although figures keep flying, there is no influence whatsoever. The image of involvement is illusion.)

"Learned helplessness" is a psychological concept discovered in animal laboratories and applicable, virtually unchanged, in human organizations. Picture two cages of rats, each with a two-sided electrified grid for a floor. In one cage, whenever a light goes on, a pulse of painful (though not harmful) electrical current is passed through one side of the grid. The rats, in this situation, are conditioned to run over to the other side whenever they see the light, and they learn quickly to avoid the shock. In the other cage, the lights and electric current have no relationship at all; each comes on randomly and it is impossible to learn how to escape the current. Wherever the rats run they get the shock and feel the pain.

The interesting point comes when both groups are placed in new though similar situations—this time, say, with a bell signaling the onset of the electrical pulse. The first group, successful with the light, is successful again, perhaps even a bit quicker in learning time. The second group, the one unable to learn with the light, is now equally unable to learn with the bell—even though it is fully possible to avoid the painful shock. The rats just freeze in a prone position. These rats have learned to be helpless.

This same attitude is all too common among people. "What's the use, it won't help anyway" is a typical response to many situations. When companies ask for new ideas, and none of them is ever considered, much less tried, employees are learning helplessness. They will be less responsive to future requests, and, if the pattern continues, eventually not responsive at all. A cadre of routiners and disengageds has been formed.

When managers are criticized constantly for performance (which, of course, can always be better), a "what's the use" attitude can be generated. Enthusiasm is destroyed; energy is sapped—commitment slides to cog and creativity to zero. When companies teach employees to be helpless, however inadvertently, it is trouble.

Meaninglessness

Meaninglessness is more empty than the mere absence of meaning. Its emotion is negative, not neutral. It connotes barrenness between the individual and the institution, an unbridgable gulf between the purpose of the person and the mission of the group. It means that nothing the organization stands for or is doing has any significance to the individual. Never expect creativity here.

Meaninglessness is cold and gnawing. It eats away at the resolve of the group member or company employee, undermining dedication, destroying motivation, dissolving the firm bond. Its poison works without haste, building in lethal power. Like a slow-growing cancer, meaninglessness must be long present internally before its symptoms become readily apparent externally.

No antagonism is implied in meaninglessness; whether the organization prospers or falters makes no difference whatsoever. The company is a blank, empty, as far as the person is concerned.

Human beings are motivated by diverse factors, but none as powerful or as robust as the search for meaning, the quest for cause. An employee devoid of meaning will be, at best, a functionary (a routiner in cog position on our commitment scale), doing assigned work with minimum involvement and maximum aloofness.

Meaninglessness is hard to generate, but meaningfulness is even harder to *re*generate. Most people begin new work in new companies with a degree of enthusiasm and excitement—if only for the newness and uncertainty. It will require progressive and persistent pressure to suck out substance and leave in meaninglessness. But once present, meaninglessness is resilient and resourceful and extraordinarily tough to replace.

Worthlessness

Esteem and pride, though often berated, are building blocks of commitment and precursors of creativity. Human beings need a positive sense of self-worth, and this applies both individually to the person and collectively to the group.

Nothing is more debilitating to initiative than feelings of uselessness and irrelevance, a low opinion of self relative to others. Depression is common to such persons; no one cares, they think, and nothing matters. A person feeling worthless will neither see any importance in life nor any reason to improve it. Worthlessness is a circular system of thinking, vicious and virulent and very difficult to break.

Performance in any endeavor is dependent on confidence, and anything that undermines the latter will inhibit the former. Worthlessness can be the most deadly of the commitment breakers as it is one of the most subtle. It is highly protective of its existence, resisting conflicting evidence and seeking constant confirmation. (Extreme conditions of worthlessness, more than the other breakers, can trigger suicidal states.) Managers are often unaware that constant criticism of a subordinate, though done to correct and improve, can erode self-confidence and thus makes correction and improvement harder.

Worthlessness has a double punch. A human being submerged by waves of worthlessness is severely handicapped in modern society, yet modern society launches massive assault on the person's esteem. It is easy to be engulfed by overwhelming events and to see oneself as trivial and irrelevant within huge organizations. Worthlessness and creativity just don't mix.

Anxiety

High anxiety is a general sense of foreboding, an unspecific fear of the future. It weakens commitment by breaking down stability, undermining confidence, and generating unease and uncertainty. Productive creativity within organizations is erased by high anxiety.

Anxiety is apprehension, and high anxiety is exaggerated or inappropriate apprehension. (We will use "anxiety" in this section to mean "high anxiety.") An employee wracked by anxiety will be in constant fear of organizational attack; there may be expectations of criticism from superiors, failure on assignments, social ostracism, even arbitrary termination or failure of the company. An anxious employee has little psychic energy available for productive activities, and less still for creative ones.

Anxiety can be defined as a present state of mind caused by the *possibility* that an action of the past, present, or future might conflict with the environment at some future date. Described in this manner, anxiety encompasses Festinger's theory of cognitive dissonance.[6] ("Dissonance" means that two or more concepts are logically opposed to one another.) Stated simply, anxiety is the anticipation of possible dissonance.

Anxiety can be characterized from several viewpoints. In psychiatric conditions, an anxious patient will exhibit pathological alertness and tension. There can be extreme eagerness that results in inept or awkward actions. The person considers each thought proof that some dire event will occur. Sometimes this event will continually change; occasionally all signs will point toward a single calamity.

Say a person has organized a club picnic three weeks in advance. Many arrangements will have to be made. With the outing a few days away, the weather bureau reports storm warnings. The picnic planner is *now*, according to our definition, in a state of anxiety. There is a possibility that his actions of the past (arranging the picnic) might conflict with the environment at some future date (inclement weather). Anxiety would not be the present state of mind if the picnic had to be *definitely* postponed for one reason or another. The emotion would then be disappointment. Anxiety is present only when dissonance is *possible;* if the dissonance occurs, anxiety is consummated and another mood takes its place.

Anxiety is more serious when no immediate cause is apparent. The person is in a continuous state of expectancy, waiting for some disaster to befall. The awful event might happen at any moment, it may assume any form. Perhaps financial loss will result from poor investments; perhaps one's job will disappear; perhaps. . . .

The magnitude of anxiety can vary widely. Apprehension is part of our biological warning mechanism. A certain degree of anxiety is valuable. We function better when we are more alert. Students do better on tests, and athletes do better on the field, with *moderate* anxiety than with either high or low levels. With the ill-fated organizer of the picnic, anxiety is beneficial. The man will now be more alert to weather reports and better prepared for alternative action. If, however, this alerting reaction becomes inappropriately strong, normal functioning can be interrupted. (Creativity, similarly, is enhanced with moderate anxiety; it is slowed somewhat by low anxiety and retarded substantially by high anxiety.)

We can assess the magnitude of the anxiety by assessing the magnitude of the dissonance since, by definition, anxiety is a function of dissonance. If two elements are dissonant with one another, the magnitude of the dissonance will be a function of the importance of the elements. For the picnic organizer, the dissonance and hence the anxiety cannot exceed the level of resistance to calling off the entire event. A washed out picnic, however, is relatively minor compared with the anticipation of a cataclysm.

Anxiety can be reduced by reducing dissonance. How to reduce dissonance?

The simplest way, though often not practical, is to alter the action. Call off the picnic. Since anxiety is the anticipation of possible dissonance, anxiety decreases as possible dissonance decreases. Although bad weather was forecast, the person might check other reports for second opinions. A humorous article recounting mistakes in weather forecasting will be read avidly, while other articles dealing with increased reliability due to weather satellites will be ignored. News reports of small craft warnings might be misinterpreted to mean that the storm was blowing out to sea. The person might begin to minimize the picnic by stressing the importance of friends getting together irrespective of place. Curiously, anxious people may be creative, but almost always unpredictably and almost never productively — at least for the accomplishment of organizational objectives.

A person with anxiety, expecting calamity, might be motivated to reduce anxiety by making the calamity *more* likely to happen. This is the strange part. Dissonance would be reduced since reality would then be in agreement with his feeling of imminent disaster. An employee overly anxious about being fired, for example, might start coming late to work or choosing projects more likely to fail. The reaction of superiors would then confirm his initial apprehension and justify his looking for other employment.

There is an inverse relationship between anxiety and security. A person rooted in a stable belief system and value structure will rarely suffer from inappropriate apprehension. Whenever such an individual confronts behavioral alternatives, he can evaluate them in light of a constant standard. He will be reasonably confident that the future environment will not be dissonant with his present behavior. Anxiety makes little headway with a secure person. (Confidence and security are not the same as contentment and complacency; creativity will flourish with the former, not with the latter.)

COMMITMENT AND CREATIVITY: THE BUILDING AND BREAKING

Creativity is rooted in the human psyche and as such is affected by feeling and emotion. Creativity in companies is not, therefore, solitary acts of fringers and wierdos; those strange sorts completely oblivious to what is happening around them are more fictional stereotypes than real prototypes.

Productive creativity accomplishes organizational objectives, and its firm strength is dependent on organizational attitudes.[7] Commitment counts, and creative companies will understand it and build it.

NOTES

1. Much of the material in this chapter is derived from Robert Lawrence Kuhn and George T. Geis, *The Firm Bond: Linking Meaning and Mission in Business and Religion* (New York: Praeger, 1984). *The Firm Bond* builds a model of commitment by combining organizational theory with extended case studies — the latter, in-depth personal histories, come from both business and religious organizations.

    The book has an organizing principle, a way of looking at the world. We believe that organizational characteristics in general, and commitment in particular, can best be studied in their purest form. This is our operating paradigm, our conceptual prism, our special lens.

    We define "pure form" as those environments where what we seek is readily apparent, where its manifestation is overt and its presence powerful. In such situations the target characteristic stands out and, though exaggerated, can be massaged and manipulated. It is one way to examine an intangible.

    What kinds of organizations do we require? Ones where the desired attribute appears in strongest and most dominant mode, where the "signal" of the target trait is highest relative to the "noise" of all other traits. Once this pure form is isolated and analyzed, then the emerging understanding can be applied. Manifestations of the characteristic in other environments, though not as overt, can then be investigated.

    Organizations exemplifying the pure form of the characteristic are the special lens, and it is through them that we look. What kinds of organizations are the special lens needed for scrutinizing commitment?

    Where is commitment best exemplified? Where is it readily isolated and analyzed? Although a critical component of all organizations, commitment appears most prominently and vigorously in *ideological* organizations — environments of religious and political passion. Here attitudes of mind are more singular, more linear, more focused.

    Furthermore, to enhance the effect, we look toward the far end of the scale, toward those religious and political settings where collective mission subjugates individual meaning, where party fidelity swamps private desire, where sect purpose crushes personal freedom. Here, at the extreme outposts of ideological organizaions, we dig for concepts and cases. These situations, tailor-made to examine commitment, we label "total organizations."

    Why are total organizations ripest for examining commitment? For one, they are both "closed" and "ideological." Closed organizations are impermeable, and often this is intended and enforced. Commitment, therefore, is both cause and effect, cause at the beginning, effect after a time. (Both "closed" and "ideological" are required for full impact. Many political movements are ideological but not closed — commitment to them need not be potent. Prisons, on the other hand, are closed but not ideological — few inmates evidence commitment.)

    We utilize total organizations — arenas of powerful religious fervor — as the analytical framework within which we examine commitment. The objective, remember, is *not* to study these situations per se; rather, we use them to elucidate the essence of commitment, which we will then apply to companies and institutions of common kind.

Religious belief enflames human emotion; with ultimate things at stake, unusual things are done. One bible college, for example, stopped playing basketball against another school when it discovered that its rival was run by another religion. (Can't play ball with the devil, you know.) A Congressional Medal of Honor holder sent back his medal because his new religion taught against war. Such stories are endless, the convictions profound.

Religious belief generates mankind's strongest, most soul-stirring feelings. How many thousands of missionaries and saints have sacrificed their lives in pursuit of their visions! How many millions give their time and their money to aid the poor and preach the Word! How much of mankind's culture—music, art, literature, morality, justice, customs—is founded on religious values and inspired by religious principles! For better or for worse, for good or for eveil, religion promotes the pinnacle of human achievement and evokes the height of human emotion.

What might we see under the magnifying glass of religious organizations? Can, for example, the attitudes of a minister in a sect shed light on the effectiveness of a manager in a company? Can understanding the devotion of church members improve the dedication of factory workers?

The psychic processes involved in the two situations are very much the same. Religion and business run parallel universes; just because commitment is more obvious in the former does not mean that it is less important in the latter. The nature of religious commitment is merely a cleaner, more overt form of the same phenomenon, the same magical mental force that binds individuals to institutions and energizes goal-directed action. Understanding what commitment means in extreme religious organizations helps us understand what it means in all organizations.

In Part I of *The Firm Bond* we use detailed personal histories to examine the components of commitment, the pillars that form its foundation—personal factors (primarily "meaning"); organizational factors (primarily "mission"); and experience factors (primarily the interaction between "meaning and mission.") These elements are combined at the culmination of Part I to construct a "commitment model."

In Part II we use the model to describe how commitment can be built and broken; how the bond between individuals and institutions can be formed and severed. The book concludes with chapters showing how understanding commitment can help individuals and improve institutions.

In both parts, points are portrayed through case and example. Real people in real organizations, from business to religion, energize *The Firm Bond*.

2. For a summary of various research definitions of commitment, see Bruce Buchanan, II, "Building Organizational Commitment: The Socialization of Managers in Work Organizations," *Administrative Science Quarterly* 19 (1974): 533–46.

3. Employees or members of closed systems often exemplify the far end of the scale, much closer to the outer than the inner locus. They affirm by their compliance the legitimacy of organizational assumption of private decision making. While such control is more potent and rigid in total organizations than in traditional corporations, the general importance of this personal variable in determining individual commitment should not be underrated.

Locus of control is one of the personal factors at work on the individual side of the individual–institution bond. It is highlighted by the magnifying glass of total organizations in which members often abdicate self-direction of their lives. Thus, *The*

Firm Bond studies locus of control in such pure form environments, in order to apply what we learn to all group environments. A similar analysis could be made of the other personal factor variables. Each is incomplete in itself, merely one part of the whole, an element in understanding the nature of commitment.

4. "Boundary permeability" is the degree to which members of an organization are able to interact with the world outside the organization. It can also include the ease with which people outside can enter inside. Most examples in *The Firm Bond* are of semipermeable groups, where inward flow of new members is encouraged but outward flow of old members is discouraged. (There are, of course, groups that restrict the flow in both directions—they don't want old members out and they also don't want new members in. Such groups are surely fewer, usually sicker, and not as relevant for corporate analogy.)

In extreme cases, almost all interaction with the outside is forbidden; the organizational boundaries are closed, shut and sealed. Why do groups erect walls so hard and high? Contact and exposure are what they fear. They worry that members can be swayed, that the taint or pulls of world will break down convictions carefully constructed and tirelessly nurtured. "Contamination," as if by infectious disease, is the word often heard. Commitment to organizational purposes must be maintained—it is their only reason for being—and the task becomes progressively more difficult in direct proportion to contact outside.

Closed or total organizations are fertile substrate for studying commitment; the component variables undergo vigorous interplay in this exaggerated environment. Low boundary permeability generates a pressure-cooker effect, boiling internal elements quickly. Circular reasoning abounds. The logic, or lack of it, is "disproofproof"; it is impossible to contradict the group since contradicting evidence is not admitted inside the system. Constructing unbridgeable barriers around the organization—sealing it off as if by medieval moat—corroborates claims of uniqueness, which in turn validates continuance of existence.

Principles pertaining to boundaries, seen in garish extract in total organizations, are common to all organizations. Specific applications may vary but general rules remain the same. Items defining the interface between "in" and "out" can range from beards to button-down shirts, motorcycles to right-wing politics. Company standards, whether recommendation or restriction, mark the boundary, distinguishing the group from the nongroup, differentiating inside from outside. (Imagine two circles, one defining the group, the other defining the nongroup. The closer the intersection of the two circles to null, the easier to maintain commitment focus.)

Business firms, as a rule, do not draw lines in the dirt and dare employees to cross them. Nevertheless, attention to the design of boundary conditions is important. Whether planned or unplanned, boundaries always exist, and whether fuzzy or clear, they define organizational essence. Just as group cohesiveness focuses on we-ness, boundary conditions stress we versus they.

5. Strong commitment is important for corporate success. But commitment in the short term should never be bought by sacrificing credibility in the long term.

Credibility is an odd animal. You start out with it free; people generally believe what organizations say. Credibility is hard to lose; people are generally forgiving and allow companies margin for error.

Why then the frequency of credibility gaps? Bureaucratic organizations seem bent on self-destruction, giving mixed signals and confusing employees. And once credibility is destroyed, it is difficult to rebuild; taken in once, people are wary of being taken in again. ("You fool me once," goes the adage, "shame on you. You fool me twice, shame on *me*.")

Organizational planning and goal-setting is an integral part of every profession-ally managed firm. In establishing objectives, inflated performance projections may give a quick fix—but the price is high and the penalty long. Overstatement and hy-perbole may whip up enthusiasm among the troops and artificially strengthen the bond between employees and company—but only temporarily. In forecasting the future, wild optimism may lead to peak levels of commitment—but only for a lim-ited period of time. In the long run, only *positive realism* can provide lasting com-mitment. When current projections and forecasts match future performance and re-sults, the firm bond is permanently strengthened.

Exaggerated claims to the company are like narcotic drugs to people. They are habit forming and addicting; the more you use them, the more you need them. With every unfulfilled expectation, the dosage required for the next round jumps up, so that soon no claims can be large enough since the discount rate in employee's minds reaches 100 percent.

Unrealistic projections may feverishly excite the uninitiated, but they carry the seeds of future destruction. The withdrawal symptoms for employees overdosed on "hype" are protracted and painful. Even the truth, when it follows hype, is not be-lieved. Executives find their power drained. A corporate credibility gap is most irk-some to close.

Commitment and cynicism, like love and hate, find close proximity around the circle of human emotions. The higher the commitment, the more potential energy available to generate cynicism. High commitment means high investment of ego, and high investment of ego turns sour quickly when insulted or ridiculed. Ease of movement around the circle depends on direction. Flowing from commitment to cynicism, from love to hate, is sadly simpler than trying to go in reverse. The trek back from cyncism to commitment is all uphill.

6.   See Leon Festinger, *A Theory of Cognitive Dissonace* (Evanston, Ill.: Row and Peter-son, 1957).

7.   Constant organizational change, for example, inhibits high creative effort. Com-panies must struggle to maintain employee commitment and creativity in the face of frequent disruptions and dislocations. (See *The Firm Bond, op. cit.,* for case his-tories illustrating the relationship between individual commitment and organiza-tional change.)

Chapter 10

RISK TAKING, INNOVATION, AND ORGANIZATIONAL ENVIRONMENT

George T. Geis

It has been said that three types of people can be found within organizations: risk takers, caretakers, and undertakers. Whether these types originate apart from organizations or whether organizations create the types is not the purpose of this discussion. Our efforts center on what is essential for organizational innovation, and our focus will be the dynamics associated with the risk taker.

Innovation as commonly defined involves the act of introducing a new discovery or change in response to or in anticipation of an environmental need. Since innovation is directly linked with the new, the unknown, or the untried, it is the first type of people in our over-generalized trichotomy, the risk takers, who are the organizational innovators.

To promote organizational innovation we must understand why individuals in organizations choose to take risks and why they refuse to do so. We must also understand how an organization can design an environment that encourages the risk taking pattern it desires.

RISK VERSUS UNCERTAINTY

In discussing risk and scientific achievement, Silver differentiates between circumstances where the odds of success can be determined with reasonable accuracy and where such odds cannot be clearly specified.[1] When the probabilities of success and failure can be gauged with some accuracy, innovative behavior is described in terms of risk. Otherwise an individual's decision to innovate is said to fall within the realm of uncertainty.

Silver uses this distinction between risk and uncertainty to explain innovative behavior in light of an individual's social position. He argues that evidence suggesting that most Nobel scientists come from the upper-middle class of society can be explained by the immediate institutional context in which most innovative scientific action now occurs. The continuing need to invest in substantial tangible resources to conduct scientific inquiry and the exchange and testing of ideas with an elite scientific community constantly pressures scientists to assess the probabilities of success in experimental design, according to Silver. The fact that the outcome of innovative action can and must be gauged with reasonable accuracy creates an environment in harmony with the values of upwardly mobile people, an environment where the odds of success versus failure in light of their economic, social, or psychological needs can be weighed. Upwardly mobile people, potentially having much to lose, are reluctant to deal in an atmosphere of uncertainty, where such probabilities cannot be measured with accuracy.

Silver contrasts the risk-assessable environment of the scientist with the highly volatile forces and largely noninstitutional context found in the world of literature. He argues that findings which suggest that comparatively greater numbers of literature laureates are from lower middle class backgrounds are consistent with the uncertainty of tastes in the literary field. The inability to gauge outcome, on a relative basis, is less suited to the upwardly mobile individual, who has more to protect and who is more prone to want to operate in an environment of assessable risk.

Whether or not Silver's hypotheses are tenable, an instructive parallelism can be drawn with the business world. Scientists and their supposed predilection to operate in an environment of reasonably assessable risk can be compared to executives in established organizations. Such executives, as their counterparts in the scientific community, have a lot to lose financially, psychologically, or socially from innovative action and consequently prefer to operate in an environment where risks can be reasonably measured.

Entrepreneurs, with perhaps less to lose in the way of organizational trappings, can be compared to the literature laureates. Both may be more willing to operate in the realm of uncertainty, which indeed may be a more fertile ground for creative innovation.

PERSONAL INVESTMENT AND ORGANIZATIONAL INNOVATION

David McClelland[2] tells the story of one of his graduate students who had just completed a thorough review of the literature on a particular topic. The student had finished his presentation detailing the current state of knowledge in this field. He showed great familiarity with and sensitivity to all of the recent research findings. After his impressive display of knowledge, McClelland asked the student what he thought ought to be done next. The student was noncommittal, stating only that since key authorities differed on the importance of the major variables, who was he to presume to provide future direction.

Seeing his reluctance as more timidity than humility, McClelland pressed him further, stressing that the student now knew as much as anyone about the field and should be willing to suggest a line of research. The student then reluctantly stated that perhaps a massive attack should be conducted on all research frontiers at the same time.

McCleland then postulates as to why some of his most promising students, with outstanding abilities and fluency of ideas, had not contributed to scientific inquiry at the level of others far less gifted. He suggests that perhaps a large part of the explanation lies in the ability to commit to and invest time, energy, and resources in a focused line of endeavor. The brilliant nonachiever may be unable or unwilling to risk commitment to a focused effort and therefore unable to create or contribute up to his or her potential.

Considerable personal investment is commonly involved in the risk of being part of an innovative process or venture within an organization. While such financial, psychological, and social investment is not unknown to the entrepreneur or poet, the context of the business organization often brings with it pressures in these three areas that are of a different level of magnitude. These pressures frequently dictate against investment of self in innovative organizational pursuits. Since commitment to a project (or organization) is directly related to the degree to which one is willing to invest oneself (both psychically and financially) in it, organizational mechanisms must be structured so as to encourage the personal investment required for the success of innovative projects.[3,4]

THE ORGANIZATIONAL ENVIRONMENT FOR INNOVATION

Risk, irrespective of whether it can be gauged, is clearly linked to innovation. Literature laureates or entrepreneurs may be, in general, more prone to take risks of a higher order of magnitude than scientists or executives operating in an established organizational environment. This does not necessarily suggest that the organizational norm should be to encourage all employees to be as unrestrained as free-form poets; the argument is simply that in order for innovation to occur in organizational settings, we must heighten our awareness of the financial, psychological, and social pressures that dictate against risk taking and creativity.

If innovative action is to occur regularly within organizations, individuals within must be willing to make the personal investments of themselves that innovation requires. The organizational environment must be structured to encourage the type of risk taking that must occur. Three suggestions for establishing such an environment follow:

1. Improve the chances of success in risk taking. Provide the professional, collegial, and financial support that will allow an individual to perceive a reduction in the odds of failure. The model of Nobel scientists with both resource laboratory and peer support is instructive. These support mechanisms can allow one reasonably to assess risk and, in a traditional organizational context, be more willing to invest the psychic energy necessary for innovation.
2. Diversify away as much risk as possible. Modern portfolio theory argues any premiuim in the required return from a financial investment is associated with non-diversifiable (systematic) risk. Risk that can be diversified away is not rewarded in the general market. Similarly, organizations need to thoroughly explore options for the diversification or sharing of risk (and gain), from both a financial and psychological perspective.[5] The company must then concentrate on succeeding in the areas of non-diversifiable risk to which it has chosen to expose itself.
3. In the areas where top management wants risk taking to occur within an organization, it must socially encourage it. The organizational motto: "If you don't make at least three mistakes a day, you're not doing your job," should be the cultural norm in departments where risk taking is wanted. Limits must be placed on the social downside of failure.

Allow me a personal note on risk taking and innovation. I recently completed a book for a major software firm in which I ventured into the area of computer programming.[6] Programming is an exacting discipline. When mistakes are made in code, error messages flash to the user, and programmer failure is as obvious as a baseball player dropping a fly in the outfield. Programming is risky business, especially for one's ego.

In writing this book/disk package I had the professional and technical support that I saw as significantly improving my odds of success in the project. The company had other areas and projects that diversified its personal risk position. (Whether or not the fact that my personal portfolio was also diversified and not solely invested in this project was conducive to innovation is a complicated matter and not within the scope of this discussion.) Finally, I had an environment where trial and error was tolerated and, at least in the development phase, even encouraged. Any claim that this project may ever have to creativity or innovation will largely rest on the presence of these three elements.

To promote organizational innovation, mechanisms that encourage individual and group risk taking within the organization must be established and implemented. In order to prevent risk takers from evolving into organizational caretakers or undertakers (or from leaving the organization), the linkage between organizational environment, risk taking and innovation must be more deeply appreciated.

NOTES

1. H. Silver, "Scientific Achievement and the Concept of Risk," *British Journal of Sociology* 34: 39–43.
2. D. McClelland, "The Calculated Risk: An Aspect of Scientific Performance," in C. Taylor (ed.), *Scientific Creativity: Its Recognition and Development* (New York: Wiley, 1963), pp. 184–92.
3. See H. Becker, "Notes on the Concept of Commitment," *American Journal of Sociology* 66: 32–40, for a classic paper on the importance of "side bets" in determining organizational commitment.
4. See R. Kuhn and G. Geis, *The Firm Bond: Linking Meaning and Mission in Business and Religion* (New York: Praeger, 1984), for a discussion of the linkage between the personal investment of time, effort, ego or money and organizational commitment.
5. See K. Faxen, "Risk Management", in A. Charnes and W.W. Cooper, eds., *Creative and Innovative Management: Essays in Honor of George Kozmetsky* (Cambridge, Mass.: Ballinger Publishing Company, 1984), pp. 155–75, for a discussion of ways to share risk and gain by labor and management.
6. The book/disc package is on personal financial management, and the software company is Ashton–Tate.

Chapter 11

PERSONALITY AND INNOVATION
How Creative Types Think and Act

Robert Lawrence Kuhn

Personalities, like fingerprints, are unique. Though composed of similar elements, the endless combinations make each pattern singular. Every human being is an aggregate sum of numerous traits, a complex amalgam of inner attitudes and outer actions. When executives build companies, when creative and innovative managers pioneer new strategies and structures, personality is a controlling factor.

Creativity, like lightning, appears unpredictable. The characteristics arrayed in Figure 11–1 describe how humans behave and can highlight the creative pro-

Figure 11–1. Human Behavioral Characteristics.

Inward	Outward
Independent	Dependent
Active	Passive
Intense	Lethargic
Dominant	Recessive
Competitive	Cooperative
Acquisitive	Quiescent
Objective	Subjective
Consistent	Capricious
Conceited	Modest

Source: Robert Lawrence Kuhn, *To Flourish Among Giants: Creative Management for Mid-Sized Firms* (New York: John Wiley, 1985).

163

cess. The grouping is a fair sample though hardly complete. As a conceptual aid, each trait is organized as a linear spectrum, with each word of the pair defining an extreme. Most people, of course, fall in the middle of all the traits, some a little more to the right on one, some a little more to the left on another. It is the combination, remember, the exquisite intertwining of elements, that makes us unique.

Each of the following trait-spectrums is introduced with a question. What is the essence of the personality element, and how might it affect the creative process? There is, of course, no right or wrong answer, just reflections on the way people feel. Creative types, remember, are rich with variety, and personality assessment should enhance, not limit, their expression.[1]

Inward–Outward

How would you rather spend an evening, reading at home or partying with friends? Those choosing the former are "inward" (or "introverted" in Jung's terminology); those chosing the latter are "outward" (or "extroverted"). Whether one is inward or outward might affect the creative process in different situations; for example, working in an "open office" environment with no private enclosures favors outward employees. Inward people generally prefer more time for private contemplation, though outward people might have a better sense of practical application.

Independent–Dependent

In taking responsibility for introducing a major new company product —with a promotion promised for success and a dismissal likely for failure —would you rather report to your superior frequently (e.g., daily) or infrequently (e.g., monthly)? Independent people are generally more creative; they care less about custom and more about content. Though independent people seem to have more status in society, companies would fragment with too many of them. Furthermore, a person dependent in one mode, say as corporate middle manager, might be quite independent in another mode, say as an officer in the Naval Reserve.

Active–Passive

Which job would you prefer (assuming equal salary and status), sales manager with the task of opening up new accounts or personnel manager with the task of maintaining proper paper flow? Actives are more creative, taking inerest in affecting their environment, not just finding a comfortable place in it. A company must have a balance between the two types: too may actives cause chaos; too many passives produce stagnation.

Intense–Lethargic

Would you ever work on Thanksgiving to get a critical shipment out to an important customer? If so, you are probably intense. Do you often have to be told what to do several times before you finally do it? If so, you are probably lethargic. Intensity correlates highly with creativity; the creative process demands high energy and persistent effort. Intensity is an important trait for entrepreneurs, who must build from nothing, but it can be disrupting for middle managers, who must maintain steady work output.

Dominant–Recessive

When serving on interdepartmental committees are you ever selected as chairman? Dominants in business, like dominants in genetics, express their traits and get their way—but too many dominants, of course, clash and cause conflicts. The revolving-door exodus of a succession of "heir apparents" in corporations run by strong though aging founders are classic cases of clashing dominants. Dominants are often creative, but the correlation may not be cause and effect. Recessive personalities, relatively unencumbered with people control, can allocate more effort and attention to novel ideas.

Competitive–Cooperative

Assume you work on the sales staff of a company selling office equipment to corporate clients. Which method of compensation do you prefer: 1) Each salesperson is free to approach any potential customer and is paid a commission, say 6 percent, based on his or her personal sales only; or 2) each salesperson is assigned to cover an equal number of potential customers and is paid a commission based on the sales of the entire sales staff, say 4 percent, as well as on his or her personal sales, say 2 percent? The balance between competition and cooperation is a difficult one to keep, as when three senior vice-presidents—over administration, marketing, and finance—are all candidates for president. Creative types are often competitive, though their arena of competition may be more achievement and recognition than remuneration and promotion.

Acquisitive–Quiescent

Do you need to build and accumulate in order to feel accomplished? Are you constantly seeking new things to buy and use? The founders of companies are more often concerned with building their firm's power than with building their personal finances. "Acquisitives," of course, are high risk personalities, often operating close to the edge of disaster. Creative managers are found on both sides of this spectrum, each with a different cast. Acquisitives are dynamos; quiescents pull the surprises.

Objective–Subjective

In selecting a new assistant vice-president, on what would you put more weight, her scores on intelligence tests and psychological profiles, or your personnel director's impressions after a fifteen-minute interview? In an age of accelerating quantification, when computers produce prodigious amounts of data, instincts and insights are under increasing attack. Others, however, speak of the importance of articulating rational analysis with nonrational (not *ir*rational) perception. Creatives come down clearly on the subjective side; an objective personality is often inhibited from seeing novelty.

Consistent–Capricious

How predictable are you? Does your boss have confidence that you will do the job as she expects? In trying to win back old customers, for example, would you give everyone the same line? Do you enjoy jumping from job to job, company to company? It is rare when consistency is not a virtue, and reliable employees are considered golden. On the other hand, firms operating in rapidly changing industrial environments need a few capricious sorts, creative types who can explode with new ideas. (They must, of course, operate under control, which poses some problems when the capricious one is the entrepreneurial boss.) While creativity and capriciousness are not synonomous, regularity and repetition stifle originality.

Conceited–Modest

Can we expect to hear all your fabled exploits every time we see you? Assuming your subordinates would never know the truth, would you rather overplay or underplay your personal relationship with the president? Society considers, if we believe convention, modesty a virtue and conceit a vice. Yet to be successful businessmen, we are told, one must flip those pairings around. The truth in business, of course, is both and neither. Few creative types hold their long suit in modesty; creatives feel their ideas are supremely important, demanding immediate recognition and instant action.

Executives concerned with the management of creative and innovative personnel must maintain awareness of personality. People differ, especially creative types, and the successful manager will be the sensitive manager.

NOTE

1. This material is derived from Robert Lawrence Kuhn, *To Flourish Among Giants: Creative Management for Mid-Sized Firms* (New York: John Wiley, 1985).

Part VI

CREATIVE AND INNOVATIVE MANAGEMENT IN PUBLIC SECTOR STRUCTURES

Chapter 12

DIFFERENT ORGANIZATIONAL FORMS IN THE PUBLIC SECTOR AS A MEANS FOR CREATIVITY AND INNOVATION

Yair Aharoni

INTRODUCTION

Throughout the developed world, the public sector has experienced enormous growth over the last three decades. Both the scope and the range of service supplied by this sector have been expanded. Citizens have assigned to their governments increasing responsibility to solve a growing array of economic, social, and cultural problems. At the same time, government has been regarded with declining confidence, and its growth has been perceived as excessive, limiting the political acceptability of increased government spending. The endless crusade against government inefficiency has gained renewed intensity, and the vision of reducing waste in government has gained appeal.

Two conflicting considerations come into play in determining the desirable size of the public sector: on the one hand, most people want the government to provide more services and to help mitigate private risks; on the other hand, there is a fear of a "big government" that is inefficient, inept, and gripped by special interest groups. The unclosed gap between demand for increasing services and public unwillingness to pay for them causes social and political tensions. It also increases the tendency of government to become invisible (Aharoni 1981b). Instead of financing public services through general revenue, governmental deficits or public debt, the government uses its coercive power to force certain parts of the private sector to finance the service or to subsidize another portion of the private sector. It also works through independent agencies, foundations, institutions, commissions, and corporations, differing in status, structure, powers, operating and financial flexibility, and in the degree of public accountability. The costs are generally absorbed by consumers, paying higher prices for protected goods or because of compliance costs of regulation. Because benefits accrue to few and costs are paid by many, those carrying the additional burden, even if they know its significant magnitude, do not bother to complain.

As one example, most governments subsidize certain declining firms to ensure employment. In Israel, when the owners of a textile plant in a development town threatened to close it, the government agreed to give them a direct subsidy from the budget. The Belgian government, in a similar situation, decided to nationalize the firm in question; its losses are not shown in the budget. The U.S. government aided its textile industry through restrictions on foreign trade. The increasing costs of clothing to the consumer are not even known.

In attempting the stimulate innovation in the private sector, government used these three organizational methods: it subsidized research and development directly; it helped innovation through tax expenditures; it directed state owned enterprises to subsidize other firms through their pricing policies (for example, by reducing the costs of electricity to manufacturing firms).

Certain government's policies fostered innovation, others impeded it. Education policy of government has been very important in creating the cadres of future scientists, direct allocation of funds for development efforts helped innovation, and aid was sometimes granted indirectly, as in the case of aeronautical industries that were assisted by military procurements covering the costs of prototype development or airline industries that enjoyed post office subsidies. (For some historical analysis in the United States, see Nelson 1982. For other countries, see Goodman 1984.)

State-owned enterprises were directed to reduce the probability of a commercial failure by procuring locally developed technologies—for example, in telecommunication (see Doz 1976) or in aircraft procurement (Trident in the United States, Caravelle in France), as well as for large utility equipment. In other cases, governmental policies impeded innovation: the British electricity system, for example, was required to purchase local coal at expensive prices, not to move to more modern substitutes (Pryke 1981); some countries preferred foreign technologies in their military procurement to the development of the locally based technologies and purchased manufacturing technology, discouraging local research and development.

The government is often a monopsony or a dominant consumer. The responsibility for the innovation and bearing its consequences moves from the supplier to the customer. The impact of government on private sector innovation, important as it is, is beyond the scope of this paper. Instead, the purpose of this paper is to analyze differences in the organizational forms within the public sector and their meaning for the ability of these organizations to innovate.

PUBLIC SECTOR AND INNOVATION

Every organization consists of tasks, structure, processes of information, communication linking departments, reward systems, and people. A sharp distinction has come to be drawn between the public and the private sectors. It is generally taken for granted that these two sectors have different goals, different modes of operations, different incentives, different control methods, and different sources for management recruitment—and that there is an inescapable contradiction between creativity and innovation on the one hand and the public sector on the other hand.

In the early stages of a new technology, product or process, performance criteria are not well defined. No one knows for sure what the market will want— even if the market exists at all—or what the product can or should do. At that stage, the development of a new product, process, or technology is to a large extent an article of faith, based on extremely weak signals with no coherent picture of market demand, ultimate costs, or even the possible uses of the new product. Competition is based largely on the performance of the product, and flexibility in production is absolutely essential. Only when design is standardized can the production process be standardized, too. Of course, once the market knows what a product is—be it a word processor, a PBX, or a video—it is the task of management charged with the product to achieve more economy and efficiency in production. At least in the early stages, however, innovation and creativity need flexibility and organic organization (Burns and Stalker 1961).

Public sector organizations are generally operating under a Webberian bureaucratic system, appropriate to stable environments. The uncertainty inherent in many changes and innovations run against the need of machine bureaucracy. The word "bureaucratic" is used here in what Crozier calls its vulgar and frequent sense. "It evokes the slowness, the ponderousness, the routine, the complication of procedures, and the maladapted responses of 'bureaucratic' organizations to the needs which they should satisfy, and the frustrations which their members, clients, or subjects consequently endure" (Crozier 1964: 3).

"Bureaucratization" can be measured along two dimensions: the degree of "formalization" and the degree of "routinization." Formalization refers to the extent to which the behavior of an individual is rule-governed; routinization refers to the extent to which the individual's work is constant and unchanging from day to day. Civil service organizations are certainly very formal, although the work is not necessarily routine.

Bureaucratic organizations and innovations, to borrow a phrase from Levine, are "strange bedfellows" (Levine 1983: 235). In a study of entrepreneurial activities in the Soviet Union, Levine found seven characteristics of bureaucratic organizations that hinder innovation: strict hierarchy of authority, narrowly specialized units, striving for stability, risk aversion, measurability of performance and reward structure, role of slack, competition and bankruptcy.

One reason for lack of innovation in the Soviet system, according to Levine, is information degradation: any proposal has to be passed through the ranks, and any level can veto it. This, in addition to the vast difference in technical knowledge between ministers and the people in the field, impedes communications and degrades the information flow on its long way from the innovator to the granter of approval: it takes a number of approvals to adopt an innovation, but only one veto to kill it.

The system is organized in narrowly specified units, and the interest of the ministry in meeting its own targets and obligations is stronger than its interest in meeting the overall goals of the economy. The narrowly defined specific units do not reward innovation and impede a close linkage between R & D and production—an essential prerequisite for innovation to be successful. Furthermore, bureaucrats cherish routine, standard operating procedures, repetitive methods that allow stability. They resist new approaches that threaten to upset the routine and standardized procedures of work. Performance of subordinates tends to be based on quantifiable measures, while innovation needs an environment that does not unduly penalize failure. Managers resist innovations and try to keep the targets low. In addition, the central planning authority applies extreme pressure, not leaving enough slack time for alertness to opportunities. Finally, the risk of bankruptcy does not exist. "The state will bail out a firm that is losing money through grants, subsidies, emergency credits, and allowed higher prices and the firm will continue to operate" (Levine 1983: 254).

Soviet enterprise managers, according to Levine, have little incentive to experiment with the new. Since this year's performance is next year's target, and since implementing new processes may interrupt current schedules, nibbling away at possible bonuses from above target production, and since, if innovation fails, the risk to the manager of lost status is very high, innovation is discouraged and the destruction of old technology by a new one fails to occur.

Most of Levine's analysis is applicable to any public sector in the world but also to any large, bureaucratic organization whose future existence is important for the achievement of state goals, be they employment or national pride. Given the past behavior of governments in bailing out large business firms in the private sector, from Rolls Royce in England to AEG-Telefunken in Germany to Continental Illinois in the United States (and hundres of like firms all over the developed world), it is at least unclear whether the managers of all large firms do not feel that the state will bail them out.

There are, however, certain public sector characteristics that impede innovation that are peculiar to it. First, opportunities for new programs are limited. Existing service levels cannot be cut without adversely affecting countless vested interest groups, and substantial real increases in governmental revenues are unlikely, as the public is unwilling to pay an increasing proportion of its income to the public pool. A private firm can decide to embark on a new program and limit its objective so that they can be achieved much more easily than the public sector can. Moreover, a private firm can work on a new program in a relatively complete secrecy, while the work of the public sector is carried out under the corrosive glare of the press (Bower 1983). In addition, many innovations are destructive to some interest groups that resist their introduction. The public sector is expected to take into account these views and pressures much more than the private sector does. In the process, the civil servants might lose their abilities to introduce any significant change.

Also unique to the public sector is the salience of public accountability. Public accountability in a democracy calls for openly declared facts and open debate of them by laymen and their elected representatives. Civil servants have the responsibility to reveal, to explain, and to justify their actions. They are expected to have authority for the exercise of discretion over resources made available to them in carrying out assigned tasks. They are also expected to render a report or a statement of the decisions and of the results arising from the exercise of their authority, together with whatever explanation is needed to justify the actions performed and the ends pursued. When the tasks assigned were not conducted satisfactorily, accountability means that discipline is exercised. Further, accountability means that every decision must be documented, explained, and approved by different echelons. It is not feasible under accountability rules to simply say: "I believe the need exists for a new product"—one has to document one's beliefs, prove them to one's superiors, and explain them to the state's auditing arm. Although accountability is extremely important, it might dampen creativity and innovation, at least when real major breakthroughs are contemplated. As already noted, at the early stages of an innovation, it is difficult to prove any need or even the existence of a market.

In addition, the public sector incentive system does not, as Levine noted, reward failures and may dampen innovation. Moreover, by the very nature of the democratic process, elected officials tend to have a short time horizon, looking for tangible results before the next elections. They can rarely afford the time or trouble to master the complexity of the situation. While the civil service provides substantial continuity, the pressure for quick fix solutions is strong, and again works against major innovation, all of which by their very nature require a long time for conception, development, and implementation.

Despite all these problems, public sector officials have often shown a strong tendency to innovate. Thus, during the first period of Mayor Lindsey in New York (for an analysis, see Yates 1977; Morris 1980) or during the Kennedy and Johnson administrations, innovative public programs and new management techniques have been attempted. Many of these were premised on a confident optimism that the most intractable and daunting problems would yield to the resolute onslaught of committed, rational, competent, and enthusiastic persons. In reality, however, many of these programs failed. Most governments invited management experts periodically, and these experts attempted to introduce methods of performance evaluation to the public sector. All these new attempts were hailed as revolutions, but they withered and vanished. New management techniques such as the zero-based budgeting, PPBS, MBO, and other attempts to introduce cost effectiveness methods were not as successful as was hoped, to a large extent because of the problems and impediments discussed above. Undaunted by the previous failures, new prime ministers or presidents have been trying again but so far with little success (for a survey and analysis, see Lynn 1981: ch. 4).

Should one despair and conclude that innovation and public sector are contradictory terms? I do not think such a conclusion is warranted. First, although many attempts failed, it is not immediately clear that the rate of failure of new innovations has been higher in the public than in the private sector. Public sector failures are well documented, but successful innovations consist of a minute proportion of the start-ups in the private sector, too. Many speculated revolutions never occurred (see *Science '84,* Jan.–Feb. 84: 34–43), and many new ideas turned into false starts and shattered hopes. Second, despite public cynicism resulting from the failure of previous—and heightened if not exaggerated—expectations, there are many examples of successful innovations coming from the public sector.

The public sector is generally accused of muddling through, and its institutional environment is perceived as encouraging minimization of risks and an incremental rather than innovative approach. Still, charismatic leaders were able to innovate new major programs, push them through the bureaucracy, and achieve fundamental changes. Think of such examples as Bismarck in Germany, who innovated and implemented the first public social security system; or President Roosevelt in the United States with the enormous basic changes in government and its structure he was able to introduce in the New Deal era, or of President Johnson's Great Society. Clearly, then, a great charismatic leader can create what Rosenbloom (1984) calls extraordinary innovation.

To be sure, in some cases the government behaved as a venture capitalist more than as an innovator. The NASA programs may be viewed in this way. Unfortunately, our definitions of terms such as innovation, creativity, or entrepreneurship are somewhat ambiguous to make a clear distinction.

We know from research on the private sector that different forms of organizations are important in allowing innovation to flourish. No organizational form is well suited for all purposes, and no organizational form consistently dominates all others. Much of the problems impeding innovation are a result of the organizational form and the incentive structure associated with it.

The public sector is composed of a plethora of ministers, bureaus, and enterprises. They each can have different structures. Innovation in the public sector can be achieved not only by charismatic leadership but also by different organizational forms, such as autonomous state-owned enterprises; different organizations for the delivery of services, such as the use of service vouchers; specialized interministerial agencies with formal authority, such as the French method of dealing with crisis situations; changes in the financial structure, reducing the centralization of resource allocation. In the rest of this paper, I shall concentrate primarily on the impact of organizational form on innovation and the role of the public entrepreneur.

PUBLIC ENTREPRENEURS

Innovation, creativity, and alertness to opportunities are needed to lead society to prosperity. The pervasive presence of state-owned enterprises (SOEs) across a broad ideological spectrum, their rapid expansion, increased significance, and the wide-ranging ramification of their performance to the achievements of economic, political, and social objectives—all caused a great interest in the methods used by them to set priorities in allocating resources among different objectives and in their role as innovators.

There are many examples in the SOEs that demonstrate the ability of these enterprises to innovate and allow entrepreneurs to flourish. An obvious example is, of course, the French theatres or the Austrian Opera: all are state owned and are certainly very creative and innovative. National lotteries are generally state owned, and some of them innovated new methods of distribution. In the public utilities field, British Gas was totally dependent on coal. It arranged with considerable enterprise the importation of liquified methane from Algeria. It also adopted an ICI invention and produced gas from naphtha with low capital and operating costs. This allowed British Gas to scrap carbonization plants: between 1963 and 1969 British Gas eliminated about half of its carbonization plants, increasing at the same time sales from 2.9 billion therms to 4.4 billion and output per equivalent worker by 43 percent (Pryke 1981). Volkswagen in Germany and Renault in France were certainly very successful, creative, and innovative organizations.

In the last two decades, European governments created SOEs in order to pick winners, moving to new high technology fields. Picking winners is intrinsically difficult and requires a mix of good information and good fortune. Yet, different governments have been promoting new and innovative industries. The Airbus is an obvious example of a very successful introduction of new technology and innovative design by an SOE. SOEs also innovated in computer designs (ICL in the United Kingdom) or in chips manufacturing (INMOS) as well as in many military applications. An innovation of a different sort has been continuously demonstrated by the French electricity SOE, Electricité de France. It innovated many new methods for the examination of pricing and of investments in a public utility. Its manager, Mr. Boiteux, is well known among economists for his new ideas on managing a public utility. EDF was also the first firm in France to volunteer and experiment on a new and innovative relationship between SOEs and government—agreeing on a "program contract" between the two parties. Under this method, the enterprise and the government sign a contract, specifying what is demanded from the enterprise, allowing the enterprise freedom to carry out its activities given these objectives.

In fact, entrepreneurs flourish in SOEs all over the world. Enrico Mattei, who turned the fledgling AGIP (up for sale by the Italian government) into the giant ENI, turned Italy around from being an oil-short country to one with energy surplus and innovating new contracts between the oil producing countries and the oil distributors, forcing "the seven sisters" to follow his footsteps. Ozira Silava headed a new organization that designed, developed, and built a Brazilian turboprop transport plane. Al Schwimmer did the same in Israel, building Israel Aircraft Industries. Robert Moses, who began his career in the state of New York in 1924 as the head of Long Island State Park Commission, was instrumental in creating many public enterprises over the next forty-four years of his career. Other SOE entrepreneurs include Pier Guliaalumet of the national oil company in France, Pierre Lafaucheaux who led Renault from third to first place in France and made the company a multinational, and Austin Tobin who was head of the Port Authority of New York for thirty years. Many more managers of SOEs have been successful entrepreneurs and innovators.

In the second BAPEG Conference, Basu reported that in India "public enterprises do not always exercise the powers delegated to them. To exercise these powers would be to assume too high a responsibility and expose them too much to the dangers of visible accountability" (Basu 1981). Bhatt (1982), however, at the same conference, reported a case study on the design of a new tractor, based largely on indigenous technology.

In most economic theories, the entrepreneurial function is a "black box." For Schumpeter, entrepreneurship was the novel recombination of preexisting factors of production where the outcome of this recombination cannot clearly be predicted (Nafziger 1977). Entrepreneurs refuse the temptation of a secure low risk return. They rarely reside in the large bureaucratic organizations, and they typically believe outcomes are contingent on their own actions (Ronen 1983). They are not gamblers, not necessarily inventors, but also not dealing only in routine and repetitive decisions. They need certain personality traits (Hagen 1975; McClelland et al. 1969; 1976), and are not necessarily owners of firms.

Some discussions of entrepreneurship have viewed the process as embedded in a competitive free market system (Kirzner 1973). In this century, entrepreneurs have changed the course of very large organizations, both private and public. To achieve change, organizations must be fluid rather than rigid, dynamic rather than static, and have organic structure (Burns and Stalker 1961). This view of organizations is important and has ramifications for their design, control, and performance evaluation. Specifically, since entrepreneurs believe outcomes are contingent on their own actions, they do not like to take into account risk-averse partners or controllers that would veto new ideas. Therefore, an SOE may lose its ability to innovate if all its activities are subject to close scrutiny, leading managers to share risks by committee decisionmaking structure.

In many cases, attempted solution for failure to solve a problem or to accomplish a task is to move the service to another organization. In several countries, post office departments were made autonomous agencies because of public complaints about the level of the service. Similarly, the U.S. government designed the Model Cities program to give responsibility to local authorities for objectives such as urban redevelopment and hardcore employment after having failed to achieve results itself. The new agencies may not have greater success in solving the problem, but the very act of reorganization shifts responsibility and gives the impression that a solution is about to be achieved. Such an experience may cause disenchantment. Still, the system design is extremely important. Hage and Aiken (1970), summarizing the existing literature on innovation, found that there are seven properties that tend to encourage the generation and acceptance of innovations in products and services. These are a high rate of professional specialists, decentralization, low formalization, low stratification, absence of high volume production, relatively low emphasis on cost reduction, and high job satisfaction.

Innovation is more likely when managers are motivated to achieve autonomy. In Kelly's (1982) terms, they should not be commissars. However, they should be less engineers and more men of vision. Even if these persons can be recruited to manage SOEs, it may well be that the structure—although allowing generation of ideas—may not allow their adoption and implementation. In several countries, the development of the telephone system was impeded by governmental restrictions of capital expenditures: telephone services are usually profitable, even lucrative, businesses. However, the funds generated by operations are generally diverted to the government. Often, the rate of change in that industry was bewildering to the civil servants. In the United Kingdom, for example, capital expenditures on new telephone equipment were restricted to a real level lower than that of 1937. As a result, the waiting line for new telephones zoomed. Moreover, as late as 1960, 15 percent of the total calls were still made through manual exchange and the British Post Office still used the Stroweger exchanges of 1899, long abandoned by the Bell system in the United States. (For details, see Harlow 1977.)

The Airbus project, already mentioned, also suffered from delays because of procrastination by governmental committees that had to finance it. Britain still has not decided how much it is willing to invest in the new A320. Thus, the hierarchical relations between SOEs and civil servants may impede or at least delay innovations.

Innovations may enhance the power of managers, who understand the new technology, relative to government controllers. Their professional knowledge enables these managers to control the resource allocation function. Therefore, power is an important consideration, to which I shall return.

Finally, success is not only due to the entrepreneurial drive of a single individual but also to the availability of alternative public-enterprise decision centers. Bhatt's analysis of the Indian tractor is relevant here: the idea was originally rejected at the national level before being picked up at the state level. It was then completed on schedule and at the cost envisioned; except for a strike, full-capacity operation would have been reached in three years as planned. Consumer acceptance and demand have been high, and innovation continued, with two new models introduced in four years. In this case and in many others, institutional pluralism substitutes for market competition in allowing innovation and in producing pressures for efficient outcomes.

In a hierarchy, the imperfection of information flows increases the uncertainty faced by top level decisionmakers. The presence of risk aversion at various levels tends to accumulate through the hierarchy, making the enterprise (and certainly the whole public sector system) more risk averse than any individual within it. The compounding effect increases with the hierarchy. In an SOE, the decision chain is typically long and discontinuous, including both the enterprise and the supervising government agencies (Tandon 1982). Lorsch and Allen (1973) have shown that the more diversity, the less likely it is that management will have the knowledge to understand detailed product/market issues. Therefore, their capacity to become involved in the substance of issues becomes very limited. In addition, their capacity to motivate through leadership will be limited by the fact that they lack the expertise that is one important basis for organizational power. Top management power is also limited by the resentment subordinate managers have to top management involvement in the substance of such issues. Meddling and interference is demotivating in the public sector as much as in the private one.

Berliner, regarding the Soviet Union, claims that "There are ways known to master bureaucrats all over the world of delaying, altering, reconsidering, and generally frustrating the intentions of higher agencies, and always supported by incontestable good explanations of why something cannot be done" (Berliner 1976: 56). By the same token, master bureaucrats, using the same methods, can frustrate the entrepreneurial drive of lower echelons, or managers of SOEs.

The entrepreneurs and innovators in the public sector are not motivated by pecuniary motives. Instead, they are driven by power, glory, prestige, the satisfaction of serving the country, and by high need for achievement. In fact, a common feature of state owned enterprises in mixed economies is a squeezing of pay scales. Workers are overpaid and managers are underpaid. The ratio of the net compensation (including all cash payments plus compensation in kind such as housing and transportation, but after taxes) of the lowest paid worker to the highest paid manager in the United States and the Soviet Union is 1:15 to 1:20. In most SOEs it is much lower. Still, to use Hirschman terms (Hirschman 1970) even though managers may voice complaints, they are loyal enough to continue instead of exercising their exit option.

There are at least three reasons why different managers are willing to accept lower incomes and manage SOEs. Some may derive satisfaction from serving the public rather than private interests. Others want to run large, modern capital-intensive enterprises, which in many countries are largely state owned; where large scale activities are not public, they are often in the hands of "family groups" where promotion opportunities for outsiders are severely limited. Third, to the extent that opportunities for promotion exist outside the public sector, the manager may perceive himself as constantly evaluated within a national market for managers where alternative job opportunities are traded. In this market, the manager's skills are evaluated. If the innovative manager is interested in the present value of his earnings, he does not succumb to temptation of "easy life" or of employing political strategies.

If indeed the last two explanations are the major reasons that attract the innovative managers, too much control may not only stifle initiative but cause them to go elsewhere. Professional managers become extremely frustrated when they see their efforts blocked by what they see as unnecessary bureaucratic interference that keeps them from managing "their" enterprise in an innovative manner.

To be sure, some of these public entrepreneurs, such as Moses of New York or Kenneth Abeyaickrama (who left a lucrative job as president of Unilever's subsidiary in Sri Lanka to turn around the ailing State Timber Corporation—see Ramamurti 1984) were independently wealthy. There were also those, such as Ibnu Sutowo of Pertamina, the Indonesian oil company, or Louis Tonti of New Jersey Highway Authority, who were found guilty of using their position to gain personal profits (Ramamurti 1984). These cases, however, are quite rare. SOE managers innovated and built empire because of high need for achievement. They may have been attracted by the ability conferred upon them to take high risks.

It seems that managerial discretion is the major numeraire of managerial rewards in SOE (Aharoni 1981a). To the extent that bonuses are not frequently used as reward mechanisms, "discretion"—the freedom to make bigger future decisions—may be identified as one type of career reward. Being successful, a manager gains a higher level of discretion in his present role, in a future role in the same organization (via promotion), or outside the organization—increase in his mobility (discretion in the selection of a future employer) and his alternative career opportunities.

Note that the risk to the manager depends on whether reponsibility is traceable. Whether, and to what degree, responsibility is traceable depends on the system design. The use of new and untested technology usually entails high project risk. From the point of view of the public manager, a success means promotion and prestige, but a failure may be regarded as an "act of God." On the other hand, the risk of system failure may be very low, but the risk to the manager is usually much higher, because of the publicity of such a failure. In an electricity generation firm, for example, the expected value of lost income resulting from a temporary system failure may be very low. Still, the managers of the firm may choose to install back-up generating capacity to avoid such incidents. The problem, therefore, is how to make innovation an acceptable risk not only to managers but also to their controllers.

MARKET FOR POWER AS FOSTERING INNOVATIONS

Competition has long been seen as the way to ensure efficient management and innovation. When competitive markets are not feasible, other markets may be used to achieve the same results. In the United States, there is a prevailing belief that competitive capital markets could substitute for other forms of competition in keeping management innovative and efficient. If management did not employ the firm's assets in an optimal way, the firm's stock price would drop. Entrepreneurial corporate raiders would then gain control of the firm through external takeover or merger and would revitalize the firm. SOE shares are not often traded on the capital market and government departments do not operate within the constraints imposed by such market. One can simulate, however, a competitive market in ideas, perception of goals and values by institutional pluralism.

One problem is to avoid resistance to change, commitments to unsuccessful decisions, hindrance to adaptation and innovation, and persistence of inefficiency. It is unlikely that governments (or headquarters of large, multidivisional, private firms) will not be committed to their point of view or to their previous strategic decisions. However, power may serve as substitute for economic markets. One may view SOEs, both within themselves and as part of a system of SOEs, as markets in which different individuals attempt to gain power and in which power is the transactions' medium of exchange. Pfeffer and Salancik argued that this view led to two implications: making information available to all participants, so that the market for power and control can work more efficiently; and keeping power and control relatively decentralized and diffuse, so that no single organizational actor or set of actors dominated the firm and could therefore institutionalize control and delimit the operation of political contests within the organization (Pfeffer and Salancik 1977: 23).

Such a design is possible in the public sector. A certain amount of conflict is built into the system. Competing perspectives — economic, social or political — are equally important and should not be subordinated one to another. This means that goal discrepancies between managers and controllers are, and should be, a fact of life. It also means that SOE managers would have more than one boss, with conflicting goals, preventing the concentration of control by a single interest.

A design of this sort may seem to fly in the face of at least some conventional beliefs about "unity of command." However, a similar design is used when projects, functions, and geographic divisions are organized in a matrix form (Davis and Lawrence 1977). Governments already introduced an internal "market" by purchasing social services from SOEs. In some cases, as in Sweden, the government does not have to procure these services within its own firms but can tender for the lowest bidder, thus permitting outside "supply" of these services. By the same token, different ministries may be allowed to "purchase" innovations. Under such a system, conflict, competition and some degree of power and political activities can be legitimized and institutionalized.

Power is an important feature in the public sector. The values, beliefs, attitudes, and ideology of different managers and different civil servants can be

heterogeneous; SOEs do not enjoy the legitimacy to operate solely as profit max-
imizers, nor do they have the resources nor the legitimacy to operate as a government bureaucracy, dispensing largesse without any regard for commercial
considerations. SOE managers, by the very nature of their job, have not only to
safeguard scarce resources but also to ensure public support and cater to diverse
demands made on them. They must recognize that their operations and their
decisions affect the interests of many groups, each of which promotes a different
set of goals. They have power because they control information and because,
assuming they are good managers, they are hard to find and difficult to replace.
Government controllers also have power, both because they often control needed
resources and because they can hire and fire the managers.

If firms are assumed to carry on routine, repetitive operations with no need
for adaptation and innovation, hierarchical structures may be appropriate. If
change occurs, however, there is very little on which to base an adaptive response. No one knows for sure at the time an innovative decision is made which
is a bad decision. In cases of this sort, an advocacy system, in which disagree-
ments are expressed and diversity of views and interests are structurally allowed
to surface may be the better design, leading to better results than the centralized "rational" systems often sought. The tendency of finance ministers all over
the world to concentrate power under their aegis may be less desirable than these
ministers would like us to think. Conflict is inevitable. It is also potentially productive by bringing into the open different points of view.

SOE managers sometimes create coalitions, sometimes present information
selectively, and often attempt to coopt. SOEs rarely operate vis-à-vis their environments in general and controllers in particular in the hierarchical structures
so often assumed. In natural selection terms (see Aldrich 1979), SOE controllers
face a dilemma in the choice between variation and retention. Structures in
which SOE managers will be left to carry on the operating decisions will have
very little variation in the decisionmaking and in tasks, but operating routines
are perfectly retained. In a world of uncertainty, need for change and for adaptation, here is a need for a great deal of variation and intrusion of other perspectives, not for unity of direction. Innovative operations need the creation of
specific markets for power, allowing experimentation and rewarding risk taking.
Such a system does not mean that the "center" is omnipotent, imposing "shad-
ow prices" and offering bonuses to get the right response. Rather it means that
different actors work together, accepting conflict as a way of life.

CONCLUSIONS

Accumulated evidence appears to indicate that economies of scale in the field
of public administration are illusory. A certain redundancy in the number of

agencies dealing with a problem does not necessarily imply inefficiency. Competition among the agencies may seem chaotic but may also result in better systems, more experimentation, and more innovation. Moreover, the larger the public sector, the more important it is to avoid the standardization and centralization of all systems, in order to preserve individual freedom. Thus, unless there is compelling evidence to the contrary, a number of competing agencies is preferable to one large agency.

If the managers of these different agencies are allowed discretion, and to the extent that they vie for power, innovation is encouraged. The rationale for the argument is very similar to that often claimed in favor of deregulation or liberalization: enterprises that are not subject to competition are subject to less pressure to innovate and to be efficient. In some cases, the desired results can be achieved by encouragement of competing private provision of services currently provided in a monopolistic fashion by the public sector: replacement of state-supplied free education by a voucher system, or private medical facilities competing with a national health service. Much more can be achieved by introducing competing publicly owned organizations and by creating a multiple system for approval of projects. Given the enormous size and scope of operations in the public sector, an improved mechanism for competition will lead to more creativity, more ideas, and more innovation.

REFERENCES

Aharoni, Yair. 1981a. "Managerial Discretion." In *State-Owned Enterprise in the Western Economies,* edited by Raymond Vernon and Yair Aharoni.

————. 1981b. *The No Risk Society.* Chatham, N.J.: Chatham House Publishers.

Aldrich, Howard E. 1979. *Organizations and Environments.* Englewood Cliffs, N.J.: Prentice Hall.

Basu, P.K. 1981. "Linkage Between Policy and Performance: Empirical and Theoretical Considerations on Public Enterprises in Mixed Economy LDCs." Second BAPEG Conference, April.

Berliner, J. 1976. *The Innovative Decision in Soviet Industry.* Cambridge, Mass.: MIT Press.

Bhatt, V.V. 1982. "Decisions Structure, Technological Self-Reliance, and Public Enterprise Performance." In *Public Enterprise in Less Developed Countries,* edited by Leroy P. Jones. New York: Cambridge University Press.

Bower, Joseph L. 1983. *The Two Faces of Management: An American Approach to Leadership in Business and Politics.* Boston: Houghton, Mifflin.

Burns, Tom, and J.M. Stalker. 1961. *The Management of Innovation.* London: Tavistock.

Crozier, Michel. 1964. *The Bureaucratic Phenomenon.* Chicago: University of Chicago Press.

Davis, Stanley M., and Paul R. Lawrence. 1977. *Matrix.* Reading, Mass.: Addison-Wesley.

Doz, Yves L. 1976. *National Policies and Multinational Management.* Unpublished DBA thesis, Harvard Business School.

Goodman, Richard Allan. 1984. "A Comparison of Industrial Policies in Five Nations: Brazil, France, Germany, Israel and The Netherlands." In *Planning for National Technology Policy,* edited by Richard Allan Goodman and Julián Pavon, pp. 138–54. New York: Praeger.

Hage, Jerald, and Michael Aiken. 1970. *Social Change in Complex Organizations.* New York: Random House.

Hagen, Everett Einar. 1975. *The Economies of Development.* Homewood, Ill.: Irwin.

Harlow, Christopher. 1977. *Innovation and Productivity Under Nationalisation: The First Thirty Years.* London: Political and Economic Planning and George Allen and Unwin.

Kelly Escobar, Janet. 1982. "Comparing State Enterprise Along International Boundaries: The Corporacion Venezolana de Guyana and the Conphanie Vale do Rio Doce." In *Public Enterprise in Economic Development,* edited by Jones, pp. 103–127.

Kirzner, Israel M. 1973. *Competition and Entrepreneurship.* Chicago: University of Chicago Press.

Levine, Herbert S. 1983. "On the Nature and Location of Entrepreneurial Activity in Centrally Planned Economies: The Soviet Case." In *Entrepreneurship,* edited by J. Ronen, pp. 235–67. Lexington, Mass.: Lexington Books.

Lorsch, Jay W., and Stephen A. Allen. 1973. *Managing Diversity and Interdependence.* Boston: Harvard Graduate School of Business Administration, Division of Research.

Lynn, Lawrence E., Jr. 1981. *Managing the Public's Business: The Job of the Government Executive.* New York: Basic Books.

McClelland, D.C., and D.G. Winter. 1969. *Motivating Economic Development.* New York: The Free Press.

McClelland, D.C., John W. Atkinson, Russel A. Clark, and Edgar L. Lowell. 1976. *The Achievement Motive.* New York: Irvington.

Morris, Charles R. 1980. *The Cost of Good Intentions: New York City and the Liberal Experiment, 1960–65.* New York: Norton.

Nafziger, F. Wayne. 1977. *African Capitalism.* Stanford, Calif.: Hoover Institution Press.

Nelson, Richard R., ed. 1982. *Government and Technical Progress: A Cross Industry Analysis.* New York: Pergamon Press.

Pfeffer, Jeffrey, and Gerald R. Salancik. 1977. "Organization Design: The Case for a Coalitional Model of Organizations." *Organizational Dynamics* no. 6: 15–29.

Pryke, Richard. 1981. *The Nationalised Industries: Policies and Performance Since 1968.* Oxford: Martin Robertson.

Ramamurti, Ravi. 1984. "The Public Entrepreneur and the Public Sector." Paper presented at the 44th Annual Meeting Academy of Management, Boston, August.

Ronen, Joshua, ed. 1983. *Entrepreneurship.* Lexington, Mass.: Lexington Books.

Rosenbloom, Richard S. 1984. "Managing Technology for the Longer Term: A Managerial Perspective." Paper presented at Harvard Business School 75th Anniversary Colloquium on Productivity and Technology, March 28–29.

Tandon, Pankaj. 1982. "Hierarchical Structure and Attitudes Toward Risk in State Owned Enterprises," in *Public Enterprise in Economic Development,* edited by Jones, pp. 245–56.

Yates, Douglas. 1977. *The Ungovernable City.* Cambridge, Mass.: MIT Press.

Chapter 13

GOVERNMENT, EFFICIENCY AND THE SOCIAL MARKET Alternative Approaches for Delivering and Financing Social Services

Michael J. L. Kirby

INTRODUCTION: THE NEED FOR ALTERNATIVES

In all western industrialized countries, government has become the largest single actor in the economy and the principal provider of the wide range of social services that are the hallmark of the welfare state. Most of these services were started in the period between 1950 and the early 1970s when government revenues were expanding rapidly and it was believed by both politicians and the public that government could afford such services and that it was morally just that they be provided.

The recent recession, however, with its severe impact on the rate of growth of government revenues, has strained to the limit the ability of government to continue to fund social programs at their existing levels of service, much less to expand them or add new services. As deficits continue to rise and debt service charges consume an inordinate share of the tax dollar (in Canada, approximately 33¢ of ever tax dollar paid to the federal government goes to pay interest on the federal debt), the problem of financing social expenditures, which are often purposely counter-cyclical, becomes increasingly serious. This problem is not unique to Canada but is besetting to a greater or lesser degree all advanced capitalist industrialized economies.

Moreover, none of the solution options usually proposed—raising taxes, borrowing more, or slashing spending—is very attractive politically. There are no simplistic solutions for solving the fiscal imbalance conundrum. What is needed are innovative approaches to both the management and the delivery of the social services that citizens have come to expect and the majority of voters believe a modern, civilized society ought to provide.

How prescient the words of President John F. Kennedy (speaking to a White House Economics conference in May and a Yale graduating class in June 1962) now sound:

> The central. . .problems of our time. . .do not relate to basic clashes of philosophy or ideology, but to ways and means. . .sophisticated solutions to complex and obstinate problems. What we need are not labels and clichés but more basic discussion of the sophisticated and technical questions involved in keeping a great economic machinery moving ahead. . . . Political labels and ideological approaches are irrelevant to solutions. . . . Technical answers—not political answers—must be provided.

THE PUBLIC MOOD

In Canada, as in the United States, there is a growing public demand that governments be trimmed in size. Indeed, there seems to be an expectation among some Canadians that a sharp reduction in the scope and size of government is imminent. This belief assumes that the deteriorating public attitude toward government represents a pronounced shift to the right; that Canadians strongly desire government to cut back on services and programs, to get out of many activities in which it is now engaged; and it assumes that this will be the prevailing political mood of the 1980s.

My own reading of the situation is that this *not* the case—at least not yet. What has been missed in all the ferment about Proposition 13¹-style proposals is this: whenever people are polled about reducing government expenditures they are all for it. Yet when the question turns to what specific functions or services should be curtailed or eliminated to achieve this reduction, the only area of government spending in which Canadians have consistently shown a desire for cutbacks is the area of welfare. To the average Canadian, this term means payments to people who are unwilling to work. Unemployment insurance payments get attacked, not because Canadians are against assistance to those in need, but because of the widespread belief that thousands of people are "ripping off' the system by taking advantage of hard-working Canadians.

Of those who insist that government deficits are too large or that government spending is too high, well over 80 percent also want to maintain or increase public spending to clean up the environment, to improve the nation's health, and to strengthen assistance programs for the elderly and the disabled. This support comes from people in all economic groups, and in all regions, regardless of political party affiliation.

When asked to explain this apparent inconsistency in their attitude toward government expenditures, Canadians say they are absolutely convinced that government could do more with less money. To prove their point, they single out the government services with which they personally deal and which they perceive as inefficient (the Post Office and Customs, for example). They then assume that the rest of the bureaucracy must be equally inefficient.

Canadians believe that if government was better managed, current services could be provided much more cheaply than they are now. This is not a desire for less government, but for more efficient, effective government.

On the basis of these observations, I have concluded that while the public accepts the need for some expenditure restraint, they also remain firmly committed to the concept of the service state. Voters do not want government to retreat, but to reform.

The Challenge

In short, the welfare state is being challenged to become more productive and cost effective in its delivery of goods to the social market. It is in this area that creative and innovative management is urgently needed.

To borrow a phrase from a former Canadian Auditor General, taxpayers rightly expect value for money — economy, efficiency, and effectiveness — in the delivery of social services. In a time of limited federal tax dollars and uncertain economic growth, the search for alternative more-for-less modes of service delivery is imperative. This means reappraising concepts of public services that have become strongly entrenched.

In the following sections we look at issues involved in such a reappraisal. We also examine several of the innovations (e.g., contracting for municipal garbage collection services, voucher systems for education) that have been tried, principally in the United States, and could have important implications for future public policy in Canada and elsewhere.

PUBLIC GOODS AND PRIVATE INTERESTS

In private markets, under optimum conditions, the consumer supposedly reigns supreme. Given free entry and freedom of choice, the invisible hand of the market will tend to produce a natural balance or equilibrium of the demand

and the supply sides. The most efficient allocation of resources will occur when consumers pay the full marginal cost for goods and services. In this way, only as much will be produced as consumers are prepared to buy. Competitive prices will reflect the true preferences of purchasers.

Of course economists' models rest on a number of assumptions that may not (indeed often do not) obtain or can at best be approximated in the real world. For example, the above model assumes perfect competition among suppliers, equality of participation in the marketplace, and the rational calculation of self-interest by consumers based on reliable information. It also assumes that the fairest, most efficient distribution of benefits results when everyone is free to maximize his or her private interests.

Government intervention is justified to the extent that these assumptions break down — in cases of "market failure" where no private supplier would be willing to undertake the costs of providing a necessary service (e.g., postal delivery to remote communities), in cases where there are significant positive "externalities" (e.g., the pursuit of a clean environment, which enriches society at large), and in cases where there are common goods which are not reducible to individual interests (e.g., maintaining national defense). Government intervention may also be necessary to enforce competition and to protect consumers in the marketplace.

One of the most ancient aims of government is to protect the weak against the strong so that laissez-faire does not result in "survival of the fittest." Gains in microeconomic efficiency may have to be traded off against the larger considerations of social justice and a more equitable distribution of income, regional employment opportunities, and so on.

In short, government intervention may be required to ensure that the externalities and distributive effects of the market system are socially and politically acceptable. As the noted economist Joan Robinson has stated, externalities and distributive effects cannot be dealt with by economic theory, yet they are the main things which are of interest to politicians.

Particularly where the output of services affects the well-being of society as a whole — as is the case with many social services — there is a strong argument that the delivery of such public services ought not to be operated solely with respect to the bottom line. There are many overriding social policy objectives, as well as practical reasons, that preclude the delivery of social services on a completely user-pay or self-financing basis.

In an important recent book, Neil Gilbert, Professor of Social Welfare at the University of California, Berkeley, explains the crucial differences between the private economic and the social markets that coexist in an uneasy balance within welfare capitalism:

Capitalism encourages competition and risk-taking behavior. Although success in the economic market-place is often well rewarded, misfortune and failure can lead to harsh consequences. There are few market mechanisms to mitigate the consequences of accident, illness, age, and vicissitudes of industrial society. And these mechanisms, such as private insurance, provide the most protection to those who are relatively well off and least in need of it. The welfare state operates through a social market that provides a sort of communal safety net for the casualties of a market economy. Ideally, as a system for distributing benefits in society, the market economy responds to individual initiative, ability, productivity, and the desire for profit. In contrast, the social market of the welfare state responds to need, dependency, and charitable impulses.[2]

Gilbert notes that at least since the 1970s the United States has been entering what he refers to as a third stage of welfare capitalism. Canada, too, has entered this third stage, although somewhat more recently than the United States.

In the first stage, providing for the social costs of industrialization was largely left to the initiative of enlightened business elites who could see the connection between a stable, healthy, well-housed work force and higher productivity. There were huge gaps in this paternalistic, voluntay social safety net that gave way completely with the onset of the Great Depression.

The second stage was that of the New Deal, which legitimized the direct shortcomings (both cyclical and structural) in the economic market. Over several decades the New Deal led to the direct, and in some cases mandatory, government provision of many social services. A massive federal bureaucracy grew up to oversee and administer the myriad of social programs and statutory entitlements.

In the third stage of welfare capitalism, a series of checks and balances operate to curtail the expansion of the centralized welfare state. In this stage, Gilbert sees a convergence of the social and economic markets as governments face increasing competition from the private sector in many areas of social service delivery. This development owes as much to the widespread feeling in both Canada and the United States that the pendulum has swung too far away from financial discipline, local control, and freedom of choice, as it does to President Reagan's New Federalism, which aims to diminish the federal role in the financing and delivery of programs.

It is precisely this entry into the third stage of welfare capitalism that has sparked the need for innovative approaches to the management and delivery of social services.

Criticisms of Current Delivery Systems

Whatever the effects of the apparent trend toward partial commercialization in the social services field (we will discuss some of the negative effects later), it is clear that existing bureaucratic arrangements have been perceived by many as inflationary, overcentralized, needlessly large, complex, and inefficient.

Government-run monopolies are being criticized for the sort of paternalism and fostering of dependency that characterized the first stage of welfare capitalism. There is also concern that the notion of free universal services complicates the task of making optimum allocations of scarce resources within the social market.

Loss of recognition of true costs due to high levels of subsidy can lead to the overconsumption or overproduction of some services and to the rationing of others. Might the consumer of social services not be better off if, instead of direct government subsidies or subsidized services, he were given equivalent compensation (e.g., in the form of lower taxes, food stamps, or education, day care or housing vouchers) that would allow him more scope to make choices in his own best interests?

The argument that user charges coupled with cash transfers would result in more efficient allocations than government-controlled subsidies rests on similar assumptions to those of the private economic market.[3] The basic idea is one of untying government assistance and transferring instead more discretionary income to individuals. In its purest form this is Milton Friedman's proposal for a negative income tax to replace all forms of direct government intervention in the social market.

Since the costs of such a system to government could well be as great, the issue is less one of restraint than of regulated monopoly versus competitive choice. The theory is that the sum of individual choices is superior (in terms of efficiency and Pareto optimality) to any centrally planned system.

In practice this theory faces many challenges in its application to social services. In such services, social costs and externalities are often very high, making user charges at best a partial solution. Such charges may simply be a way to increase revenues to government or to service providers with no trade-off in more efficient resource use.

In addition, some consumers of services (e.g., the sick, the mentally incompetent) are in no position rationally to calculate their self-interest but must rely on the good judgment or expertise of service-providers. Moreover, many social problems require cooperative resolution and action "in the public interest."[4]

The provision of public services also entails values other than efficiency, such as universal access and equality of treatment.[5]

Finally, the introduction of competitive forces into the social market will be strongly resisted by the monopoly sector, by public service unions, and by those who benefit most from existing subsidies, quotas, regulations, and other forms of direct intervention. To paraphrase a point made earlier: no matter how much a citizen favors a policy of greater competition in the marketplace for social services, he likes nothing so little as its application when it affects him personally.

Without understanding the difficulties inherent in the character of the social market, there remains a strong case for reforms that seek to give consumers of social services more value for money and more control over the decisions that affect their lives. There has to be a balance struck between the values of equality and universality and those of choice and efficiency. A mere proliferation of costly government social programs will not solve the dilemmas of social policy in the 1980s.

SERVICE DELIVERY: THE OPTIONS

What does this mean for the management of government in the 1980s? It means, first and foremost, that the way in which many goods and services are provided may have to be changed. This does not mean that I support the simplistic argument that more services for the public should be provided by the private sector (even if they are financed by government) because the private sector is always more efficient, for I do not believe that this is necessarily the case (see below).

Moreover, public sector versus private sector is far too simple a dichotomy to represent adequately the spectrum of ways in which services can be delivered, for in most cases there are several different mechanisms that can be used. Let me give some examples.

At one end of the spectrum, a government department or crown corporation[6] can be used to deliver a service directly to the public—as CN Marine provides ferry services, for example.

Secondly, a service can be contracted out from one level of government to another, as RCMP police services are contracted out by the federal government to most provincial governments.

Thirdly, a service can be contracted out to private sector companies or private nonprofit agencies, municipal garbage collection in Halifax being an example.

Fourthly, a private company can be granted the exclusive right to provide a service under regulation, as is the case with Bell Canada telephone service in Quebec and Ontario.

Fifthly, the government can sell an exclusive franchise to provide a service to the highest bidder. This means of service delivery is not used much in Canada but is the way in which cable television licenses are granted in some cities in the United States.

A sixth delivery mechanism is a subsidy to the provider of a service to permit the service to be sold at a lower price than otherwise would prevail. Universities are a good example here.

A seventh mechanism is the voucher system, giving the subsidy to the consumer rather than the producer. This approach is more widely used in the United States than it is in Canada, food stamps or housing vouchers rather than subsidies to home builders being examples.

An eighth approach is to have a service delivered through voluntary associations, such as volunteer fire departments.

A ninth approach is self-service, or noninstitutionalized forms of self-help — for example, hauling your own garbage to the municipal dump as happens in many parts of rural Canada.

A tenth mechanism is the free market, whereby the consumer of a service purchases it directly from any one of a multitude of suppliers.

The role of government is different in each of these delivery mechanisms, as are the roles played by the private sector and the consumer. The mechanisms differ in their degree of competition and of consumer choice, and the mechanisms have different economies of scale, hence the unit cost of delivering the service will vary with the delivery mechanisms that is used. The delivery mechanisms also differ in their political characteristics; each results in different winners and losers.

Moreover the ten delivery mechanisms are not mutually exclusive. As E.S. Savas has pointed out,[7] multiple and compound arrangements are also possible. For example, in Indianapolis five different arrangements are utilized for the collection of municipal refuse: municipal service, contract service, voluntary service, free market, and self-service. Compound arrangements are also possible, such as a franchised bus line that receives an operating subsidy from a state or local government.

Since the ten delivery mechanisms (and their variation through multiple and compound arrangements) differ in a variety of ways, the question arises: which is best for a particular service and why? Or put another way, how does one choose among the mechanisms to ensure that a service is provided as efficiently and effectively as possible?

There are no easy answers. Indeed, this is the area where considerable research, experimentation, and innovation are needed. Governments have been unimaginative and have not experimented sufficiently with alternate delivery mechanisms for a given service.

Public Meets Private I:
The Case of Municipal Refuse Collection

There is one service — solid waste collection service — that has been studied extensively in over 300 North American cities, including several in Canada. If the results of the study be E.S. Savas[8] are any indication of what can be learned by systematically examining alternative methods of delivery, then much reform is possible. Let me illustrate.

The study showed that for cities with populations larger than 50,000, the cost of garbage collection by municipal employees is 60 to 70 percent higher than the cost of contracting these services out to the private sector. (The free market option is even less efficient than the public sector monopoly because of lack of coordination and diseconomies of scale, separate billings, etc.)

However, the study also demonstrated that if garbage was contracted out to a single private sector firm (so that a private monopolist rather than a public monopolist was providing the service), the private sector service was every bit as inefficient and costly as the service provided by the municipality itself.

Thus the study showed that it is the *competitive* environment that provides the appropriate incentive for efficiency, not merely the fact that the service is provided by the private rather than the public sector. After all, private sector employees are not *inherently* more efficient than their public sector counterparts; their efficiency depends on the circumstances under which they are operating.

In order to achieve a 70 percent reduction in garbage collection costs, it was necessary for a city to be divided into regions or districts, with the right to collect garbage in a region being awarded on the basis of competitive bidding by a number of private sector firms. In addition, municipalities with the lowest average garbage collection cost found it useful to have the garbage in one district collected by municipal employees, so that the municipal government would have some feel for the true cost of collecting garbage. In this way, the private sector competitors in other regions would be dissuaded from colluding to raise their bids beyond a level that gave them a reasonable profit.

As Savas points out:

Montreal has a splendid system of both snow removal and refuse collection. They break up the city into small areas. They contract out under vigorously competitive conditions. About 10 per cent of the work is done by municipal agencies, which prevents collusion among the private suppliers and gives the city the ability to move in, in case a contractor's performance starts to decline, and to expand its own operation in case there is collusion and the price of the private contractor starts going up. The result is high quality service at very low cost. Comparing Montreal to American cities in terms of cost per capita, it has the lowest refuse collection cost of any major city. . . .[9]

Savas discounts the fear that marketplace competition will lead to layoffs in the public sector and a net loss of jobs. He argues that it makes no sense to subsidize inefficiency. Instead, if public job creation is the goal, the savings from increased efficiency can be used to create these jobs by providing additional services.[10]

As the Montreal example illustrates, competitive systems allow for flexibility in choosing an appropriate mix of public and private participation and in choosing among financing and delivery alternatives. A summary of the advantages of mixed systems would include increased efficiency, decreased vulnerability to employee actions and contractor failures, protection against monopolistic behavior, yardsticks with which to measure and compare performance, and improved knowledge of service delivery and what can be achieved through innovation. Savas concludes:

> Good management of public services requires more than tidy organization charts. The implicit belief that the public interest requires public services to be delivered by public agencies has given way to the recognition that the private sector is able to deliver services effectively and efficiently while under contract to public agencies. It is appropriate to look ahead to the next step, and to recognize and appreciate the advantages of dual, mixed or competitive systems in which both the public and private sectors provide services, and where a competitive climate is deliberately fostered to improve the delivery of services. The evidence at hand rests firmly on a foundation of solid waste but the underlying principles appear applicable to numerous other public services.[11]

Garbage collection is not an isolated example of a government service that could probably be provided more efficiently by the private sector on a contract basis. The following list (derived chiefly from government examples in the United States) demonstrates how extensive the range of applications of contracted-out services can be:

- Computer services (Orange County, California);
- Lawyers to serve as public defenders (Phoenix, Arizona);
- Fire protection (notably Scottsdale, Arizona);
- Bus shelters (Houston, Texas, and elsewhere);
- School custodians (New York, New York);
- Hospital administration (Butte, Montana);
- Parking meter operations (Milwaukee, Wisconsin);
- Window washing in public buildings (Milwaukee, Wisconsin);
- Security for public buildings (Houston, Texas);
- Paramedical services (Hawthorne, California);
- Vehicle and fleet maintenance (Gainesville, Florida).

Vending machine services in public schools and urban transit systems are two of the other service areas where contracting-out is widespread. In each of these cases, better or equivalent services at reduced or similar costs were the objective of the exercise, and while the success of such an approach has been difficult to quantify on a national scale, particular instances of success are prevalent.

I have detailed this example because it underscores the point: there is a variety of different ways in which a government service can be provided more efficiently and effectively and these alternative service delivery mechanisms should be explored when government is deciding on the way in which a new or, indeed, an existing service will be delivered.

Revenue Dependency, Tax Credits, and Vouchers

Recently proposals have been put forward for ways to make the public sector more revenue dependent.[12] The concept of revenue dependency is to increase the economic efficiency of government departments and agencies, and other public institutions such as universities, by making them more dependent for their revenue on the sale of their services than on the revenue they receive through appropriations. In effect, revenue dependency is an attempt to apply the principles of "user-pay" to services currently provided directly by the public sector itself (including government departments).

Revenue dependency is based on four principles:

- The principle of full costing: public sector operations should be fully costed;
- The principle of revenue dependency: all services should be priced and sold on a fully costed, cash transaction basis; services provided by a department would increase or decrease depending on consumer demand for the department's services;
- The principle of direct competition: direct competition between public and private sector producers of a service should be fostered by eliminating the impediments created through existing governmental funding, regulation and administrative practices.
- The principle of consumer subsidization: to the extent that subsidization is required to equalize social and regional consumption patterns, such funding should be provided directly to the consumers of the service rather than to the producers of the service.

The essence of the case for revenue dependency is that the full costing, pricing, and selling of public services would provide for major increases in efficiency in their production, more competition among suppliers, thus better levels of service in their delivery and greater public choice in their selection of how and by whom the service would be provided. Because, under revenue dependency, these developments would be the only means of a government department ensuring operational survival in the face of competition from the private sector, the survivors would be the most economically efficient suppliers. This means that such a system would make government managers subject to the strong economic incentives that now exist only in the competitive business world. This would make at least part of government decisionmaking subject to the same kind of discipline that governs decisionmaking processes in the competitive private sector.

In short, revenue dependency would apply the lessons learned from the garbage collection example to a wide range of services that are now provided directly by government.

Using the private sector to deliver public goods is part of the drive for efficiency, decentralization, and a loosening of bureaucratic constraints that marks Gilbert's third stage of welfare capitalism. While restraining the growth of government is one objective, at least as important is that of enlarging consumer choice through a partial "deregulation" of the social market.

These two objectives—restraining of government growth and enlarging consumer choice—can be seen as complementary in the sense that done in this way government restraint leads to transferring decisionmaking power from public bureaucracies to consumers. It must be emphasized, however, that expanding consumer choice does not necessarily entail a reduction in the amount of money spent on social services. In fact, it could have the opposite effect.

There is also growing interest in alternatives "to supplant the public provision of social welfare services by tax credits, vouchers, and cash grants, which would enable consumers to purchase services of their choice on the private market."[13] Both tax credits and vouchers are sector-specific; that is, they have a structured exchange value within a designated service sector.

Tax credits are more progressive than tax deductions. But to benefit from such credits one must first have the money to purchase the service and, unless the credit is fully refundable, one must be in a high enough income bracket to owe taxes at least equal to the amount of the credit. Vouchers on the other hand are distributed prior to purchase.

In both cases—tax credits and vouchers—the recipient is free to choose from among any bona fide supplier of the particular service. In the case of straight income transfers, there are no strings attached as allocative decisions are entirely an individual responsibility.

Public Meets Private II:
The Case of Voucher Systems in Education

Economist Milton Friedman was the first to introduce the idea of educational vouchers in 1955.[14] Instead of funding schools directly, parents would be given vouchers equal to the average cost of educating a child in the public school sys-tem. There would be no restrictions on parents' choice of schools or on schools competing for the patronage of parents. Parents could supplement the vouch-ers with their own income if they wanted to obtain above-average schooling for their children.

Notwithstanding the inconclusive results in the United States, the idea of vouchers has recently attracted favourable attention in Canada. In a study for the Ontario Economic Council Glenn MacDonald and James Davies argue that the educational system must adapt and become more responsive to market forces.[15] They contend that, while government support for education is justi-fied on efficiency grounds because of positive externalities, central planning of educational choices is likely to be extremely inefficient.

Choices should be available to consumers of educational services which corre-spond to real job and income opportunities. For example, there should be more investment in on-the-job training that benefits a majority of school-leavers and children of low-income families. Rigidities in the post-secondary system (e.g., fixed fee schedules, quotas) should be reviewed so as to achieve a better fit be-tween (a) program offerings and enrollments and (b) changes in demand and employment prospects.

MacDonald and Davies see the growth of private schools as reflecting dissat-isfaction with the quality of state-provided education. Their solution is to open up the whole system to competition with the goals of efficiency and equity being served through government transfers to individuals rather than to education providers:

> The point of the voucher and tax credit schemes is that they would force schools to adopt efficient methods of production and induce them to innovate to offer programs attractive to students. In equilibrium one would expect to find that certain 'bad' public schools would disappear while others become 'good'; 'good' schools would be-come larger, and the relative importance of private schools would grow. The result is predicted to be a general improvement in the quality of education, with no need for increased state expenditure.[16]

Richard Bird and Enid Slack make the further argument that the only way to justify increased funding for education may be to make it more responsive to consumer demand. They concur that vouchers provide the best market-oriented alternative to monopolistic bureaucratic provision of education while retaining the compulsory and subsidization aspects of the present system.

The amount of vouchers could be made inverse to income, so that "the de-gree of redistribution through education could even be enhanced."[17] Bird and Slack admit that in an unequal society the rich would still be in the best posi-tion to take advantage of educational opportunities. But they suggest that "the opportunity to create centers of different kinds of excellence will no longer be confined to the very well-off alone, which in turn might be taken to improve opportunity."[18]

The idea of vouchers is not new. (Housing vouchers have been proposed since 1935.) But there is renewed interest in such schemes as part of a trend toward giving recipients of government assistance more choice over how they use this assistance to obtain services.

Vouchers can be viewed as a compromise between in-kind transfers, in which allocations are the result of decisions made by government elites and service-providers, and simple cash transfers in which there is a concomitant transfer of discretionary power to individual consumers.

For a number of practical and policy reasons, voucher systems would have to operate within some important guidelines—for example, there is the question of accountability and the assurance that the assistance provided is in fact used to improve the standard of service (in education, housing, or any other sector of the social market).[19]

The use of vouchers involves to some extent "privatizing" decisions with respect to large sums of public money. For voucher systems to be politically acceptable it must be demonstrated that the indirect beneficiaries—the private service providers—can be trusted to increase services, not only profit margins, and that the direct beneficiaries can be trusted to make choices that in the aggregate are consistent with the overall objectives of social policy.

Much of the debate on social services delivery systems that will take place in Canada and the United States during the next few years will focus around these two issues of trust—trust that the private sector service providers will not charge excessive prices, and trust in the collective wisdom of service beneficiaries. Because these issues are not capable of being resolved analytically in advance of new delivery systems being tried and practiced, the political debate on these issues will almost certainly be couched in ideological rather than analytical terms. Unfortunately, this will do little to illuminate the issues involved.

The Dangers of Excessive Privatization

Over the last decade in the United States, Neil Gilbert concludes, "the distinction between financing of services through the public and the private sectors of social welfare has faded close to the disappearing point."[20] He cites several specific developments that have encouraged this trend: the use of purchase-of-service arrangements whereby public agencies contract out to the private sector,[21] and the invasion of profitmaking organizations into the human services market.

The commercialization of this heavily subsidized social market is already very far advanced in some areas:

> Proprietary agencies are prominently represented in many social service program areas including: homemaker/chore, day care, transportation, meals-on-wheels, and employment training. The most conspicuous area is that of nursing home care. Between 1960 and 1970 the number of nursing home facilities increased by 140% and the number of beds tripled. Close to 80% of these facilities are operated for profit; public funds, mainly from the Medicaid Act of 1965, account for $2 out of every $3 in nursing home revenue. This area of service is typically referred to as the nursing home "industry": the child-care "industry" looms just over the horizon.[22]

The case of nursing homes and private hospital chains, some of which have evolved into huge multinational enterprises, shows that there are handsome profits to be made in the social market and that large corporations may be better placed to take advantage of economies of scale and the environment of government subsidization and regulation than independent nonprofit and community-run institutions.

In fact, Bergstrand[23] signals the dangers of state subsidization being used to further corporate takeovers and "monopoly capitalism," adding that:

> Even if the monopoly sector of the health care industry no longer needs a governmental regulatory apparatus to enhance its growth, it is not true that they are therefore in favour of free enterprise. There is every indication, in fact, that they do not intend to put up with 'competition', and free enterprise to them means freedom to totally dominate their economic and political environment.[24]

Apart from the moral question of whether certain basic human needs should be exploited for profit, there are fears that corporate concentration could take place in the social market as it has in the economic market. This could well increase rather than control the costs of service delivery. In fact, the evidence presented by Bergstrand suggests the corporate health for profit does not effect real savings for society.

In comparing the Canadian and American systems, there is also the familiar argument that the Canadian public Medicare scheme provides much more complete and even-handed coverage at lower administrative cost than does the U.S. health care system. This would appear to be a major advantage that is often not fully addressed by those who favor a more "mixed competitive" approach.[25]

Moreover, profit-oriented service providers might be tempted to "skim off the cream" by focusing their attention on the most profitable clients. As Bergstrand cautions, the tendency is that:

> Expensive or 'unprofitable' patients will increasingly be 'dumped' on nonprofit and publicly supported hospitals with fewer private-pay patients to offset these losses.

The result will be an intensification of fiscal crisis among these hospitals, increased costs to the taxpayer, cutbacks in services to the poor, and eventually a two-class system of health care delivery.[26]

The consumption of many social services is not like other economic transactions. As Gilbert points out:

There is a charitable ethos associated with public and private nonprofit social welfare agencies that stands in contrast to the capitalist spirit of profit-making organizations.

'Caveat emptor' may be an appropriate principle to guide business transactions in the market economy. In the field of social welfare, however, where the consumer rarely purchases the service and is often in a vulnerable life situation, the responsibility for regulating the quality of service remains largely in the hands of the providers. It is here that the charitable ethos of nonprofit agencies is likely to exercise a positive influence on the quality of response to social welfare needs.[27]

The Dilemma of Social Service Delivery

Despite such considerations, there are strong pressures toward more competition, "entrepreneurial" innovation, and "consumer sovereignty" within social services delivery. Some of these pressures are coming from professionals in what have traditionally been considered nonprofit public services. Gilbert notes that:

Despite ideological reservations, private practice holds considerable appeal for many social workers. It is seen as a way to free professional practice from the bureaucratic constraints of agency settings. Cast in opposition to bureaucratic obstructions to service delivery rather than in pursuit of profit-oriented activity, attractions to private practice assume the moral legitimacy of being in the client's best interest. One argument, drawing upon the market economy doctrine, asserts that clients would additionally benefit from heightened competition among independent service providers, as social work practice shifted from bureaucratic to entrepreneurial enterprises. In the bargain there are, of course, increased professional recognition and financial rewards as an extra fillip to private practice. In regard to financial rewards, over the last two decades the growing prospects for reimbursement of social work services through third-party vendor payments provided by public and private health insurance schemes have intensified the lure of private practice.[28]

Recognizing these pressures and the arguments against impersonal bureaucracy, there have been experiments to expand individual and community initiative while remaining within a public agency setting. Gilbert gives the example of the Kent Community Care Project in Great Britain set up as an alternative to institutionalization of the frail elderly. The aim is to bring together public employees and their clients in such a way as "to tap the energies and resourcefulness associated with entrepreneurial activity."[29]

The challenge to large, centralized state-financed institutions and other public sector monopolies comes at a propitious time in terms of the post-Keynesian debate over the role and limits of government in general. Faced with fewer federal tax dollars relative to expenditures and a skeptical public, agencies whose mandate is to serve the public are being forced to innovate and to do so in a cost-conscious way.

Even foes of cutbacks in government social spending recognize the need to explore decentralized low-cost alternatives that can deliver services efficiently through empowering individuals, families, neighborhoods, and local communities to help themselves. Simply adding to public service bureaucracies is not necessarily the best way to reach those who need help the most.

Bertram Beck argues that the climate of retrenchment which has taken hold in the United States may, paradoxically, provide the opportunity to return to a more participatory, grassroots-oriented social service system that relates benefits directly to need and is therefore less beholden to a "middleman" elite of heavily subsidized service providers:

> For those for whom formal human services are required, service should not be shaped in Washington and then planted in the neighborhood. Those of us who resist Reagan need a new service plan. Such a plan cannot ignore the social and economic context in which services exist. Obviously federal taxation is needed to redistribute wealth, but there is nothing inherently wrong in block grants distributed in a fair and equitable manner. Returning power to local government, of course, required vigorous federal enforcement of civil rights, for without the parochial interests may deny benefits to the oppressed. A national negative income tax or Family Allowance Plan is a first step toward income redistribution that takes priority over redistribution of wealth by taking from the middle class to employ middle-class service providers.[30]

Bertram Beck makes the further comment that

> The growth in interest in what are called natural helping networks and self-help, which antedate the current (Reagan) Administration, represents a recognition that formal service structures manned by professionals may actually destroy the capacity of people — including families — to help one another. Is it not odd that Alcoholics Anonymous, which is practically without paid staff, is universally acknowledged as the most effective program dealing with a disability, while practically every effort to measure effectiveness of professional social counselling as a measure to reduce deviance has had a negative outcome?[31]

Some privatization of the social market is no doubt preferable to having all services delivered by government employees with little input from the public. However, a large degree of government intervention will continue to be justified on both equity and efficiency grounds. It is the form of that intervention that is increasingly at issue.

Mobilizing the private sector to deliver more public goods at less cost to government is a potentially progressive option but not an unproblematic one. Any radical reshaping of the current hodgepodge of social programs will not be easy. As already mentioned, it will be resisted by a wide coalition of client groups, bureaucratic, professional and other vested interests.

Social policy is especially sensitive to political pressures because it serves many different objectives and constituencies. Measuring its output—the comparative evaluation of competing delivery arrangements—is usually a difficult, risky exercise even when there are shared assumptions. When there are not (which is the case in liberal democratic societies such as our own), who, if not elected officials or social planners, should decide what is efficient or what is in the public interest?

Ideally governments, service providers, and consumers will act so that everyone is better off (or at least no one is worse off) than before. But in the real world of hard choices, one cannot assume that the social market will operate as a positive-sum game.

CONCLUSION: A RESEARCH AGENDA

In this paper I have argued that two factors—the size of government deficits and changing public attitudes—require that government become more efficient in the way it delivers services, particularly social services that consume the largest portion of the budget of all state and national governments in Western industrialized countries. But these factors do not automatically mean that government should stop delivering these services. Far from it. What the public wants is more efficient, effective administration, not necessarily fewer services.

I then argued that this will require that government review the ways in which services are delivered; that government should no longer accept in blind faith the assumption that public services must be provided by employees of government departments or agencies. Other methods of delivery exist, and they should be examined before a decision is made on how a service will be delivered.

I outlined ten different delivery mechanisms, each of which differs in its political characteristics, the choice it gives the consumer, and the economies of scale it permits. Moreover, combinations of these ten methods are possible, thus considerably enlarging the scope for innovation.

What is needed now is more experimentation and more research. Various hypotheses should be tested, as they were in the municipal refuse collection example. We need to test hypotheses such as:

- Efficiency will be the greatest where the consumer pays the producer directly for the service he receives;
- Total cost will be higher when government is the producer;
- Consumer satisfaction with a service will be greater when he is also the arranger of the service (i.e., makes decisions about when, how, and by whom it is provided).

These and other important policy questions represent a research agenda, for relatively little systematic work has been done thus far in this area.

The need for such research is demonstrated by the impact that the work of Savas on the municipal refuse collection has had on the way in which garbage is collected in cities in North America. Several have changed their method of collection as a result of Savas's research results.

This is an indication of the demand for this kind of research. It is also a challenge to the public policy-oriented management scientist. Clearly innovative management in government is needed today—needed perhaps more than it has ever been.

NOTES

1. California referendum dramatically reducing property taxes and, as a result, public services.
2. Neil Gilbert, *Capitalism and the Welfare State: Dilemmas of Social Benevolence* (New Haven: Yale University Press, 1983), pp. 4–5.
3. For a discussion of some of the issues relating economic utility to public services delivery see Richard Bird, *Charging for Public Services: A New Look at an Old Idea,* Canadian Tax Foundation, Toronto, Paper 59, 1976; Michael Krashinsky, *User Charges in the Social Services: An Economic Theory of Need and Ability,* Ontario Economic Council, Toronto, 1981; Krashinski, "User Charges and Government Restraint" in Aucoin, *The Politics and Managment of Restraint in Government,* The Institute for Research on Public Policy, Montreal, 1981.
4. The meaning of "the public interest" is not at all clear, in spite of its frequent use by almost every proponent of a particular government action. A few years ago W.T. Stanbury of the University of British Columbia compiled a list of twenty-three different definitions of "the public interest" that had appeared in the academic literature. Each definition was in at least partial conflict with the other definitions. As Humpty Dumpty retorted in *Through the Looking Glass:* "When I use a word [the public interest], it means just what I choose it to mean—neither more nor less."
5. Even the meaning of a term like "efficiency" is neither self-evident nor value-neutral. Krashinsky defines efficiency in economic terms as simply a matter of "getting the most output for the least input" ("User Charges and Government Restraint",

p. 201). But this assumes costs and benefits can be evaluated on the basis of universally accepted criteria, which is seldom the case where human service "outputs" are concerned. (See also the critical comments on the Krashinsky paper by James McNiven, op. cit., pp. 206–11). On the more general problems of defining social utility, with examples drawn from American public policy decisions, see Virginia Held, *The Public Interest and Individual Interests* (New York: Basic Books, 1970).

6. A crown corporation is a government-owned corporation.

7. E.S. Savas, "Public Policy, Systems Analysis and the Privatization of Public Services," in Brans, *Operational Research '84*, p. 94.

8. E.S. Savas, "Private Enterprise Alternatives to Public Services," in Aucoin, *The Politics and Management of Restraint in Government*, pp. 215–21.

9. *Ibid.*, p. 220.

10. *Ibid.*, p. 221.

11. E.S. Savas, "Intracity Competition Between Public and Private Service Delivery," *Public Administration Review* (January/February 1981): 51.

12. See, for example, A.R. Barley and D.G. Hull, *The Way Out: A More Revenue-Dependent Public Sector and How It Might Revitalize the Process of Governing*, Institute for Research on Public Policy, Montreal, 1980.

13. Gilbert, *Capitalism and the Welfare State*, p. 32.

14. Milton Friedman, "The Role of Government in Education," in Robert Solo, ed., *Economics and the Public Interest* (New Brunswick, N.J.: Rutgers University Press, 1955).

15. J.B. Davies and G.M.T. MacDonald, *Information in the Labour Market: Job-Worker Matching and Its Implications for Education in Ontario*, Ontario Economic Council, Toronto, 1984, especially chapters 4 and 7. (See also the comments of the authors cited in the front-page article in the *Globe and Mail*, 8 August, which followed the public release of this study.)

16. *Ibid.*, pp. 89–90. On this question see also M.E. Manley-Casimir, ed., *Family Choice in Schooling: Issues and Dilemmas* (Lexington, Mass.: Lexington Books, 1982).

17. Richard Bird and N. Enid Slack, *Urban Public Finance in Canada* (Toronto: Butterworths, 1983), p. 97.

18. *Ibid.*, p. 98.

19. Jill Khadduri and Raymond Struyk, "Housing Vouchers for the Poor," *Policy Studies Review Annual* 6 (Beverly Hills: Sage Publications, 1982): 550. (This study was first published in the *Journal of Policy Analysis and Management* 1:2 (1982): 196–208. See also Struyk and Bendick, eds., *Housing Vouchers for the Poor* (Washington: Urban Institute Press, 1981), pp. 555 ff.

20. Gilbert, *Capitalism and the Welfare State*, p. 7.

21. Under the 1974 Title XX amendments to the federal Social Security Act, private agencies were able to qualify for the states' 25 percent share of social service grants. In 1976 it was estimated that between 50 and 66 percent of the $2.5 billion spent under Title XX involved purchase-of-service arrangements, with little effort to distinguish between private nonprofit and proprietary agencies. With regard to the former, by 1980 federal programs accounted for over 50 percent of their total financial support. (Gilbert: pp. 8–9.)

22. *Ibid.*, p. 9.
23. See Curtis Bergstrand, "Big Profit in Private Hospitals," *Social Policy* (Fall 1982): 49–54.
24. *Ibid.*, p. 53.
25. See, for example, Ake Blomqvist, *The Health Care Business: International Evidence on Private Versus Public Health Care Systems* (Vancouver: The Fraser Institute, 1979).
26. Bergstrand, "Big Profit in Private Hospitals," p. 53.
27. Gilbert, *Capitalism and the Welfare State,* pp. 16–17.
28. *Ibid.*, p. 24.
29. *Ibid.*, p. 26.
30. Bertram Beck, "New Patterns of Service," *Social Policy* (Fall 1982): 2.
31. *Ibid.*

Chapter 14

NEW VISIONS FROM THE PUBLIC SECTOR

Bertram S. Brown

I take pride in this volume because much of its genesis took place between Robert Kuhn and me on a train ride from Philadelphia to Washington early in my presidency at Hahnemann University. At the time, Dr. Kuhn was serving as my creative and innovative management consultant. He was a major stimulus, pointing out ways to energize a complex organization such as a university — a place of high technology, opportunity, talent and competition. He made it clear that while mobilization of talent across the board, of departments and constituencies, was essential, it was also necessary to focus energies in an organized, visible manner.

Hence, as part of our program, he introduced the concept of building a sports science research center, modeled after the Soviet Union and East Germany. It was an extremely creative focus around which Hahnemann could rally, yet it failed to meet our high expectations.

At the time, the Olympics were coming up in Los Angeles, and we had several key Hahnemann alumni involved, such as Irving Dardik, who was chief physician of the U.S. Olympic Committee, and Tony Daly, who was the chief physician of the Los Angeles Olympic Committee. In addition, key faculty at Hahnemann were working on basic biology as it relates to high levels of human performance.

But, as we proceeded swiftly with the project, we soon faced the turbulence of the Soviet boycott, the issue of drug use by athletes, and other problems that, despite the support of Jack Kelley, the Philadelphian who was the likely candidate to succeed William Simon as president of the United States Olympic Committee, distracted us from raising adequate funds for scientific work.

However, built into our project was a plan to cut our losses in case of insufficient progress. I present the incident here as a learning experience, because planning for potential failure is a subject we should address in the context of creative and innovative management.

During our association at Hahnemann, Dr. Kuhn and I, on the aforementioned train ride, discussed the first conference on creative and innovative management, which we had both attended in Austin, when I was professor of Social Policy and Mental Health at the University of Texas. We looked at the concepts of creative and innovative management pioneered by George Kozmetsky and the broad arenas to which they could be applied in the private sector, public sector, the federal government, state governments, and companies big and small. During the discussion I raised the issue of the management of creative enterprises such as the Woodrow Wilson International Center, the Max Planck Institute, the Rand Corporation, and the scientific settings at the National Institutes of Health. What, if anything, I wondered, was special about the management of creative enterprises, whose primary goal is discovering new knowledge and new ways of thinking, rather than the production of automobiles, steel girders, and the like?

In Part VI we examine creative and innovative management in the public sector as compared with the private sector, which is not the same as looking at creative enterprises. But, it is an issue I am well familiar with, in the public sector as director of the National Institute of Mental Health for many years and now, in the nonprofit private sector, as the president of a university.

Creative and innovative management, public or private, government or nongovernment, is significant because resources are diminishing in the face of an exploding population. Forests and plains, water and food, are being used up faster than renewal and resupply can take place. The challenge of the day is creative and innovative management on a worldwide scale.

On a smaller scale, resources available for social service, health, and other human services are leveling off. Hence, as Senator Michael J.L. Kirby of Canada states so clearly, we must strive for greater efficiency in the use of our resources. The public demands the provision of services by the government and the public sector. The real demand is not for fewer services but for more efficient provision of services. And the major road to efficiency and proficiency is creative and innovative management.

If one looks at the two papers presented several differences emerge, to which I would like to add some from my own knowledge and experience. A primary difference concerns public accountability and visibility. There is a fishbowl-like public accountability for the leader in the public sector. There are no secrets. They are quickly found out because of investigative journalism. This problem does not exist in a private, family, or closely held corporation, where one has the chance to plan and think without public scrutiny and exposure.

Another aspect is that of rewards, of psychological motivations and payoffs. In the public arena, visibility and prestige are the reward, as opposed to the bottom line, the large personal income, the size and growth of the company, which constitute the reward in the private sector.

Managers in the public and private sectors have different power needs. The contrast is an interesting one. Most people in the public sector need their power to be visible, while most of their counterparts in the private sector need their power to be invisible, or visible only to an elite. There is, of course, some overlap, as in the case of Lee Iacocca, a leader in the private sector who wants to be known to the public. But, the basic difference in the constellations of power between leaders in the two sectors remains.

Examples can be illustrated by the contrasting management of the media. In the public sector, managing the press becomes a primary tool in accomplishing one's goal. By contrast, the private sector turns to the press as a secondary task for marketing and visibility. In the public sector you must be aware that the media is watching you, and you as the manager must manipulate and counter-manipulate it to accomplish your goals. In the private sector, you deal with the media either when you want to utilize it for a specific purpose or when you are playing defense.

A key issue in public sector management is the search to reduce overlap and duplication. Organizations or agencies pulling diverse programs together under a single rubric are created constantly. The National Science Foundation concerns itself with the nation's science. But, this is inherently difficult by the complex nature of things. Science obviously belongs to both health and education, for example, two cabinet-level departments. You cannot have health without science or education without science.

Moreover, overlap and duplication are necessary for innovation in the public sector. I learned in twenty years of experience in government that competing government agencies enabled researchers to obtain grants much more easily as administrative bureaucracies fought for power and prestige than if government had been streamlined for the sake of efficiency. Streamlining would be deadly for the innovative process.

I remember many a grant application in my own field, psychiatry, for training mental health manpower, that could not be funded by NIMH but could be by the antipoverty agency. It is a point of view that Dr. Aharoni expresses when he notes, "...success is not only due to the entrepreneurial drive of a single individual, but also to the availability of alternative public enterprise decision centers."

In the private sector, however, overlap and duplication are clearly the mark of inefficiency, leading to increased costs and reduction of profit, if not loss.

If we look at the public sector strictly from a single perspective, we shall be missing a great deal. As we examine creative and innovative management in the public sector, we must consider different cultures to get a complete picture. While there are regional cultures to consider, we must look at cultures in a more traditional national, or even anthropological way. If we want to add an important subject to our research agenda, we have to look at the public sector in the Soviet Union and others of the Communist bloc.

I had the opportunity to study the public sector in the Soviet Union close up. During my eleven years as deputy director and later director of the National Institute of Mental Health, I headed a division which participated in the U.S.– Soviet Health and Science exchange, which, in a sense, was a most delicate and difficult one because it concerned the use and misuse of psychiatry. (My study was published by the U.S. Senate Committee on Foreign Relations in preparation for the SALT talks.)

Subsequently, as a member of the Kennan Institute of Russian Studies, I read about the formation of the prison and slave labor camps and the extensive rocket and missile research conducted in the gulags. I had to face the fact that one can have great outbursts of creativity under the most barbaric conditions. It is a far cry from the careful, rewarding, nurturing, supportive ways of enlightened management. It would appear that a threat to life can make one think creatively and productively, using the brain as a tool in order to survive.

I would hazard a rather dramatic guess that studies of the holocaust and concentration camps would yield information about equally great creative acts by a small minority under extreme circumstances. This does not mean that I advocate the formation of slave labor camps in order to promote productivity. I am, rather, highlighting a unique research activity for those interested in creative and innovative management. I am suggesting a careful look at counterintuitive settings, particularly labor camps, concentration camps, prisons, asylums, and similar institutions, and the types of creativity that have taken place under dire circumstances. Comparing these with institutions such as the Woodrow Wilson International Center, the Rand Corporation, and Hahnemann University could make a dramatic contribution.

In looking at the psychology of creativity under trying circumstances, one overall concept I put forth is the use of the brain as an instrument for survival. Perhaps there are subsidiary issues, such as the use of creativity, fantasy, and dreams as a means of dealing with unbearable surroundings. For example, it was found that those who kept their pianistic and musical skills alive by playing with their fingers on tables for several years, practicing in their brains, took only six months to regain their former level of performance. Others, who had not kept their skills alive, found they had lost them forever during years of horror and mental and physical abuse.

Dr. Aharoni points out the lack of innovation and entrepreneurship in the Soviet Union, where the characteristics of the bureaucractic organization hinder innovation by striving for stability, strict hierarchical authority, and narrow specialization. This may explain the most glaring example of inefficient social and health services in a modern society. The Soviet Union is the only advanced industrial nation in which mortality in general and infant mortality in particular are climbing and where health in general is declining.

Having played a role in the genesis of this volume let me be so bold as to make a few suggestions for the next. They are topics that make excellent research issues to benefit creative and innovative management.

So far, little attention has been paid to sex differentiation. In what ways are women different managers than men? How are changing sex roles and mores affecting women's opportunities as managers? One got the impression from the first volume that creative and innovative management is the exclusive property of men.

Women and how they relate to creative and innovative management is but one subject we may wish to address, under the rubric of The Nature of the Person in Creative and Innovative Management. Another topic we should deal with is age. What is the nature of the aged who remain fruitful executives and leaders well into advanced old age? The current president of the United States is the oldest ever to have occupied the White House. Konrad Adenauer was chancellor of West Germany at eighty-nine. Remarkable musical managers such as Stokowski, Toscanni, and Ormandy continued productive lives into their eighties, as did Ben Gurion. Golda Meir exemplified both factors: a woman leading an active life in the international arena at an advanced age.

Conversely, what is the nature of the child prodigy in creative and innovative management? We have learned from creativity studies in physics that persons in their early twenties can make Nobel laureate-level contributions. What is the equivalent in creative and innovative management? What types of leadership come from the very young?

Finally, on a personal note, I suggest as another research issue, the successful leader and manger in the public sector who moves to the private sector and is often unsuccessful due to the change in environment. Such a person often cannot tolerate the lesser visibility and misses the goldfish bowl. Money is not as motivating as it had been thought. During my own experience in the private sector, I missed the lack of opportunity to share, in the cold light of harsh competition.

After moving from NIMH, where I had been a public figure, to the Rand Corporation and later to ownership of a for-profit health care corporation, I discovered in the private sector many aspects that felt good. I liked the fast pace of accomplishment; I liked the quick decision. It was important to move rapidly in order to obtain certificates to build hospitals.

But I found one aspect which, for me, became impossible. In twenty-five years of public service I had been socialized to share my knowledge as fast as I had acquired it. I wrote papers and books. I held consultations. At all times my raison d'être was to teach, to lead, to share.

Suddenly, I was in the private sector, where anything I shared would make my competition stronger. Suddenly, the motivation was to hold back. There even was a subtle reward for being duplicitous. Knowing something simple like a regulation number would make it easier for someone to look up the regulation, so why tell him or her? Let the person search instead of using the time to compete with me. To me, competition in the private sector meant that you mislead — and you must not look as if you are doing it. I found the competitive environment jungle-like, making me extremely uncomfortable. Eventually, I gave up the potential for personal wealth to go back and become a professor at the University of Texas before coming the Hahnemann, where my current position as president is similar in many ways to my role in the public sector.

For me, the shift from the public to the private sector was a trying experience, personally and psychologically difficult. My story is far from singular, although it goes against the trend. Most people move from business into government. But, there are a number of us academic-government-bureaucrats who moved into the private sector. I think such an experience is worth investigating for its implications for creative and innovative management.

In summary, creative and innovative management is a field that necessitates the gathering of experience and the development of a research agenda.

DISCUSSION

Bertram S. Brown

Yair Aharoni: The question of who does what is ideological. The United States tends to use more regulation and less government compared to more government and less regulation in other countries — and not enough studies have been done to show whether one system is better, more efficient, or more innovative. One innovation in the United States is to move the cost of the public sector to the private sector. The public sector in the United States is a smaller percentage of GNP than it is in some other countries. It is simply that certain things are done through regulation and as a result the cost in the national income figures shows up in the private sector not the public sector. You could theoretically have a system of national accounts in which the total cost of tax collection, as one example, would be written in the public sector. Under such an accounting system, the public sector of the United States would be much bigger because, in this example, the cost of the whole witholding system would be borne by the private sector. This is not a value judgment. I am just making the point that not all the costs associated with public programs are shown in the national income as part of the public sector. There have been many important changes in the public sector, especially the creation of new institutions, new enterprises, and new organizations. Government is striving to find both diversity and efficiency, to provide specialized needs with minimum costs.

Michael Kirby: Growth at the state and local level everywhere is essentially people. I'll give an example: the largest growth in federal employment in Canada has been in only two areas, accounting for about 95 percent of the growth in the last five years. One is RCMP, the Royal Canadian Mounted Police, who provide provincial police service; and two is postal workers, because every time you get a new suburb, you must deliver the mail.

On Dr. Aharoni's point, the reason you cannot look at international comparisons of government expenditures is not just the regulation issue; it's the tax expenditure issue as well. If, for example, you want to subsidize an oil company because its oil is a nonrenewable resource, there are two ways to do it. One is to tax the firm like any other firm and then give it a subsidy. If you do it that way, the subsidy will show up as a public sector expenditure. If, on the other hand, you give the oil company a tax break (so they can get the same amount on their bottom line), the government never collects the money and the subsidy does *not* show up on the public sector accounts. That is what I mean by a tax expenditure, subsidies not counting as public sector expenditures. And what we are finding in this so-called "era of restraint" is more and more governments using this system. It is like a value added tax. You can never find it unless you know the tax system. Since more governments are converting to tax expenditures instead of cash expenditures — not collecting tax revenues from companies and people for sundry reasons — international comparisons of government expenditures are becoming progressively more meaningless.

Robert Kuhn: What about the disruptions of political change?

Michael Kirby: The governance issue is the toughest issue facing all countries and the one in which, quite frankly, all of us are groping for answers. My concern, in particular, is that as problems become more complex, and the need for quick decisions becomes more crucial, and people are less able to understand the nature of the issues on which they have to decide, then people will look more and more for simplistic solutions. As a result we will see more and more ideological approaches from politicians and others who are attempting to market themselves. Unless government is improved, we will move over the next twenty years to a situation very much akin to what, in my view, has happened in the United Kingdom where they oscillate between a demagogue of the right and a demagogue of the left. (An ideological answer seems to be a total answer, and, however wrongheaded, such seems satisfying.) Violent ideological swings between radical extremes is a real concern of premiers, presidents, and prime ministers. This is what they worry about in private.

Bert Brown: A "big bang" innovation in government is sometimes called a political revolution.

Jack Borsting: In the private sector, one can shift organizational structure fairly easily. Such change is difficult to effect in the public sector.

Michael Kirby: Within any given government you can change the administrative bureaucratic apparatus. You can kill departments and create departments. Changing the political decisionmaking system is a much more complex problem, requiring constitutional amendments and other such political miasma. The problem, of course, is that any change creates winners and losers. And since losers do not like giving up power, they frustrate the system. If there's one overriding fundamental difference between the public sector and the private sector, it is that there is nobody in the public sector with the power to say "yes" and a hell of a lot of people with the power either to say "no" or at least to stall.

Comment: We have an entirely new sector of increasing importance in the United States—the private not-for-profit sector. It includes some of our most distinguished foundations and schools. How does the private not-for-profit sector compare to public or for-profit sectors, and where does its future lie in terms of creativity and innovation?

Bert Brown: A few years ago, Brian O'Connell (who had left the Mental Health Association) and John Gardner teamed up to form an "independent sector" that is moving along as a new institutional force. They are working on the issues of innovation, accountability, vigor, and so on. If we take the three giant sectors—for-profit, independent, and public/governmental—a matrixed research agenda begins to craft itself around the issues of innovation, management, differences, personalities, and we begin to see a taxonomy that lends itself to scholarly study.

Yair Aharoni: The importance and vibrancy of the independent sector is a good example why ownership is not always the most critical variable in explaining innovation. I think we ascribe too much to ownership. We talk about public sector versus private sector as if this dichotomy were the only variable to consider in our deliberations. We forget to take into account all kinds of other variables from competition to industrial structure to organizational structure, accountability, and so forth. I do not know of any research showing differences in academic excellence between universities in the public sector and universities in the private sector. I suspect this is true for hospitals, too. There are municipally owned hospitals, federally owned hospitals, private not-for-profit hospitals, private for-profit hospitals. Is the level of medical services different? I am not aware of any such data. We need rigorous analysis comparing similarities and differences between sectors. What are the variables that explain these similarities and differences, and how can various sector-specific enterprises be managed optimally, whether through alternative governance structures, accountability methods, and so forth. We still seem to believe that the world is divided between Adam Smith and Karl Marx.

Michael Kirby: I agree completely that enterprise ownership does not determine innovation. The fundamental difference is in the risk you're prepared to take in the public sector when failure means being on the front page of the newspaper and national television news; it is the public exposure more than anything else that causes governments to be more risk averse. So wherever innovation is needed in the public sector, we need some system where it is understood in advance that some failures, as well as some successes, will occur. To facilitate governmental innovation we must mitigate the stigma, the political costs, and the bureaucratic costs attached to failure.

We have an interesting example in Canada. About five years ago, the Ontario Provincial Government set up an enterprise designed to help fund innovative ideas (called the Idea Corporation). This innovative enterprise, working like a venture capital fund, has survived some failures. How? First, it has had enough successes, and second, the politicians have been able to escape the heat by simply arguing that they have announced in advance that it you're going to take chances, you're going to have to expect failures. How can we exend this principle to a whole variety of other public sector institutions in a way in which the media and others will accept that no one can bat a thousand all the time? This is the fundamental problem with innovation in the public sector.

Part VII

JOINT PUBLIC/PRIVATE ORGANIZATIONS AND ACTIVITIES

Chapter 15

RESEARCH IN SEARCH OF RELEVANCE AND EXCELLENCE
The Management of Creativity in the Social Sciences

Meinolf Dierkes

INTRODUCTION

Social science research is a newcomer to discussions about the institutionalization and management of creativity. This is not surprising: only relatively recently has the need for large-scale and long-term research in the social sciences
been recognized; little experience has been collected in the field, and too little
time has passed for conducting serious evaluations of different models.

In the natural sciences the pressure to achieve specific goals (e.g., in defense,
space, energy, health) and the inherently large-scale and long-term nature of
several undertakings made the management of such endeavors felt much sooner:
as early as after World War I they stimulated the creation of a diversity of institutions in a variety of countries and generated the need to examine and evaluate
the problems of research management that demand priority in such settings.

Social science research, on the other hand, was conducted almost exclusively
by individual or small teams in university-type contexts until the 1960s. The
demand for social science knowledge in the 1960s and 1970s underwent both
quantitative and qualitative changes (Frankel 1976a: 4). Not only was *more* social science information sought after, but also information of a *different* kind,
requiring more extensive data collection and empirical research. In order to meet
these demands, large-scale and long-term projects were undertaken and special
institutions were established outside the traditional university departments.

These changes posed new management problems for the social sciences, which, due to the dominant small team type of structure, had generally left research to the motivation of the individual researcher. Through the introduction of new research styles in larger institutional contexts, it became necessary to explore how creativity in the social sciences can actively be managed. Specifically, what kinds of institutional conditions and which management approaches are most suited for stimulating innovation?

The search for answers to these questions must still rely largely on the analysis of case studies and the experiences of individual managers, because no thorough evaluation has yet been conducted cross culturally, across the board of diverse experiments, in different countries. This article is intended to help answer these questions by examining the experiences of a major social science research center, the Wissenschaftszentrum Berlin (Science Center Berlin). This particular institution is of interest because, on the one hand, the kind of research to which it is devoted—problem-oriented basic research—is becoming increasingly important, so that its pioneering efforts provide valuable insights into the challenges and risks involved. On the other hand, its very size, and the fifteen-year span of its operational history, represent an unusual wealth of experience in social science research to draw on.

The Wissenschaftszentrum Berlin was founded in 1969 by members of the West German Parliament, the Deutsche Bundestag, to attract high-level social science research to Berlin. Later, in 1976, the ownership was transferred to the Federal Republic of Germany and the State of Berlin, which were represented by the Federal Ministry for Research and Technology and by the State Ministry for Science and Research in Berlin. The Parliament, however, kept a strong influence on the institution: seven out of twenty-one board members come from the Deutsche Bundestag. In the course of this change in ownership the basic mission of the Wissenschaftszentrum Berlin also changed: the intention then was to use this large center of social science research outside the university system to meet government needs for research and policy advice.

Deviating from the traditional university structure, the Wissenschaftszentrum Berlin was organized around institutes focusing on different problem areas and policy fields: labor market policy, environmental policy, industrial policy, labor policy and global developments. A central characteristic of the research approach of the center is its internationally comparative and interdisciplinary perspective. In the course of the early 1980s the mission of the center was again reexamined and reoriented away from immediate policy relevance to obtain a more long-term perspective. This process of defining the purpose and nature of the institution involved a complex set of discussions and adjustments and correspondingly complex interplay between the institution itself and its constituencies.

The result of the process was the development of an institutional identity focusing on the search for *relevance* and *excellence,* combining the goals of contributing to the solution of social problems and attaining highest academic standards. For a more detailed description of the institution, its current structure, size and areas of concentration, see appendix.

This article aims to abstract from the experiences of the Wissenschaftszentrum Berlin in dealing with three of the central management tasks involved in establishing an institutional setting conducive to innovation: 1) defining the vision of the institution; 2) specifying the organizational and structural prerequisites for fulfilling such a mission; and 3) designing the appropriate procedural and cultural mechanisms to promote a creative working environment. In this manner, an examination of the experience of the center can serve to illustrate to operationalization of these various tasks and provide a springboard for generalizing on the nature of the challenges to the management of creativity in social science research.

Accordingly, the next section of the article deals with the need for defining the mission of an institution and discusses how to determine, based on the experience of the Wissenschaftszentrum Berlin, where the specific contribution of such an institution should lie in view of the intellectual and institutional landscape in which it is situated. The next section then deals with the process of defining and establishing the institutional prerequisites for this mission. It discusses the need to determine the conditions required in order to meet the goals of the institution and illustrates this through the prerequisites the Wissenschaftszentrum Berlin defined for its purposes: autonomy, medium-term programs, and a strong planning function. Finally, the article examines the management tasks involved in developing a culture oriented to the kind of innovation and creativity envisioned by the institution. It discusses the sources and potential problems in achieving this goal in terms of the concept of "creative tensions" underlying the search for relevance and excellence in social science research. Individual tensions are identified and mechanisms for dealing with them, based on the experience of the Wissenschaftszentrum Berlin, are presented.

COMBINING RELEVANCE AND EXCELLENCE: THE NEED FOR INSTITUTIONAL INNOVATION

A primary task in institution-building is the development of an identity. What, exactly, is the nature of the potential innovative contributions of the institution? A sense of uniqueness is central to the life of an organization: on the one hand to establish its position in the relevant landscape and to legitimize its existence vis-à-vis its various external constituencies and the public at large; and, on the other hand, to guide and motivate the efforts of the internal constituencies, the members of the institution, who need to understand the mission they are intended to contribute to fulfilling. The key function of management in this process is to define and communicate the vision by exploring the needs to be responded to and by formulating the goals to be striven for.

Reviewing the nature of social science research—its goals and traditions, as well as current forms of institutionalization—two characteristics become apparent that are relevant to the definition of a vision for an institution seeking to identify deficits and to achieve creativity. First, the social sciences have historically always been shaped by a dual goal structure: relevance and excellence. Second, however, while it would have been inconceivable for many of the great scholars around the turn of the century to separate the intention to conduct societally relevant research from that of striving for the highest scientific quality, in the course of the last decades the two goals have increasingly been viewed and pursued as polar opposites. An examination of the implications of this development highlights what can be learned and where new innovative impulses can be sought.

A brief glance back at the turn of the century shows that problem-oriented research was at the forefront of conceptual and methodological developments in the emerging social sciences (Nisbet 1976: 104). Examples can be found in the work conducted by the "Verein für Socialpolitik" in Germany on the housing and working conditions of workers in the 1890s and 1900s that spearheaded the development of social science research (Kern 1982; Gorges 1981). The same holds true for the community-oriented policy research in the United States in the first two decades of the twentieth century; for such early British social researchers as Charles Booth, too, research aiming at social relevance could not be achieved without meeting the highest theoretical and methodological standards (Bulmer 1980; 1983).

The later development of the social sciences in the phase of rapid expansion was characterized by increasing differentiation and specialization. A strong tendency emerged to split the community of researchers along the two goals of relevance and excellence. As political and economic decisionmakers gradually increased their demand for social knowledge and as cores of theoretical knowledge crystallized various aspects of social life along disciplinary lines, *two separate markets* came into being. Part of the research addressed itself to its actual or potential customers or contractors, and part exclusively to the academic community. While the latter strived for rewards given by peers' opinions and acknowledgements, the application-oriented researchers headed for practical usefulness or, at least, new contracts or continued funding. This separation of the intellectual markets is mirrored in a differentiation in the network of funding sources.

Analyses of the social science research systems in the various European countries showed that this dual demand and funding structure corresponded rather closely although not perfectly to *institutional specialization* (von Alemann 1981; Knorr et al., 1981; see also the distinction made by Trist 1970). Applied research intended for instrumental use by specific clients was to be found in commercial or government- or interest group-oriented research centers, whereas basic research with an academic orientation retained its traditional place in the universities. Similarly, *communication structures* were also largely differentiated, thereby again intensifying the separation: researchers, who directed their findings in "grey literature" type of reports directly to decision-makers or sought publication in newspapers or in journals specializing in fields of knowledge application, naturally developed concepts and standards different from those publishing in disciplinary journals of high but exclusively academic reputation. This development was convincingly characterized by Shils as "the current dilemma of the social sciences: search for truth or for public service?" (Shils 1976: 287).

Is the dichotomization of goals and institutions, accompanied by the dichotomization of funding and communication processes, of incentives and rewards for research, a necessary consequence of growth of the field? Was the combination of relevance and excellence, which was characteristic of social science research at its origins, only possible at such an early stage and neither possible nor desirable at later stages of conceptual and methodological development? Some observers might claim that research oriented at relevance and research seeking excellence are essentially different, even belonging to worlds apart: the world of action, where political interests reside and guide the analytical work, and the world of truth, governed by the values of disinterested scientific inquiry (Coleman 1972). The necessary conclusion, of course, is that belonging to each of the two worlds is equally legitimate, but that the two normally do not meet or even fall into one. This view, however, largely ignores the respective deficiencies of unidimensional goal structures in social research, of which many of the forefathers had been so well aware.

Finding answers to these questions might not be so urgent or problematic in a period when the interests and intentions of individual research personalities shaped a scientific field. It can, however, become one of the most serious challenges to social science research in a phase of large-scale institutionalization. Each institution then has to be assigned a well defined place in a research system which as a whole has to guarantee the overall perspectives of the social sciences.

In this context, organizing a research infrastructure, which is solely oriented to the needs of decisionmakers, prevents the cumulation of research findings and cumulative learning because all research projects have an immediate constituency expecting only a timely analysis of the specific problem it is concerned with. There is little incentive for the communication of research findings among researchers and, consequently, hardly any development of broader conceptual categories or even social theories.

In the separate subsystem for "excellence" there is a tendency for disciplinary research to narrow in on highly specific theoretical issues, which is accompanied by the danger of becoming detached from societal reality by devoting too great a share of resources to theoretical, methodological and technical refinements. Theory-building in the social sciences, however, requires that research be in constant contact with the dynamics of society; this essential historical character of the social sciences is one of the central elements distinguishing it from theory-building in the natural sciences. A conception of excellence that does not take into account the importance of dealing with the realities of social change and does not consider examining the resulting social problems to be within its sphere is too limited and therefore destined to fall short of its goal.

The understanding that social research is most relevant when it can be applied immediately in political action proves to be equally restrictive. It only captures the short-term perspective of the policy-makers' demand for social knowledge. It does not take into account the need for medium- and long-term information and analysis in policymaking. Neither conception does justice to the scientific and social potential theoretically informed social knowledge can have.

What implications are to be drawn from this analysis? In sum: an exclusive orientation of researchers and research institutions to these two poles is unsatisfactory. While there is no question but that the universities will continue to play an essential role in providing the basis for consolidated disciplinary science, that policy information needs will continue to be served by research organized in a more commercial market manner, and that some types of research (such as long-term continuous data gathering) may be rather well located in government bureaucracies, there is a definite need for institutions combining the goals of relevance and excellence. This relates to the increasing recognition of the need for problem-oriented, long-range social science research that "combines work on societally relevant problems with the best that scholarship has to offer: high quality standards, complete with replication and verifiability; methodological rigor; and theoretical continuity" (Wittrock et al. 1984: 2.25).

In meeting this need lies the mission of an institution whose vision is the search for creative contributions through the joint pursuit of the two goals otherwise kept separate by other organizations: relevance and excellence. The specification of this vision is a continuous management challenge. The task lies in elaborating exactly how the institution can contribute to meeting the information needs and the theoretical challenges as well as how it can determine in which areas it will concentrate its efforts.

Defining the vision of such an institution in more specific terms, as in the case of the Wissenschaftszentrum Berlin for example, means identifying and selecting the long-term societal information needs to which it will devote itself. In order to ensure both that knowledge can be built up over an extended period of time and that the institution can do justice to its aim of reflecting changing social reality, the process of setting and revising thematic priorities in the research is a primary concern of management.

Defining the vision also involves specifying the implicit: for example, problem-oriented research implies applying a multi- and often interdisciplinary perspective since social reality does not organize itself into clear disciplinary categories (Yarmolinsky 1976: 270). Furthermore, problems do not respect national borders: there are problems of a global and transfrontier nature (e.g., pollution); there are problems that appear earlier in one nation than in another (e.g., unemployment); there are problems and actions in one country that influence the policymaking of other countries (e.g., inflation). To deal with such cases, a cross-national approach to information collection and analysis is essential. At the same time, theories claiming universal validity also require a cross-national research perspective (see Dierkes, Weiler, and Antal, forthcoming). Therefore, an institution focusing on problem-oriented basic research is implicitly characterized by an interdisciplinary and comparative mode of research (which has implications for the organization of research and the selection of staff as well — namely, it requires team research of an interdisciplinary and international composition).

Once the vision of the institution has been defined and its implications clarified, the next management task is to establish the institutional prerequisites for pursuing the desired objectives. This task is in itself an innovative challenge in the case of the creation of a new type of institution such as that represented by the Wissenschaftszentrum Berlin. Since its context remains dominated by the split between policy research and academic research, a continued balancing of the institution is required to develop fully the potential of the vision.

ESTABLISHING PREREQUISITES FOR INSTITUTIONALIZING THE SEARCH FOR RELEVANCE AND EXCELLENCE IN SOCIAL SCIENCE RESEARCH

Under what conditions can problem-oriented basic research be conducted? The call for new institutional settings for problem-oriented social science research has been made more than once, and attempts to create and support such an orientation have been undertaken time and again in various countries; but in most cases they have not been built on a clear understanding of the conceptual and organizational requirements for successfully developing institutions that try to find their place between the two strong poles that structure the field of scientific inquiry in the social sciences. For instance, the idea of a nonprofit research institute alone does not suffice as it will always tend to drift either in the direction of dependence on its funding-source, when deciding on its research programs and approaches — as in the majority of cases (see Orlans 1972: 92 ff) — or in the direction of a return into the academic sphere hardly to be distinguished from university research (see in general the discussion in Perry 1976).

The reverse attempt to dissolve a prevailing academic orientation by a science policy of "contractualisation," in which an increasing share of research funding is distributed via client-oriented contracts, undermines the required distance from short-term political interests and leads to a highly fragmented research community and to the erosion of academic criteria of research quality (Pollack 1976). An examination of the experience of the Wissenschaftszentrum Berlin shows that striving for excellence and relevance in social science research implies three essential requirements: the institution must be autonomous, its research must be structured around medium-term programs, and a strong planning function is needed to determine the future directions of research.

A research organization that seeks to be innovative while straddling several constituencies that have different goals, interests, and standards must be independent from all of them. If a high degree of self-determination with respect to defining research goals and managing research progress is not guaranteed, the institution risks being paralysed or at best producing only mediocre compromises as a result of the tugging and pulling by the different constituencies. "It is only a strong scientific institution — coherent and independent, yet responsive and responsible — which has the strength to maintain its views, even when they may be unpopular or contrary to conventional wisdom" (Weinberg 1974: 17).

Autonomy has structural and financial aspects. While mechanisms for channelling the input from external constituencies must be foreseen, the decision-making structures of the institution must ensure that the power to determine and implement research policy resides in the institution. At the same time the vision of the institution cannot be achieved if research priorities are in effect determined by funding arrangements that distort the time perspective of the research policy and also allow external constituencies too much influence over decisionmaking. The pursuit of cumulative knowledge, long-term goals, and a type of research that often falls between the cracks of existing market mechanisms requires the establishment of a high level of long-term institutional funding. The possibility, however, of securing additional short-term funding for specific projects is desirable when it is consistent with the research strategy.

Second, if the research institution is to achieve its multiple aims, it needs to structure its research in such a way as to focus on the cumulation of knowledge in selected areas over time and yet also allow for flexibility in the medium term to adjust research priorities both to changing social reality and to changing academic needs for knowledge. The organization of research around programs running five to seven years has been found to permit both the concentration and synthesis of knowledge on the one hand and the review of priorities on the other.

Among the key management tasks required by a program-orientation are:

- Planning the research programs;
- Specifying the research projects to be conducted under the program umbrella;
- Promoting the aggregation of project-level knowledge into larger conceptual frames in the interest of supporting the development of middle-range theories; and
- Communicating the results to the various constituencies.

The planning of research programs involves the identification of potential research needs and the selection of areas of concentration. As a first step, an intense process of communication has to be organized with relevant societal actors and representatives of important institutions, with distinguished scholars of the various social science disciplines and with program managers of research funding organizations. An analysis of its results leads to the selection of a social problem area according to the societal demand for knowledge in the field and the theory-guided research interests in academia. Following this, the key-sectors of interest are defined by juding the prospects for important contributions to disciplinary theories and to the development of conceptual tools, which may be at the roots of interdisciplinary theory-building.

When pursuing problem-oriented research in those key sectors of interest, it is a constant task to aggregate project level approaches into larger conceptual frames and thereby contribute to the formation of middle-range theories as well as link the findings of often interdisciplinary projects to developments in traditional disciplines, thus contributing to mainstream academic progress. Besides promoting these efforts in the pursuit of excellence, an active communication strategy informing constituencies and society at large about the research results and the frequent summarizing of knowledge and data generated on the problem area are key elements in achieving a high level of relevance in such programs.

It is obvious that an institution for problem-oriented basic research to meet these requirements needs a strong research planning function to organize and coordinate the networks of external links to societal actors and academia; to organize and coordinate internal cooperation and scientific exchange between project teams with regard to the institution's objectives; and to decide on the establishment, continuation, reorientation, or termination of research work in specific problem areas. Whereas the success of steering problem-oriented basic research institutions towards achieving their ambitious objectives ultimately hinges on particular management issues to be specified in the following section, a high degree of autonomy, medium-term program orientation and a strong research planning function are necessary preconditions for dealing with the challenges to research management.

CULTIVATING CREATIVITY: THE MANAGEMENT OF TENSIONS

These prerequisites are the institutional basis for stimulating and developing creativity in a research organization striving for both relevance and excellence. Beyond this, however, every institution requires the cooperation of its members in order to be able to fulfill its mission. The task for innovative and creative management is to find the appropriate structural conditions and the set of values and beliefs necessary to ensure such cooperation. The optimal mix of both depends on the kind of products, the production processes, the modalities of diffusion, as well as the unique vision of the individual organization. While in factory work, for example, detailed production operations largely determine the passive compliance of employees, in a research organization the support must be more than tacit. When the purpose of the institution is to be creative, formal structures are of relatively lesser significance. It is more important that the members actively promote the mission of the organization and share its vision.

There are a number of reasons why the identification with the goals and values of the organization is particularly important in a research setting. As studies of organizational culture show, shared beliefs and values imply shared ways of doing things and thereby reduce the need for explicit procedures and bureaucratic processes, which are stifling to creativity (Sathe 1983). In addition, research indicates that a sense of commitment plays an important role in creativity. "Studies of outstanding individuals in various fields almost always reveal that such persons seem to be impelled by feelings of mission or purpose (Uenishi 1984: 223). When individuals "believe that what they are doing is tremendously worthwhile...[they] are aroused to all-out effort" (Uenishi 1984: 223).

Such a sense of common purpose is especially central to an institution that does not fit the traditional mold. A research organization attempting to achieve excellence and relevance simultaneously—which requires that its members deviate from accepted paths and ways of thinking, career patterns, and developments in academics—must transform traditional thinking into a feeling of uniqueness and impart a special set of values in order to gain their support. Therefore, an important task of the research manager is to communicate the vision of the institution to its members. Weinberg recognizes the significance of the organizational cultural factor when he writes "the key to making an institutional policy effective is the creation of a proper mood in the members of the institutions. This requires that the director of an institution. . .instill into his staff an unswerving commitment" (Weinberg 1974: 16).

The nature of the management tasks in an institution striving for relevance and excellence in social science research is well captured in the concept of "creative tensions" introduced by Kuhn (1963) and researched by Pelz and Andrews, among others (Pelz 1967; Pelz and Andrews 1976; Andrews 1979). This concept draws on two observations: first, "a creative act ocurs when a set of elements not previously associated is assembled in a new and useful combination" (Pelz 1967: 161), and second, "achievement often flourished in the presence of factors that seemed antithetical" (Pelz 1967: 157). In terms of this concept, an institution attempting to achieve a symbiosis between relevance and excellence thrives on the fundamental tension between these goals. It implies a departure from the traditional distinction between the two frames of reference that up to date have been perceived to be contradictory and seeks innovation in their combination.

To make use of such tensions, the research manager must develop ways to reap the benefit for creativity that can come from associating the ideas from the two worlds while at the same time protecting the researchers from the problems that can stem from the often contradictory demands and incentive and reward systems of the various constituencies. The task, therefore, is to establish which specific tensions and possible contradictions are involved in the vision of the organization and then, rather than eliminating them, to design a balanced system to develop an innovative and stimulating research environment.

Identifying Creative Tensions

Experience indicates that the following specific tensions emanate from the basic vision of such an institution:

- Disciplinary versus multi- and interdisciplinary perspectives;
- Short-term versus long-term views;

- Flexibility versus continuity;
- Freedom of individual researchers and teams versus program coordination;
- Production of knowledge versus its diffusion.

Problem-oriented basic research requires a *multi- and often interdisciplinary perspective:* social problems and society's information needs for understanding and solving those problems do not simply correspond to the way academia organizes its knowledge (Orlans 1972: 75). Studying social problem areas therefore often requires the input of more than one discipline, and it can promote the development of knowledge outside traditional disciplinary boundaries. The need to draw on a variety of disciplines proves to be a significant stimulus to creativity and innovation. Whereas theory-building in the social sciences usually builds on disciplinary knowledge, the new insights that can be gained from different disciplinary perspectives and their combination can contribute to the enhancement of the explanatory power of a hypothesis or theory. In this sense, research oriented to social problems not only provides insights of relevance to policy making but can also enrich the scientific search for concepts of more universal validity. Herein lies the creative potential of this tension.

The tensions between disciplinary and interdisciplinary perspectives also has a significant impact on the recruitment and career development responsibilities of research managers. In order to achieve academic recognition, to be properly evaluated and integrated into the body of existing knowledge, research output striving toward excellence must be fed into mainstream academic disciplines. Only rarely does interdisciplinary knowledge per se gain academic recognition—for example, when it is "adopted" by a discipline (e.g., urban sociology) or when it is recognized as a new field (e.g., implementation research). This implies that the researchers conducting interdisciplinary research confront serious difficulties in achieving professional academic recognition for their work. Therefore, problem-oriented institutions, when not properly managing the tension, have often not been "successful in attracting first-class specialists that are best recognized and rewarded by their peers" (Levien, in Orlans 1972: 76).

An institution striving at relevance and excellence simultaneously, however, has to be attractive to those first-rate specialists. An important challenge to such an institution, therefore, is "to provide careers of equivalent security and prestige to those in the disciplines for those working outside them" (Brooks 1976: 257).

Relevance and excellence often imply quite different *time perspectives* (Yarmolinsky 1976: 259). Society's information needs in attempting to understand and tackle major problems tend to be immediate and short-term in nature. To generate the relevant knowledge quite often requires more time than is available to decisionmakers and their constituencies. If it is to prepare itself to meet future information needs, and if value is placed by decisionmakers on the quality of the information received, research has to operate on a significantly longer term perspective. The challenge is to allow both for the stimulation to be derived from recognition and meeting short-term information demands and for the insulation needed to accumulate a sound knowledge basis over long periods of time. In other words, the necessary level of creative stimulation must be found in a balance between buffering an institution and its members from the immediate demands of constituencies and exposing them to these demands.

The importance of this second specific challenge to creative research management is also supported by Pelz's research: he observed that "it seems reasonable to say that the scientists and engineers in our study were more effective when they experienced a "creative tension" between sources of stability or security on the one hand and sources of disruption or challenge on the other" (Pelz 1967: 157).

Related to this is the tension between *flexibility and continuity*. As indicated in the argument above for a strong research planning function as an institutional prerequisite, information needs and research priorities change over time. On the other hand, the development of competence as well as theoretical knowledge beyond the project level requires a relatively high degree of continuity. The research institution must therefore be managed in such a way as to allow it to respond flexibly to emerging ideas and new opportunities but also to guarantee a stable, continuous development. Both the personnel policy and the research program must take this tension into account.

Another tension lies between the needs of researchers and research teams for *freedom* and independence and the institutional interest for *coordination* (Brooks 1976: 254). Independence, the freedom to follow one's own ideas, is an important motivational factor for individual researchers. The need for independence includes the choice or (at least) a voice in the selection of projects, based on individual interests and the logic of individual professional development. Following these individual needs exclusively would undermine the institutional interest to pursue a coherent research program in the interest of cumulative knowledge generated on problem areas as well as on areas of theoretical and conceptual development. Such an institution, therefore, has to find an optimal way to manage the tensions between individual motivations and institutional needs regarding the determination of projects and programs.

Finally, a specific tension in a research institution whose mission it is to conduct problem-oriented basic research can be seen between time and resources allocated to the *production of knowledge versus the diffusion of research results*. Problem-oriented research requires the active communication of research results to the various groups of social actors and the general public. The purpose of an active communication strategy is to contribute to enhancing society's knowledge about the existence of a specific problem, its structure and nature, as well as to provide insights into ways of finding appropriate solutions. More than any research organization exclusively trying to meet high professional standards, an organization devoted to problem-oriented basic research has to spend time and energy on the diffusion of knowledge. Despite the growing demand, social science research "must still compete for the society's attention and respect" (Frankel 1976: 30).

How much time and energy should be spent for this purpose is a key problem to research management. Since the diffusion of scientific knowledge also has to involve the researchers who generate the knowledge in the first place, and since society learns only slowly, attempts to be relevant could easily drain on researchers' time and energy. The communication of research therefore competes for resources with those dedicated to generating new knowledge and meeting high academic standards.

Managing Creative Tensions

Having identified these tensions inherent in conducting social science research aimed at both relevance and excellence, how can they be managed? As long as the dichotomy between these goals is maintained in the perceptions, institutional arrangements, incentives, and reward systems outside the research institution, it will be the task of management to deal with these tensions. How can a culture supportive of the goals of the organization be instilled and institutionalized to promote the kind of creativity sought? What kinds of institutional arrangements can be developed to maximize the benefits to be drawn from these tensions so that the unique contribution of the organization can be achieved?

As indicated above, the support for the vision of a research organization is essential to this success. The researchers need to identify with the mission and value the goals of the organization: their production cannot be ensured through technical mechanisms; their creativity needs to be motivated and channelled in the direction of the aims of the specific organization through cultural identification. As explained by Kluckhohn: "Culture consists in a patterned way of thinking, feeling and reacting, acquired and transmitted mainly by symbol, constituting the distinctive achievement of human groups, including their embodiments in artifacts" (Kluckhohn 1951: 86).

In the case of a vision such as that held by the Wissenschaftszentrum Berlin, for example, cultural identification implies sharing the belief that the multitude of tensions described above are a worthwhile and managable challenge as well as a real source of creativity. If the members of the organization (particularly the researchers, but also to some extent the supporting staff) cannot identify with this mission, all structural measures supporting the management of these tensions will fail—or a best have only marginal success. The need for multi- and interdisciplinarity, the importance of flexibility as well as continuity, the significance of combining relevance and excellence must be perceived by the members of the organization to be key elements to its existence, a reason for collaboration.

What insights can be gained into the process of developing a cultural identity for a research institution from anthropological and organizational studies and from the specific experience of the Wissenschaftszentrum Berlin? Research shows that culture is *transmitted* primarily through the involvement of members of the organization in the specification of goals derived from the mission, in the operationalization of values in the planning of research activities. In addition, shared values and beliefs, common understanding about the ways things are done in the organization, are *reinforced* by symbols, stories, staff selection, and examples set through the behavior of senior members of the organization (Wilkins 1983: 24; Pettigrew 1979: 575–77).

In practice, this means, for example, that *participation in team-type structures* seems to be central to the development of an organizational culture striving at relevance and excellence. A constant task in such an institution is the discussion of plans and the integration of overriding goals into individual projects. The participation of the researchers in this on-going process is essential for their understanding and identification with the values of the organization, on the one hand, and serves as a stimulus for creativity, on the other hand. The experience that participation in the elaboration of projects has a positive influence on the achievement of researchers is supported by Pelz's study (Pelz 1967: 162) as well. Not only does it help to motivate the researchers, as Pelz found, but it also utilizes the capacity of the individuals to serve as "organs of perception," sensing and probing future challenges, an essential function in such a research institution. Participation and involvement, there, specifically help to manage tension between freedom of the individual researchers and the needs of the overall institution for coherence of research programs.

The team-type structure not only promotes participation, it also facilitates the *operationalization of interdisciplinary approaches* to problem-oriented basic research. Depending on the nature of the research in question, teams are composed of researchers from different disciplines (and often from different countries). Managing such diverse teams to generate the new perspectives needed for a creative contribution is a continuous challenge, the pull from the individual perspectives tending to be centrifugal even when strong cultural support for the value of interdisciplinary and international research exists in the team. Among the management mechanisms to be implemented in this context are:

First, the integration of knowledge from multi- and interdisciplinary projects into traditional disciplines by requiring relevant publications as a regular element of the planning and execution of the research program and the individual research projects. Such a structural device helps to enhance the individual researcher's professional development by a periodic exposure to standards and knowledge of the discipline. At the same time, the unique potential of such research for the development of individual disciplines is systematically explored.

Second, a periodic effort also needs to be built into the planning and execution of research programs to synthesize project-level knowledge into overarching middle-range theories. Specifically institutions with longer term research perspectives over and above the project level can exploit this resource and contribute to theory building, thereby striving towards high academic standards.

These kinds of mechanisms help to deal with the tensions involved in conducting problem-oriented basic research by *building bridges between the tensions,* between demands of the different worlds. They enable the "counter-culture" (which the organization represents in relation to established institutions) to pursue its goals while fitting into and meeting the demands of the outside world. Such mechanisms as ensuring the publication of research results in both reports for decisionmaking purposes and in disciplinary journals, conducting individual problem-oriented projects and then synthesizing their results into middle-range theories satisfy the different types of needs for knowledge. At the same time, they help the individual researchers to establish their credentials according to traditional career standards while they devote themselves to achieving goals based on different understanding of the world.

A major task of management next to the transmission of cultural values and beliefs to the members of the organization is their *communication to the external constituencies.* In order for the institution to be allowed to function and its products and members to gain recognition outside its walls, the various external constituencies must learn to value the uniqueness of the institution. Key actors in relevant institutions in the decisionmaking community, for example, have to understand the implications of the concept of relevance when combined with excellence. It means that some of their specific information needs can be optimally served by such an institution but others cannot: knowledge on long-term developments, options for actions in areas of social concern, for example, are more likely to be provided than short-term and ad hoc formulated information. It is necessary to communicate to them that ensuring the stability of research programs over a significant period of time will serve their interests by providing cumulative knowledge on an area of social concern. Academia, as another key constituency group, also has to understand and support the unique opportunity of such an institution to contribute to scientific progress, specifically from the perspective of multi-disciplinary basic research, and to the development of new fields within or outside traditional disciplines.

Seen from the perspective of organizational culture, then, the management of creative tensions involves the "education" of internal and external constituencies to appreciate the different values and ways of doing things envisioned by the institution, and the design of specific supporting mechanisms to help the different worlds to meet where necessary.

A central role in this bridge-building task is the *establishment of feedback processes*. In each of the different stages in the research process, ranging from the problem identification to the final presentation of results, inputs and feedbacks must be planned for from the different constituencies. Means of achieving this, for the academic constituencies, include encouraging researchers to teach at the university, either in a mono- or interdisciplinary setting, and to contribute to conferences having both a disciplinary or problem-oriented perspective. The results of the research projects need to be disseminated to the scientific community in the appropriate publications. At the same time, the input and perspectives of other decisionmaking constituencies also need to be sought and integrated in the research process, both through formal structural mechanisms (e.g., advisory boards, conferences) and informal discussions. Similarly, the results of the research projects must be made available to these constituencies in a form they are able to use.

The final stage of the feedback process is the evaluation of the results. An institution like this cannot rely on traditional evaluation mechanisms, since they are specific to each constituency and thereby too narrow and inappropriate for the overall mission of the institution. An institution attempting to combine relevance and excellence therefore needs a multidimensional evaluation approach both for the performance of individual researchers and for the evaluation of its overall output. To take into account the complex goals and related tensions involved in the pursuit of the innovative mission of the institution, evaluation procedures must involve various external constituencies who also have an understanding of the nature of the challenge.

Besides providing feedback on the quality of the research output, evaluation reports also help the institution to rethink and, if necessary, to reconsider its definition of an optional mix of structural and cultural efforts to manage the various tensions. Experience indicates that this mix has to be seen as a constant process of adjustment based on trial and error, which can only work effectively in an environment and a culture that stimulates a continuous discussion of the basic mission of the institution, the specific ways it defines the various creative tensions involved, as well as the effectiveness of concepts it uses to manage those tensions. An open and comprehensive external feedback system, specifically designed to serve this purpose, is an essential element of such a process.

APPENDIX

The Wissenschaftszentrum Berlin as a case study for institutional innovation and an experiment in innovative management in social science research

The task of the *Wissenschaftszentrum Berlin* (WZB) is to conduct problem-oriented social science research of a basic nature in selected policy fields and to communicate the results to members of the scientific and decisionmaking communities. Founded in 1969 by representatives of the political parties in the *German Bundestag,* the WZB presently consists of three institutes with a total of five research units: the International Institute of Management, with research units in labor market policy and industrial policy; the International Institute for Comparative Social Research, with research units in global developments and labor policy; and the International Institute for Environment and Society, with a research unit in environmental policy.

The WZB is a nonprofit corporation. Since 1976/1977 the Federal Republic of Germany and the *Land* Berlin have been the shareholders.

The Board of Trustees establishes the basic directions of research policy and is involved in all important matters bearing on the corporation's research policy and financial affairs.

The president represents the WZB as managing director of the corporation, plans the research units, and coordinates the institutes.

The WZB has 142 permanent positions, of which 86 are for research fellows. In addition, visiting fellows, doctoral candidates, temporary personnel, and staff members working on externally funded projects are engaged in the research at the WZB.

At the WZB, scientists from different disciplines collaborate, usually conducting their research in the framework of international comparative projects. As a rule the project teams are composed on individuals from a variety of countries. There is extensive cooperation, particularly with the universities in Berlin and with similar institutions and universities in the Federal Republic of Germany and abroad.

The WZB informs many different groups and institutions in the scientific and decisionmaking communities of its research results in a variety of ways, including conferences and seminars. The results of the work done in the projects are reported in articles published in professional journals, in the WZB's book series, and in numerous information materials.

INTERNATIONAL INSTITUTE OF MANAGEMENT

The International Institute of Management was founded in 1970. Its research centers focus on the interaction between the state and the economy in highly developed industrialized societies.

Research Unit: Labor Market Policy

The persistence of high unemployment and the altered constraints and opportunities of labor market policy and employment policy constitute the starting points for the new research program of the IIM's research unit on labor market policy. It emphasizes the analysis of the institutional and economic conditions required to achieve a maximum level of socially acceptable employment opportunities.

In addition to investigating the possibilities for development offered by new technologies and by initiatives from within the business community, studies examine the influence that industrial relations and regulations of the welfare state have on the number and distribution of employment opportunities and investigate the international altered conditions affecting the national economies as well as the factors determining the impact of promising labor market and employment policy.

Research Unit: Industrial Policy

Industrialized western countries are concerned about low economic growth and the persistence of high levels of unemployment. The research unit is currently investigating whether there are structural causes of, and policy solutions for, this economic stagnation.

The research focuses on the economic interrelationship between the legal and institutional framework, and economic processes and structural development. By employing theoretical and applied microeconomic models, the impacts of government regulations and the relationship between individual actions and markets are investigated. This provides a basis for a better understanding of macroeconomic processes.

Current activities also cover research in health economics, the formation and allocation of human capital, and industrial economics. The work at this research unit is supported by the traditionally international profile of its staff, a feature providing the necessary framework for international comparative research projects.

INTERNATIONAL INSTITUTE FOR COMPARATIVE SOCIAL RESEARCH

The International Institute for Comparative Social Research began its work in 1977. Its task is to investigate at both the sectoral and global levels the developmental trends and the potential for change in highly industrialized societies.

Research Unit: Global Developments

With the aid of the macroquantitative long-term computer simulation model — GLOBUS — that has been developed here, this research unit examines causes of, and relationships between, economic and political issues. Existing world models were reviewed for their usefulness in predicting key problem areas over the next twenty-five to thirty-five years. Building on this foundation, the research unit began developing its own model (GLOBUS), which departs from earlier models by including special economic and political questions and utilizing a broad political and social data base.

The model, which simulates the behavior of governments reacting to domestic and international economic and political developments, encompasses twenty-five nations that are politically and economically interlinked in the international sphere. The model outlines some of the consequences of alternative decisions that governments might make.

Research Unit: Labor Policy

The institute's research unit on labor policy deals with the problems of development in labor, particularly paid work, and the way in which it is regulated by society. The rapid change that new market situations, technologies, and work structures have brought about in the world of work alters the social setting, qualifications, and health of the employed, redefining the substance and form of industrial relations. Regulation through social policy is used in part to reinforce, compensate, and counteract such developments.

Central issues therefore include:

The identification of the physical and psychological consequences that processes of industrial rationalization entail through changes in the organization of work or through technology, and the impacts such processes have on qualification, wages, and the social welfare network; and

Strategies and measures developed by employers, employees, their representative organizations, and government authorities to address these problems of the individual and society.

INTERNATIONAL INSTITUTE FOR ENVIRONMENT AND SOCIETY

The International Institute of Environment and Society began its work in 1977. Its task is to respond to the urgent need for social research on environmental problems.

Research Unit: Environmental Policy

The program of this research unit covers the following project areas:

- Environmental monitoring and assessment: including the development and improvement of concepts and methods of media-specific and trans-media environmental monitoring and assessment on the regional, national and international level.
- Environmental impacts and environmental behavior: examining the conditions governing the perception of environmental problems and of people's involvement in environmental issues (environmentalism, environmental learning).
- Evaluation of environmental policies: identifying the most efficient regulatory systems in conventional, media-specific environmental policy, especially air-pollution policy.
- Evaluation of selected policy areas from environmental perspectives: the focus of research is on the ecological orientation of other relevant sectoral policies like energy policy, and technology policy.

REFERENCES

Alemann, Heine von. 1981. *Sozialwissenschaftliche Forschungsinstitute. Personalstruktur, Forschungsprojekte und Spezialisierung der Sozialforschung.* Opladen: Westdeutscher Verlag.

Andrews, Frank M., ed. 1979. *Scientific Productivity. The Effectiveness of Research Groups in Six Countries.* Cambridge: Cambridge University Press.

Brooks, Harvey. 1976. "The Federal Government and the Autonomy of Scholarship." In *Controversies and Decisions — The Social Sciences and Public Policy,* edited by Charles Frankel. New York: Russell Sage Foundation.

Bulmer, Martin. 1980. "The Early Institutional Establishment of Social Science Research: The Local Community Research Commitee at the University of Chicago 1923–30." *Minerva* 28: 51–110.

——. 1982. *The Uses of Social Research. Social Investigation in Public Policy-Making.* London: Allen and Unwin.

Coleman, James. 1972. *Policy Research in the Social Sciences.* Morristown, N.J.: General Learning Systems.

Dierkes, Meinolf; H. Weiler; and A.B. Antal, eds. Forthcoming. *Comparative Policy Research: Lessons from the Past and Challenges for the Future.* Aldershot: Gower.

Frankel, Charles, ed. 1976. *Controversies and Decisions — The Social Sciences and Public Policy.* New York: Russell Sage Foundation.

Gorges, Irmela. 1980. *Sozialforschung in Deutschland 1872–1914. Gesellschaftliche Einflüße auf Themen- und Methodenwahl des Vereins für Socialpolitik.* Königstein: Hain.

Kern, Horst. 1982. *Empirische Sozialforschung.* München: Beck.

Kluckhohn, C. 1951. "The Study of Culture." In *The Policy Sciences,* edited by D. Lerner and H.D. Lasswell. Stanford, Calif.: Stanford University Press.

Knorr, Karin; Max Haller; and Hans-Georg Zilian. 1981. *Sozialwissenschaftliche Forschung in Österreich. Produktionsbedingungen und Verwertungszusammenhänge.* Wien: Jugend und Volk.

Kuhn, T.S. 1963. "The Essential Tension: Tradition and Innovation in Scientific Research." In *Scientific Creativity: Its Recognition and Development,* edited by C.W. Taylor and F. Barron. New York: Wiley.

Nisbet, Robert. 1976. "Max Weber and the Roots of Academic Freedom." In *Controversies and Decisions — The Social Sciences and Public Policy,* edited by Charles Frankel. New York: Russell Sage Foundation.

Orlans, Harold. 1972. *The Non-Profit Research Institute. Its Origin, Operation, Problems and Prospects.* New York: McGraw-Hill.

Pelz, D. and F. Andrews. 1976. *Scientists in Organizations: Productive Climates for Research and Development.* Ann Arbor: Institute for Social Research, University of Michigan.

Pelz, D. 1967. "Creative Tensions in the Research and Development Climate." *Science* 57: 160–65.

Perry, Norman. 1976. "Research Settings in the Social Sciences." In *Demands for Social Knowledge. The Role of Research Organisations,* edited by Norman Perry and Elisabeth Crawford, pp. 137–90. London and Beverly Hills: Sage.

Pettigrew, Andrew. 1979. "On Studying Organizational Cultures." *Administrative Science Quarterly* 24 (Dec.): 570–81.

Pollack, Michael. 1976. "Organisational Diversification and Methods of Financing as Influences on the Development of Social Research in France." In *Demands for Social Knowledge. The Role of Research Organisations,* edited by Norman Perry and Elisabeth Crawford, pp. 115–136. London and Beverly Hills: Sage.

Sathe, Vigay. 1983/84. "Some Action Implications of Corporate Culture: A Manager's Guide to Action." *Organizational Dynamics* 12 (1983/84): 4–23.

Shils, Edward. 1976. "Legitimating the Social Sciences." In *Controversies and Decisions — The Social Sciences and Public Policy,* edited by Charles Frankel. New York: Russell Sage Foundation.

Trist, Eric. 1970. "The Organization and Financing of Research." In *Main Trends of Research in the Social and Human Sciences,* part one: Social Sciences, edited by UNESCO, pp. 693–812. Paris/The Hague: Mouton/UNESCO.

Uenishi, Roy Katsumi. 1984. "Creativity and Originality in Science." *Impact* 34: 221–29.

Weinberg, Alvin M. 1974. "Institutions and Strategies in the Planning of Research." *Minerva* 12: 8–17.

Wilkins, Alan L. 1983. "The Culture Audit: A Tool for Understanding Organizations." *Organizational Dynamics* (Autumn): 24 ff.

Wittrock, Björn; Peter deLeon; and Helga Nowotny. 1984. *Choosing Futures: Evaluating the Secretariat for Futures Studies.* MS. September.

Yarmolinsky, Adam. 1976. "How Good Was the Answer? How Good Was the Question?" In *Controversies and Decisions — The Social Sciences and Public Policy,* edited by Charles Frankel. New York: Russell Sage Foundation.

Chapter 16

CAN ANACHRONISTIC INSTITUTIONS BE SAVED?

Donald M. Kerr

Three trends have a dominant influence on the environment in which national research and development programs are carried out. First, meeting critical needs for new technologies to address pressing defense, energy, and health problems is increasingly more complex and interdisciplinary. Second, at the same time, traditional boundaries between the sciences are vanishing. While much is to be gained in well-established areas by specialization and intense focus on critical issues, there is much more interest in combining concepts or techniques from different fields to either detour around the old roadblocks or to advance in new regions of the frontiers of science. Third, public support of applied research brings with it an implied commitment to maximize long-term economic benefits as well as solve near-term problems. Public support also brings with it requirements for visible accountability and unprecedented openness in operations which make planning a far more difficult process.

These three trends bring an important challenge to management — the challenge to maintain an environment where creative interdisciplinary collaboration can flourish, where new institutional ties can be developed, and where anachronistic impediments to effective performance can be removed.

A number of large, publically funded, applied science laboratories like the Los Alamos National Laboratory evolved as part of the growth of U.S. science and technology since World War II. There laboratories function under very special contractual relations with the government — they are government-owned-contractor-operated and have technical management responsibilities with great flexibility. The initial research and development problems they confronted in defense, nuclear technology, and space science were unprecedented in scope and magnitude. Initial successes soon led to participation across a broad set of applied problems, and the laboratories became multiprogram in nature. Even greater demands were placed on creative and innovative individuals to contribute to large and complex endeavors that required close coordination and new management techniques to succeed. One now must ask if these institutions have become anachronistic given the rapid advance of science and technology and the three trends I have mentioned.

The National Laboratories have established a tradition of interdisciplinary work, but that tradition must continually be modernized, improved, and expanded in order to meet the challenge created by the three trends I have mentioned. Similar efforts are needed in other institutions, such as universities, laboratories staffed by agency personnel, and industrial laboratories. If the National Laboratories do not make such adjustments, the promise that flows from their interdisciplinary tradition will slip away, and they will become another anachronistic institution swept aside by the forces at play in the rapidly changing environment facing us today.

I shall discuss that challenge related to defense and energy programs and in four areas of technology that cross disciplinary lines. The end products of a national R & D establishment are few in number and often either one of a kind or less tangible than industrial products. Solutions often require close coordination with interrelated government, university, and industry efforts to succeed. Complex problems require integrative systems for their adequate solution. In many cases no clear cut, acceptable solutions may exist. Typical examples of great current interest in the defense field are:

- Strategic weapons systems
- Strategic defense initiative
- Emerging technologies (advanced conventional munitions)
- Arms control verification.

Similar examples in the energy field are:

- Civil nuclear power (safety, safeguards, waste)
- Controlled fusion
- Synthetic fuels.

All require large inputs of technical and intellectual resources — scientists, engineers, and other professionals supported by service personnel and technicians. Those who lead the efforts need the ability to identify and formulate problems and to manage the technical, intellectual, and information resources needed.

The changing availability of natural resources and global political and economic competition create a demand for new technologies. The creation of new technologies and entirely new products opens up new human vistas. I focus on four areas of technology that cross traditional disciplinary lines and, I believe, will be the driving forces in the next two decades: materials science, information technology, biotechnology, and health and medical technologies.

MATERIALS SCIENCE

New materials are already revolutionizing the transportation, aerospace, communication, and construction industries. Composite polymers, new ceramics, and the metallic glasses are especially worthy of note. Both the new composite polymers and new ceramics are in use. They will be of great importance to the transportation industries. The composite polymers such as the carbon fiber reinforced plastics are stronger than steel and lighter than aluminum. Body weight is being reduced and structures are being made stronger through use of these materials.

These same properties have led to the use of composite polymers in military and space vehicle applications and attempts are being made to introduce carbon-fiber-reinforced plastic components into automobiles and aircraft, in order to reduce fuel consumption. Boeing is using major quantities of these polymers in its new 757/767 series of airliners. Also, now that component manufacturers have developed more sophisticated and automated production processes, they are intermixing glass and carbon fibers to increase strength at a lower cost. The use of ceramic whiskers instead of graphite fibers to reinforce metals or glass-ceramics offers even greater potential.

The new ceramics are important for high temperature applications such as engines, industrial heat exchangers, and energy conversion systems. Ceramics provide high strength at high temperature along with good oxidation, corrosion, and erosion resistance. Higher operating temperatures and higher operating efficiency can, therefore, be achieved with ceramic components. They are also lighter in weight than high temperature metallic alloys, and the basic elements that comprise the new ceramics such as silicon nitride and silicon carbide are found in plentiful abundance, unlike the increasingly short supply and increasing cost of the elements cobalt and chromium that are critical for metallic alloys.

Super plastic alloys—the oxide dispersion strengthened metals—have some unusual characteristics. They are creep resistant and stress resistant because they withstand heat better than almost any other metal. They will be very important where high temperatures are involved. Under other conditions, these remarkable alloys are soft and highly deformable. While many production problems remain to be solved, it seems clear that we are well on the way to a new generation of super metals.

Another area of materials research, membrane technology, promises to produce some remarkable breakthroughs within the next decade. Synthetic membranes imitate biological membranes that separate chemicals in living organisms. These new membranes are already replacing a whole range of industrial separation processes, from distillation to drum filtration. They are increasingly being used to filter out pollutants, to purify and concentrate substances, to recover rare minerals, and to produce pure antibiotics. Their major economic benefit may be in the petrochemical industry where new separation procedures for H_2, CO_2, and N_2 will increase the conversion efficiency for production of useful products from crude oil at less cost in feedstock and energy input.

INFORMATION TECHNOLOGY

In the past decade we have witnessed spectacular advances in information technology. At the heart of these developments is a tiny device about which we have all heard a great deal, the microelectronic circuit. Its manufacture makes possible the remarkable cornucopia of information processing and handling possibilities that both delight and confuse us. Already the marginal cost of adding substantial information processing capability to manufactured products is small. By 1990 that cost will be virtually zero. By then, some experts predict, almost anything that costs more than $20 and plugs into a wall will contain a microprocessor.

Because of microelectronic circuitry, an important change in perspective is occurring that will determine the thrust of technology in the 1980s. In the broadest sense, this change can be viewed as a shift in emphasis away from optimizing the efficiency of systems and toward optimizing the efficiency of *people*. Microelectronics allows us to decentralize our systems to a level at which they can provide support capability to individual workers. This change may appear in the form of a modular management or office work station that offers a menu of services on command. Or it may appear in the form of an "intelligent toolbox" that allows people to carry the resources of their profession with them wherever they go, just as plumbers or carpenters carry their tools with them today. The man–machine interface is the critical element here in order to make the device "user friendly" as well as useful and therefore widely accepted.

Computer-based automation technology will soon be able to provide the United States and other advanced economies with the means to change their mode of industrial production radically and beneficially. Major batch production industries — automobiles, earth moving and construction equipment, aircraft, and electrical and electronic equipment and appliances — will constitute the greatest market for this technology and will be the most affected by it.

If the true factory of the future is a decade away, the true office of the future is just around the corner. All the necessary technologies are here now. They require only to be refined from a "user-friendly" point of view and to be integrated into compatible systems.

The office of the future will not be a silent room full of workers hunched over computer keyboards. Conversation will thrive. With voice recognition technology now becoming available for mini- and microcomputers the average user will instead speak commands to the machine and listen to the machine's response. New capabilities will expand accessibility of computers and eliminate delays from syntax error or typing mistakes. Voice recognition units will be "trained" by the user to respond to a given set of commands.

Finally, the conduct of scientific and engineering research has been transformed by access to large-scale computing, access that will increase rapidly as a consequence of advances in microelectronics. The emphasis will be on large-scale simulation using numerical models made predictive through theoretical and experimental tests.

BIOTECHNOLOGY

Many say that the 1990s will belong to biotechnology, the third driving technology I single out. (I believe most biotechnology applications will come in the twenty-first century, which of course is not far away.) Eventually, biotechnology's contributions will be truly revolutionary in their impact. The human ability to understand and harness nature's basic life process through technologies such as gene splicing could alter the course of industrial evolution.

Genetic engineering and recombinant DNA are two important components of biotechnology. Recombinant DNA technology excites the imagination because it offers the possibility of directing living organisms to carry out a desired chemical reaction or synthesis. Novel gene constructs are produced. Even the simplest bacterium is capable of making chemical products and carrying out elegant chemical conversions. If a microorganism can be instructed to make a product inexpensively from common raw materials in an energy efficient fashion, the economic possibilities can be substantial — particularly if the product in demand cannot be made cost effective by any other technology. The driving forces that spur interest in biotechnology include potential process improvements that will reduce energy requirements, increase product yields, and enable researchers to use inexpensive raw materials or perhaps waste products as energy sources.

Despite the economic importance of biotechnology, product commercialization will encounter four major obstacles: technological barriers, government regulations, patent questions, and social pressures. Formidable technological barriers will delay some applications until the late 1990s. Indeed, multidisciplinary teams will often be necessary to overcome scientific and technological hurdles. The future possibilities are awesome, but the timeframe for their realization is longer, I suspect, than most people realize.

HEALTH AND MEDICAL TECHNOLOGIES

Finally, significant advances in health and medical technologies in the next decade will enhance our abilities to identify, and to treat and prevent disease. Microprocessor technology applied to bioengineering technology will make it possible to manufacture instruments that are far more accurate in diagnosing disease conditions.

Research in the field of immunology will yield banks of monospecific antibodies for the rapid diagnosis of infectious agents, vaccines to prevent a number of diseases, and may provide immunotherapy for cancer.

Monoclonal antibodies are starting to be used routinely for a number of clinical diagnostic tests (pregnancy, infectious disease) because they are cheaper, simpler or quicker to use. In the case of chlamydia (the most common sexually transmissible disease) where there was no prior method, they now provide the only technique. They are also being used in clinical trials as imaging agents (heart attack and tumor assessment) and are being tested as therapeutic agents (cancer, bacterial infection).

Such new techniques as positron emission tomography, microwave and nuclear magnetic resonance hold promise for future medical applications in imaging. Another exciting research area is organic electronics. Biosensors, an early product of the marriage of biochemistry and electronics, offer a compact means of measuring glucose in diabetics blood; sense the presence of the common ions of Ca, H, K and Na; and are the basis of new instruments to detect nerve agents. The sensors consist of coatings, including enzymes, that react chemically with certain ions and a field effect transistor built into a silicon chip.

In the future, it may be possible to grow the equivalent of electronic semiconductors in protein substrates. These organic chips would be many times smaller than silicon or gallium arsenide semiconductors. Theoretically, they would interface directly with the human body's biological systems, by measuring the electronic potential of nerves—or even individual cells—through tiny sensors implanted under the skin. Such organic electronic systems could be used for medical diagnosis or as alarm systems that would react to subtle changes in the body's chemistry or function. They could, for example, trigger the release of drugs in case of an impending heart attack or insulin shock. All this sounds far out, but much theoretical work supports the concept and several companies have already undertaken the development of practical organic electronic technology and applications.

These four technology areas, with their evident promise, share their multidisciplinary nature. All will require teams of basic scientists and engineers in order to achieve useful products for defense, energy, and, in fact, our general economic well-being. One way, of course, that many of them can be advanced is through the work of the national laboratories. That possibility focuses attention on the issue of public accountability and the need to create an environment where the greatest technical success might be achieved.

Accountability in the near term, of course, means solving the sponsors problem. And there I think one can quite simply say that quality performance depends on quality people with appropriate internal and external reviews. Rather than dwell on the obvious, I speak to the longer term notion of accountability—that is, the expectation that federal research and development will in fact provide long-term benefits to the United States.

In that area the primary aim of industrial initiatives at a laboratory like Los Alamos is to develop mutually beneficial interactions, including work for and with industry and industry staff, private consultations by staff, and ultimately entrepreneurial spinoffs. One initiative is cooperation with the Los Alamos Economic Development Corporation, which is attempting to provide through an incubator and consulting assistance to potential entrepreneurs all of the support that we can reasonably provide to make their ventures a success.

In the area of major industry, we have performed, subject to noncompetition restrictions, work for companies such as Westinghouse, IBM, ARCO, 3M, and Schlumberger in areas including laser-induced chemistry, electronics, special explosives, reservoir modeling, and materials technology. We now have over a year and a half of history with staff exchanges; our first agreement was with Tektronix and we have subsequently had people at ARCO and 3M. In the collaborative mode, for example, we work with Bolt, Beranek, and Newman to be the host for the national DNA sequence data base called *Genbank,* which provides the assembled knowledge in the United States of the human genome. More recently we have been working with the American Iron and Steel Institute on laser-based instrumentation for steel furnaces and provided for an industrial staff member from Armco Steel.

And one of the most exciting things is our so-called Quest for Technology where Control Data Corporation did a technology inventory in our Material Science and Technology Division that yielded approximately 190 technologies that they felt were ready for transfer to industry. The results were widely announced, and over 200 companies have received copies of the report. About ten have visited for more details, and a several-day conference will be planned to provide for an efficient means of establishing the necessary person-to-person linkages between the laboratory and industry.

In the small business and private initiatives area, we encourage private consulting, and over 200 of our technical staff engage in it. Two awards under the Small Business Innovation Research Program have been based on our technology. One company called Scientific Systems International has as its product fast electronics for nuclear energy and weapons tests. A second, Technical Programmers, Inc., is to develop a small high-current accelerator for positron tomography for medical diagnostic purposes. Five small businesses have been started in the last year in New Mexico that have as their basis patents that are either licensed to the inventor or where the University of California has provided for licensing to the new business.

Finally, in terms of making our long-term efforts more accessible, we are participating in a major development in New Mexico called TECHNET, which will be a high bandwidth communications system along the Rio Grande from Los Alamos through Santa Fe to Albuquerque and on the Las Cruces, linking the federal research and development institutions such as Los Alamos National Laboratory and Sandia National Laboratory and White Sands Missile Range to the state's universities and technical business community. We hope to provide teleconferencing capability, technical courses, and to nurture in-state scientific collaboration, particularly the new State of New Mexico Centers for Non-Invasive Diagnosis, Explosives Technology, and the Plant Genetic Engineering Laboratory.

It seems to take too long to establish these relationships, but we and industry are different types of institutions. Cooperation has not normally fit well with the national competitive spirit. The interest of the federal government in productivity and innovation and their roles in economic competitiveness is combining with the interest of some opinion-leaders in industry to bring about a rapid strengthening of laboratory–industry cooperation.

With regard to providing the environment within which these new institutional relationships can be nurtured and developed, we have created many new kinds of arrangements within the laboratory that are not organizational in nature but, in fact, umbrellas or meeting places for people with common research interests. One such is the Center for Material Science to provide for university and industrial participation and collaboration in fundamental materials research.

We have had over 150 university participants, eighty from national laboratories and fifty from industry, in recent workshops on subjects like "Polymers as Synthetic Metals," "Picosecond Photoconductors," "Thermal Plasma Synthesis of Materials" — in fact, a total of ten such conferences in the last two years. We are also actively pursuing a collaborative program in computational materials theory where advances in computational methods and access to Los Alamos supercomputers have opened up a new era in computational materials theory. This program is becoming a strong attractor for university collaborations.

A second such center has been our Center for Non-Linear Studies, which holds about ten workshops per year, has over 200 visitors, supports about three to four post-doctorate fellows, and initiates and supports new research themes such as "Chaos in Dynamical Systems," "Theoretical and Experimental Dynamic Properties of Polymers (particularly synthetic and biological polymers)," "The Theory of Cellular Automota," and "Fundamental Studies in Turbulence and Instabilities at Interfaces." These are interdisciplinary topics, which in fact will be very important for understanding chemical processes, astrophysical processes, and the whole range of basic to very applied research.

A third such initiative has been to found at Los Alamos a branch of the University of California's Institute for Geophysics and Planetary Physics where the focus, of course, is on the solid earth sciences and space science. But one of the most exciting things has been the two summer camps for applied geophysics experience; we call it SAGE. It is a six-week course. Three of the major oil firms have contributed to the costs in 1984. We had forty students in 1983, and fifty in 1984, for an intense study of the Rio Grande Rift and the surrounding geological phenomena in New Mexico. The IGPP has also been involved in deep, seismic sounding of the Rio Grande Rift, mainly a collaboration between NSF, UCLA, and the Laboratory. We have had some twenty-nine proposals for joint collaborative research by campus and laboratory scientists supported in 1984.

A second area where a national research and development facility like Los Alamos has been able to play an important role is in support of international programs. Our geothermal activity is carried out with the International Energy Agency and provides for the governments of Japan and Germany to join the project to explore the potential for hot dry rock geothermal energy. The laboratory has always played a major role with the International Atomic Energy Agency in providing the technology for nuclear materials control and accountability safeguards for nuclear facilities around the world. We also provide for the training of all of the IAEA inspectors that are drawn from the member countries worldwide.

Most recently we have been heavily involved in Central America in support of the Caribbean Basin Initiative where the laboratory has been asked by the

Agency for International Development to play a lead role in transferring energy technology to our neighbors in the Caribbean Basin area. We have done mineral assessments of St. Lucia and St. Vincent, worked on the peat resources of Costa Rica, looked at geothermal energy in St. Lucia, Costa Rica, Guatemala, and El Salvador. At the same time we have ongoing scientific and technical exchanges with the Institute for Petroleum Research and the Institute for Nuclear Research in Mexico. These initiatives, of course, both support U.S. foreign policy as well as provide for more effective transfer of technology in areas that may be quite useful for our neighbors to the south.

Finally, we try to recognize that both our very applied programs as well as our technology development programs have a need for people who are not purely disciplinary in nature but, in fact, can also play the new role of integrator, mediator, catalyst, or translator, whose technical breadth is required to work on these multidisciplinary activities, whose depth of knowledge has to be sufficient for them to be effective. We recognize that such people are more often found in the work place and trained on the job than produced through a traditional scientific or engineering education.

We see a long-term need to find a mechanism to encourage these people, to identify them, to give them the opportunities to develop their capabilities as they move from small to larger programs, both in basic research as well as in more applied development. This, we think, coupled with the way in which science is increasingly done, taking advantage of large-scale computer simulation, will provide for effective and efficient research and development in the future on a timescale commensurate with national needs. The National Laboratories can adjust to meet the challenge I posed at the beginning, but it requires more effort than in the past — more willingness to experiment with new structures and processes, and more willingness to reach across boundaries to create partnerships with industry, financial institutions, and universities. The goal is continually to renew a creative anachronism to focus on multidisciplinary problem solving, enhance productivity, and create a pool of talent for the future.

DISCUSSION

Barry Munitz

Barry Munitz: Of all my roles, the one that offers the most intriguing management responsibility is president of the Houston Grand Opera. If you have ever tried, on the one hand, to raise $5 million a year from the corporate community, and, on the other hand, to deal with the world's finest creative artists, you really get a sense of juggling the public and the private.

In dealing with joint public/private initiatives, I'd like to discuss a report submitted to the association of university governing boards. The commission, on which I was happy to serve, was sponsored by the Carnegie Foundation and chaired by Clark Kerr and David Reisman. In completing this report, and at the same time planning this public/private section, I noted some linkages. Our basic concern was that the college and university president was being driven inward in recent times. Twenty years ago, strong university presidents were very much involved in social issues, whereas today, with few exceptions (like President Cyert), most college and university presidents are nowhere near as visible, nor as active, nor seemingly as committed to issues beyond their own campus. There are many reasons, of course, financial demands being not the least of them. But the trend concerns us deeply. Furthermore, the search process for finding new college and university presidents is becoming increasingly bifurcated: a strong faculty-based search committee that does much of the screening work and a board selection committee that tries to make the final decision. The problem is that the faculty committee tends to screen out those people that the board committee is most intrigued by, and the board committee then tends to choose people in upside down order from the list prepared by the faculty screening committee. We were attempting to address some specific recommendations to those search and screening apparatuses to mitigate that tension. We wound up being convinced that a vast majority of people who want to do research or pursue learning in this day and age still must pursue those activities within a unit of society that is organized for that purpose. It is very hard to be an isolate in intellectual activity. Scholarship and learning requires some formal organized group and a formal organized group requires a leader. We were concerned that in order to maintain student access to first-rate teachers and researchers, we had to stop the brain drain to industry. We had to provide opportunity for strong faculty to engage unmolested in their research activities and to be well compensated for those research activities as well as to consult with private enterprises, which would allow them to both apply their knowledge and augment their income. (Pockets of innovators can survive for years before anyone in the university bureaucracy discovers where they are, much less what they are doing. Unfortunately, higher education is often *reverse* Darwinism — that is, the survival of the *least* fit. If you're good and strong, you move up and out.)

Two dilemmas concern me: first, the nature of administering creativity and innovation; second, a particular question about power and governance. Being a creative manager, in my opinion, is fundamentally different than managing creativity. All too often, we erroneously assume that the two concepts are identical. It may be, for example, that a very traditional administrator may be a better leader for a highly innovative organization than a highly innovative leader. Take a political analogy. Just as President Nixon broke new ground in China because he was the last person on earth people expected to be imaginative about China, President Reagan might now take on arms control because of his tough stance against the Soviet Union. Thus it may be that a better governor of high-risk innovation and creativity is a person whose credentials, indeed whose instincts, are far more traditional than the people that he or she has to manage. The talents required to provide such leadership are fundamentally different than the talents required to be a risk-taking entrepreneurial researcher or an imaginative entrepreneurial businessman. The trap is superimposing rather than distinguishing these two sets of divergent qualities. Therefore, to use Abe Zaleznick's concept of the holding environment, I offer the hypothesis that the ability to design or sustain that holding environment requires substantially different skills than the ability to create within that environment.

On the governance issue of the joint public/private venture, the two key players bring fundamentally different perceptions of running the partnership. (A university–corporate venture is my model.) As a matter of fact, one is the opposite of the other. A university and a company are opposite images of each other. A university is an inverted hierarchy. (I always enjoyed the notion that, as the academic vice-president of the University of Illinois System, I made less money than the chancellor of the Medical Center Campus, who made less money than the dean of the College of Medicine, who made less money than the chairman of the Department of Surgery, who made less money than all but two of the full professors in his department. My corporate colleagues can't understand this—except for the investment bankers who love to see the brokers and dealers make more money than their presidents.) It is very hard to explain a university's inverted hierarchy to corporate types, since each side has a profoundly different sense of governance. What does this all mean for the management of creativity and innovation?

It probably means that we ought to consider leadership more as a partnership than as a dictatorship. This puts great tension on the board of any joint entity to understand both worlds in which they have to operate, to be sensitive to differing approaches to seeking funds, distributing funds, and setting priorities. It surely means that there is serious tension on the linkage between risk and reward. There is greater risk in joining a public/private entity from either side of the partnership but there is also greater opportunity to be creative.

Michael Kirby: We have an enormous literature on managing private sector companies and an enormous literature on managing public sector agencies, but little on managing mixed public/private enterprises. This, in my view, is the growing sector of the economy. If one looks around Western Europe, Canada, and elsewhere, one finds that government is a share owner of some proportion in major enterprises, sometimes at 60 percent, sometimes 40 percent, but it is often a major player. There is no theory from the academic community that answers such questions as what is the role of a government nominee on a board of directors, or how does a public/private company deal with fundamental problems since public and private sectors' objectives are in fact substantially different. The growth in the future will not be in a simple dichotomy of 100 percent privately owned companies and 100 percent government-owned agencies; rather it will be mixed enterprises (for example, the result of many bailouts will be government taking equity positions). Here seems to be fertile area for a whole range of really interesting work in creative and innovative management.

Donald Kerr: I think the U.S. situation is different than it may be in some other countries. There is, I think, little interest in having part government ownership of private sector companies. We have enterprises that are quasi-public, but the issues of governance are so diverse that you cannot deal with them in an aggregated way. The governance, for example, of the Brookhaven Laboratory with nine associated universities forming a company to operate that laboratory is very different than the University of California operating the Lawrence–Livermore and Los Alamos Laboratories. The buck stops, of course, with the Congress, which in all cases plays the role of senior board, if you will, and examines the programs for which it appropriates money. Thus we have a double board structure with regents of a university at the first level and congressional committees at the second level. (For Los Alamos, some fourteen committees are involved.)

Part VIII

AGENDA FOR BUILDING CREATIVE AND INNOVATIVE MANAGEMENT INTO A FIELD OF ACADEMIC ACTIVITY

Chapter 17

BUILDING A NEW ACADEMIC FIELD
An Act of Management Approach

George Kozmetsky

INTRODUCTION

The development of creative and innovative management as a new academic field can be an important academic experiment. Like many experiments, the things learned during the course of its progress can lead to successful innovations before the field becomes recognized. These spin-offs can be both academic as well as practical. The excitement of the experimental process is embodied in the fact that creative and innovative spin-offs can lead to the development of new strategies for other academic developments, research, teaching, and curricula. The reason that there is a high probability of such successes is that establishing an experimental goal for the field requires the initiation of multidisciplinary programs that are consonant with the goals of the field.[1]

As background, I would like to summarize some of the early IC[2] Institute literature review project related to the development of creative and innovative management as an academic field. The selected review of books was based on the key terms "creativity," "innovation," "creative management," and "innovative management." These publications cover the years 1955–83. Works relating to creativity in the title began appearing early in the period; those with innovation in the title appeared in 1970–71; and both creativity and innovation were included in titles after 1971. Chapter titles in the books focused on examination of environments necessary for creativity, definitions of creativity, how creativity

Table 17-1.   Frequency of Key Words by Function.
Current Awareness—January–July 1984.

Functional Area	Creativity	Innovation
Finance	5	11
Insurance	1	3
Marketing/Retailing	2	6
Purchasing	1	–
Public Administration	–	1
Travel	–	1
Real Estate	2	–
Manufacturing	1	4
R & D	–	1
Health Care	1	2
Production/Distribution	–	1
Advertising	1	1
Personnel	–	–
Legal	–	–
Management (general)	8	6
Telecommunications	–	1
TOTAL	22	38

Source: "Creative & Innovative Management Literature Sample Analysis." Compiled by Patricia L. Roe, IC² Institute Research Associate.

can be applied to problem solving, characteristics of creative individuals, and creativity in groups. The academic fields/topics most represented in the selected literature were management psychiatry, science, research, and engineering.

Another selected sample was taken of the articles in the INFORM current awareness listings. Again the key words "creativity" and "innovation" were used to identify the articles. A total of approximately sixty entries were found for the period January through July 1984. Table 17–1 shows the frequency by functional areas in business as well as by the key words "creativity" and "innovation." The preponderance of citations are on innovation and especially in finance.

Table 17–2 shows the number of articles on innovation by functional business fields found in the Business Index Selections covering the period from December 1982 through June 1984. Finance, again, had the preponderance of the citations.

A preliminary review of the literature clearly establishes that from an academic experimental point of view there are recognized quality refereed journals

Table 17–2. Number of Innovations by Function.
Business Index—December 1982–June 1984.

Functional Area	Innovations
Finance	28
General Management	12
Marketing/Retailing	8
Manufacturing	6
Insurance	5
Travel	5
Advertising	5
Health Care	3
Personnel	3
Real Estate	2
R & D	2
Production/Distribution	2
Purchasing	1
Public Administration	1
Legal	1
Telecommunications	1
TOTAL	85

Source: "Creative & Innovative Management Literature Sample Analysis." Compiled by Patricia L. Roe, IC² Institute Research Associate.

in which academicians in business, liberal arts, psychiatry, and engineering can publish. Most of these journals publish articles on creative and innovative management rather infrequently. Those journals that published three or more articles in the last decade are *Harvard Business Review, Administrative Science Quarterly, Academy of Management Journal, Journal of Creative Training, Research Management, Supervisor and Supervision,* and *American Economic Review.*

There are European journals in which one can publish. The Japanese have tended to publish within their own journals and books, a number of which are available in translation. Those who are interested in publishing in the more professional journals (in contrast to those who have a more academic bent) will find that there is a plethora of opportunities. Periodicals that have published two or more articles between January and July 1984 are *International Management* (UK), *Business Week, Savings Institutions, Pensions and Investment Age, Retail Control, Chain Store Executive,* and *Hospital Forum.*

In the area of science and technical innovations, the Social Policy Research unit at the University of Sussex have published an outstanding bibliography entitled *Science, Technology, and Innovation.*[2] It contains over 2,000 entries on the most important books, journals, and articles that reflect the diversity of research. The reference covers:

1. Measurement of Science and Technologies
2. Inventions and Patents
3. Innovations
4. Economics of Technical Change
5. Social and Political Aspects of Technical Change and Innovation
6. Management of Technical Change and Innovations
7. Technical Change Innovation and Government
8. Technical Change and Work
9. Other Bibliographies on Technical Change and Innovation.

Item 3 bibliographies are classified into (a) Innovations and Economic Developments: Case Studies and Theory; (b) Diffusion of Innovation: Firms and Countries; (c) Specific New Technologies; and (d) Social Innovation and Technical Change. Item 6 bibliographies are: (a) Organization and Management of R & D and Scientific laboratories; (b) Project Evaluation in R & D; (c) Technology Assessment; and (d) Other Aspects of Management.

There are rich data bases available for various aspects of creativity and innovation. Among these are the reports issued by the Congressional Office of Technology Assessment, Department of Commerce Bureau of Industrial Economics, National Science Foundation Science Indicators, Commission of the European Communities Reports, Japanese periodic White Papers by MITI and Japan External Trade Organizations. There are a huge number of private data bases and countless other special reports.

The *Economist* publishes *Innovate,* a new science and technology magazine for top corporate managers. Articles appearing in the first issue include space hardware, test-tube plants, synthetic vaccines, metals and plastics, and supercomputers. The American Academy of Sciences and the American Academy of Engineering publishes *Issues in Science and Technology.* The journal covers policy implications of developments in science, technology, and health, and is intended for decisionmakers in industry, finance, government, and education.

What all this tells me is that there currently exists, in Kuhn's terms, the need for "coordination of myriad quantas of information . . . beyond any person's capacity." From an academician's point of view, Professor Tim Ruefli states that in the future each distinguished professor will have his own knowledge base of data, his or her private information with which to do research and to publish.

Professor Ruefli's research at IC² has done a great deal in this direction. He has built what he calls a "Macro-concentration Data Base" for his research in the policy area of management. Building knowledge data bases including its hardware, software, and system engineering aspects is a growth industry. (IC² is currently preparing an extensive bibliography for researchers interested in creative and innovative management. In addition, Robert Kuhn, as senior research fellow of the IC² Institute, has been commissioned by McGraw-Hill to prepare the *Handbook for Creative and Innovative Managers.*)

There is now a vast unstructured body of professional and academic literature and data and knowledge bases in the area of creative and innovative management. There is need to structure them for more effective utilization by academicians, professionals, and managers.

Some key conclusions for an academic agenda experimental perspective in creative and innovative management are:

1. Discovering Reasonable Conditions to Conduct Experimentation;
2. Approximating a Framework of Reference for Experimentation;
3. Choice of Alternatives for Successful Experiments and Evaluation;
4. The Next Steps and Future Directions.

DISCOVERING REASONABLE CONDITIONS

The pursuit in academia of experimental research is seldom a budgetary process or a contractual/grant process. These processes generally fit those academic research areas that are recognized and thereby subjected to peer review through the department, college, and total university. Peer review is also generally utilized when proposals for outside funding of research are requested from foundations, corporations, and the cognizant government agencies. Most world-class universities have set aside research funds for experimental research. These, as one would expect, are limited and are appropriately subjected to keen review and thereby viewed from an individual researcher's point of view as very competitive and difficult to get in an embryonic stage of research. Such funds are extremely hard to attain when one is on a campus with very outstanding researchers. It is doubly difficult to have such scarce funds allocated to developing a field that has no home. As indicated earlier, "creative and innovative management" is highly unstructured in terms of its expertise, literature, and data bases. No department nor academic discipline nor professional society has emerged to embrace it as being clearly in its province of interest, with the subsequent support and usage of results.

Since the First International Conference on Creative and Innovative Management in 1982, I have not found the "Garbage Can Model" applicable to the field of creative and innovative management. Put in terms of the model, there are no solutions looking for the problem building of a creative and innovative management field. In fact, there has been little academic interest to make incremental changes (adding new and dropping older materials) in functional fields of business to incorporate the innovations found in the academic and professional literature surveys. The hidden agenda of the Second International Conference on Creative and Innovative Management was to influence academic champions to hasten the development of the field. The opportunity for extraordinary participants to present papers together should encourage the academicians who best work in interaction with manager and executives.

At this point, I would like to report on my own experiment that was set forth in my keynote paper for the First International Conference. At that time, I indicated that it was possible for a tenured professor to teach a course on "Measuring the State of Society." To quote from the paper:

> Many have already told me that the measurement of the state of American Society is an impossible task; they end their remarks by saying, "Good Luck!" But that, after all, is the beginning state for all significant innovations. To see its significance, we only need to observe that it is necessary to know where we are if we want to plan rationally and set goals to advanced the state of our society. It is a good challenge for our new discipline."[6]

After teaching this course for five semesters, I found many personal and professional satisfactions. However, it was evident that the course posed problems in terms of reasonable condition for academic experimental research. The major difficulty was use of a nontraditional course title. The department chairman, budget council, and dean had difficulty evaluating the course's contribution to the more traditional existing fields of concentration. Moreover, the topics such as demographics, social indicators, attitudes and concerns, historical perspectives (including economic, philosophical, sociological, political, religious, and technological), functions of wealth and the commercialization of science and technology were not traditional business chunks of knowledge. On the other hand, from the point of view of the students, the course was important to establish a point of departure necessary for creative and innovative management. In terms of Herb Simon's paper, they were given large chunks of knowledge outside of the traditional management curricula that at least met some of his requirements for creativity.

Let us now turn to developing what can be reasonable conditions for academic experimentation under current academic administrative policies and procedures. Some of these are:

1. Professors are encouraged and permitted to teach graduate seminars and/or topical courses.
2. Professors are allocated research and teaching assistants. They can be used to structure the data and bibliographies for the professor. This provides materials for publication and classroom use.
3. Summer research grants and other support can be utilized by the professor.
4. Colloquia can be held to discuss early research results. Hopefully these can be multidisciplinary.
5. Networking can be initiated with other interested faculty members in other universities, domestic and foreign. Their identification is available from bibliographies, attendance at academic and professional societies, symposia, and conferences.
6. Many universities permit the grouping of interested professors to apply for approval of establishing research institutes or centers. While most universities do not provide funds for such entities, it is still important to have official sanction to raise the necessary funds or to obtain a "hunting license."

The above are reasonable internal conditions. There are also a number of reasonable external conditions for academic experimentation in building a creative and innovative management into a field of academic activity. Some of these conditions are as follows:

1. Many academic and professional societies have provided means of holding special sessions at their normal conferences and meetings. These sessions can help give credibility and legitimacy to an experimental agenda.
2. Selected workshops and executive development programs for business, government, and other institutions can also provide reasonable ways to provide experimental research and practical applications as valuable data for scientific study and analysis. In addition, such activities provide legitimacy, ability to place selected graduate students, and part-time financial support to the faculty. Other byproducts can well lead to private corporate support, consulting, and expert witness activities.
3. Locations outside the traditional discipline can contribute to academic experimentation. In fact it may be a necessary condition. Outside locations can even include visits to other academic institutions, think tanks, or research centers, domestically and internationally.
4. Joint appointments help in developing multidisciplines as well as transfering and extending traditional bodies of expertise necessary to build a new field.
5. There are a number of ways that faculty can form cross-disciplinary teams for experimental research in this field. Some require less funding than others.

Underlying both external and internal reasonable conditions is the institutional environment for encouraging experimentation. Richard Cyert addresses important criteria for establishing the appropriate environment from the perspective of a total university. George Huber examines strategies for the adoption of innovation from the department's and dean's perspectives.

The point of Part VIII is that while there are many barriers impeding development of a newer academic field, reasonable conditions do exist to conduct experimental research for building the required agenda. There are good historic reasons for academia to maintain the status quo for academic disciplines. When there is a sound environment that encourages experimentation in curricula, that means it is possible to take an unstructured field such as creative and innovative management and eventually transform it into a structured field when it meets the critical tests of success.

The magnitude of such an experiment is, in Herbert Simon's terminology, "writ large" and requires creativity. Using his definition of creativity, if the experiment proves successful in toto or in significant parts it will be novel, interesting, and valuable.

Because the field is unstructured, a framework of reference for academic experimentation is required to build a field of creative and innovative management. This is an act of management strategy. A framework is necessary if we are to utilize current reasonable academic conditions to conduct experimentation. Currently, the literature encompasses at least four or more academic disciplines (business, engineering, science, and psychiatry). The methodology for the experimentation will require additions of a number of other disciplines including computer sciences, mathematics, statistics, history, economics, econometrics, political science, law, health sciences, psychology, communications, and philosophy. It is difficult to envisage such an experiment as an individual act. It is also difficult to envisage such an experiment as an innovative single group research effort. This volume is designed to help identify a broad research agenda and issues for consideration. Until these are generally accepted, I believe it will be difficult to secure support for a single group research program.

What then is a workable framework of reference within the context of an act of management approach? Management, as used in this context, does not connote that there is a manager or a director. Rather, it connotes that there is a way for synergy to develop around a new academic discipline. Such a synergy does not require the individual academicians to be in one discipline, one department, one college, or located at one university. As an act of management, it mandates that disciplines be assimilated. Most of our world-class universities do not have on their campuses the required expertise, experience, or determination, and even if they did, not all would want to engage in the experiment.

Modern telecommunication and transportation makes it feasible for the development of such a synergistic experimentation across geographic and institutional lines.

A major requirement for conducting the academic experiment is that there must be some kind of duly constituted organization such as an institute or center that reports university-wide, that is recognized to be interdisciplinary and cross-disciplinary, and that focuses on theoretical and applied constructs. Such an institute or center could even take on an independent organizational form such as a consortium of universities. An act of management strategy under such conditions becomes more a process rather than a function.

Approximating a framework for academic experimentation can now be developed. In its simplest form, an on-campus institute or center or consortium can provide for academic research and developmental projects. The framework must provide for two major thrusts; namely, academic research and development projects. The inputs to academic research are the interests of key researchers, issues generated from development projects, and identification of unstructured problems. The outputs are advances in theory and methodology; publications, including academic and professional journals, academic and leadership books, and theses and professional graduate reports; and interactions, including colloquia, workshops and conferences. The inputs to development projects are unstructured problems. The outputs of development projects are advances in methodology, publications including academic and professional journals, academic and leadership books, public/private policy and initiatives, and interactions including workshops and conferences. Figure 17–1 diagrams these relationships.

An act of management strategy recognizes that the experiment requires the process of linking creative management and innovative management. (Creative management, by definition, means new concepts, ideas, methods, directions, and modes of operation. Innovative management, by definition, consists of the ability to implement, develop, and move successfully.) Coupling creative management and innovative management is an act of management. The above framework can give structure to what is seemingly unstructured, yet be within acceptable conditions for experimentation. Also, it helps to develop the processes necessary for coupling the two dimensions of academic research and development programs with creative and innovative management.

We can now approximate some of the couplings. Academic research and development project results, when viewed as new, can flow through a process that provides linkages to move successfully from academic research to development projects and back again. Figure 17–2 shows how the framework, working through the process of coupling, can provide a dynamic environment that is perceived to be conducive to creativity and innovation.

Figure 17–1. Framework for Academic Experimentation

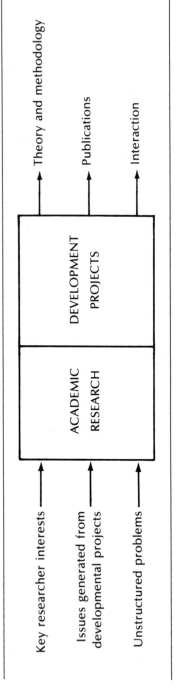

Source: George Kozmetsky.

Figure 17–2. Approximating a Framework for the Process of Academic Experimentation.

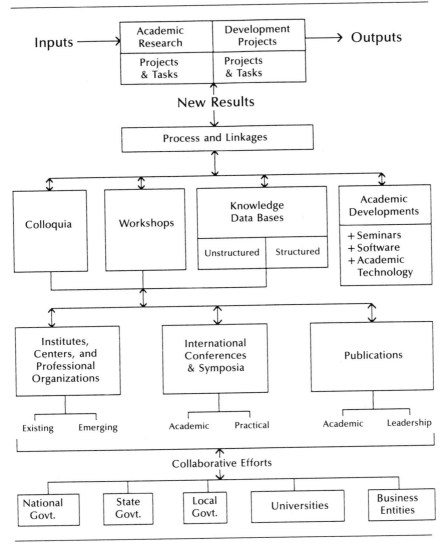

The coupling process basically links new concepts, ideas, methods, directions and modes of operation—first to academics through colloquia and workshops and then to practitioners who are leaders in their respective fields—builds knowledge data bases (both structured and unstructured), and assures that new results enter academic development under reasonable conditions conducive to experimentation. From these couplings, it is then possible to establish relationships with other existing and emerging institutes, centers and professional organizations, to conduct academic and practical conferences and symposia, and to publish works for both academic and nonacademic leaders. The process in turn allows for collaborative efforts between academics on the one hand and those in national governments, state governments, local communities, universities, and business entities on the other hand. Because there is continual feedback and interaction, the process is dynamic.

CHOICES OF ALTERNATIVES FOR SUCCESSFUL EXPERIMENTS AND EVALUATION

There are a multitude of alternatives for joining in experimental research. Individuals and institutions can participate in the coupling process at any point in the process. For example, it is possible for individual academics to participate under reasonable conditions in pioneering academic research. They can enter into the process through their own research or by attending colloquia, conferences and symposia, or by attending meetings of institutes, centers or professional organizations, or by collaborating with other universities, federal government, state government, communities or businesses, or by becoming a member of development projects that work on these matters. This permits individuals, groups, institutions, and other collaborative arrangements to have freedom in both selection and degree of participation in the rich menu presented by the framework. The range of knowledge resulting from the coupling process must contribute to academic development. Otherwise the experiment of developing creative and innovative management into an academic field will not be successful.

Given the framework of academic experimentation, how does one measure success in the utilization of an act of management strategy? The clearest measure is, as Herbert Simon indicates, that the output of the experiment must be novel and valuable. Whoever wants to use the results in the process may well determine that the output has value. The users can be other academicians, various participants in the experiment, outside individuals, students, government officials and agencies, businesses and other institutions. If the new outputs are not used, they do not meet the test of success.

The successful use of the experimental results can be determined in a number of ways. Academic participants can evaluate their own individual success in a number of ways:

1. Publications in refereed journals or through books;
2. Development of knowledge data bases—personalized as well as more general.

3. Academic development applications for classroom supplements including case material, other teaching material, software, and so forth.
4. Participation in colloquia, workshops and symposia — locally, nationally, or internationaly.
5. Involvement in institutes, centers, and professional organizations — as members and officers. They should participate locally, nationally, and internationally. They can even become founding members of new organizations, which in turn give legitimacy and credibility to the experimental process.
6. Active participation in collaborative efforts at their discretion that develop the couplings to other institutions.

Other institutions and individuals can evaluate the success of the experiments in a number of ways:

1. Workshops and conferences are ways of determining the utility of the focus of research and its subsequent usage. They serve to identify priorities and areas of opportunity that can contribute to the short-, mid-, and long-term development of creative and innovative management as a field.
2. Successes from workshops and conferences can be measured by what the participants have done to "make things happen" as opposed to the attitude "nobody has done a thing about it." The dynamics of "making things happen" transcends the act of the research. It must be embodied in subsequent actions. The process of coupling becomes important and self-amplifying in terms of action taking. The action is only successful when something concrete and meaningful happens.
3. Initiatives generated from conferences and symposia provide a standard by which to measure success. Namely, can they be implemented in terms of new laws and regulations or opportunities being used within the private sector or in academia?
4. Another measure of success includes continued collaboration and support. If additional collaboration occurs, that too can be viewed as success within the experimental research process.

Administrative heads — chancellors, presidents, deans, departmental chairmen, and institute and center directors — can evaluate the success of the experimental research as follows:

1. Assess accomplishments of faculty members in the traditional manner and under existing policies.
2. Evaluate the feedback from academic developments, colloquia, workshops, symposia, conferences, and publications.

3. Assess the effectiveness of collaborative efforts in terms of acceptance of the overall institution, incremental increase in support (financial and otherwise), and attraction of graduate students and their subsequent placement.

What are the motivational factors that encourage faculty members to participate actively in an experimental research process? Creative and innovative management research clearly involves academic, personal and professional risks. There is a paradox here. While getting involved is a risk, the process itself reduces risk.

The process provides for an integrated set of motivational forces. These include:

1. *The perception of success.* Individuals in the process feel as though they are participating in successful academic research that at the same time has positive impacts on development projects. The perception of success spreads across disciplines and traditional institutional barriers. It brings credibility and legitimacy to the entire process and builds acceptance for the new discipline.

2. *Entrepreneurial opportunity.* Faculty members have the opportunity to exercise their entrepreneurial bent. The process encourages risk taking within a supportive environment so that the individual faculty members can produce services for the classroom and develop a reputation in their discipline.

3. *Prestige.* The framework provides a sense of prestige to those invited to participate. Faculty, through titles, special awards including fellowships, and participation in key events feel important, and rightly so, in setting new directions.

4. *Ties to key people, associations, and organizations.* The collaboration with prestigious scholars and other important individuals and institutions is not only personally satisfying but also provides insights into the thinking and action of creative and innovative individuals.

5. *Incremental Financial Rewards.* Many of the experimental choices provide additional financial sources such as holding fellowships, commissioned papers at conferences, participating in funded developmental projects, and expert consulting fees.

THE NEXT STEPS AND FUTURE DIRECTIONS

In a real sense, building creative and innovative management into a field of academic endeavor is still a pioneering task. Let us proceed with imagination, hope, and daring to chart the direction of this emerging discipline through an act of management approach. In this task, as in most earlier explorations, our map of this previously uncharted territory leaves much to the imagination.

Among the next steps that must be initiated are:

1. Continue the series of international conferences on creative and innovative management. We must expand the focus and examine the area from different management perspectives, academic disciplines, institutional frameworks, geographical locations, and current to long-term macro as well as micro needs and demands.
2. Develop and publish the agenda of issues emerging from the Second International Conference.
3. Complete and publish the state-of-the-art Handbook for Creative and Innovative Managers.
4. Complete and publish a relevant, up-to-date, and multidisciplinary bibliography.
5. Initiate, complete, and publish relevant, up-to-date knowledge data bases.
6. Encourage the teaching of courses or parts of courses that examine in an integrated way the issues related to creative and innovative management.
7. Foster and support research projects in universities.
8. Establish prizes or awards recognizing outstanding achievements in and contributions to creative management, innovative management, and/or creative and innovative management.
9. Encourage research for discovering—as well as research for invention—within an academic setting of creative and innovative management.
10. Identify and extend development programs that can contribute to the understanding of and use for creative and innovative management.
11. Encourage the collaboration of government, business, and academia to more effectively couple theory and practice in creative and innovative management.
12. Encourage the study of the feasibility of establishing university consortiums to study creative and innovative management for large-scale programs, dynamic growth institutions, small businesses, entrepreneurial ventures, planned cities, industrial complexes, regional development projects, and outer space programs.

I firmly believe that we are at a great watershed in advancing creative and innovative management into an important field of academic activity.

NOTES

1. One set of such goals is set forth in A. Charnes and W. W. Cooper, eds., *Creative and Innovative Management* (Cambridge, Mass.: Ballinger Publishing Company, 1984), p. 23.
2. F. Henwood and G. Thomas, eds., *Science, Technology and Innovation* (New York: St. Martin's Press, 1983).

Chapter 18

CREATIVE AND INNOVATIVE MANAGEMENT
A Manifesto for Academia

Timothy W. Ruefli

INTRODUCTION

There is a specter haunting the management schools of America. It is the unsettling notion raised first by a handful of academicians and practicing managers that managerial education is not fulfilling the primary role that is required of it by society. Having made the transition in the middle of this century from schools of commerce, training the future clerks and secretaries of America to schools of management, training the future managers of the giant corporations and large bureaucracies, the more externally attuned individuals in schools of management are perceiving hints that a second, and even greater, transition in management education is facing them. There are indications, as yet faint, that society is formulating demands to be placed on schools of management for them to go beyond meeting the requirements of large traditional corporations and government agencies. New age schools of management must produce knowledge and future executives that will serve as catalysts for and directors of creative and innovative solutions to the current and emerging societal demands. It is the objective of this paper to provide a rationale for and outline of the strategic elements of a framework for activities that will establish creative and innovative management as a viable academic area of research and teaching.

As a starting point in this manifesto, creative and innovative management is defined to be management that in ambiguous circumstances effectively sur-

passes competitors in markets for inputs and simultaneously strategically sur-
passes competitors in markets for outputs by providing existing and new products and/or services for existing and new markets more efficiently. This definition is both functional and structural, avoiding being a trivial characterization
of all management by including the qualification that the circumstances of
management be ambiguous and that performance be measured strategically. In
an article analyzing corporate development under ambiguous circumstances,
Ruefli and Sarrazin define ambiguous circumstances to be a situation where: (1)
information ranges from nearly certain to highly ambiguous on multiple dimensions; (2) goals, objectives, and constraints are vague and ill-perceived; and
(3) there is a diffuse decisionmaking process involving multiple levels of the
internal hierarchy as well as external stakeholders (Ruefli and Sarrazin 1981).
The authors showed that given ambiguous circumstances a control approach to
management is more appropriate than is a rational planning approach. That
implication is carried over into the present paper.

EXTERNAL FACTORS

The general motivation for the up-coming change has been well established in
the proceedings of the first symposium on creative and innovative management,
notably in the papers presented by Kozmetsky (1984), Kuhn (1984), and Kirby
(1984), and will not be repeated here. Rather the focus will be on the impacts of
that transition on academia, specifically on schools of management, primarily
business schools, but also including schools of public affairs, educational administration, health administration, and the other professional schools. This
manifesto reflects the attention paid by the press and popular literature to business schools, but the problem and motivation for change extend to all academic
programs dealing with management functions; this generalization, to be sure,
is direct.

FRAMEWORK

In developing this paper, and in designing an agenda for creative and innovative management as an accepted academic field, the strategic control model developed by the author and Jacques Sarrazin (1981) will be used. In brief, the
problem is recognized as being strategic in nature and the circumstances are
characterized as being ambiguous. That means that we are faced with a situation in which information reliability falls off at a rapid rate over time, varying

in this behavior by decision dimension. The usual rational planning paradigm of setting precise long-range goals and constraints and programming resources over the time horizon to achieve that goal is inappropriate under these circumstances. Therefore, the strategic control approach suggests that rather than a precise long-range goal, a fuzzy long-range goal be established, and the development space be partitioned into that short-run segment in which information is reliable enough for decisionmaking and a longer run segment in which information is inherently unreliable and unsuitable for planning (see Figure 18–1).

To incorporate the effects of long-run fuzzy goals on short run decisions, the strategic control approach establishes a development window at the end of the segment of reliable information. The dimensions of this window are developed by factoring the long-range fuzzy goal into an appropriate number of strategic dimensions and using them to establish threshold events that determine the development window. Short-run activities are then programmed forward to attempt to reach the window in the specified time. If this is possible, then the system will be in a position to reach the long-range goal at the end of the development period.

Continuing the structural approach it can be observed that the demand for the outputs of management schools ultimately comes from a society demanding goods and services and the need to manage those, but this demand is moderated through existing corporations. In the past two decades that demand has been channeled through the corporate infrastructure — the top thousand corporations and the financial and other service organizations that support them. These corporations have the resources, employment positions, and networks of influence to affect the curriculum and research programs of the management schools.

IMPLICATIONS

Given that the demands for creative and innovative management come ultimately from society and these demands are being actualized by a small but growing number of managers and organizations, one implication is that to give creative and innovative management academic legitimacy, research must become more managerial, more in touch with real-world management problems; furthermore, the results of this research must be translated into the classrooms for the prospective manager at a faster rate. Channels must be opened from creative and innovative managers to academia so that external influence can be brought to bear, not to permit outside influences to direct academic programs, but to expose academics to a new and exciting set of problems and opportunities.

Figure 18–1.   Strategic Control of Systems Development: Fuzzy and Nonfuzzy Spaces of Systems Development in Relation to Strategic Control.

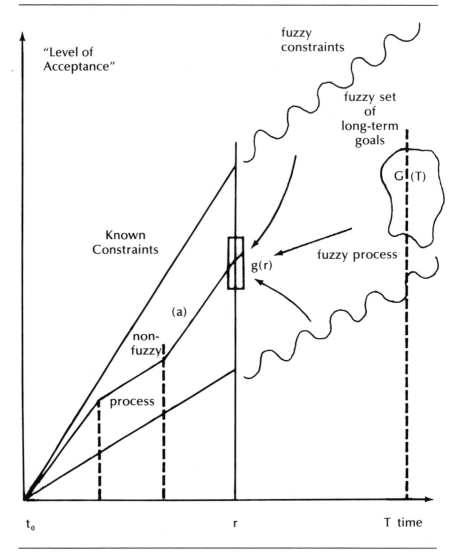

(a) = development of system in the period [t_0, r]
g(r) = intermediate non-fuzzy goals for time 'r'

To accomplish this, creative and innovative managers, faculty, and administrators must make their voice heard over the demands created by the more traditional managers. The latter are more numerous, have more history, and are more coherently organized. Right now academicians hear about creative and innovative managers and organizations on an anecdotal or isolated instance basis, with an occasional book like Peters and Waterman (1982)—hardly the degree of influence necessary to generate a revolution in the underlying paradigm. Creative and innovative managers need to respond to questions like: Where are the professional societies of creative and innovative managers? Where are the endowed positions dedicated to creative and innovative management? Where are the leading creative and innovative senior executives speaking out on the deplorable state of creative and innovative management in business schools? Where are the creative and innovative executives lobbying for new directions in business education? Where are the creative and innovative managers who are willing to return to academia to help train a new generation of creative and innovative managers?

Too often creativity and innovation are regarded as being strictly future-oriented when they are better regarded as having solid roots in historical processes. If we are to avoid creativity and innovation that are generated for their own sake —the management education equivalent of pop-art—we need to see that we and our students and future managers have a thorough regard for history. Just as corporations emphasize the last and next quarter's performance, politicians the last and next election, management schools emphasize the most recent textbooks and most current articles as being worthy of students' attention. Thus students are often not given a sense of perspective, a foundation upon which to evaluate and make changes. Where are the management programs that incorporate general trends in society and culture as a context for management? Similarly, we have in management schools backed away from courses in the future — technology forecasting, and so forth—leaving our students to live in the present only. Who then is surprised that when they graduate they manage from the same perspective?

Creative and innovative management are not fostered in an atmosphere of generalities, universal theories, and models that are applicable to all management situations. Creative and innovative management are fostered in regard to specifics of structuring operations and implementation of decisions. The implication here is that we need niche strategies for management schools. The low-cost across-the-board producer of MBAs is not likely to be the source of creative and innovative managers.

Before turning to a set of issues and the preliminary specification of the milestones for the legitimization of creative and innovative management as an academic area, it is worth examining the strengths and weaknesses that will impact on the ability of management schools to undertake the necessary strategic change. Ostensibly, academia is characterized by a tradition of seeking out and developing new ideas. In fact, like the scientific community characterized by Thomas Kuhn (1970), new ideas are welcome as long as they fit and support the existing paradigm. There is in place, however, the mechanism to allow acceptance of a new paradigm once it appears—the principle of academic freedom that will allow individual researchers and teachers to change directions of intellectual effort. Thus another strength of academia is the significant number of trained researchers and teachers that can be attracted to the new area. A substantial number of these academics have significant contacts with practicing managers through consulting, research studies, and just general acquaintanceship and can document the changes as they appear in management practice.

On the negative side, academicians seem to operate on the principle of sunk intellectual costs and will likely require significant external pressure before they will yield recognition of a new paradigm, especially if the new paradigm threatens their existing intellectual investment. The current demand on the part of existing and prospective students for existing forms of management education can also act as an inhibition of academic change. The sheer numbers of such students places a strain on the academic system and leaves little slack for change. Academia's past successes in serving the demands of both traditional management and students wanting such positions coupled with a "don't fix it if it ain't broken" mentality also militate against change.

ISSUES FOR THE AGENDA

Issues cluster around the four goal areas of research, curriculum, dissemination, and professional activities identified above.

Issue: Can creative and innovative management be taught?

One of the objections that academicians raise to the suggestion that creative and management be introduced into the curriculum is that creativity and innovation cannot be taught. In this objection they are partly correct; creativity and innovation in the sense of genius cannot, to the best of my knowledge, be taught. But if one examines carefully the proposals being made and the concepts being developed with respect to creative and innovative management, what is being called for—while not excluding genius—does not require it. Given this more modest proposal, it is clear that the possibility of being able to teach creative and innovative management exists; the strategies for operationalizing this pedagogy, however, are not self-evident, and developing them and selecting from among the alternatives is the true heart of this issue.

Issue: What concepts and techniques available today can form the basis for a theory of and the practice of creative and innovative management?

American managers created a style of management that was both creative and innovative until it stagnated in the 1970s. After a brief period of self-castigation and casting about in the late seventies, the threads of a new creative style of management have appeared in the more innovative of American corporations and in prescient academic literature. The concepts of managers as operators/ strategists, logical incrementalism, multiple points of view, strategic profit and loss statements and balance sheets, comprehensive audits, information technology, artificial intelligence, and so forth are emerging in these corporations. These concepts have been noted by management schools as being of peripheral academic interest, and the connection to and impact on the curriculum has not been made in most cases. These may be categorized by faculty as being worthy topics for Ph.D. dissertations, but they are not perceived as relevant to turning out large numbers of MBAs for the corporate infrastructure. This list of concepts should be enlarged and linked as a step in synthesizing a theory of creative and innovative management.

Issue: What specific sources of creative and innovative management in academic programs can be used as a basis for a more general creative and innovative program?

Most management programs have sub-areas of curriculum and research that incorporate creative and innovative management. Management schools have often relegated creativity and innovation to the small business/entrepreneurship and fringe areas of the curriculum, conveniently ignoring the need for creativity and innovation in our larger organizations. This models the naive conventional view of the real world wherein little in the way of creativity is expected from the producers of basic goods and services until they are pressured by domestic or foreign competition. Innovation and creativity are often seen as the province of small and high-tech firms. Less frequently, creative and innovative management is included as part of courses in the area of mangement of macro-projects—large-scale efforts involving multiple organizations on a cross-institutional basis. These and other pockets of creative and innovative management need to be identified and evaluated as sources for and bases from which to introduce creative and innovative management into the mainstream curriculum.

Issue: What is the role of quantitative techniques in creative and innovative management?

The conventional wisdom is that quantitative approaches to management are strictly deductive in nature (and therefore scientific) whereas creativity takes place in strictly an inductive cognitive mode. This is, in fact, the case if the teaching of quantitative methods is limited to the teaching of quantitative techniques and ignores design aspects of problem structuring and implementation of solutions. Unfortunately, this latter situation is often the case in management schools. Recent understanding in mathematical research and the philosophy of science have, however, shown the interrelationship of deductive and inductive reasoning and the creative aspects of each (Davis and Hersh 1981). Mathematical techniques have proven to be a help to management when placed in the proper managerial context. Perhaps if schools of management spent less time in teaching the mechanics of quantitative techniques and more time in developing the managerial context for using and evaluating the results of such techniques, the creative and innovative management content of the curricula would thereby increase.

Issue: Must a creative and innovative management program abandon teaching of the more traditional management approaches?

The teaching of creative and innovative management has been regarded as an either/or proposition vis-à-vis traditional management teaching. This does not necessarily have to be the case. Creative and innovative management is not likely to do away with the role of more traditional management activities nor with the need to educate future managers in that role. We must, however, cut down on the time it takes us to teach the traditional ways of doing business to leave more time to teach our students to go beyond those ways and develop new ways of managing.

Changes in the traditional environment of managers must be taken into account. The advent of large data bases moves the locus of and context for creativity from the making of data-free hunches (a process that is difficult to teach) to the creative use of data that already exists (a process that is teachable). The rise of service organizations and information technology-based corporations means that intellectual and informational capital have become more prominent and cannot be managed under traditional management approaches; just ask the corporation that has acquired a high-tech company only to have the key personnel leave after the acquisition, leaving little in the way of tangible assets.

We must, for instance, teach our Ph.D.'s to apply their academic training to the problems of management (as opposed to only the problems generated by other academicians) and to learn more about the practice of management, if we in academia are to participate in the creative and innovative management of the future. Simultaneously, we must train future managers to be managerial researchers—giving them more of a research education so they understand the process of intellectual creativity, at least at an operational level. Prospective managers must be taught to evaluate new and creative ideas in the management area. One place to start is to expose them to the best of the recent managerial research done by faculty and Ph.D. students and have them evaluate these findings in light of their knowledge of historical management practice.

Teaching creativity and innovation in the classroom should lead to students who demand creativity and innovation as an ongoing part of their educational process. That means more creativity and innovation on the part of faculty, administration, and associated business executives. Room should be left for students to design part of their own curriculum. Interdisciplinary teaching concepts should be dusted off once again and retried but this time with a new focus—that of creative and innovative management. Contacts with other professional schools, the liberal and fine arts, and the sciences should be encouraged.

Issue: What academic standards can be used to evaluate creative and innovative management education?

One of the fears of academics is that in admitting creative and innovative management into the curriculum, standards by which student and faculty performance is evaluated must be drastically changed. To allay that fear we must develop evaluation procedures that do not require a change in standards of academic excellence to allow for innovation and creativity but, rather, recognize that those standards have a wider range of applicability that heretofore have been implemented and that only new measures are required to enforce standards.

Issue: Can creative and innovative management be taught on an across-the-board basis or must elites be generated?

Initial efforts, at least, will most likely not be on an across-the-board basis. Elites are going to have to be created in the form of pilot programs where selected students and faculty explore new ideas in pedagogy. Perhaps the best place to start is with executive programs where managers with a record of creativity are combined with faculty and regular students to design and implement a program in creative and innovative management.

Issue: What are appropriate strategies for schools of management to take with respect to creative and innovative management?

While the next section of the book deals with appropriate strategies at the program level, this issue addresses the question of strategy at the level of the school or college. Given the formidable barriers to entry, it seems clear that creative and innovative management must appear first as part of an existing management curriculum. There is, however, a question as to whether there is a need to have some of our management schools focus on the area of creativity and innovation in management the way that Harvard and Stanford focus on the Fortune 500, to make creativity their strategy, and to have as a goal the production of creative managers who are hired by companies for their creativity and ability to innovate. This creativity should have a sound basis in the business principles and a thorough grounding in the functional areas, but the market focus should be on the firms on the American Stock Exchange and smaller.

Issue: In what areas of creative and innovative management does the business community lead the academic community and vice versa?

There was a time when management schools lead the business community in terms of techniques and concepts (operations research, information systems, behavioral science, etc.) and many faculty and administrators are living in the reflected afterglow of that period. But that time is gone; business firms have better computers, more sophisticated O.R. models, bigger data bases, more complex organizational arrangements and so forth than exist or are well under stood in schools of management. It is time for schools of management to be creative and innovative themselves. They have never been particularly good at practicing what they preach, but the call is not for a restructuring of management schools, rather for a redirection of research and programs within the existing structure. The first step is to go out into the business world and document the existence and dimensions of creative and innovative management. Use the problems and opportunities facing managers as the basis for academic research. The hope is to leapfrog the business world and to lead the next cycle.

Theory is needed to provide a basis for flexibility (i.e., creativity and innovativeness in the future management), but the old theory will not do. New theory is needed, and this must initially be based on descriptive material. What is called for is not a repeat of the traditional cases that provided much of the basis for the last revolution in management education. These cases were static in nature and generally theory-free. There is now available a wide body of knowledge on traditional business practice, and this knowledge should be incorporated into the descriptive material. We now have the capability to link descriptive material to data and knowledge bases to yield a series of dynamic narratives that can serve not only as teaching devices for future creative and innovative managers but also as the basis on which the new round of management theory can be based.

Issue: What trends need to be monitored in determining the employment possibilities of future creative and innovative (as well as traditional) managers?

While management schools have not been noted for the application of sophisticated market research technique in determining the availability of jobs for graduates with specific skill mixes in traditional areas, if they attempt to educate prospective creative and innovative managers, they will have to monitor a different set of trends if they are to anticipate demand for this program. Alternatively, the same trends might be monitored but interpreted differently. For example, predictions are that future jobs for humans will either be more menial than those suitable for computers and robots, be a more creative tandem operation with computers, or be far more creative than computer capacity. Middle managers doing routinized decisionmaking are prime candidates for computer-driven obsolescence or even more routinization tending computer systems, while this same trend will increase the demand for creative and innovative managers. While middle management will not disappear, the truly creative jobs will be open to those with better training in creative and innovative management than those coming out of most traditional management programs.

Similarly, the demand for traditionally trained management graduates has come historically from the largest corporations and the supporting infrastructure. However, this source of demand has not provided most of the rest of the managerial employment. For example, in the period 1965–84 population growth in the age group 16–65 years of age was 38 percent. Jobs in that period increased 45 percent. Government employment did not grow much past the 1970s; the Fortune 500 have a net loss in jobs since 1970; high-tech created only 10 percent of new jobs and will not be a significant factor until the 1990s (if then). The growth in jobs in this last decade has been due to small- and middle-sized low-tech or no-tech companies. This trend is projected to continue for the next decade and may well provide the most likely source of employment for creative and innovative managers. Strategically significant trends must be identified and monitored if academic creative and innovative management programs are to be given the direction they need.

Issue: Who should set the creative and innovative research agenda and how?

The academician's standard response is to claim authority for the academic community. But since this new area is directed at management practice, it might be wiser and even academically sounder to set the research agenda with an eye to real world problems. We have historical evidence that academics in professional schools can so divorce their research efforts from professional practice that not only do they lose the interest of the managers, but, in their increasing irrelevance, they even lose the interest of their colleagues. While the precise combinations of academics, managers, funders, and other interested parties needs to be determined, it seems clear that setting the creative and innovative management research agenda should be a joint effort. As for the question of how the agenda is to be set, in the discussion of a previous issue the need to determine the areas where business leads academia and vice versa suggests one approach. Other alternatives need to be developed and analyzed.

Issue: Who should fund research and curriculum development in the area of creative and innovative management?

Very often the traditional areas of funding are not available to those engaged in research in nontraditional areas. Even if these funds are available, they may not be there in the form or quantity necessary to produce the needed progress in the field seeking the funds. For example, it might be best if a program similar to the Ford and Carnegie Foundation programs for business schools in the 1950s and 1960s that gave impetus to the behavioral and quantitative areas of management were to be established for the area of creative and innovative management.

Issue: Which professional learned societies, if any, should take responsibility for the development of creative and innovative management?

One of the cachets of an accepted academic area is to have its own or the sponsorship of another professional learned society. In the case of creative and innovative management there are several possible existing societies that could serve as possible sponsors for an embryo society or institute of creative and innovative management. The problem is to chose among them or to decide to form a new society or institute specifically for the area.

The issues raised above are not exhaustive of those needed in the process of creative and innovative management becoming an accepted academic area. They are representative issues that touch most of the key points necessary to develop an agenda for the academic respectability of the area. In the next section of this paper just such an agenda, based on the foregoing issues, will be presented.

AGENDA

A set of suggested milestones to measure the acceptance of creative and innovative management in academia is presented in Figure 18-2. This figure is a detailing and extension of the diagram presented by Kozmetsky. In developing an agenda for acceptance of creative and innovative management as an academic area, four areas must be addressed: research, teaching, service, and dissemination. Aspects of each of these appear in the diagram. Following the strategic control paradigm we have established a long-range fuzzy goal: academic acceptance of creative and innovative management by the year 1999. This fuzzy goal can be translated into more precise terms by noting that such acceptance can be defined to mean that by 1999 we will see (1) the establishment of an ongoing research program formally supported by industry, private foundations, and government; (2) the establishment of a graduate school of creative and innovative management; (3) the existence of a national professional learned society of creative and innovative management; and (4) an international creative and innovative management journal.

Figure 18–2. Acceptance of Creative and Innovative Management in Academia.

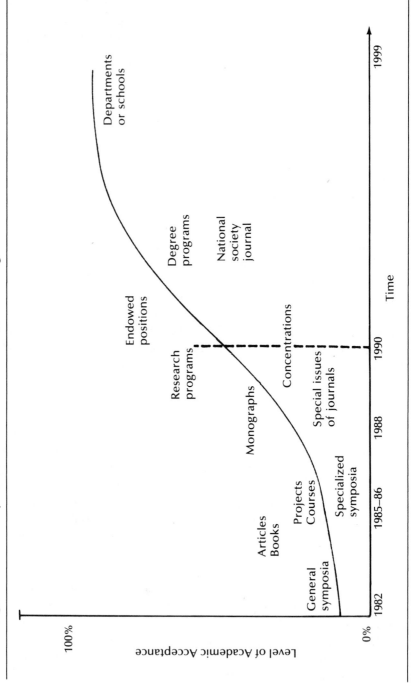

Given this long term set of goal measures we can then continue the strategic control approach by establishing a nearer term development window for the acceptance of creative and innovative management. We can set this window at 1990 and specify by that time in order to be in a position to reach the long-term goals the following dimensions of the window must be in place: (1) ongoing creative and innovative management research programs with individual support; (2) the establishment of one or more graduate management programs permitting a major in the area of creative and innovative management; (3) groups of sessions devoted to creative and innovative management at national meetings of existing learned societies; and (4) special issues of existing academic journals devoted to creative and innovative management research findings.

The dimensions of this development window allow us to specify what steps must be taken in the short run to be in a position to go through the development window by 1990. The necessary first steps in this process have been taken by the holding of the first creative and innovative management symposium in 1982, the publication of the proceedings of that symposium, the holding of the second symposium and the publication of its proceedings. The next steps to be taken are: (1) to hold a series of symposia devoted to creative and innovative management in specific contexts; (2) the development of a number of courses on creative and innovative management; (3) the publication of articles on creative and innovative management in leading academic journals; and (4) the presentation of sessions on creative and innovative management at regional and national meetings of learned societies.

The concept of the next set of symposia needs some elaboration. I suggest that the next step in carrying out the agenda is to convene two different sets of symposia in the area of creative and innovative management. I believe that the previous symposia on the general issue of creative and innovative management have been desirable and necessary first stps in the process of achieving legitimacy. However, based on the observation that creative and innovative management must start from particulars of management situations, the next set of symposia in this area should be sponsored by academia and should be built around a theme of examining creative and innovative management in corporate strategy or marketing or personnel or organization, or alternatively, creative and innovative management in a selected industry. The second set of symposia would be directed at the observation that external influence is needed to encourage academic acceptance of creative and innovative management as a legitimate area. These symposia would be organized by funding agencies and academicians in conjunction with creative and innovative managers and would address the problem of developing and allocating the resources necessary to generate the required changes in academia.

Schedules of Strategic Milestones

Curriculum

1. Course sessions
2. Courses
3. Pilot programs
4. Specializations
5. Programs
6. Schools
7. Continuing education programs.

Research

1. Projects
2. Programs
3. Centers
4. Institutes
5. Ongoing research programs supported by business, government, and foundations.

Dissemination

1. Symposia devoted to specific areas
2. Articles in leading journals
3. Monographs
4. Special issues of leading journals
5. Journal of creative and innovative management.

Professional

1. Sessions at regional and national meetings of learned societies
2. Program area at national meetings of national learned societies
3. A professional learned society devoted to creative and innovative management.

CONCLUSION

This paper has outlined a manifesto for change in schools of management to make creative and innovative management an accepted academic area. The dimensions of the change noted by others and repeated here suggests that such shifts will require a substantial and continuing external input to reinforce the agents for change within academia. A set of prescriptions, ideas, issues, and strategic milestones have been outlined to suggest an agenda to bring about the required change. The next step in the process of academic acceptance is to refine and revise simultaneously the proposed agenda and to develop alternative strategies to resolve the issues raised and to reach the systems development window generated in the agenda-setting process.

REFERENCES

Charnes, A., and W.W. Cooper, eds. 1984. *Creative and Innovative Management.* Cambridge, Mass.: Ballinger Publishing Company.

Davis, Philip J., and Reuben Hersh. 1981. *The Mathematical Experience.* Boston: Houghton Mifflin.

Drucker, Peter. 1984. "Why America's got so Many Jobs." *Wall Street Journal* (Jan. 24).

Kirby, Michael J.L. 1984. "Innovation in Government: Problems and Possibilities." In *Creative and Innovative Management,* edited by A. Charnes and W.W. Cooper. Cambridge, Mass.: Ballinger Publishing Company.

Kozmetsky, George. 1984. "Creative and Innovative Management: A New Academic Frontier." In *Creative and Innovative Management,* edited by A. Charnes and W.W. Cooper. Cambridge, Mass.: Ballinger Publishing Company.

Kuhn, Robert L. 1984. "Creative and Innovative Management—A Challenge to Academia." In *Creative and Innovative Management,* edited by A. Charnes and W.W. Cooper. Cambridge, Mass.: Ballinger Publishing Company.

Kuhn, Thomas. 1970. *The Structure of Scientific Revolutions.* Chicago, Ill.: University of Chicago Press.

Peters, Thomas J., and Robert H. Waterman. 1982. *In Search of Excellence.* New York: Harper & Row.

Ruefli, Timothy W., and Jacques Sarrazin. 1981. "Strategic Control of Corporate Development Under Ambiguous Circumstances." *Management Science* 27: 10 (October).

DISCUSSION

Abraham Charnes

Abraham Charnes: Creativity and innovation, insofar as developing into a field of academic activity, need to be considered for what they are, the functions of individual and groups of individuals joined together for intellectual activities involving knowledge and/or experiential bases beyond the competency of a single individual. As far as the teaching is concerned, the generation of creativity is a function of searching for and discovering the talents of individuals and/or group combinations by means of problems posed to them for possible solution or possible failure. The problems have to be real, current, and new, at least to the individuals. At The University of Pennsylvania years ago, they used to have a problems seminar, and every once in a while, unsolved problems would be snuck in. The faculty would be warned to keep the secret, and regularly new results would come forth. The students did not know that these problems were unsolved, and therefore they went ahead and solved them.

Another kind of structural mechanism that can be adapted is that of the technical committees in Esso. These innovative groups were started after Esso/Humble did not license the thermal cracking process and a year later found itself in a great bind. They decided to do their own research in thermal cracking; but since they did not want to be caught again without having evaluated the latest ideas coming out in the field, they established these technical committees. They were set up across the whole institution and operated like professional societies. The composition of the committees combined older experienced persons and younger persons. The papers submitted were not to be reviewed by

294

anyone's boss, and the results were sent up to top management for further action.

Question: Do you see graduate schools of management being replaced by graduate schools of creative and innovative management? If not, what are the separate roles for the two different institutions?

Thomas Ruefli: That's a choice that must be made. If we look at the mass of business schools in the early part of this century (not the leading ones), many of them were just training clerks and secretaries. When the transition was made to train managers, the new schools of management supplanted the old schools of commerce. I do not think such a similar supplantation is demanded by introducing creative and innovative management. The two can coexist within one framework, although there are significant advantages for having a distinctive school that has as its specific strategy the production of creative and innovative managers.

Comment: If we take Professor Simon's construct, creativity and innovation permeate the entire business curriculum rather than being segregated into separate fields.

Thomas Ruefli: There's a trade-off here. Just as we need mass production for economies of scale to reduce costs and establish quality standards, if we allow creativity to run rampant on an assembly line with workers and machines inputting innovations as items pass, we would end up with a very expensive process. Creativity and innovation are disruptive; that has been adequately documented. The question is, therefore, can we tolerate that much disruption throughout the business curriculum? We have some business schools that are oriented towards low cost and mass output. Should we ask those schools to alter their success strategies? Should all schools become creative and innovative? I think not.

George Kozmetsky: I have strong opinions on this topic. We are going to get bogged down by structure and miss the whole point. Academic territoriality erects high barriers to new ideas. Let's not worry about where creative and innovative management belongs, at least not yet. Who gets upset that sociologists, psychologists, scientists, engineers, mathematicians all use operations research? O.R. had to be hauled in kicking into business schools. Why are we so concerned in which direction graduate schools of business are going? How can you be a modern manager if you don't know science, technology, and all the liberal arts as well as the quantitative and qualitative skills of business? The more we argue about the name of a college or graduate school, the more we miss the point.

Let's go back to my framework. Get started. If creativity is in certain companies already, let's find out what their constructs are. Let's see if we can distill general principles. Let's start teaching the best of today's practices. Let's see if we can find ways for our students to jump a generation. If you need to get 50,000 chunks of knowledge, how do you get that experience? Nobody stops me as a professor. You have all the conditions necessary to start. Stop arguing about the need for an institute or the name of the college. Get started.

Part IX

STRATEGIES FOR ACADEMIC DEVELOPMENT: RESEARCH, TEACHING, AND CURRICULA; PUBLICATIONS AND PROFESSIONAL ACTIVITIES

Chapter 19

THE DESIGN OF A CREATIVE ACADEMIC ORGANIZATION

Richard M. Cyert

The problem of designing organizations to achieve particular objectives or characteristics has long been an occupation of students of organization theory. As more knowledge has been gained of organizations, the desire to structure the organization to achieve a specific result has increased, and over the last twenty years, there has been a major preoccupation with developing an organizational form that would lead to a creative organization.

"Creative" is a somewhat ambiguous word. In the context of an academic organization, creative means the ability of the organization to develop new approaches to the problems of education and research (Mohr 1969; Henderson 1970). The new approaches have to be based on ideas about education and research. These ideas, when implemented, lead to methods of teaching, to the process of learning, and to an educational environment that are all different from those in the more conventional academic institution. For an historical perspective on innovation see Smith (1954).

Thus, the creative organization is one dominated by new ideas that are implemented and, as a result, is characterized by change. In research the creative organization may undertake problems that are different from the conventional ones in the standard disciplines. It may attack these problems in an interdisciplinary fashion that does not respect conventional classifications of knowledge (Simon 1967).

It is difficult to characterize the general nature of innovation, almost by definition, but is is clear that the creative organization looks for new ways to achieve the old goals of the university — the creation of knowledge and the dissemination of knowledge. This paper is concerned with a design for making the total university creative, not merely a department or a college.

SIGNIFICANCE OF THE CREATIVE ORGANIZATION

Higher education needs institutions that are innovative if our society is to make progress. Yet, as we show below, all the pressures on the university are conservative ones. Clearly there is a tension between an administration that wants an innovative organization and a faculty that wants a conventional one. Thus, an extra effort is required by the central administration to make the university a creative organization, as I have defined that entity. Perhaps this requirement is the reason that the literature on universities and the university presidency ignores the problem of creativity (Ortega y Gasset 1944; Balderston 1974; Cohen and March 1974). Some research has been done on designing innovative organizations, but no research has been done explicitly on universities (Khandwalla 1977: 551–67).

Thus, the university president attempting to design an organization and organizational policies that will be innovative is moving into a relatively unknown area. He or she does, however, have the body of organization theory with which to begin (Simon 1947; March and Simon 1958). This theory does lead to a recognition of the variables that are important but not to the specific ways in which these can impact the organization to achieve the desired results. This paper will be based on my deductions from organization theory as to the important variables and the actions that I have come to believe, through some organizational experimentation, are effective in achieving the design of a creative organization.

NATURE OF A UNIVERSITY

The university is a highly decentralized organization (Wallis 1966). In essence, each faculty member is an individual entrepreneur. He or she is in business to produce services in the classroom and to develop a reputation in a particular discipline. A scholarly reputation is produced primarily through research. As a result, the individual's basic reference group is the professional association that is related to the discipline as well as his or her peers working in the field (Cyert 1975).

The disciplines generally tend to be conservative of the knowledge and the traditions that have developed within the disciplines. They are not, by nature, innovative. There is in each discipline a main line of thought. Those people deviating from the mainstream are generally viewed as critics of the discipline and as a threat to those who have previously learned the field. As a result, critics are not generally welcomed in professions. Therefore, it is unlikely that, left alone, a faculty member in an orthodox discipline will be a highly innovative individual. Those individuals who deviate from the main line will attract criticism from their colleagues in the discipline and may have difficulty getting jobs. Thus, it is clear that all of the pressures on the individual faculty member are antithetical to innovation.

Faculty members are organized into departments in a university. The nature of the department is to be concerned with promoting the discipline on which it is based. Department heads are evaluated by their faculty on the basis of the resources that they can get for the department. A good department head, in the view of the faculty member, is able to get the dean to allocate increased resources to the department; he or she would also have the ability to get resources from the outside. The department must protect itself from those people within the university who want the members of the department to function in some way that is different from accepted practice in the discipline. Thus, the department head will tend to resist any pressure for innovative activities that would be viewed as deviations from the main line of the profession.

The department, in turn, is a member of a college. A college in a university is one of several colleges. The college is, however, organized around the larger set to which the disciplines belong. At the college level the department heads expect the dean to promote the set of disciplines in the college in the same way that they attempt to function for their departments.

In short, the university has all the pressures from the world pulling its faculty, its departments, and its colleges away from university innovation and towards preserving the status quo. There probably is no other organization that has the same pressures for decentralization and conservatism with respect to change that a university does (McCorkle and Archibald 1982). Under these circumstances, therefore, the question of how the university can be designed to become an innovative, creative organization becomes a difficult one.

VARIABLES

Frequently in attacking the design problem, the organization theorist will concentrate on the formal reporting structure of the organization (Boning and Roeloffs 1970). In the case of the university, this approach does not seem to be fruitful. The current structure of departments and colleges is so well established that it is difficult to eliminate. Further, it is not clear that structure is the most important variable. There are, undoubtedly, many structures that can enable an organization to achieve particular objectives.

There are other variables of great significance that have not been emphasized as much as structure. The set of goals of the organization must clearly reflect the importance of innovation.

The attention focus of the participants in the organization is another prime variable. The attention focus is closely connected with behavior, and activities influencing the attention focus will, thereby, influence behavior.

The reward system is, of course, a well-known variable. Strangely enough, it is difficult to tie the reward system as closely as desired to behavior. There have to be a number of variables affecting the decision on rewards, and it is, therefore, difficult to emphasize only one variable and produce a particular kind of behavior (March and Simon 1958). The designers of executive compensation systems have long experienced this kind of frustration.

Another variable of importance is the information flow in the organization and the action taken on it. This variable is closely related to attention focus but is also of importance independently.

These variables affect the attitude of the participants in the organization, and attitude has some relation with behavior. It has to be emphasized, however, that the connection between the variables with which we must work and actual behavior is tenuous at best. Our aim has to be to design organizational policies that will tend to produce the type of behavior desired.

INNOVATION AS A GOAL

The goals of an organization are usually established through a process of strategic planning (Keller 1983). In an organization that is being designed for creativity, it is critical that innovation be specifically listed as a goal of the organization. Innovation should be listed as a goal, and the reasons why it is a goal of the organization should be specified. Once the goals are established, the president should make a point of stressing innovation as a goal of the organization and point to the established set of goals in the plan. As the point is emphasized in discussions, participants in the organization begin to accept innovation as a way of life. They take pride in being part of a creative organization.

ATTENTION FOCUS OF PARTICIPANTS

As we have seen, the attention focus of the participants of the university is generally on their own disciplines, departments, and colleges. Yet, if the university is to be a creative organization, the attention of the participants has to be focused on innovation.

Role of President

An important variable in changing the attention focus is the action of the chief executive officer of the organization, the president. If the president is committed to innovation, his or her actions can influence the attention focus of the participants in the organization, even in a university.

The first action that can influence the attention focus is oral interaction with the faculty — on an individual basis, in larger subunits, or to the total faculty. The president should aim in these talks to change the attitude of faculty members. The president must find ways to emphasize the importance of innovation in the organization. The concept of innovation must be viewed by the participants as a goal of the organization. The president can achieve this result through the informal process of talks to individuals, but he or she can also do so by influencing the formal planning process in the university. Through the president's conversations, the concept of innovation must be emphasized. The president must stress this point not only with the faculty but also with department heads and deans. These talks have to be viewed as ways of altering the orthodox attitudes of the environment.

Secondly, the president must be receptive to new ideas and must demonstrate that receptivity. The environment the president creates must be one in which faculty members are able to speak with him or her directly. Bureaucratic deference to a chain of command can effectively kill new ideas and new idea generation.

When a faculty member presents a proposal for change, the president must be open-minded and careful in the appraisal. The usual reactions of "we're doing that already" or "that won't work" should never be used by the president. No matter what the initial reaction of the president is, nothing should be said that would in any sense make the initiator of the idea feel foolish or frustrated. Getting faculty members to introduce new ideas is difficult but is only a first step. Once the idea is presented, the reception must be positive. Every idea presented to the president must be treated as an important contribution, and feedback as to its disposition must be given ultimately to the person who generated it.

Thirdly, the president must make sure that actions are taken to implement the new ideas. If a proposal needs to be studied further to determine whether or not it has merit for the organization, that action should be taken as soon as possible and as visibly as appropriate. Frequently, it is desirable to appoint a committee and make a public announcement of the appointment and the reason for it. The committee should be chosen with care and should have people on it who have a reputation for receptivity to new ideas. As soon as possible, action should be taken to put the idea into motion or to have valid and justifiable reasons why the idea cannot be utilized.

To project the proper attitudes, the president must avoid the reaction that a new idea is a criticism of the way the university is being operated. Actions based on such assessments will tend to kill innovativeness in the organization quickly. Another emotional reaction that is antithetical to innovation is the resentment the president may have at not having thought of the idea. Such reactions will tend to reduce receptivity and impair the ability to evaluate the idea properly. The president must be a secure and confident person if his or her actions are to produce the attention focus of the faculty, staff, and students on innovation.

Finally, it is desirable for the president to be innovative. By this statement, I mean that the president must initiate some innovations that are seen as coming from the central administration.

The president, however, must be careful in the way in which the innovation is implemented. He or she must resist the effort to impose a change on the faculty but should not hesitate to initiate a change and proceed to get faculty discussion of the proposal. Ultimately, as this process is utilized, the faculty will acknowledge the recognition of an innovative president and central administration. The net result is a positive stimulation of faculty attitude and attention focus toward innovative activity.

In general, in this section we have been utilizing the concept of the president as a role model for forming faculty attitudes toward innovation and, in particular, to get the attention focus of the organization on innovation. The president is in a leadership role, and the attitudes projected by him or her will influence the attitudes of the faculty, staff, and student body (Golembiewski 1962). Therefore, if a president wishes to develop an innovative organization, steps along the lines that I have described should be followed.

Senior Faculty

The senior faculty have a role similar to that of the president in regard to innovation. They should represent the same attitudes and values with respect to innovation that the president does. They must be people who have participated in innovative activity and are still interested in doing so. Their emphasis on the importance on the goal of innovation stimulates the younger faculty to give attention to creative ideas as a goal of the university.

More importantly the senior faculty must make certain that the results of creative actions of the junior faculty will be taken into account when faculty evaluations are being made. Such recognition by senior faculty of particular behavior will have the effect of reinforcing the behavior. The role of the senior faculty is especially important because they represent an internal reference group that is critical to the younger faculty members. Positive response to innovative actions encourages the younger faculty to behave in ways that are desired by the university even though the actions may not be in the main line of the particular discipline.

Clearly one of the obstacles to making an organization innovative is the conservatism of most disciplines and their professional associations. Young faculty members in particular must worry about deviating from the "party line" of the discipline since future jobs at other institutions may be dependent on the extent to which the faculty member is accepted and evaluated by others in the profession. Thus, there is a tension that develops in the innovative university, and most of the burden falls on the young faculty members who do not have tenure. The behavior of the senior faculty can significantly help to reduce this tension.

The type of problem we are discussing is exacerbated when the innovation involves a research area that may be interdisciplinary or teaching that requires a faculty member to learn something about another discipline (Hutchins 1953: 22–48). When the faculty member is young and untenured, he or she may be worried about the resulting effect on future career moves. The help of an established faculty colleague to quell the uncertainties may give the necessary courage to enable the young faculty member to proceed.

REWARD SYSTEM

We have discussed some of the ways to capture the attention focus of the participants in the organization on innovation and creativity. A second factor that is important in inducing the kind of behavior that is desired in an organization is the reward system. We want the reward system to be related as directly as possible to innovative behavior (March and Simon 1958). There are three basic forms of the reward system that are relevant to our discussion—salary, promotion, and public recognition.

Department heads and deans have the most authority in establishing salaries. The usual criteria for setting salaries relate to publication performance and the amount of research money that the individual has brought into the university. The importance of teaching tends to be overlooked. The weighting that these factors are given in determining salary influences the behavior of the faculty members. For example, if teaching is really weighted less than publications and grants in the promotion process, faculty members will tend to put less attention on teaching. Too often, the concept of creative and innovative activity is not even looked upon as one of the variables determining the level of salary for the faculty member.

In order to change this situation, the department head must give different signals to the faculty from the usual set of signals. The department head must make it clear that innovative activity is important, and he or she must define what is meant by innovative activity. Then the faculty members that are receiving their increases must be clear on the role that innovative activity has played in either increasing their salaries or reducing the level of increase that they have been given.

In turn, this means that the president must be working directly with the department heads to change attitudes from the conventional value system that would not include innovative activity. There has to be a number of direct meetings between the president and the individual department heads as well as the department heads as a group. It is a problem similar to the one described earlier. The attention focus and attitude of the department heads must be changed. Most have spent their working lives in academic institutions and have absorbed the values of the conventional academic organization. Those values do not include an understanding of innovative activity nor a heavy weighting on innovative activity for setting salaries and allocating other rewards.

The problem of promotions is similar. It is critical that innovations be credited to a faculty member being considered for a promotion and that such innovations be taken into account in making promotions. Again, this approach requires a change in traditional attitudes. It means that innovative activity must be given weight in promotions. Traditionally, the heavy weight put on publications for promotions swamps all of the other variables that are being utilized (Jencks and Riesman 1968: 18–19). If the organization is to be an innovative one, promotions committees must be trained to give weight to innovative activity. Changing attitudes requires the intervention of department heads, deans, and direct statements of the president. But an organization will not encourage creative and innovative people if it does not reward them in salary and promotion.

Another way in which innovative activity can be stimulated in the organization is through public recognition. Awards, including cash awards for innovative activity, can show participants in the organization that innovative activity is valued. The awards should be made in public before other faculty members, and a great deal of internal publicity should be given the awards. The aim is to capture the attention focus of participants and to show them that such activity is actually rewarded.

UPWARD COMMUNICATION

One of the most difficult kinds of communication in any organization is upward communication. The belief among participants lower in the hierarchy that they can speak to the president is an important value for innovative activity. Ideas can be killed by people lower in the hierarchy. Where upward communication exists, it is possible for an instructor or assistant professor to bring his or her ideas directly to the president for discussion. Similarly, the president must ensure that the deans and department heads are equally available and receptive to new ideas.

The aim of increasing upward communication has to be a reduction in uncertainty in the minds of the participants in the organization as to the receptivity that will be given to new ideas. In addition, there must be a rapport between the president and the faculty that gives the faculty confidence and ease of mind with respect to upward communication.

Conditions that promote communication can be established in a variety of ways. The president should be an academic. He or she should be someone that has served as a faculty member and has come through the ranks. Such a person will have a strong identification with the faculty members themselves. Secondly, the communication must go out to the colleges and the departments to meet with faculty on their grounds. This kind of action can develop a familiarity that makes it easier for faculty members of all ranks to communicate ideas to the president without fears and with some assurance that the ideas will receive a good hearing.

Of equal importance with getting the ideas transmitted upward is the way in which the ideas are dealt with when they are discussed with the president, dean, or department head. In all cases, the ideas should be treated with respect and seriousness regardless of what the initial reaction may be to the idea. More good ideas are killed, as I've said, and more people are discouraged by such phrases as, "we already tried that"; "it doesn't work"; "that's an old idea." There are many other similar expressions. Clearly, an individual greeted in this fashion will never again present an idea to anyone in the organization. The word will soon spread that it is difficult to get new ideas listened to within the organization.

Each idea should be treated as special, and there must be a serious attempt to deal with it. Sometimes this can be done on the spot through further discussion, and the individual may decide the idea needs further work. On the other hand, with greater exploration, the president may realize that what looks like a poor idea is, in fact, a good one. So, the first step must be to have a serious discussion of every idea brought to the president's office. Secondly, there must be a way of clear disposition.

Frequently having a small group explore the idea further is a good way to deal with the matter. Where an idea is to be examined further after the initial conversation, it is also useful to have the originator of the idea participate in the development of the procedure by which the further investigation is to take place. The reputation of the university for the receptivity of ideas will depend on how the president treats those ideas that are brought to his or her office.

SOME SPECIFIC TECHNIQUES

We have described a number of policies that can be followed to affect the three variables on which we have concentrated — attention focus, reward system, and upward communication. There are, however, additional management actions that can be taken to further the incentive within the organization to innovate. These techniques have been ones that I have tried and have shown some promise.

Internal Foundation

One of the ways to make the goal of a creative organization operational is to make funds available internally for innovative activity. These funds must be visible to all participants in the organization, and they must be funds dedicated to innovative ideas. One of the most effective ways to accomplish this task is to establish an internal foundation (Cyert 1977).

Internal foundations should be managed whether the funds come from inside, or out, by an internal board. The objective of the foundation should be to finance innovative activity. The innovative activity could be in a specific area such as new ideas for increasing productivity in teaching or some other specific area. Another alternative is to have the internal foundation willing to support any activity that meets the task of being innovative whether it is in education or research.

Formation of the internal foundation gives the president another opportunity to emphasize the importance of innovative activity. The latter can be accomplished through the specification of creative ideas in the guidelines for making proposals. It is also an excellent idea for the president to be one of the group making the selection for financing proposals at least in the beginning of the foundation. There should also be a great deal of internal recognition of the participants who receive innovative grants, and much should be made of the fact that the innovative activity will have implications beyond the campus.

The objective of the internal foundation is to emphasize the importance of new ideas within the organization, to show the president's interest in creative thought, and to show that the organization is prepared to put some of its own resources into stimulating them. Activities of this kind will help emphasize the importance of innovative activity to the members of the organization as well as stimulating the desired goal.

Information Gathering

One of the requirements for designing a creative organization is the inclusion of antennae for the organization. The organization has to be alert to developments in the world or, more specifically, potential developments. In an academic environment, there is a tendency to rely upon the senior faculty members to keep abreast of developments in their field. Frequently these faculty members may not foresee what the developments will be. An innovative organization needs to be futuristic. It needs to be looking at prospective developments in fields for both research and educational purposes.

Another way for the president to emphasize innovation and to keep track of development in the world is to establish a series of seminars in which people from a variety of fields outside the university are invited to the campus. The objective of the visit should be to talk with a selected group of faculty members on the future of a particular area. It is desirable to get the participants to forecast what is going to happen and to identify where new areas of importance to research are going to be. In small seminars, which the president chairs, excellent discussion between visitor and faculty can result. The outside visitors resemble antennae that sense developments in the world and bring information to the university.

Out of such meetings the university will be able to determine some areas in which it can be a leader. It is possible to find some areas where the university has a comparative advantage or where by being first, it can establish a comparative advantage. Ideas of this kind require a great deal of discussion, but committee work can be an important source of creative solutions. Further, however, it establishes the importance of innovative behavior and emphasizes its importance for the organization.

Reporting Systems

One of the interesting control mechanisms that controllers in corporations use is the reporting system. W. W. Cooper, for example, has pointed out the effects on behavior of the management of a subsidiary of the requirement of monthly financial systems. The reports become a written record of performance.

A somewhat similar mechanism can be used within an organization to stimulate innovation. A periodic request to deans and department heads for a report on their innovations in teaching and research can have a salutary effect. There is always a danger that such requests can lead to descriptions that are nothing more than window dressing. Thus, the president must read the reports carefully and give feedback to the reporting unit that evaluates the worth of the innovations to the university.

It is obvious that significant innovations do not occur with predictable frequency nor do they occur often. Regular reports may lead to definitions of innovations that are not helpful. Thus a reporting system for innovations, in contrast to an accounting controls approach to reporting, should probably be done on an irregular basis rather than routinely.

CONCLUSION

I have tried to indicate some of the elements of an organization that is designed to be innovative. It is clear from the analyses that the variables that must be affected are attitude and the attention focus of the participants. One of the critical ways of affecting these variables is through carefully planned activities of the president and, to a lesser degree, other officers such as the provost, deans, and department heads. The organizational structure itself is probably not a significant variable in designing an innovative organization. An innovative organization requires a real team effort. The desire to be innovative must be pervasive in the organization, and to make any attitude pervasive requires significant team work. It is clear that organizational design becomes increasingly important in our society. The notion of being able to design organizations that will exhibit one or more specific characteristics is a challenge to our ingenuity and imagination. Much work remains to be done in the area.

REFERENCES

Balderston, F.E. 1974. *Managing Today's University*. San Francisco: Josey-Bass.
Boning, E., and Roeloffs. 1970. *Innovation in Higher Education: Three German Universities*. Organization for Economic Co-operation and Development.
Cohen, M.D., and J.G. March. 1974. *Leadership and Ambiguity*. New York: McGraw Hill.
Cyert, R.M. 1975. *The Management of Nonprofit Organizations*. Lexington, Mass.: Lexington Books.

————. 1977. "Effective innovation and increased productivity in an organization." *Innovation and Productivity in Higher Education,* edited by David T. Tuma. San Francisco: San Francisco Press.

Golembiewski, R.T. 1962. *Behavior and Organization: O & M and the Small Group.* Chicago: Rand McNally.

Henderson, A.D. 1970. *The Innovative Spirit.* San Francisco: Josey-Bass.

Hutchins, R.M. 1953. *The University of Utopia.* Chicago: University of Chicago Press.

Jencks, C., and D. Riesman. 1968. *The Academic Revolution.* Garden City, New York: Doubleday.

Keller, G. 1983. *Academic Strategy.* Baltimore: Johns Hopkins.

Khandwalla, P.N. 1977. *The Design of Organizations.* New York: Harcourt Brace Jovanovich.

March, J.G., and H.A. Simon. 1958. *Organizations.* New York: John Wiley.

McCorkle, C.O., Jr., and S.O. Archibald. 1982. *Management and Leadership in Higher Education.* San Francisco: Joseey-Bass.

Mohr, L.B. 1969. "Determinants of innovation in organization." *American Political Science Review* 63: 111–26.

Ortega y Gasset, Jose. 1944. *Musion of the University.* Princeton: Princeton University Press.

Simon, H.A. 1947. *Administrative Behavior.* New York: Macmillan.

————. 1967. "The Job of a college president." *Educational Record* 48: 68–78.

Smith, J.W.A. 1954. *The Birth of Modern Education.* London: Independent Press Ltd.

Wallis, W.A. 1966. "Centripetal and centrifugal forces in university organizations." In *The Contemporary University: U.S.A.,* edited by Robert S. Morison, 39–49.

Chapter 20

STRATEGIES FOR INDUCING ACADEMIC UNITS TO ADOPT INNOVATIONS*

George P. Huber

There is clear reason to believe that in the decades ahead society will have a much greater need for creative and innovative management than it has in the past (Charnes and Cooper 1984; Huber 1984).

The purpose of this chapter is to propose strategies that will induce academic units to adopt innovations. It focuses in particular on strategies for encouraging college or department-sized academic units to design and implement teaching and/or research programs devoted to creative and innovative managment.

RECEPTIVITY OF ACADEMIC UNITS TO INNOVATION

With few exceptions, universities today do not explicitly attempt to develop creative and innovative managers. Convincing university units and their faculties to adopt this goal, and to design and implement the associated strategies, will not be easy. Yet it is an idea whose time has come.

There are natural forces that we can channel to aid in achieving this goal, and there are features of the academic setting that actually facilitate the introduction of innovations. We must temper these optimistic assertions, however, with direct recognition of five important obstacles to creating change in academic units.

* The author wishes to acknowledge the support of the U.S. Army Research Institute for the Behavioral and Social Sciences in carrying out the literature review that underlies this chapter.

Obstacles to Innovation in Academic Units[1]

Change, in whatever form or magnitude, tends to threaten secured positions. Both faculty jobs and organizational power positions are involved in this threat. Today's age of scarce resources for higher education worsens this condition.

The entrenched convention of shared power between faculty and administration, combined with the multidepartmental nature of curricula, commonly inhibits the pace and implementation of academic decisionmaking.

Traditional academic values are often resistant to new conceptions of curriculum, teaching methods, meritocracy systems, research priorities, and so forth.

There are few tested and accepted methods for measuring the success or failure of research or teaching programs and therefore for estimating the worth of a potential program change.

Academic units and programs have considerable inertia. Any curriculum must "stay in place" until all students admitted under the curriculum have had a chance to graduate. Research programs take years to complete. Faculty have long periods of training and become conditioned to view certain topics as appropriate for research and teaching. In addition, they have tenure, so firing them because of unfashionable standards is not an alternative.

The above five obstacles seem formidable but they can be overcome. To the contrary, the 1960s and 1970s were decades of major change in higher education, and during the 1980s we observe still more changes.

What accounts for this contradiction, where on the one hand we have several sources of resistance to change and on the other hand we see change taking place in almost every major university in the country? It seems that there are two explanations. One is that there are social forces that are offering universities strong incentives to initiate change. Private industry, for example, is providing funding for research and teaching in the areas of computing and manufacturing technology at a level unimaginable a decade ago. This new source of resources is having considerable impact and staffing. Similarly, the decrease in the population of traditional-age university students combined with an increased demand for professional education has caused many universities to seek and serve new clientele. Thus while universities clearly possess change-resistant characteristics, society possesses change-inducing forces of sufficient strength to overcome some of these characteristics.

The second explanation for the contradiction of considerable change in spite of significant obstacles is that universities and their faculties possess characteristics that facilitate the introduction of innovation. These are not readily apparent in some instances, and since we must draw on these features in selecting or developing strategies for inducing innovation, I describe them here.

Characteristics That Facilitate Innovation in Academic Units

One characteristic of great importance is universal adherence to the belief that faculty members should carry on creative and innovative pursuits. This is apparent in the requirement, for example, that to attain tenure in any major university, a faculty member must demonstrate successful creative or innovative behavior in the form of published research or the equivalent. Salaries, too, are significantly related to successful creative and innovative activity (if this activity conforms to professional norms). Organizational culture is receiving a good deal of attention in the business world today, but in the form of belief in the importance of creative pursuits, it has been a recognized force in academia for centuries.

A second characteristic that facilitates change, when change must involve faculty activity, is the flexibility of time allocation. There seems to be no compelling reason to believe that faculty members work more or fewer hours than do other professionals, but they tend to have much more discretion over when they work and on what. This enables them to concentrate their energies for relatively extended periods of time on individual projects, a condition that case histories of creative and innovative individuals suggests is facilitative of innovative outcomes.

Organizational science research suggests that the availability of organizational slack facilitates creativity and innovation. Most major universities possess and distribute on a regular basis organizational slack in the form of funds for research resources, sabbatical leaves, or — to a lesser extent — time off from other duties to undertake curriculum or course development. This is a third characteristic that helps universities facilitate, if not induce, change in their research and teaching programs.

In contrast to the availability of slack research resources, most research-oriented faculty seek nonroutine research resources. Routine resources, such as summer salary support and computer support, come from organizational slack. Nonroutine resources such as funding sufficient to carry out a focused program of research rather than just a project, or access to field research sites generally come from outside the university and are relatively scarce. The faculty's need for nonroutine research resources is a characteristic of universities that facilitates innovation in that it renders them amenable to innovations that are closely linked to these nonroutine resources.

A characteristic of university research projects and programs that facilitates change and innovation is that they are, at most, loosely coupled. Faculty have great autonomy in the initiation and conduct of their research (as contrasted with curricula). This fact, complemented by the fact that university administrators favor faculty acquisition of extra-university research resources, is a characteristic of the university setting that facilitates change in research thrusts when individual faculty decide to address topics not previously part of the academic unit's research endeavors.

The last characteristic less facilitates change than leverages it. Faculty members conducting research in an area tend to direct their teaching in the same area, either by introducing the research topics into ongoing courses or by initiating new courses. This enables them to achieve dual payoffs from their reading, educates students to help with the research, and enhances the visibility of the research. Thus research in an area prompts teaching in the area. Further, teaching about a topic tends to lead to research on the topic, as students become interested in the topic and choose to study it further when fulfilling thesis or dissertation requirements. Faculty supervising such theses and dissertations tend to get caught up in the work and continue it on their own. Thus teaching in an area prompts research in the area and vice versa. Resource invested in promoting either teaching or research about a topic have a dual payoff and thus are leveraged.

THE SHORTAGE OF USABLE KNOWLEDGE

Major changes come to most organizations only infrequently. This is especially true of individual academic units, buffered as they are from many societal forces by protection-minded boards of trustees, by inertia-prone superordinate bureaucracies, and also by their perceived traditional responsibility to take "the longer view." In addition, the tenure in office of university-unit administrators is extremely short. The half-life of business-school deans is perhaps three years, and many academic departments require a rotation of the chairmanship every two, three, or four years. In combination, the facts that changes are infrequent and that administrative tenure is short result in academic-unit administrators being generally inexperienced in introducing major changes, especially changes of any particular type. As a consequence, we can have little hope that any administrator's "experience" will be a source of usable knowledge in getting university units to adopt programs in creative and innovative management.

What of hand-me-down or codified experience? For example, administrators in industry know a great deal about how to bring innovations to the marketplace. In general, they did not learn this personally. Rather they obtained their knowledge from "the organization." Their organizations had carried out the innovation introduction task many times and had learned how to do it well.

There is no parallel here with the situation we face. In industry the success or failure of an innovation, either external or internal to the company, is generally quite determinable and is available in a relatively short period of time. Unambiguous fast feedback facilitates learning; in contrast, "there are few tested and accepted methods for measuring the success or failure of new innovations within the traditional setting of the college campus" (Redman 1982). Thus "feedback" is ambiguous. Further, the aforementioned availability of slack resources and organizational inertia lead to "delayed failures" and cause feedback about failure to be slow. As a consequence, because feedback is both ambiguous and slow, organizational learning from accumulated experience is less characteristic of academic units than of industrial units.

When usable knowledge from either personal or codified experience is unavailable, where can we turn? Academics have the universal answer: turn to "theory." What usable theory is there?

Knowledge about Organizational Innovation

In determining what theory could guide the introduction of innovations into academic units, I was surprised that most of the literature on innovation was simply not applicable to the situation at hand.[2]

A good deal of the literature is focused on designing organizations to generate innovative ideas and action (Duncan 1976; Hedberg, Nystrom, and Starbuck 1977; Weick 1982). For example, the large literature on the design of industrial R & D units fits here (see Tushman and Moore 1982). In contrast, (1) we already have an innovation in mind that we want adopted, the undertaking of academic activity in creative and innovative management, and (2) we face already designed organizations. Consequently this large body of literature is of little use.

In addition, the innovation and change literatures deal with introducing changes in technology, structure, or process. This is as true of the literature on innovation in higher education as it is of the less specialized literature (see Daft and Becker 1976; Davis, Strand, Alexander, and Hussain 1962). Although the innovation that we want to see adopted may cause or rely on such changes, it is to a great extent a change in goal. There seems to be no literature on how to get organizational units to change their goals, especially in an academic setting where superordinate units are unsure of what subordinate unit goals should be and where the imposition of goals from above is a violation of traditional norms and values.

Finally, there is the literature on government-promoted innovation in education (Altbach 1982). What this literature tends to deal with, however, is governmental goals and governmental change processes, not university or academic unit goals or change processes. Fortunately some of this literature describes how governmental strategies were used to induce innovation adoption in universities by inducing changes in university processes (Lantz 1984). (I have drawn on this material in developing some of the guidelines contained in this chapter.)

While a review of the literature in innovation resulted in interesting but mostly disappointing surprises, a review of the literature on organizational decisionmaking identified some useful concepts. In retrospect, this should be expected, since the organizational innovation paradigm includes as a conspicuous component the "decision to adopt."

Knowledge about Organizational Decisionmaking

A number of concepts helpful in thinking about how to get university units to adopt innovations are found in the "Garbage Can Model" of organizational decisionmaking. This model was first delineated by Professor James March of Stanford University (see Cohen, March, and Olson 1972) and has been found to be quite useful in interpreting decisionmaking in academic institutions (Daft and Becker 1976; March and Romelaer 1976). While more traditional models of organization decisionmaking, such as the Rational Model, the Political Model, the Bureaucratic Process Model, and the Incremental Adjustment Model (see Allison 1969, 1971; Lindblom 1959), are collectively valuable in interpreting a large proportion of decision processs, for many types of organizations such as educational institutions, the Garbage Can Model is especially well suited to interpreting the decision formulation process. Here is what the model, in essence, says:

> Organizational decisions are the consequence of problems looking for solutions, solutions looking for problems, choice opportunities arising, and decision makers looking for work. When a suitable set of elements from each of these streams encounter and cling to one another long enough, a decision is the outcome.

The name "Garbage Can Model" came from its originators, who envisioned elements of the four streams as being dumped into a garbage can where, occasionally, they encountered one another and generated decisions.

I suspect that most observers of organizational life would agree that the Garbage Can Model is a useful interpretative framework in almost all organizations some of the time. And so are each of the earlier mentioned models—the Rational Model, the Political Model, and Bureaucratic Process Model, and the Incremental Adjustment Model. What is of relevance here is that research has shown the Garbage Can Model to be relatively more useful for understanding decisionmaking in educational institutions than are the other models.

As we will see, the model is quite useful as an interpretive framework in understanding and influencing an academic unit's decision to adopt an innovation. Let us move on to considering strategies for causing academic units to engage in researching and teaching creative and innovative management.

STRATEGIES FOR OBTAINING ADOPTION OF AN INNOVATION

The idea that universities should adopt as a goal researching and teaching in the area of creative and innovative management is a novel one. We must realize that very few academic units are presently committed to this goal. Further, as Altach notes in his review of 336 publications concerning reform in higher education, "universities are notably conservative institutions and have a long historical tradition — a tradition that is respected by members of the academic community. As a result, academic institutions have been difficult to change and the process of reform and innovation is inevitably a complicated one" (Altbach 1982: 5). Undertaking activities in creative and innovative management will consume administrative effort and other resources. Such activities will be initiated and endure only if some organizational members see the researching or teaching of creative and innovative management as a goal worth pursuing. At present it apparently is not viewed as such a goal. What can be done? What strategies are particularly appropriate for obtaining adoption of an innovation in that peculiar organization, a university? We examine four such strategies. The first follows directly from the Garbage Can Model.

Find a Problem for Which Funding Creative and Innovative Management is a Solution

Where should we look to find a university problem for which funding for activity in creative and innovative management is a solution? One answer is to look inside of rich but impoverished universities. Many universities are today rich in terms of talented personnel but impoverished in terms of operating budgets, slack resources, and nonroutine research resources. Their *problem* is lack of money. A *solution* for this problem is funding for activity in creative and innovative management. We must be thoughtful in choosing among these universities. Some may have become impoverished because they lacked creative faculty or because they had inept leaders. On the other hand, many universities and their subunits are having serious financial problems in spite of the efforts of creative faculty and competent leaders. Their historically dependable resource streams, such as state revenues, have simply disappeared. These universities are likely candidates to take on innovative activities in order to obtain funds with which to reverse their decline.

Another place where funding for activity in creative and innovative management may be a solution to a problem is in dormant units seeking to erupt. As we noted earlier, academic units tend to be buffered. As a result it is not unusual to find them not in rapid decline but rather in more gradual decay. In some instances their faculty and administrators have not dealt with this problem because the deterioration is unnoticeably slow or because the people involved expect to leave the organization before the situation becomes intolerable. In considering dormant units as candidates to take on innovative activity, we must again be careful. Many will be hopeless cases—no matter how hard you blow on cold coals, you can't expect fire to burst forth. For such sites to be good candidates, we need two conditions. One is the presence of some faculty who are frustrated with the lack of action in their immediate professional environment. These people are likely to become *innovation champions.* The other condition is the relatively recent placement of new administrators at some level who seem likely to support new faculty initiatives. These people are likely to act as *innovation sponsors* and to encourage and reward faculty entrepreneurship.

For example, a dean (especially a new dean) in one of these stagnant ponds might initiate a "strategic planning project" for the college, with faculty study teams, committees, subcommittees, reports, presentations, plans, publicity, and so forth. Such groups invariably find unexploited opportunities or other "problems looking for solutions." If during the same time interval the dean has informal conversations, invited speakers, and distributions of material dealing with both the need for activity in creative and innovative management and the funding available to support such activity, it is highly likely that the eventual strategic plan will include activity in creative and innovative management as either a goal or a means to a goal. A recent study supports this approach:

> In sum, the best strategy for encouraging innovation (other than offering substantial amounts of incentive funding) may be to encourage the development of formal plans. The study seems to suggest that large monetary incentives may not be the only way to encourage implementation. In fact, small monetary grants may not even be essential. What may be essential is an incentive for the planning process, which may or may not be monetary. (Lantz 1984)

Of course, according to the Garbage Can Model, activity in innovative management is a "solution" suited to the "problem" of having to find something strategic to do; the enactment of the strategic planning effort is the "choice opportunity," and the task force members are the "decisionmakers" doing work.

Portray the Goal of Engaging in Creative and Innovative Management Activity as a Means for Fulfilling Higher Order Goals

How to change organizational goals is a subject about which little is known. A review of two familiar cases provides a working hypothesis, however. First, consider the March of Dimes. Here was an organization whose announced goal during much of its early years was the elimination of polio. But did the March of Dimes organization dissolve itself when a successful polio vaccine was developed? No, it turned to the new goal of reducing the incidence of birth defects, and today survives in much the same form as before. Did the March of Dimes change goals or did it change its means for fulfilling other goals?

Second, consider the case of AT & T. Here was an organization whose resource allocations and personnel promotion patterns suggested that its long-term goals were related to research, development, and production. Today, one of its primary goals is championing its service over that of its new competitors (Nadler 1982; Tunstall 1983). AT & T appears to have changed its goals, but has it? Perhaps it has simply changed its means for attaining higher order goals. Both these examples suggest that it may be helpful if reorientations in curricula can be introduced as changes in *means* rather than as changes in *goals*.

Specifically, I suspect that we would be wise to put our innovation in an evolutionary perspective. We can cite the evolution of managerial training from a focus on the accounting and production functions to a focus on a broader set of managerial functions and staff responsibilities (e.g., marketing, human resource management, and information systems management). We can also cite the evolution of such training from a focus almost solely on goods-producing industries, including health care, public administration, and other specialized service industries. This approach leads us to viewing academic activity in creative and innovative management as simply another means for addressing academia's higher-order goal of fulfilling society's need for managers with foresight.

Create Innovation Champions

Research and experience teach us that successful innovations, innovations that get and stay implemented, have "champions." We can safely assume that a program of research or teaching in innovative management is not going to be implemented or have staying power unless some faculty member is actively supportive.

But such champions will have to be created. We have no reason to believe that there are hundreds or even dozens of potential "creative and innovative management" harbingers running around our universities. They are not there to be found. Neither can you just go out and buy them. Most faculty have relatively full employment and a backlog of organizationally valued projects to occupy them. They have little motivation to take on the uphill climb of selling innovations in order to obtain a paycheck.

Successful champions must be committed to their idea or product. Commitment helps to give them credibility and tenacity, both important characteristics of internal change agents. How do we create commitment to a new cause? How do we create champions? Two of the university characteristics mentioned earlier are helpful in addressing these questions. The first is the idea that faculty have a need for nonroutine research resources. The second is that researching a subject prompts teaching of the same subject, and teaching a subject promotes researching of the subject. Thus we can initiate activity in either teaching or research by initiating activity in either research or teaching. These ideas suggest two approaches to creating innovation champions.

One approach is to make use of the fact that research-focused faculty need and seek salary for summer research projects, grants and fellowships for Ph.D. students, and field sites in which to collect data. Support for projects in creative and innovative management that provides one, two, or three of these resources is likely to lead to a significant degree of faculty interest and involvement. Related articles will be read, conversations with Ph.D. students about innovative management will occur, and conversations with innovative managers in the field will take place. The faculty member's initial interest will be reinforced, and commitment will likely follow.

The second approach capitalizes on the fact that many faculty are eager for interaction with managers and executives. This interaction gives faculty members credibility with students and deans and occasionally access to consulting opportunities or field research sites. Building on this, a corporation or public agency could sponsor a workshop on innovative management where both its managers and invited champion-candidate faculty members would participate. The faculty would be paid to prepare and to manage the workshop and to make presentations. This effort would get the faculty involved in the topic. To maintain involvement, follow-up projects could be commissioned, such as surveys or exercises, or a second workshop could be set up with the caveat that new ground would have to be covered.

Focus on Processes

A number of authorities have concluded that a low-key strategy to introducing changes, especially in academia, is more effective than is a more dramatic approach (March and Romelaer 1976; Weick 1982). Three tactics follow from this conclusion.

In his insightful article, "Footnotes to Organizational Change," James March reminds us that "Neither success nor change requires dramatic action. The conventional, routine activities that produce most organizational change require ordinary people to do ordinary things in a competent way" (March 1981). This suggests that we may want to adhere wherever possible to conventional processes. Since most academic units are "old" and must answer to tradition, this approach is especially relevant to inducing change in universities.

I alluded earlier to the consensual nature of decisions regarding courses and curricula. Since curriculum changes can, and often do, lead to either formal or informal reallocations of status and other more tangible resources, significant curriculum changes have difficulty getting consensual approval. This suggests the third tactic, that we must be especially attentive to employing the well-known change strategies (e.g., gaining the participation in the planning stages from those who will be affected and allowing sufficient time for the process to take place).

In universities, as elsewhere, resistance is generally inversely related to relevance. Small changes tend to be less relevant. Research and our own experience tell us that innovations will be accepted more readily if they seem to be unimportant. A study of four changes in the structure or processes of a university highlighted as a feature of the change process "the importance of unimportance" (March and Romelaer 1976: 259). Small changes, in general, are less likely to appear important than large changes. We should therefore make changes that appear to be of low relevance inside the university. This is especially important in university settings, as in these settings low relevance "is a characteristic and consistent feature of university decisionmaking" (March and Romelaer 1976: 271). Thus high relevance changes are more likely to be viewed with alarm.

CLOSING THOUGHTS

We know that resistance to change is generally less if the change appears to be small, and the smaller the better. On the other hand, we know that to maintain the good will and flow of resources from external proponents of a change, we must provide visible indicators that progress is being made, and the more visible and public the indicators the better. This poses an obvious dilemma for those who will seek to establish creative and innovative management as an academic discipline. Appropriately enough, the particular nature of academic organizations and the scarcity of relevant knowledge makes the pursuit of this goal itself an ideal exercise in innovative and creative management.

The second thought is associated with the idea that what we become is often a consequence of our acts. The idea is captured in a number of clichés. Clichés survive in part because they contain an element of truth. Consider, for example, "Act enthusiastic and you'll be enthusiastic"; "You are what you eat"; and "Smile and the whole world smiles with you." Might another of this family be "You become what you do?" It seems quite possible that, if we can catalyze university units to research and teach in the area of creative and innovative management, they may well become creative and innovative themselves. If this happens, we will have achieved two important goals, not just one.

NOTES

1. Several of these obstacles are discussed more fully by Redmon (1982).
2. For a critical review of the literature on the "Effectiveness of Strategies to Encourage an Innovative Education Program," see Lantz (1984).

REFERENCES

Allison, G.T. "Conceptual Models and the Cuban Missile Crisis," *The American Political Science Review,* LXIII (1969), 689–718.

Altbach, P.G., "Reform and Innovation in Higher Education," *Educational Documentation and Information,* N223: 12–51 (1982), 5–55.

Charnes, Abraham and William Cooper, eds. *Creative and Innovative Management,* Vol. 2. Cambridge, Mass.: Ballinger Publishing Company, 1984.

Daft, Richard L., and Selwyn W. Becker. *The Innovative Organization.* New York: Elsevier, 1978.

Davis, Robert H.; Rich Strand; Lawrence T. Alexander; and M. Norrul Hussain. "The Impact of Organizational and Innovator Variables on Instructional Innovation in Higher Education," *Journal of Higher Education,* 53, 5 (1982), 568–586.

Duncan, Robert B. "The Ambidextrous Organization: Designing Dual Structures for Innovation," Chapter 9. In R.L. Kiman, L.R. Pondy, and D.P. Slevin, eds., *The Management of Organization Design: Vol 1.* New York: North-Holland, 1976.

Hedberg, Bo; Paul C. Nystrom; and William H. Starbuck. "Designing Organizations to Match Tomorrow." In P. Nystrom and W. Starbuck, eds., *Prescriptive Models of Organizations.* New York: North-Holland, 1977.

Huber, George P. "The Nature and Design of Post-Industrial Organizations," *Management Science* 30, 8 (August 1984): 928–51.

Lantz, Alma E. "Effectiveness of Strategies to Encourage an Innovative Education Program," *Educational Evaluation and Policy Analysis* 6, 1 (Spring 1984), 53–61.

Lindblom, C.E. "The Science of Muddling Through," *Public Administration Review,* XIX, 2 (1959), 78–88.

March, James G. "Footnotes to Organizational Change," *Administrative Science Quarterly* 26, 4, (December 1981): 578–96.

March, James G., and Pierre J. Romelaer. "Position and Presence in the Drift of Decisions," Chapter 12. In James March and Johan P. Olsen, eds., *Ambiguity and Choice in Organizations,* 2nd edition. Bergen, Norway: A/S Repro-Trykk, 1979.

Nadler, David A. "Managing Transitions to Uncertain Future States," *Organization Dynamics,* 11, 1 (Summer 1982), 37–45.

Redmon, Thomas. "Policy and Academic Innovation," *The College Board Review,* 124 (Summer 1982), 19–23.

Tunstall, W. Brooke. "Cultural Transition at AT & T," *Sloan Management Review,* 25, 1 (Fall 1983), 15–26.

Tushman, Michael, and William L. Moore. *Readings in the Management of Innovation.* Marshfield, Mass.: Pitman Publishing, Inc.

Weick, Karl E. "The Management of Organizational Change among Loosely Coupled Elements." In P.S. Goodman and Associates, *Change in Organizations: New Perspectives on Theory, Research and Practice.* San Francisco, Calif.: Jossey-Bass, 1982.

DISCUSSION

W. W. Cooper

W.W. Cooper: As R.M. Cyert notes, the classics on higher education from John Stuart Mill and Cardinal Newman to Thorstein Veblen and Robert Maynard Hutchins, Ortega y Gassett and A.N. Whitehead have generally regarded universities as preservers and transmitters of knowledge and civilizing values— and especially the value of rationality that the Greeks believed to be the distinguishing feature of civilized man. These classics, therefore, provide little assistance to President Cyert when seeking to encourage creativity and providing the innovations needed to give practical form to the resulting ideas. Today's college president must find new ways to facilitate dynamic and applicable learning, even though the universities have been major sources of knowledge at least since the time of Galileo. Indeed, Galileo's storied clash with the established church provides an excellent example of the impact of new ways of reasoning on the values as well as the knowledge of society.

President Cyert's paper provides a new direction or at least a new emphasis in thinking about our institutions of higher learning and how they should be organized and directed. Especially important, he believes, is the role of the university president in encouraging and initiating innovations. I think this also extends to deans, or whatever titles are used to designate the heads of relatively independent schools within a university structure. Once one reaches the department head level, however, the job becomes much more one of protecting the discipline. This is perhaps not surprising since, at this "firing line" level, much time must be spent in ensuring that present faculty and student needs are met while also trying to secure what is required from a relatively remote and unsympathetic bureaucracy.

As Professor Huber finds, after his search through the literature, the idea that universities should initiate researching and teaching in the area of creative and innovative management is a novel one. I believe that one inherent obstacle to such a goal lies in reliance on movement at the departmental level for the needed initiatives. Change is not likely to occur in most cases unless the president or at least a dean is willing to provide the necessary leadership and resources. This means that the latter levels must be mindful of the problems and opportunities involved in initiating such changes and should be willing and able to do what is needed along lines like Dr. Cyert is suggesting.

How then are we to begin developing programs of education and research in creative and innovative management? As Dr. Huber notes, conferences such as the one underlying this volume should prove helpful in signaling the need for such programs. They can also begin to remedy the lack of suitable teaching materials and stimulate research opportunities. The real development will begin, however, when one or two schools really "grab hold" and show that the job can be done and is worth doing. Other schools will then surely follow to supply the broader base of activities that is really required.

This course of development is the one that was followed in "case teaching" and "analytic approaches" to management. Yet, programs for creative and innovative management raise special problems. How can we ensure that, once started, programs will continue to provide what is needed for creativity and innovation? I suspect that one solution will lie in providing new channels for student and faculty responses to the world of active management.

Achieving these goals while preserving the character of the university as a transmitter of knowledge and civilizing values will also require innovative attention at the level that President Cyert is addressing. A successful program will almost certainly strive to convert these influxes of new problems and opportunities into research that will impact other parts of the university as well as provide the necessary materials for the departments concerned with teaching creative and innovative management. If this can all be done, the university will not only be preserved, but it will also be enriched, extended, and made more pertinent to the kind of society it will help to shape.

How to do creative and innovative management in the university? We have to look in new directions. One such way is new kinds of institutions, such as Stanford Research Institute (SRI). I was there in the early 1950s when there was a big flap over separating the institute from the university because it was likely to "contaminate" the university with the kinds of problems it was attracting and dealing with. Those problems may be part of today's solutions. I suspect that it is the ability to bring in new problems that becomes the continuing force for creative change.

Professor Dierkes presented his government-supported institute in West Berlin, The Science Center. It is an innovative institution, devoted to social science, that is raising this peculiar, problematic combination of *excellence* (of which the disciplines are always very fond) and *relevance* (of which the disciplines are often less fond). It is the ever-changing relevancy issue that is, I believe, the energizing source of creative and innovative management.

Question: What is the current attention focus of university administration?

Richard Cyert: Sadly it is often survival. We must change this climate: Universities should stress innovation, which itself will help the survival problem.

Question: What happens when you encounter an immovable force in attempting to alter the attention focus of faculty in implementing creativity and innovation?

Richard Cyert: You don't ever expect to have 100 percent of the senior faculty with you. But they may not be negative. The real point is whether you have enough to help achieve the end that you want. Department heads are the ones that you need to work through, and I have regular meetings with them stressing the importance of innovation. We use the budget allocation process as a definite facilitator of the process. This is a very practical matter. We are not willing to put large amounts of money into units that do not have a chance of achieving a high level of excellence.

Question: On the one hand we would like to induce changes that are small and appear to be unimportant. On the other hand, change is often required to be rapid. How can we make large radical changes appear unimportant?

Richard Cyert: Making change seem small and unimportant is only one particular tactic. A more critical notion is that change can take time. To introduce the idea of radical change and then allow some time for discussion, criticism, and so on as the idea becomes assimilated within the organization is often the best strategy possible. And the more radical the change, the more likely that this is the most effective way to introduce it.

George Huber: Don't forget the strategy of introducing innovative ideas in the context of accomplishing an important and always held goal. Thus the innovation appears less radical. One should also allow time for people's mental set to get adjusted.

David Hertz: Change occurs when a problem, small or significant, faces a prepared mind. Difficulty in organizational change relates to the "will" as opposed to the intellect or the design of an organization.

Richard Cyert: A final point backing up George Kozmetsky's plea for action. The distinction between a businessman and an academician is that the businessman says, "Ready, fire, aim!", while the academic says, "Ready, aim, aim, aim, ..."

Part X

IMPLICATIONS FOR PUBLIC POLICY, ECONOMIC PRODUCTIVITY, SCIENCE AND RESEARCH

Chapter 21

STRATEGIC THINKING AND THE PUBLIC POLICY ENVIRONMENT

Robert H. Kupperman and David Williamson

Strategic thinking, like so many other sly phrases, tends to be pronounced without definition, without mutual agreement as to what either the speaker means or the audience understands. "Strategy," of course, has been applied as a noun to virtually every field of human activity, from chess to crime and from war to business. "Thinking" is such a common concept it is seldom considered in precise terms of inclusion and exclusion. Together, the words "strategic thinking" have been used to embrace almost everything from family planning to preparation for apocalypse. Here, however, the intended meaning is more modest in scope and quite sharply focused on the political behavior of great nations. More specifically, strategic thinking means the study of the dynamics of great forces in motion—the net national interests of sovereign states, and fluid relationships among these independent nations, and the powerful influence of available resources and new technologies in the global equation. Strategic thinking deals with the coupling of these elements in various practical formulations to enlighten the selection and pursuit of public policy.

For the United States, strategic thinking presumes a working knowledge of the most important national objectives in some rough order of priority. It presumes a realistic and reasonably accurate assessment of the objectives and priorities of the other participants on the geopolitical scene. It presumes a good understanding of basic makeup of civilization—such as population, food, water, materials, climate—and the key role technology plays in extending civilization beyond its otherwise natural limits of growth. It then presumes to analyze these elements in relation to each other in order to offer insights into the implications of various public policies; most critically, strategic thinking strives to cover *all* the probable outcomes of an act, to press outward the natural human boundaries of time to a point that eliminates the possibility of surprise. It is not by any means a monolithic discipline whose proper exercise will always produce the same right answer; it is quite the opposite, a lively activity dedicated to a heterogeneous output within the constraints of declared assumptions and logic. And, since 1945, strategic thinking has further been conditioned by the deployment of nuclear weaponry sufficient to extinguish global life.

It is this last aspect that makes strategic thinking something more than the specialized field for military staff officers and their gifted professors; it puts a different value on error than was ever apparent in the days of Mahon or Clausewitz. Strategic thinking should not be confused with examples of great tactics on the battlefield or in the political arena; such tactics, to be called successful, must contribute to safe progress within the selected strategy that supports fundamental national ends. The kinds of errors that can be made are legion: misestimating national will, overlooking underlying social forces, targeting technical and political leadtime, relying on mirror-image assumptions, suppressing inconvenient facts — all these can creep into a process of strategic thinking that then, inevitably, will be skewed in a direction that will lead to flawed public policy. When the issues involved are those of national security and the choices ultimately involve peace or modern war, the premium on the quality of strategic thinking becomes incalculably high.

Unfortunately, there is no guaranteed litmus test for "good thinking" in this business. There is no laboratory proof or sorting logic that allows national management to come to rest upon the one "right" concept or select the one "proper" mechanism, or even to pick the one "correct" thinker. It seems that an assurance of quality in this case comes from the degree of universality that can be entertained in the process: by analogy, a pyramid of all good ideas is more stable in the support of its pinnacle of best ideas than is any other, more selective, and less inclusive construct.

The first order consumer of strategic thinking on the macroscale is the government — the federal establishment that has the responsibility for crafting, proposing, and executing policies that further our net national objectives. When the Second World War came to an end, U.S. economic, technical, and military superiority appeared so overwhelming that little competitive thought was felt necessary to analyze the global options; our national predilection for near-in horizons denied us an early appreciation of the almost inevitable future: a world of power shared in ever smaller proportions with the ever increasing appetites of a larger and larger body of claimants. We did not even look far enough into the probabilistic future to identify the rapid acquisition of nuclear explosives and high technology delivery systems by the Soviet Union as a long-term determinant of future U.S. policies, foreign and domestic.

But that moment did come, and the United States had to respond. The wartime lessons of mobilization of intellect were still young; the clear and present challenge was unmistakable; the rewards for wrestling with the new complexities introduced by technical progress and political confrontation were high. The U.S. response was enthusiastic and innovative—and successful. Although in retrospect it is clear that there was no single master plan for the organization of talent appropriate to the new environment, the rapid evolution of institutions and processes and mechanisms soon was able to offer the policy selecting function of government a rich and substantive menu of choices. The pyramid of all good ideas capped by the best began to form.

Strategic thinking in the 1950s and early 1960s was characterized by a ferment of ideas from a wide spectrum of sources. There was a real hunger in the White House, on Capitol Hill, and in the public for enlightened perceptions of what the events of the day might mean for the far tomorrows of the world. These were the days of PSAC (the President's Science Advisory Committee) that provided for absolutely top-level communication between government and the energetic post-war scientific community. At the same time, each major department and agency had its own external advisory structure, organized to make specialized talent easily and immediately available. This was the period when the cream of the technical community was learning to grapple with intractable questions of political reality. This was the heyday of the independent "think tanks" and federal research centers—the Institute for Defense Analysis and its related evaluation groups; the Hudson Institute and Herman Kahn; the earliest incarnation of today's RAND Corporation.

This was when operations research, mathematical modeling of geopolitical events, and game theory became important tools in the process of sorting out the full range of "what if" scenarios. This was the period when, from the research viewpoint, "a hundred flowers blossomed." Universities and research groups had ready access to financial support from the Defense and civil agencies without the later encumbrances of red tape, cost-sharing, "mission-relatedness," and insistence on competition virtually at any cost. The research and development base of the nation was broad, strong, inventive, and optimistic; the same sense of energy and intellectual ferment was felt in the world of ideas as was visible in the world of things. Ideas found ready markets in the federal establishment; and the establishment had unfiltered access to the intellectual critical mass of the country. This past was certainly not perfect—hindsight often focuses through rosy lenses—but it was effective. Even in the most sensitive security issues, where classification rigorously limited access to important areas of knowledge, the "system" as a whole encouraged informed debate and invited many independent outsiders to participate; policy options did not become the captive of security compartmentation.

Looking back, the ease of doing business then seems incredibly streamlined in the light of today's ponderous procurement process. At the same time, of course, everything appeared to be slow, balky, bureaucratic, and in the hands of senior clerks still wedded to the quill pen and sandcaster. In those not-so-far-past days, a dollar in the market of ideas probably bought ninety cents' worth of thinking and ten of management. The federal centers were fully funded; they could afford the luxury of full-time problem solving without having to market themselves in the world of commerce. They could pay salaries commensurate with the importance and quality of their work, not constrained by artificially depressed federal pay scales. Universities and the like received grants—not contracts, with the multiplication of paperwork that that implies—that covered the institution's real costs; cost-sharing for the privilege of doing the government's work was not a policy then. Sole-source transactions were recognized as the simplest means of engaging talents of external experts and analysts; competition of ideas came after they had been formulated and documented, not before. The federal procurement system in those days was designed primarily to buy what the government needed, not to be an instrument of social change or an arbiter of social justice.

In this environment, strategic thinking was really possible, if never easy. The overwhelming problem of a U.S.–Soviet political competition, made deadly dangerous by the ability to resort to ultimate arms, captured some of the best minds in the country.

The United States developed, under the external stimulus of events and the internal stimulus of analysis, a quite successful and workable national security posture. The roles and priorities the United States assigned to such policy elements as intelligence, alliances, technology, weapons development, arms control, civil defense, and the relative emphasis due to offensive and defensive systems did not occur by accident: they were, for all the freight of compromise they carried, the end elaboration of an important policy process. And that process retained its integrity—and thus its apparent value—as long as it remained dynamic, as long as both the nation's problems and its possible courses of action remained the subject of lively intellectual interrogation from an ever-renewed body of participants. It is important here to repeat the point: strategic thinking will be valid only under conditions when neither the issue nor the solution are dictated and when the process is continuously perfused by new talent and new ideas.

Today, it appears that strategic thinking is not in the best of health. Some hold it is no longer being practiced. At the very best, strategic thinking has become a temporary victim of temporary aberrations of style and perception; at worst, the once-successful process has reached a point of self-fulfilling, entropic collapse. Whether one is optimistic or pessimistic, the symptoms are there to see: there is a kind of petrification of strategic thinking, at the top and at the bottom. This is the end result of a closed-loop circular process which, for descriptive purposes, can be entered at any point. The cause-and-effect flow may be something like this:

- good ideas are diminishing in number because —
- the number and quality of outside and inside practitioners is diminishing because —
- budgetary and program management ground rules make it difficult to get good people involved because —
- resources and the flexibility to use them sensibly have been cut by both the executive and legislative branches and because —
- good ideas are diminishing in number.

When the dynamics of a useful strategic thinking process are interrupted, one of the results is an aging of the work force: the seniors stay in place beyond their time because no challenging juniors are pressing forward and upward with new visions, new interpretations, new analyses. Nothing turns to concrete quite so quickly as an unchallenged old guard of experts. This leads to the institutionalization of both problem perceptions and solution proposals. In a nutshell, an original quest for understanding devolves into a cult, complete with arcana, priesthood, and devotees. Orthodoxy becomes an end in itself; the insider hierarchy has a corner on revealed wisdom; the school solutions brook no questioning.

Were the problems of today identical with those that led to the creation of the current canon of strategic thought, the calcification of process would perhaps be tolerable; too large an effort on too limited a problem set is certainly wasteful. What is not tolerable is that the calcification of process also has the dangerous side-effect of freezing problem perception in the minds of the practitioners. When the elite, *because* it has become a certain kind of elite by default, insists on defining the realities of today and tomorrow only in the terms of conditions twenty years ago, then society is faced with double dangers: those that really exist and the fact that they are being overlooked in favor of comfortable attachment to an earlier credo.

An interesting characteristic of this process, even when arrested in mid-development, is that it continues without difficulty to absorb and respond to new technology. For example, today's technological debates are quite up-to-date in the military matters of new high-precision conventional weapons possibilities, of new sophisticated aircraft delivery systems, and of new survivable nuclear retaliatory systems with CEP's measured in meters rather than kilometers. Like late medieval philosophy, this is a focus on detail rather than a reaching for a new threshold of understanding. The process seems trapped by its own past, a kind of societal monotony that cannot shake off a twenty-year old perception of the shape of the world. A single example may suffice: why does the United States continue to pour its limited treasure of money and men into preparations for the least likely of military eventualities? It seems clear that a great Soviet land attack driving through Germany to the Channel is the remotest of possibilities — there are few if any net national needs of the Soviet system such a military adventure could meet — yet the U.S. planning and programming machinery continues to regard this possibility as a paramount driver of military requirements. This situation does suggest a discontinuity between reality and its perception, between the strategy being followed and its putative national objectives.

The security problem set that we and the world must deal with has evolved over the past two decades. It now includes the new phenomena of great power powerlessness, of collapsing norms of international behavior, of sophisticated "have not" insistence on sharing material wealth, and of the emergence of violence as the first resort of political disagreement. The intellectual apparatus to illuminate the merits and demerits of basic policy options needs to evolve as well. The traditionalists still focus on NATO, on land-based missile and related force structure equations, on Mutual Assured Destruction (MAD), on counter-value and counterforce arguments. Our strategy seems constrained by old ideologies with a negative flavor: deterrence, not constructive action; status quo and nonproliferation, not a recognition of the inexorable dynamics of the history of technology; confrontation, not maneuver and flanking and correlation of forces. It seems time to revitalize strategic thinking in America, to start afresh with a look at the whole world rather than just the linear East–West axis, and to test entire new generalizations about the aims of American society and the most constructive ways to meet them.

And it is not too soon to start; it may, in fact, already be too late. The mechanisms that served so well in the past are probably beyond reach. The hope of reverting to federal rules of procurement that are not based on presumptions of perfidy and incompetence are faint. Management of this aspect of the federal enterprise has gone beyond the ability of the federal establishment to cope — the end product of decades of meddling with the procurement process has probably created a most durable sacred low immune from internally energized reform; we must turn elsewhere to find a cutting edge that can slice through the tangle of process and allow for a new, unfettered environment of intellectual excellence constructively focused on the greatest problem of our era—moving from a tenuous absence of war to a new concept of world peace and security.

The outlines of a proposal for such a plowing of the nation's intellectual seed-bed do suggest themselves at this time. It is to the Congress we can turn, using successful models of previous legislation to support the contention that new ideas flourish in new environments. (One significant example is the early success of the space program given a fresh start with no preconceptions; another is the success of unversity-based development laboratories like Los Alamos; another is the unconventional new corporate–state–federal partnerships in research for the fifth generation computer.)

As a start in revolutionizing attitudes, the Congress might consider chartering an experimental institute—sunshine legislation might provide an initial life-time of seven years to reduce politicization of the debate on continuation—dedicated to strategic thinking. A single lump-sum endowment-cum-revolving fund appropriation would guarantee independence and, more importantly, would reduce consumption of funds by overhead and marketing to an absolute minimum. A major element of managerial experimentation would be in the institute's freedom from the traditional and conventional rules that typically control the respending of government funds: the MacArthur Foundation's support of excellence might be an archetype of the institute's management philosophy.

The institute should be run neither as a business nor as a university, in that both have their own bureaucracies that hamper action. It should rather be run as a modern analog to the Renaissance patrons of the arts and sciences, dedicated to the sole proposition of bringing out of the best minds in the country the best strategic thinking for the country. To support five hundred people a year—not necessarily always the same people—for seven years could probably be guaranteed with an endowment of $500 million, even if invested in government securities.

The choice of agent for establishing and running the institute would pose the most thorny political barrier unless it were already inherent in the proposal itself. A Smithsonian regent structure comes to mind, one that involves both parties and all branches of government but retains real independence for the operation itself. An inspired choice for director is obviously needed—not necessarily a scholar but one whom scholars respect; not necessarily a practitioner of strategic analysis but one familiar with it as a user—George C. Marshall might be a model. Perhaps the ranks of former congressmen and senators hold such a person available to this new experiment in public service.

The structure of this suggested first step aimed at a change in national attitude toward, and investment in, strategic thinking is far less important than the recognition that the problem itself is important. At this juncture, any step that brings intellect widely to bear on the nation's agenda for security and progress would be welcome.

Chapter 22

REFLECTIONS ON ACADEMIC LEADERSHIP

Joseph S. Murphy

It might be useful for me to discuss some of the decisions made during my twenty years as an academic manager. I have to say that very few had anything to do with my having been personally innovative. In general, my experience in public life suggests that it is the kiss of death to any enterprise for the president or chief executive officer to propose a good idea. My best advice is to plant a good idea someplace else with someone else, and then to nourish and fertilize it — preferably at night and at a distance. Should the idea become identified with the chief executive officer, the suspicion inevitably arises that a secret, nefarious, outrageous intent is behind it, bearing no resemblance to its explicit description and portending no good to anyone.

The only kind of issue a president can safely and candidly espouse from the outset is something that others can identify as a harmless eccentricity. For instance, a sudden concern about cruelty to small animals would be acceptable. Everyone would say, "It's a reasonable position for him, and it's not threatening to us." (It is also, essentially, of little interest to most.) That is the kind of idea you can propose with impunity.

What is it then that the manager of a public institution can do, other than oversee the mundane daily life of the organization? What beyond the allocation of dollars, the negotiation of contracts with unions, the representation of the university to its political and public constituencies, and the perpetual seeking, day and night, of money for the nourishment and sustenance of everyone in the institution?

While the example of practices at work in private industry is not apropos, it is likely that our heightened interest in creativity and innovation is directly related to the threat to American corporations and industries and our economy posed by Japanese assertiveness and ingenuity. Consequently, we are all suddenly trying to fulfill the dictum of the governor of New York to "do more with less." As consumers of the profits of other people's labor, public institutions clearly do not measure innovation and creativity by profit and loss statements, though it is generally not a good idea for public servants to overspend their budgets—even if it were possible, which in most cases it is not.

Now, is there any kind of innovative action that one can hope to see fulfilled; and just how are the ideas generated? It seems to me that there is a whole dimension of psychological and subjective variables that must be taken into account in a public institution that are not relevant in private industry.

Our experience suggests that the energy for creative ideas is often generated by frustration, anger, and resentment. These emotions can be powerful catalysts in motivating people and provoking creative and innovative activity and behavior. There is also much to be said for the advice given me when I was a young man by a veteran of long-term planning: "Remember, the objective of a planner is not to let anyone know how complicated or how expensive an undertaking is going to be; in short, you must learn how to protect your project early in the game so that no one will put a damper on your efforts at the outset."

The example of the growth of my own university—which now consists of some twenty different colleges, plus professional schools, including medical schools and a law school—is a case in point. As a consumer of approximately $889 million in operating expenses in one year and roughly $300 to $400 million in capital construction funds at any given time, the financing of the university is a formidable item in the state and, to a lesser extent, the city budgets. It is not surprising that there is always serious opposition to the expansion of the university's activities.

To illustrate some of the strategies we have used in the past to promote new ideas against all odds, I offer the case of launching an innovative professional school. The idea arose during a discussion of the difficulties many of our able but needy graduates had in gaining admittance to professional schools. At the same time, many people in our poorer neighborhoods were experiencing just as much difficulty in getting the professional services they needed.

We decided what was needed was a professional school that would reach out to a special kind of student—one committed to the care of the underserved and the broad public interest. The idea of providing wider access to professional education was a logical extension of the university's historic commitment to meet the educational aspirations of all the people of New York City. The idea of creating a professional school committed to educating students who would use their professional skills to meet humanitarian needs was new.

The following year a proposal was advanced by a group of people far removed from the president's office. Many people struggled for years to enlarge the numbers of people whose interests would be served by having this school. First, the idea was planted in the minds of local politicians. Next, we did something comparable to the ploy of the presidential candidate who promised the job of secretary of state to fifty different people. We dangled the deanship of the new school before at least that many people, many of whom were influential in the state legislature.

Another tactic involved making it clear that no one in a position of power or authority was in favor of the idea. This posed just the right challenge to the convictions of the supporters of the school. It confirmed their original hypothesis that this must be a good idea when they viewed the caliber of the opposition. I think it is important that there be an impediment to the dynamics and a vigorous dialectic in the development of creative and innovative ideas. It should not be easy. There ought to be an awareness that an innovative idea cannot have not much value unless it really does threaten someone's interests or at least disturbs someone's inertia. A little bit of resistance is usually the first thing that whets the appetite of someone pursuing a good idea.

It can take many years for such an enterprise to get underway, and obviously one of the most difficult things is finding an established academic leader in the country who is willing to risk a respected reputation in so precarious an undertaking. We found the old traditional appeal to be the most effective. One need only say, "We are offering you something absolutely new." Now, to have something new is to be able to do things that can never be done with something that is old; that is, to put one's private, subjective, personal mark on an institution. It is an appeal, frankly, to ego, perhaps even an appeal to one's hopes for immortality. (I might add that it is not the kind of tangential appeal that elicits the contributions of those donors whose names are engraved on a good many buildings on many campuses in the United States.) To have a new academic entity to establish is just a tremendous incentive for a creative educator; it was our final stratagem for getting our professional school underway.

There are many other nonrational, accidental, almost marginal considerations that go into the development of new and innovative ways of dealing with the world that should not be ignored. In an institution such as mine, which does not require that I be particularly innovative but does require that we try to attract, recruit, and hire presidents who are creative and innovative, we have learned a bit from our mistakes and successes. Choosing the right manager is more complex in the public arena where there are no objective standards, such as a profit and loss statement, to guide you. You must identify something more than the character, experience, and background of an individual to whom you are entrusting one of your institutions. Clearly, the competence of the individual is important, as well as the background, the experience, and the ability to do everything from reading a budget to negotiating a contract; but there is a whole other spectrum of qualities that are equally important and are often overlooked.

We look for someone who shares the values of our institution, above all a commitment to our two primary goals: broad access to educational opportunity and academic excellence. These objectives are not easily meshed as everyone knows. We have found that a president who has strong sense of himself or herself as an individual, a strong commitment to a set of social and public values, is more likely to succeed in this kind of task than someone without those qualities.

There are other standards which have also proven useful in selecting managers. We like them to be psychologically healthy. That does not mean they have to be terribly sane; it means that, even if they are mildly neurotic, they will at least have had some familiarity with the psychodynamics of human behavior. They tend on the whole to be a little more sensitive toward the people they work with.

A recent event reminds me of another important consideration. A friend of mine, a college president, was in need of finding a wife. The board of trustees would have been happier if he had a wife, and his mother would have been happier if he had a wife, so he did what every good manager does: he created a search committee. I had asked him what charge was he about to give to the search committee. He said he had the usual preferences: he wouldn't mind if she were attractive and he wouldn't mind if she were intelligent, interesting, and if she were wealthy; but he said there was one thing he really wanted very much—he wanted someone who was cheerful, had good humor, and an even disposition.

We have added a pleasant personality to our list of qualifications for college presidents. It is terribly important to avoid having an institution run by a depressed person, no matter how qualified. A cheerful person is more apt to take chances and risks.

We have come to shun those who are too preoccupied with their own ego, or appearance in the world, tendencies that do not enhance the performance of a manager of an institution. A manager should know which things in life are and are not necessary to take seriously. It is a valuable quality in a college president. Also, one ought to look for a leader who has a sense of the historical role of the institution and of himself as an individual. We think of our institution as part of a railway that stretches from Portland to Portland, with our having charge of a small expanse in Indiana; and we think we ought not exaggerate the importance nor underestimate the opportunities that it presents. We like managers and presidents who feel that way, as well.

I have one last word about creativity and innovation. I believe a good deal of what happens, happens serendipitously. There is an old Hegelian principle called "the cunning of reason"; all of mankind thinks, thinks, thinks, chooses a particular set of policies; then something altogether accidental supplants all expectations. My favorite example is reported in a *New York Times* editorial of 1900 in which it was stated that the population of New York had reached its maximum capacity of three million people. The argument stated that there was no conceivable way we could provide all the horses three million people would require. Clearly, no one at that time could have predicted that the automobile would become what it became. Many of our own prognostications will be equally off base.

In conclusion, I would say that innovation and creativity depend upon the ability to identify a likely opportunity. That happens more often when one is clever enough or smart enough or quick enough to read in other people's eyes what it is they want, will support, and value.

Chapter 23

MICRO VS. MACRO
The Firm Benefits of Creative Management*

Robert Lawrence Kuhn

"Industrial policy," the new buzz among political partisans, tickles our ears in media debate. It is, we are told, the national economic panacea for international competitive sickness. "IP," to those on the in, would direct and control from Washington the thrust and focus of American industry. IPers believe that the free market system is no longer efficient and that the government must intervene to prop up business and support jobs. Coined by intellectuals and caught by politicians, IP is a symptom of economic illness and political fever.

One cannot deny the appeal to industries suffering decline and workers without work. Nor can one negate the fact that in a tightly wired world foreign governments can shift the commercial balance of power by giving home-grown companies unfair advantage. Thus IP sparks the hope that federal funds might aid outmoded and out-priced companies regain former glory.

But numerous industries will vie for the golden tap. Which to promote and which to protect? Which to ignore and which to forget? When the government picks "winners," it must, by that same decision, also pick "losers." To sustain

---

* Much of this material is taken from Robert Lawrence Kuhn, *To Flourish Among Giants: Creative Management for Mid-Sized Firms* (New York: John Wiley, 1985). See also Robert Lawrence Kuhn, *Commercializing Defense-Related Technology* (New York: Praeger, 1984); Raymond Smilor and Robert Kuhn, *Corporate Creativity: Robust Companies and the Entrepreneurial Spirit* (New York: Praeger, 1984); Eugene Konecci and Robert Kuhn, *Technology Venturing: American Innovation and Risk Taking* (New York: Praeger, 1985).

one, we must shun another. An increase of jobs here must result in a decrease of jobs there. If automobiles are chosen, why should textiles be condemned? Who is to decide that employment in the Midwest should go up while employment in the Southeast should go down? Why should large steel mills in the north be subsidized if small steel mills in the south can be so profitable? One conjures up tortuous visions of procedural miasma, politicking and lobbying of unprecedented magnitude. Resources, we have come to learn, are not unlimited; available subsidy is only finite. (What, by the way, happens to IP when favorite industries do not make the Federal Hit Parade?)

Socialism, it is said, is a wonderful concept; the dream of economic equality and financial fairness is utopian. The only problem, of course, is that it just doesn't work. Theoretical idealism breaks up quickly against the rocks of pragmatic realism. Human beings function best when they are controlled least, when they prosper in proportion to personal initiative and self-driven intensity.

American business is still burdened by archaic regulations codified two generations ago. There were right and rigorous reasons then. We were fast becoming, in those heady days, the world's premier industrial power; our growth was unimpeded, domestic markets were burgeoning and foreign markets beckoning. Industries and industrialists became intoxicated with their new-found powers, and consumers and workers, at the mercy of these mammoths, needed protection. Yet times shift and paths twist. What worked then won't work now.

Is passivity the answer? Is public policy perfect? Should national debate go quiescent? The status quo be bronzed? By no means. What American industry needs is simple: not more control by government but more confidence in management. Not centralized planning by bureaucrats but aggressive leadership from businessmen. Not industrial policy but creative management. More micro and less macro.

American industry must be freed from constraints, not encumbered with more. American business must be invigorated, not suffocated. The mold for forging the future? Independent management, not centralized command. (For every rule, there is an exception. In certain areas of the economy, especially in high risk advanced technology, individual companies cannot afford to invest and America cannot afford to abdicate. Supercomputers, for one, have huge development costs and uncertain commercial revenues. Yet the United States must not lose world leadership, certainly not by default. Here is fertile substrate for an industrial policy.)

The ends of industrial policy are desirable; it is the means that are questionable. It is not sufficient to deny IP for American business. To critique is always easier than to construct. Industrial policy will not work. What will? It is one thing to describe the illness, quite another to prescribe the remedy. Alternatives proffered usually stress macroeconomic manipulations, like looser money, tighter budgets, and the like. Yet something is missing. We've heard all this before.

Economists dominate economic thinking. Logical, at least at first. But economists, when one thinks about them, do not run companies. They do not manage budgets and do not direct staffs. They never formulate corporate strategies and never build corporate structures. "P & L," "personnel," "product positioning" are terms they do not use. Meeting payrolls is something they do not do. Making enterprises work is responsibility they do not have.

Yet enterprises — for-profit businesses and not-for-profit institutions — are the components of the economy. Like cells in a body, the *are* the economy; and to treat the economy only by macroeconomics is to treat an epidemic only by epidemiology. Building businesses in the former, like curing people in the latter, must be addressed. To leave the economy solely in the hands of economists is to leave the sick solely in the hands of statisticians.

We must listen to the gross national product. We must hear the rhythms of small businessmen, middle managers, corporate executives. We must feel the beat of individual needs, wants, desires. The world works because some have vision and brilliance, with the tenacity and temerity to produce and provide. Business, to my mind, is the economic substance of human knowledge, the molding of value and substance out of concept and form.

Creative and innovative management is what America needs, and government policy should be directed toward building it. But this is not a topic of macroeconomics; one does not study it in doctoral programs; there is little research, no Nobel Prizes, and minor media. It is local not global, micro not macro.

Yet the stakes are big not small: Creative and innovative management is the economic pulse of American health. It is the life blood for sustaining the strength of the economy, for improving the quality of management, for securing the robustness of business. It is the fulcrum for the final fifth of the twentieth century. If America is to build a muscular national economy, benefitting all citizens and leading the world, the mechanism must include creative and innovative management.

Though words flow easily, precise definitions come hard. *Creativity* is the process by which novelty is generated, and *innovation* is the process by which novelty is transformed into practicality. Creativity forms something from nothing, and innovation shapes that something into products and services. To nurture and develop creative and innovative management is to engender America with the power to prosper.

Both collective policy and individual business are involved. If creative and innovative management can build industrial abundance in America, it will do so on two pillars: the macroeconomic environment and the micro business structure—macro and micro. But such flourishing will not happen by accident. It is a way of thinking new and hard. No one risks for little reward. Only within a proper environment will American management make the right moves and take the right risks.

This environment has two elements: an economic climate responsive to creativity and innovation, and a corporate culture conducive to such novel management.

CREATIVITY AND THE ECONOMIC ENVIRONMENT

Encourage Risk by Strengthening Reward

Proprietary ownership is a powerful human motivator; it is capitalism's great advantage over communism, and we must pound it without pause. We should strengthen our patent laws now to include new forms of invention in the information and knowledge-based sciences. Government contracts should be structured to encourage recipients to reach and to risk, whether defense contractors, university science departments, or government laboratories. Both institutions and individuals must benefit from their toil. Federal R & D funds, perhaps our nation's chief asset in building comprehensive national security, should embed economic as well as military forces, deriving maximally efficient value from each. Government contracts, for example, might be awarded to firms that generate original ideas or products, or firms adept at commercializing defense-related technology, whether the firms be large or small.

Facilitate Information Transfer

Creativity and innovation are resources that increase with use: the more you use it, to quote Dr. George Kozmetsky, the more you have it. To enhance applications, we must publicize and promote. Although creativity and innovation are private processes, they can be fostered by information sharing and situation setting. Centers for innovation and invention should be established, funded by state and federal government and administered by colleges and universities. The commercialization of defense-related technology should be encouraged. National data banks can enable active researchers and potential entrepreneurs to access ideas and information.

Focus Government Fiscal and Tax Policy

Many words are spoken in Washington; millions every year are written into record and law. None are heard more clearly, none are read more carefully, than those dealing with taxes. By tax law the federal government directs public policy. A clear message for developing creative and innovative management will be given only when tax policy is the medium. We should reward creative and innovative companies through lower taxes, rather than penalize their profit with higher taxes. Tax credits for incremental R & D is a first, albeit halting step in the right direction. We might consider, say, tax credits for new patents, for new products, for R & D expenditures above industry norms. Capital gains, as another example, might be dropped further, perhaps to zero, but only if, in my opinion, the holding period is increased. (The recent reduction of the holding period to six months, while personally productive, is socially counterproductive; it flies off in the wrong direction by encouraging financial manipulations not productive development.)

Understand the Creative Process

Public policy should support research and education in creative and innovative management. Studying the process should become a national goal — not a curiosity, but a necessity. America's finest researchers should be funded and interdisciplinary work encouraged — from organizational psychology and the decision sciences to artificial intelligence and the neurosciences. The arts, too, offer much and should not be neglected.

In concert with research, we must stimulate creative and innovative management in our schools. Principles of creativity and innovation can be taught at every age, in parallel with enhanced math and science, from early education through high school and college. Schools of business should take the lead, instilling motivation to shift and change rather than drilling techniques to trend and continue. One danger of making business more rational, more analytical and computer-based, is the subtle pressure to stifle the new and inhibit the fresh. Businessmen must be prepared to make nonrational (not *ir*rational) decisions, gambling on instinct and perception. Though business should become more of a science, it must never cease being an art.

Promote Interaction Among Sectors

Creative and innovative management is not sector specific. It occupies a unique place at the union of industry, government, and academe. Each sector must make its contribution, and critical mass can be generated nationally only when all focus their force on the interface. Intersector interaction is not just a current fad, it is the white-hot focus — and government policy should catalyze the reaction. The Department of Defense policy of rewarding companies with university ties higher scores for independent R & D funds is an excellent prototype. State government, too, must participate; they may, for example, offer matching incentives for state-based R & D, increasing operational leverage and financial appeal.

CREATIVITY AND THE CORPORATE CULTURE

Encourage Risk by Strengthening Reward

Most companies give mixed signals about risk. They praise new ventures with lofty words and reward failure with career wipeout. One such derailment incinerates the whole house of corporate cards. We must shift this risk–return tradeoff by decreasing the risk and increasing the reward. Incentives for originality and invention must be internalized and believed by the company underground. The organizational structure must support it; the informal networks must promote it; the grapevines must confirm it. Participating in new ventures, not just making them successful, must be the pinnacle of corporate achievement. "Have the Guts to Fail"—the corporate motto of MacDermid (a mid-sized specialty chemical company)—should become the national battlecry.

Creativity and innovation has expression, one should note, in all areas of corporate life, not just high technology and new products. Managers who look beyond the traditional, who see the unusual, who dare to be different—upon these does posterity rely.

Facilitate Creative Types

Egalitarianism, the belief that all are equal, is a fundamental American value. While wholly appropriate in politics and society, it is inappropriate in economics and business. People differ in every respect, with the capacity for creativity at the top of the list. A company must respect its creative types. They are a breed apart, absorbed in their quest, dedicated to intensity, oblivious to others. Creatives are often difficult to control. They work strange hours in stranger places. They don't want supervision and demand personal satisfaction for personal achievement. Proprietary participation, especially financial reward, is an essential motivation. How to find them? A word of caution. Creative and innovative people may not be the smartest or brightest; they may not be aggressive or assertive or even realize their own gift. The best firms will treasure them.

Focus Corporate Fiscal Policy

Companies that talk innovation and invest elsewhere dig credibility gaps. Promoting creativity is no mean task. A firm must evidence its commitment, putting cash on the line. Nothing energizes more than the movement of money. You cannot talk creativity and fund tradition. The resource allocation process must encourage creativity and innovation; new procedures must skew dollars to more risky ventures. Most critically, results cannot be expected quickly. Corporate executives must see beyond the horizon, beyond the quarterly reports, beyond the street called Wall.

Understand the Creative Process

Creativity and innovation happens by itself, but not all the time. Since innovators are often not the brightest or most aggressive, the firm must find them or, more accurately, help them find themselves. One cannot train people to be inventive, but one can develop educational programs to facilitate the process. Creativity appears with infinite variety. In a high-tech firm, for example, a person with a new method for inventory control may not think herself creative, yet the benefit to the company may exceed most scientific study. One good idea covers a lot of ground.

Promote Interaction Among Divisions and Departments

Scientific advance depends on constant communication among diverse disciplines. Likewise for the best businesses. When problems are attacked by divergent approaches and disparate facts, a wider range of solutions emerge. Task forces composed of different departments are not unusual in corporate life, but these are often established for coordinating current programs rather than creating new ones.

Interdepartmental cooperation in companies, like interdisciplinary work in academics, is fraught with suspicion and worry about territoriality and dominance (the sociobiology of ant hills and wolf packs does not encourage creativity).

A firm's new products division does not want manufacturing sticking its nose in; manufacturing says it's ridiculous to develop products that can't be made. Mechanisms must be found to break these barriers. The catalyst is often the person to whom the departments report; the boss must become actively and aggressively involved. If he or she "recommends" the interaction without personal participation, it will surely fail.

What is creative management? More, to be sure, than external analysis and internal intuition. Psychological motivation and political positioning is also involved. "Stakeholder analysis" is a qualitative technique that segregates out the relevant parties and projects the personal attitudes of each. What's everyone's driving motivations, his or her "stake" in the matter? Crucial here is an assessment of individual feelings and hidden agendas. What's the private bottom line? Potential political standing and perceived career paths are often lurking just beneath the surface and must be considered in all creative management decisions.

Compromise, said to be golden, is sometimes a weak manager's failure to choose between contradictory positions or people. As such, the "in-between" solution can be worse than either of the extremes — and be no solution at all. To allocate to each of two competing projects half the money requested dooms both to certain disaster. Collaboration, on the other hand, brings the opposing parties onto the same side, encouraging interaction and establishing the conditions for innovation. The dialectic of dissent, carefully controlled, is a marvelous antidote for the poison of group-think.

The critical test of creative management is *internal consistency*. Does the overall plan pass rigorous evaluation of all functional components? Does it resonate well with all issues and areas? Does it make common sense? Is, for example, the decision to launch a new product consistent with all functional departments: is production ready to make it; marketing ready to sell it; financing ready to pay for it? (How often an ever-eager sales force promises delivery months before the plant can product the stuff!)

Will computers help? Will they be making more creative decisions? For certain operational issues, computers are essential: record keeping and data base management; minimizing costs of ingredients and inventory levels; maximizing efficiency in component scheduling and travel routes; and so on. Even for the organization and integration of long-range planning, computers are vital. But here, they are only a notebook. True creative management demands original insight.

The executive computer, symbolizing not money but brains, represents the new wealth of a new world — information. But who wants all that data? Who needs all those numbers? Today's most critical need is not more information but *less*. We need data reduction techniques, systems of selection and discernment, the intelligent search for meaning. We have enough numbers; what we need is understanding.

Computers are deterministic, preset by circuit and code; though the software be most intelligent, electronic pathways are still hardwired to spark a known output. Brains are probabilistic, patterned by design and chance; in the gray matter of the cerebral cortex semi-random processes can trip new thresholds. It is impossible to program computers, however large the data base and however "expert" the system, to devise creative ideas — that is, ideas that are original in essence and unique in vision. The two dimensions are forever incompatible. Computers can crunch vast numbers and sift complex algorithms by brute force, but only brains can search imaginatively for order and innovation amidst chaos and tradition.

The opportunity is here, the time is now. What we have is nothing less than the restructuring and recrudescence of American industry. Economists and executives must work together in building both a macro/economic foundation and a micro/corporate structure. In the new realities approaching the year 2000, to achieve domestic vitality and world leadership, the American trick is creative and innovative management.

Chapter 24

COMPREHENSIVE NATIONAL SECURITY
The Creative Power of American Science

Robert Lawrence Kuhn

Science separates present from past. It is the critical difference between savages living like animals and humans living like people. Science is more than a subject in school; it is the foundation of our world, the progenitor of present-day society, the source of contemporary civilization. Science, in short, is axial to our way of life. It is also the personification of creativity.

Science is both process and content, the mechanism of discovery as well as the thing discovered. The scientific method is the core paradigm of modern man; it is the shortest distance and surest route to factual truth, the line of thinking most logical and reproducible. The scientific method is perhaps mankind's finest creative tool: unbiased data collection; creative hypothesis generation (induction); rigorous analytical reasoning (deduction); comprehensive hypothesis testing; and independent repetition and confirmation—all are necessary irrespective of content area, whether "science" in the traditional sense or any other facet of human awareness.

Science is not a field of knowledge, it *is* knowledge. The advancement of science is the enrichment of mankind. What we call "human progress" is quite literally the historical sum of innumerable creative scientific steps. Derived from the Latin *scientia* meaning knowledge, science, in its broadest sense, conceives most concepts and sculpts most objects.

There is one area, however, where science is controversial, where inquiry is questioned and advancement criticized. Science in the service of national defense triggers hot debate. Some would say that scientists have the moral right to control the potential use of their personal creativity, and the moral imperative to prevent their innovative output from producing weapons of war. This lofty position bespeaks high tone and laudable ideals, yet it is fatally flawed.

The simple syllogism, framed for America, is thus: 1) Such dissenting positions can be espoused only in a free society; 2) A free society will remain free only by military strength; 3) Military strength will be guaranteed only by state-of-the-art science. This is the real world. (Examples of free societies flourishing devoid of military strength? They only prove the point: all rely, at last resort, on the United States.)

National defense demands technological superiority. Parity in military science, for a nation without expansionist designs, is not good enough; equality just will not do—it's too close, a slight error and you're behind. Being behind is no place to be, not in this game, not with all the chips in the pot. In an electronic fairyland of blinking black boxes, where battlefield microprocessors command, control, and communicate, "leapfrogging" is the ever-present problem and creativity is the only solution.

In past wars we could survive a slower tank or shallower sub, but in future encounters missing a scientific breakthrough in missile defense or sub-location technology could be disastrous. Our country is committed upfront: we will not be the aggressor. When the other side picks time and place, we had better field superior weapons and surer systems. When we concede quantity and number, we had better stress quality and expertise. The issue, of course, is more deterrence than triumph. We must *prevent* the next war, not win it.

Yet the world moves on. Subtle shifts redefine the nature of power. Today, well into the final fifth of the twentieth century, American security stakes out broader boundaries than ever before. More is encompassed within our vital needs as a nation. The economic thrust of Japan, for example, is a threat every bit as real as the military menace of the Soviets. Not the same, of course, but every bit as real. Computers and communications are also extending security boundaries. The profusion of information amplified by the ease of transmission lowers entry barriers for those with disruptive intent.

The battles of the future will be fought on vastly more complex terrain, contested more with ideas and products than with armies and navies. Confrontation among nations—attacks, provocations, insults—will assume new forms and novel shapes. Troop movement across Europe is virtually an anachronism—superpower nuclear standoff has seen to that. We must secure the standoff with military strength through technological supremacy, but that is not enough. An irrefutable defense capability, in the words of the logician, is "necessary but not sufficient" for national security.

This, then, is the *new* vision of national security, a broad concept embedding economic, social, education, cultural, and intellectual components as well as military ones — a concept increasingly being called "*Comprehensive* National Security."

Creative scientific superiority must maintain America's comprehensive national security just as it must assure the subset of preeminent military might. The first nation, for example, to mass produce future generations of integrated circuits will capture high ground and strong position. The country that pioneers genetically enhanced food production will wield commanding influence in world politics, well in excess of Arab oil's peak power.

Comprehensive national security must become our redeployed concept of self-protection. Mechanisms of competition, not machines of warfare, is now the critical concern. We must construct a *comprehensively* secure country, and creative and innovative management is our primary building block.

Following is the domain of comprehensive national security, with each area evincing the central role of science.

Military.   Maintaining technical superiority in weapons and delivery systems is the sine qua non of national security. Responsiveness, reliability, and redundancy are also cardinal characteristics. American science should be proud to participate in sustaining freedom.

Economic.   Strengthening the industrial base of the United States is a quintessential component of comprehensive national security. In past centuries countries could make up with military aggressiveness what they lacked in economic resourcefulness. This is no longer possible. Countries will survive and prosper or suffer and fall in direct relation to their productive capacity and commercial acumen. The premier growth industries of the next decade — telecommunications, personal computing, biotechnology, and health care — are all science-based, all driven by creativity and innovation. Scientists are not only involved in creating novel high-tech ventures but also in developing fresh approaches to traditional businesses. Both are prescribed for American economic health.

Social/Political.   Structuring society for the benefit of all people is our contemporary mega-problem, labyrinthian in complexity, long-term in solution. We must be able to meet our oft-stated goals of equality, opportunity, care and concern for citizens of every age, sex, race, creed, religious belief. A populace well-pleased is an intrinsic part of comprehensive national security. Though human systems are fiendishly more intricate than material systems, social scientists are as clever and inventive as their physical science counterparts. The use of sophisticated techniques in sociology, political science, and the like provide a core of hard data, certainly superior to the self-serving rhetoric of political palaver.

Educational.   The minds of the young are the blueprints of the future. What we teach, and how they learn, will plot America's course—with the trajectory now being set in our schools. Science, here, contributes more than tools, though the personal computer will revolutionize both teaching and thinking. (Free enterprise has given the United States a jump of at least half a generation over the Soviet Union in acclimating children to personal computers.) Science teaches logic, how to use it, when to overrule it. It catalyzes enthusiasm for investigation and analysis; it teaches respect for proper rationale and confirmed proof; it offers the thrill of exploring unchartered areas, of using insight, of making discovery, of finding truth. Science replaces rote by rigor and memorization by reasoning. Science is no longer the exclusive domain of the elite; it is the language of all.

Cultural.   The identity of a nation affects its cohesiveness; self-image determines self-confidence. Building American culture buttresses American security. Science, the complement of culture, supports its promulgation and propagation. Culture thrives on wide accessibility, and science provides the nutrients of transmission—television, radio, cable, satellite, video discs/cassettes, motion pictures, computer networks, interactive video. Science has also fashioned marvelous techniques for enhancing effect, making culture more pleasurable and more veritable, conveying emotion and making impact.

Intellectual.   In the twenty-first century information will be the new medium of exchange. (Money, that archaic commodity, will be bytes in computer memories and numbers on computer screens.) International leadership will be framed in terms of cerebral skill not military prowess. A nation's prestige will be built by its intellectual endowment and creative output, not by the number and size of its bombs and rockets. Scientists from all disciplines will contribute, from philosophy and astronomy to mathematics and music; new information will be prized, even from fields without direct economic benefit—human values will have changed and human worth redefined.

A word, here, for *pure* science. Basic research is the foundation of science, the platform for progress, the precursor of revolution. One cannot know in advance where seminal breakthroughs will come and what application technologies may be. Instinct and intuition, not program and project, are the requisite sources of energy. Basic research is a stimulant for creativity; it is, in all fields, an absolute necessity.

Sensitivity to scientists as well as appreciation of science is vital for optimizing national output. Scientists, by personality, are not easily coerced, not easily directed. Indeed, such is their strength. Scientists must be free to wander and explore, to confront blind alleys and to shatter tradition. Society must establish incentive systems to encourage scientists, giving them maximum motivation to imagine and construct. We must enhance creativity and facilitate innovation. We must nurture and develop America's premier natural resource.

DISCUSSION

Jack Borsting

Jack Borsting: Let me give an example of incremental innovation in the public sector. David Potter was head of the research lab at General Motors in Santa Barbara; he was appointed assistant secretary of the Navy for research and development and then undersecretary of the Navy; ultimately, he went back to become a Group Vice President of General Motors. Dave said that he was at first frustrated in the policy arena in his Navy job because he had set his goals much too high. It took him several years before he stepped down and targeted incremental innovation rather than radical change as his way of affecting the system; and once he decided to work in this manner, he really began to make some progress. I think incremental innovation is a primary theme of this volume.

How do you get group creativity in the Congress? Botkin talked about power, vision, implementation. Certainly the power in the Congress has been diffused in recent years due to weakening of the seniority system. Is this a good thing? It is now difficult to move on any important public issue unless there is a crisis. The huge federal deficit is a classic example. With social security problems, the only way we could move was to establish an outside commission; Congress couldn't handle it themselves. Military retirement? Congress doesn't even want to think about military retirement, certainly not face it; the unfunded liability of the military retirement system is half a trillion dollars, and it's not funded on an accrual basis but is merely paid (hopefully) year to year. Medicare has its own hosts of problems.

The executive branch has some of the same problems as has academia: people come and go; the average tenure of a political appointee, like myself, is about eighteen months — a short time. The senior level civil service are very hard working, very conscientious, but they are also very resistant to change. Consequently, just like in academia, old programs are difficult to cancel; all current government programs have their own special constituencies both in the Congress and in the bureaucracy, and new programs are difficult to start.

People often stress the "fear component" as being big in the public policy arena; it is indeed most important. Because of the media, because of the goldfish-bowl effect, there are powerful disincentives for anyone to try anything at all that might lead to public censure. The procurement problem that we have been hearing about — thousand dollar hammers and seven thousand dollar toilets paid for by the Defense Department — what is the cause of this? The primary reason is that we have straitjacketed the procurement system with so many rules and regulations that nobody can think; nobody can be creative. But why should anyone bother being creative — it could only mean trouble. Band-aids, please note, will not fix bureaucracies; nor will complex regulations enhance creativity and innovation in government.

A final thought. Being chancellor of a large university system — such as those of New York, California, and Texas — is much like being Secretary of Defense, with all the corresponding departments, services and staffs. I once drew this analogy for the chancellor of the University of California; to which he commented, "You're right, but I'm not sure either organization would like it."

SUMMATION

Robert Lawrence Kuhn

Frontiers in Creative and Innovative Management brings together leaders and scholars of intellectual institutions, organizations whose output is knowledge and information. We have two parallel and interdependent purposes: first, to make creative and innovative management relevant and useful for on-line businessmen and executives; second, to develop a new academic field in creative and innovative management, one that is rigorous and theoretical as well as anecdotal and practical.[1]

We start with definitions, and we struggle. Is there a difference between creativity and innovation? George Kozmetsky and Abraham Zaleznick think yes, Herbert Simon and David Hertz think no. Is the issue one merely of semantics? Is the controversy, pardon the pun, only academic? I think not. Precise definitions are critical for defining new fields, and this particular struggle is no exception. Thus we confront a series of terms: creativity, innovation, creative management, innovative management, the difference between creative management and management of creativity, as well as the conundrum in question, any difference between creativity and innovation. Hard issues, these. But progress requires precision.

Let us start with the simple one. Being a creative manager is fundamentally different from being a manager of creativity. The crux of this difference lies in the locus of the creativity and the process of management. A creative manager is himself or herself creative, producing creative content personally in the conduct of managerial tasks. A manager of creativity is a facilitator of the creative

365

process, working to produce creative content in others. The skill sets for each are not the same — indeed there is little overlap — although either one can also be the other.

When we get to questions of differences between creativity and innovation, the road gets rougher. Professor Simon states that creativity is novel, interesting, and valuable — high quality problem solving requiring risks to generate novelty. We note definitions (from Dr. Kozmetsky and me, for example) that differentiate creativity and innovation — stating that creativity is the generation of novelty while innovation is the transformation of such novelty into products, processes, and practical implementation. Professor Simon (and others) aver that there is no difference between creativity and innovation. Do we have a contradiction here? (Nothing wrong with a contradiction.) I suggest that there is no contradiction, because the two classes of definitions are operating on different levels. Professor Simon talks about fundamental processes and mechanisms; what is the deep structure that makes creativity and innovation work in the human mind? Dr. Kozmetsky and I are not categorizing fundamental mind mechanisms, but rather creative and innovative activities within the confines of management, within the specific, narrowcasted domain of business enterprise organization. Consequently, the terms "creativity" and "innovation," much like "slack" or "scarcity" or "elasticity," take on specific meanings within a contextual field that is different from other connotations of the same terms in other fields. Rigorous definitions are an important part of the process, and we should continue to pursue them vigorously.

We discuss creativity in the stream of the history of ideas, finding perspectives and traditions that are both unexpected and illuminating. We looked at creativity in the context of religion, the arts, the sciences, as well as management. Management itself is not a new concept. If you check the original text on the subject, a certain Jethro taught a certain Moses about management (specifically about organizational hierarchies and delegation, see Exodus 18: 13–27; Moses, a creative, hands-on sort, was not much of a delegator).

Many of us, coming from the natural sciences, tend to equate creativity and innovation with high technology. Indeed, "innovation" is often identified with engineering and connotes fiddling around to make better products. Engineering new ideas is innovation, but more is subsumed here. One can check high-tech history and find that a creative approach in inventory control has had ten times the bottom-line effect of fifty scientists working in R & D. Corporate creativity extends across the board, functionally, industrially, sectorially. We should not fall into the trap of assuming that creativity and innovation apply only to R & D, or only to science and technology industries, or only to the private sector.

We must *decouple* creativity's exclusive link with high tech just as we have decoupled its exclusive link with music and art. Sure, creativity is very much involved in high tech, just as it is in music and art, but it is not a subset of those areas. Creativity is a large essence of human life, *within which* we can discuss high tech, the arts, the sciences, and, indeed, management.

We talk about creative and innovative management as being both "contingent" and requiring the process of management. Possible contingencies to consider are industrial organization, competitive position, and product life cycle. The risk requirement for creative and innovative management is one area to engender agreement; "the right to fail" we propound as virtually a right of life, liberty, and the pursuit of happiness. But the high failure rate elicits the query "Can only the rich be creative?" I think the question fascinating. If 80 or 90 percent of creative and innovative activities promote failure, can only rich people and rich companies afford to be creative and innovative?

One need not speculate the answer. History defends the opposite argument. Why? The key may be the risk/reward ratio. It seems a peculiar penchant of human nature that as organizations (or people) get more and more rich, they get more and more chicken; they have more to lose and therefore less to risk. The rich have further to fall, so they take surer steps. Entrepreneurs, on the other hand, go for the big hit since they have little to lose. President Cyert commented that if he had a billion dollar endowment, he'd be a follower. Terrific!

What are some *personal* drivers for creative and innovative management? Money, power, public recognition, competition, commitment. What are some *environmental* drivers? In a stable environment, creative and innovative management is more incremental; in a turbulent environment, it becomes "Big Bang" (our business analog of cosmological or political explosion).

What about changing organizational goals? They are difficult to deal with and largely unstudied. Dr. George Geis and I examined recently what happens in organizations when fundamental truth must change. We used as our model and paradigm closed-system ecclesiastical groups, extreme religious organizations, and determined what happens in these organization when fundamental doctrines change. We then compared our case data to what happens in commercial organizations when founding strategies must change. (The analogue was between fundamental doctrines and founding strategies.) The similarities we found were remarkable.[2]

We address interesting issues such as the paradox that creative and innovative management is what CEOs need in abundance, but apparently it is not a prime category for CEO selection. We consider the private and public sectors and what happens as the boundaries between them blur. We see the need for multiple decision centers for funding, and that too much "efficiency" could kill creativity. Creative and innovative management, we believe, is a key for comprehensive national security that must embed, as the next century approaches, economic, social, educational, and intellectual elements, as well as military ones.

What are some issues of creative and innovative management?

1. Individual or collective? Is creativity isolated to individuals or can groups be creative?

2. What are the similarities and differences between creativity in different fields? Are we fundamentally flawed not having the president of Julliard or a musician contribute to this volume; or is creativity pandemic and consistent no matter where we find it?

3. The articulation of practice and theory. How can research be both rigorous and tied to reality, both excellent and relevant?

4. How do we control research with confidence?

5. How do we expand our data base and allow both public and private institutions to participate?

6. What kinds of institutions should we develop? What new kinds of research institutes can bridge gaps and monitor interfaces?

7. What about intellectual property rights? What about the proprietary rights of corporations?

8. How do we encourage high-risk projects? What about the internal corporate environment? Companies that talk innovation and fund tradition dig credibility gaps. Nothing motivates more than the movement of money. How about the external public environment? No words are read more carefully than new tax policy.

9. How do we identify talents? Creative and innovative people may not be the brightest, and they are often not the most aggressive. (Sometimes, they're the most obnoxious.)

10. How do we teach creative and innovative management? We need new educational technologies. Multiple billions are being spent by industry today and little, sadly, has proper focus. The fault is ours: if we claim leadership of creative and innovative management, we must do a better job of communicating as well as researching.

Regarding our research agenda—a primary goal of this book—we must stress the search for *rigor* and *relevance*. We cannot have success unless we build an analytical field. If we are not rigorous and theoretical, creative and innovative management will be forever anecdotal and repetitive. We must develop a body of knowledge.

We need multimethodological design. Qualitative work alone lacks confidence. Quantitative work alone lacks relevance. We must articulate the quantitative with the qualitative. We need cross-sectorial design; public and private; joint public/private; not-for-profit. We must have cross-cultural design looking at different geographic regions as well as different corporate cultures. We must develop theory from both directions: build the database on empirical knowledge and induce general principles; and the other way around, deducing specific applications from logical assumptions — the two methodologies being iterated recursively.

A few words about the senior management of creativity. What are the requirements for CEOs of innovative institutions? What must they know? Surely enough to earn the intellectual respect of their staffs. Nothing less will do. The chief executive of such organizations should be able to converse fluently virtually at the state of the art of current thinking in each content area of his or her purview. He or she must be able to make independent judgments about the long-term implications of the information being generated and should have the self-reliance to devise innovative structures and marketing concepts in order to optimize development. Similarly, to generate comparative strategic advantage, a CEO must have broad intellectual reach and be able to sense interdisciplinary and cross-sector relationships before they reach the academic journals and well before they hit the mass media.

In order to make long-range decisions, a CEO of an innovative organization must be able to distance himself or herself from current paradigms and be divorced from common ways of thinking. What will the environment require in ten to fifteen years? And how can one prepare the organization to provide it? That's the strategic key. The management of intellectual resources is a fascinating subject. To nurture and develop creative and innovative management is to imbue institutions with power to prosper.

Directing creativity and innovation is no textbook task. Great feeling and empathy, not sympathy or apathy, is required. One must have special sense for the priorities of an academic, the concerns of a scientist, the intensity of an inventor, the rage of an artist. Managing mental types demands content knowledge and process sensitivity. People who produce scholarly output have little concern for anything else, not managerial issues, not organizational problems. Their work is their world and upon it alone does the sun rise and set. Creativity is impossible to coerce; it must be coaxed, stroked, and shaped. The leader of an intellectual, innovative institution must get his or her people to internalize whatever they do or tasks will just not get done. Though management is becoming a science, it will never cease to be an art.

Creative strategies must take into account the nature of an organization: how to cut a company is essential for understanding the strategic process and making the innovation ring right. Numerous dimensions are involved. Strategic decisionmaking is a function of the social structure and corporate culture. Is the sector for-profit or not-for-profit? The organization large or small? The product original or replicative? The level of managerial decision top or middle? The personalities assertive or passive? The procedure individual or collective? For example, in a high-technology company, how should the chief operating officer direct the key research scientists? In a university music department, what dollar value should be placed on subsidized concerts for poor children? In a manufacturing firm, what level of losses can be sustained before a division be dispatched? In the media, should a magazine publisher stop an editor from printing a story criticizing a top advertiser? All of these creative decisions, though superficially similar in form, differ fundamentally in substance. The scientist is a creative self-starter unaccustomed to close supervision. Artistic enrichment of the kids defies quantification. The manufacturing division may become a vital resource in future years. The magazine may not exist without editorial freedom.

Often, as we noted, one associates creativity with the arts and sciences and innovation with technology and engineering. Although appropriate in these contexts, creative and innovative management attains its potential as a *strategy-making mechanism* even more than a decisionmaking one. Thus, a difference emerges between strategy making and decisionmaking, the former assuming much larger scope and substance, especially when amplified by creativity.

One might believe, by reading erudite arguments and counter arguments in the press that industrial revival in America is linked to some new economic policy whether monetary and supply side on one hand, or increased taxes and government spending on the other. A cardinal mistake here—and it permeates contemporary thought—is the notion that economic solutions to industrial problems will yield business success and competitive advantage. Macroeconomics surely has its place, but, please, not the whole place. To treat the economy only by macroeconomics is to treat the sick only by epidemiology. Macroeconomics should and can modulate the pace and proportions of the economy, but it cannot make marketable products nor produce positive financial returns. It is like trying to coach a basketball team by planning the theoretically proper mix of heights, weights, and talents of players without teaching any of them how to pass, dribble, or shoot. What we need, coach, is creative and innovative management.

NOTES

1. Each purpose will be supported by a publication: this present volume continues the academic development begun by the first volume; a *Handbook for Creative and*

Innovative Managers, with pragmatic contributions from leading corporate executives, is forthcoming from McGraw–Hill.
2. See Robert Lawrence Kuhn and George T. Geis, *The Firm Bond: Linking Meaning and Mission in Business and Religion* (New York: Praeger, 1984).

ABOUT THE RGK FOUNDATION

The RGK Foundation was established in 1966 to provide support for medical and educational research. Major emphasis has been placed on the research of connective tissue diseases, particularly scleroderma. The Foundation also supports workshops and conferences at educational institutions through which the role of business in American society is examined. Such conferences have been cosponsored with the IC² Institute at the University of Texas at Austin and the Keystone Center for Continuing Education in Colorado.

The RGK Foundation Building, which opened in October 1981, has a research library and provides research space for scholars in residence. The building's extensive conference facilities have been used for national and international conferences including the International Conference on Scleroderma and the Symposium on Current American Economic Policy. Conferences at the RGK Foundation are designed not only to enhance information exchange on particular topics but also to maintain an interlinkage among business, academia, community, and government.

INDEX

ABOUT THE EDITOR

Robert Lawrence Kuhn is a strategist, scientist, author, and lecturer specializing in corporate strategy, financial strategy, commercializing high technology, and creative and innovative management. He is an investment banker with expertise in new business formation, venture capital, mergers and acquisitions, and the structuring of innovative financial transactions. He works with diverse companies and organizations developing managerial skills, designing financial models, creating novel enterprises, formulating business strategies, and implementing corporate structures. He is noted for his radical restructuring of Eagle Clothes, now a national retail consultant. Previously, he ran a foundation operating concert series, international research projects and cultural programs, and national media and publishing operations.

Dr. Kuhn is at home in the complementary worlds of academic institutions, business corporations, and government agencies. He has advised the United States and Israel on commercializing defense technology; he served as the American consultant for the Jerusalem Economic Conference (1984) and works on international finance and marketing. He is Senior Research Fellow in Creative and Innovative Management at the IC² Institute at the University of Texas at Austin and is Adjunct Professor of Strategy and Policy in the Department of Management and Organizational Behavior at the Graduate School of Business Administration of New York University. Dr. Kuhn holds a B.A. in Human Biology from the Johns Hopkins University (Phi Beta Kappa), a Ph.D. in neurophysiology from the Department of Anatomy and Brain Research Institute of the University of California at Los Angeles, and an M.S. in Management from the Sloan School of Management of the Massachusetts Institute of Technology. At MIT he was a Sloan Fellow in Management and taught in the Psychology Department.

Dr. Kuhn's recent books include: *To Flourish Among Giants: Creative Management for Mid-Sized Firms* (a book club main selection and being translated into Japanese); *The Firm Bond: Linking Meaning and Mission in Business and Religion*; *Commercializing Defense-Related Technology*; *Corporate Creativity: Robust Companies and the Entrepreneurial Spirit*; *Technology Venturing: American Innovation and Risk Taking*; *Managing Take-Off in Fast-Growth Companies*; *Industrial R & D in Israel*; and *Regulation Reform*. Dr. Kuhn is Contributing Editor to the *Journal of Business Strategy* and Senior Editor of *Texas Business* magazine. He is Editor-in-Chief of the forthcoming *Handbook for Creative and Innovative Managers*.

LIST OF CONTRIBUTORS

Yair Aharoni is the Issachar Haimovic Professor of Business Policy and the Director of the Jerusalem Institute of Management, Tel Aviv University.

Jack R. Borsting is the Dean of the Graduate School of Business, University of Miami, and is former comptroller for the U.S. Department of Defense.

James W. Botkin is Director of the Technology and Group in Cambridge and the author of several books on innovation.

Bertram S. Brown is President of Hahnemann University. He is the former Director of the National Institute for Mental Health.

Abraham Charnes is University Professor Across the University of Texas System, the John P. Harbin Centennial Professor, Director for Cybernetic Studies, The University of Texas at Austin.

William W. Cooper is the Foster Parker Professor of Finance, Management and Accounting in the Graduate School of Business of the University of Texas at Austin and holder of the Nadya Kozmetsky Scott Centennial Fellowship in the IC² Institute.

Richard Cyert is President of Carnegie–Mellon University.

Meinolf Dierkes is President of the Wissenschaftszentrum, Berlin, West Germany.

George T. Geis is Research Coordinator for the Center for Human Resource Management, Institute of Industrial Relations, University of California at Los Angeles. He is the author of numerous publications in organizational development and personal computers.

Frederick W. Gluck is a director and senior partner of McKinsey & Co. where his practice stresses strategies for large corporations.

David Bendel Hertz is Distinguished Professor of Artificial Intelligence and Director of the Intelligent Computer Systems Research Institute, University of Miami.

George Huber is the Eddy Clark Scurlock Professor of Management, The University of Texas at Austin.

Donald M. Kerr is Director of the Los Alamos National Laboratory.

Michael J. L. Kirby is the Senator from Nova Scotia in the Canadian Senate. He was formerly the Senior Corporate Vice President of Canadian National and also the former cabinet secretary for Federal–Provincial Relations under Prime Minister Trudeau.

George Kozmetsky is Director of the IC² Institute, Chairman of the RGK Foundation, Executive Associate for Economic Affairs of the University of Texas System, and the Marion West Chair Professor of Constructive Capitalism.

Robert Kupperman is Executive Director for Science and Technology, Center for Strategic and International Studies, Georgetown University.

Gerhard O. Mensch is Professor of Management, Weatherhead School of Management, and Professor of Economic, Economics Department, Case Western Reserve University.

Barry Munitz is President of Federated Development Company and Vice-Chairman of the Board of MCO Holdings, Inc. He is the former Chancellor of the University of Houston.

Joseph S. Murphy is Chancellor of the City University of New York.

W. Arthur Porter is President of the Houston Area Research Center in The Woodlands, Texas. He is the former Director of the Texas Engineering Experiment Station at Texas A & M University.

Gerard R. Roche is Chairman of the Board of Heidrick & Struggles, a leading executive search firm.

Timothy Ruefli is the Fayez Sarofim Centennial Professor of Management and IC² Institute Frank Erwin Centennial Fellow, The University of Texas at Austin.

Maurice Saias is Professor of Business Administration at the Institut d'Administration des Enterprises at the Universite d'Aix-Marseilles.

Herbert Simon is the Richard King Mellon Professor of Psychology and Computer Sciences, Carnegie–Mellon University. Professor Simon is a Nobel Laureate in Economics.

Gerald Schmitz is in the Research Branch of the Library of Parliament in Ottawa, Ontario.

David Williamson is Senior Fellow in Science and Technology Policy in the Center for Strategic and International Studies, Georgetown University.

Abraham Zaleznick is the Konosuke Matsushita Professor of Leadership at the Harvard Business School and the author of numerous publications on organizational psychodynamics.